There are so many things I miss.
Like clouds in the summer sky, cold rain showers,
the scent of the autumn breeze,
the softness of the earth in spring,
the way a convenience store feels safe
in the middle of the night,
the cool air in school after classes are out,
the smell of a blackboard eraser,
the distant sound of a truck driving through
the night...

I wanted to keep feeling those
things with you forever.

voices of a distant star

Story: Makoto Shinkai
Art: Mizu Sahara

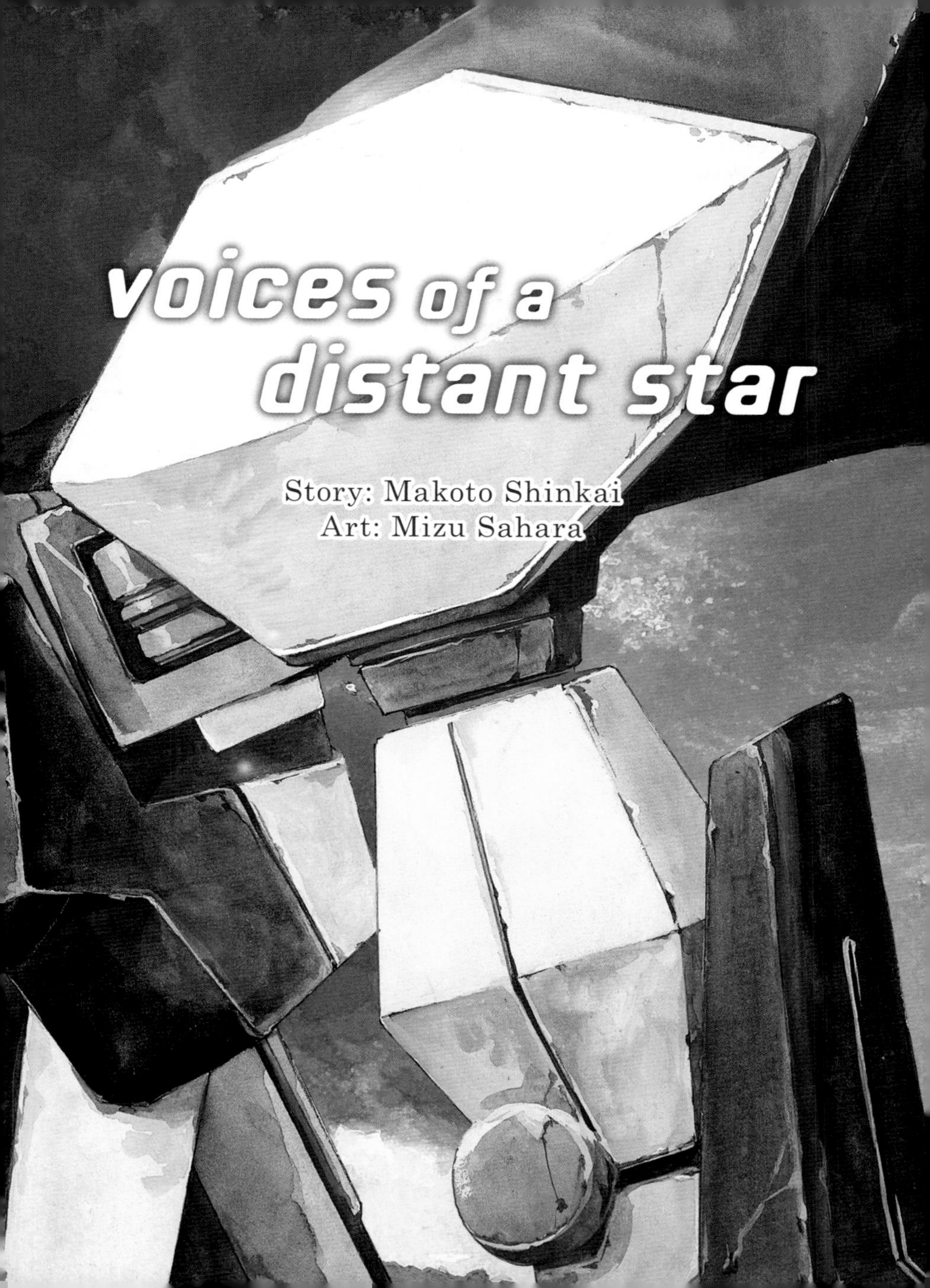

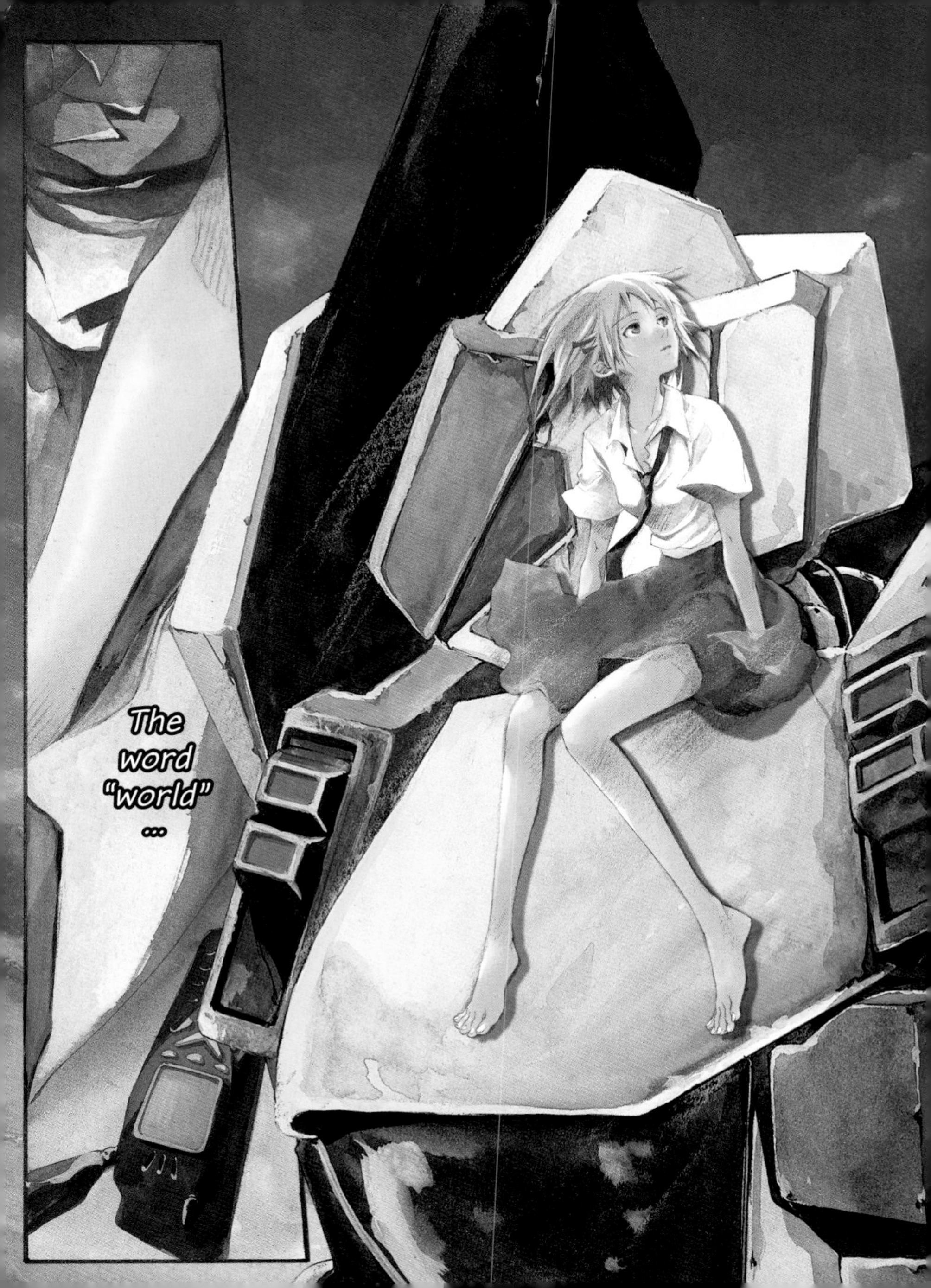
The word "world" ...

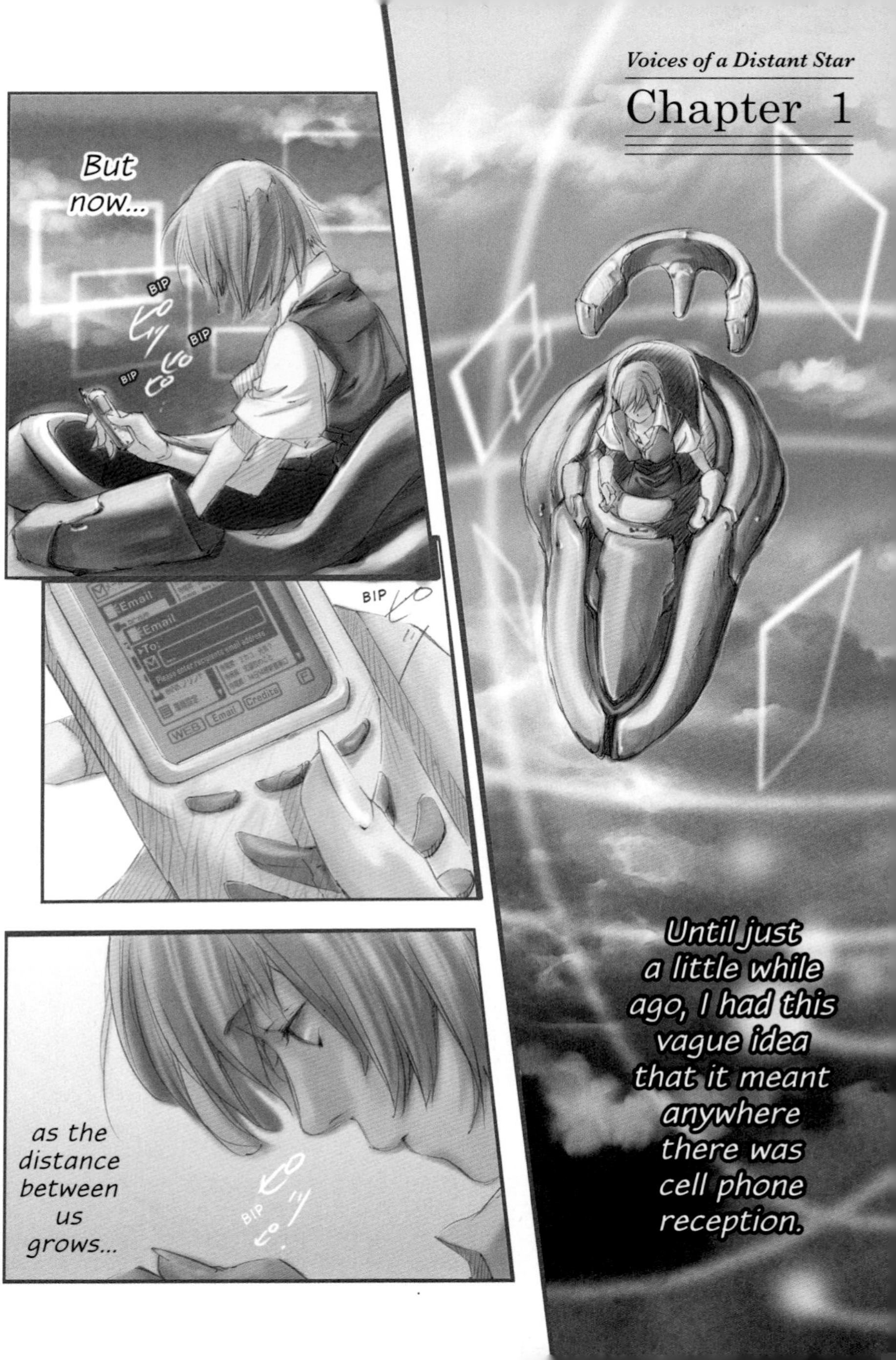
Voices of a Distant Star
Chapter 1
Until just a little while ago, I had this vague idea that it meant anywhere there was cell phone reception.
But now...
BIP
BIP
BIP
BIP
Email
Email
To:
WEB
Email
Credits
as the distance between us grows...
BIP

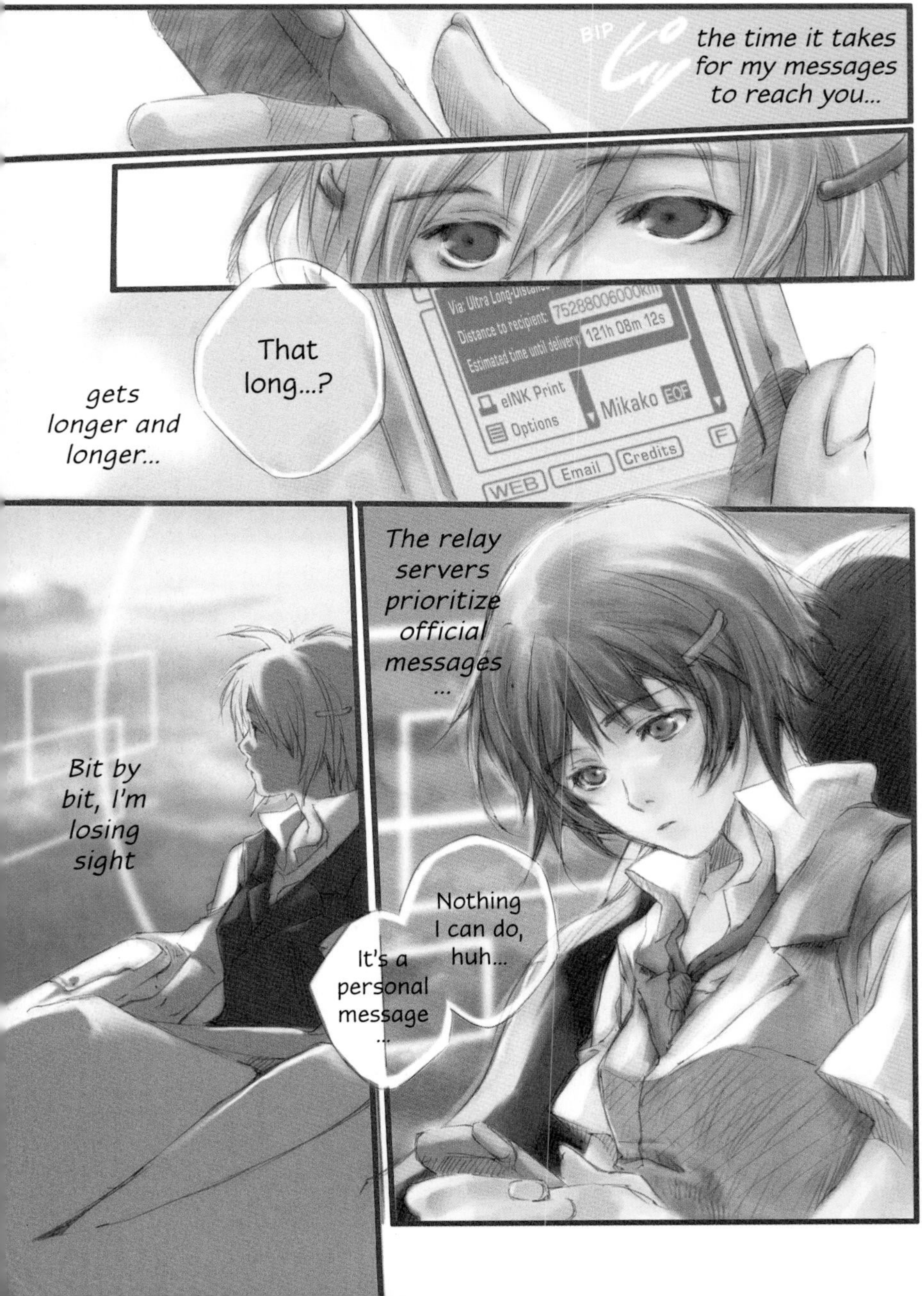
BIP
the time it takes for my messages to reach you...
Via: Ultra Long-Distanc
Distance to recipient: 75288006000km
Estimated time until delivery: 121h 08m 12s
eINK Print
Options
Mikako EOF
F
WEB
Email
Credits
That long...?
gets longer and longer...
The relay servers prioritize official messages ...
Nothing I can do, huh...
It's a personal message ...
Bit by bit, I'm losing sight

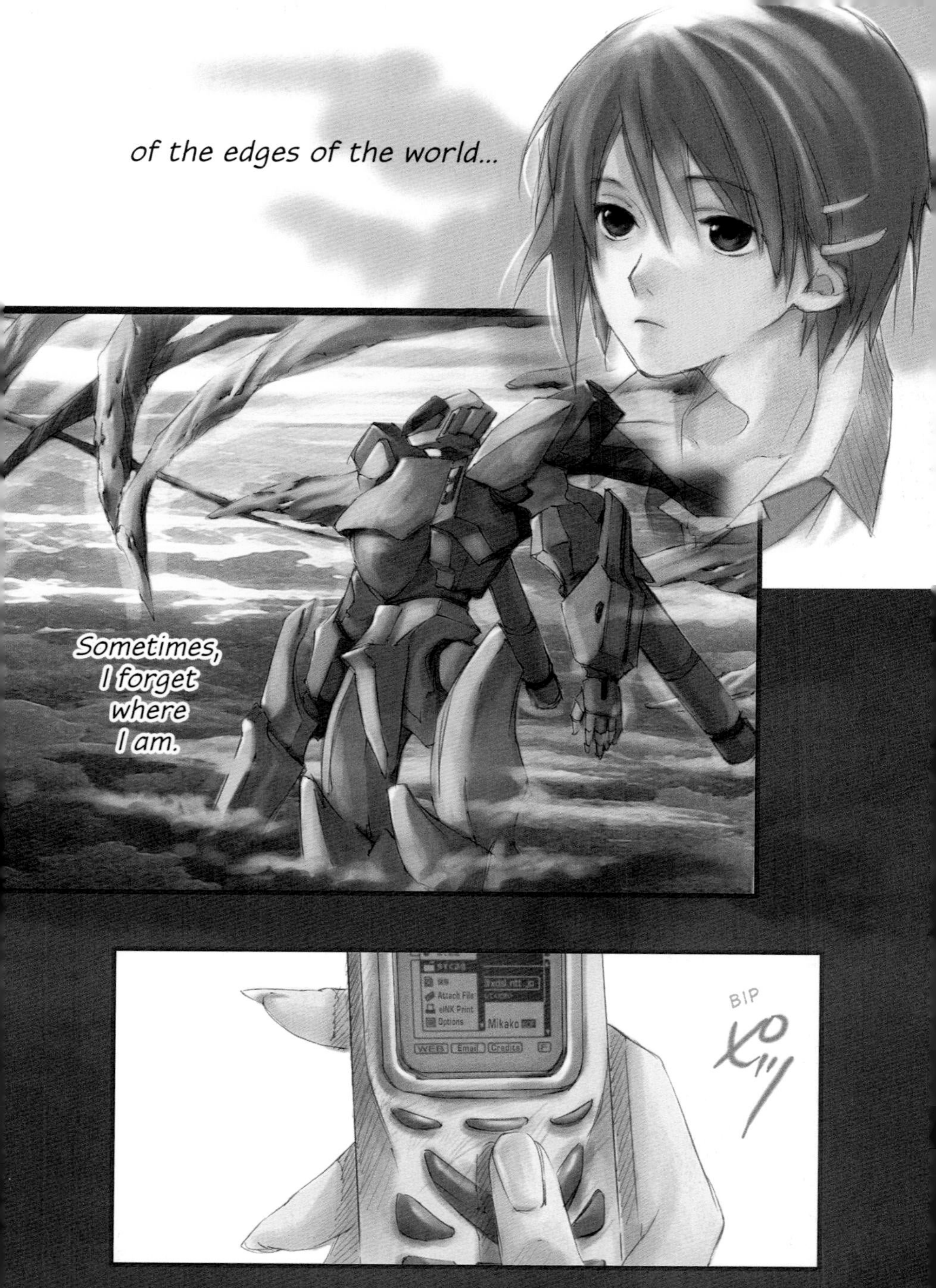
of the edges of the world...
Sometimes, I forget where I am.
Attach File
eINK Print
Options
Mikako
WEB
Email
Credits
BIP
ピッ

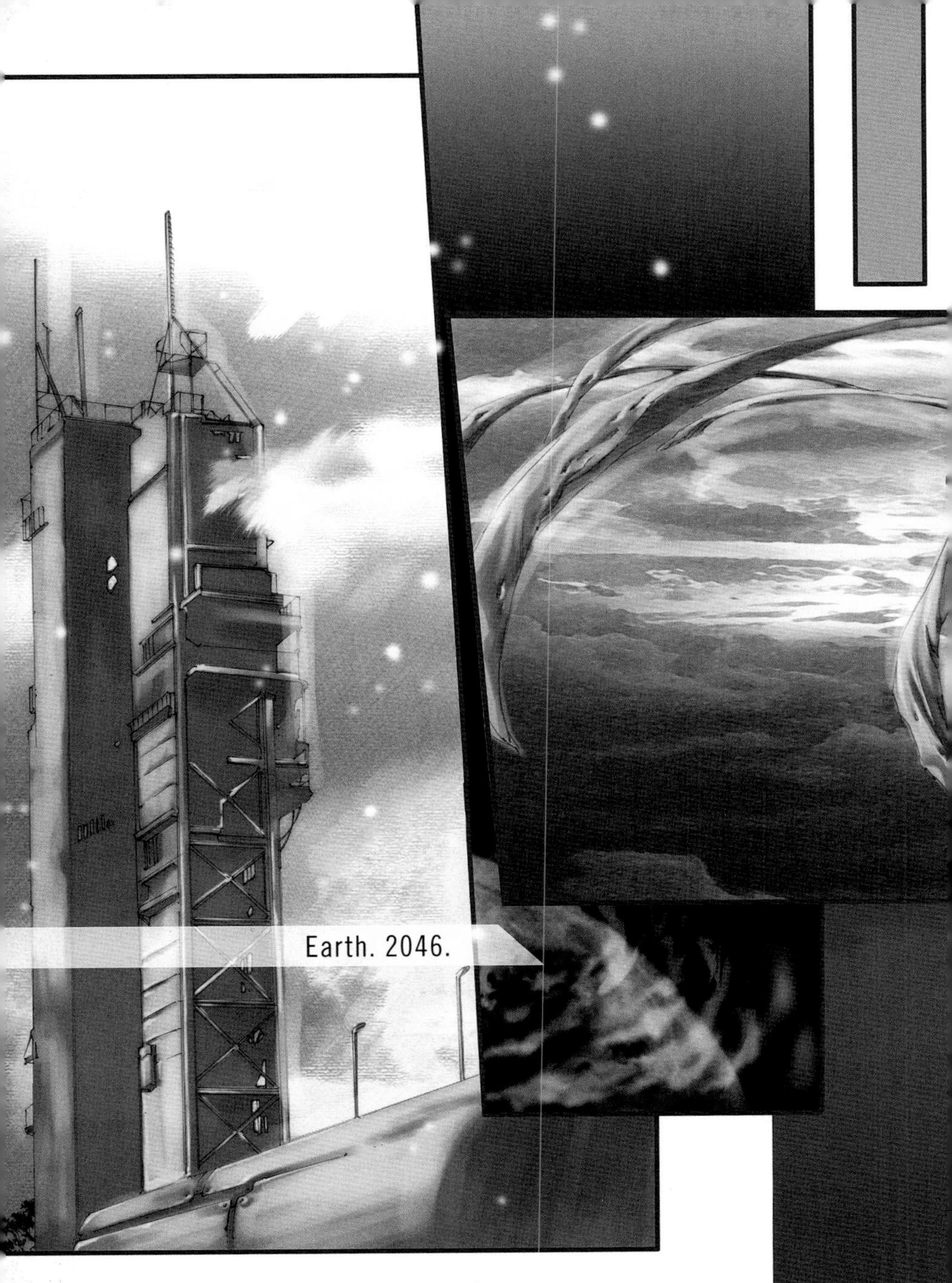
Earth. 2046.

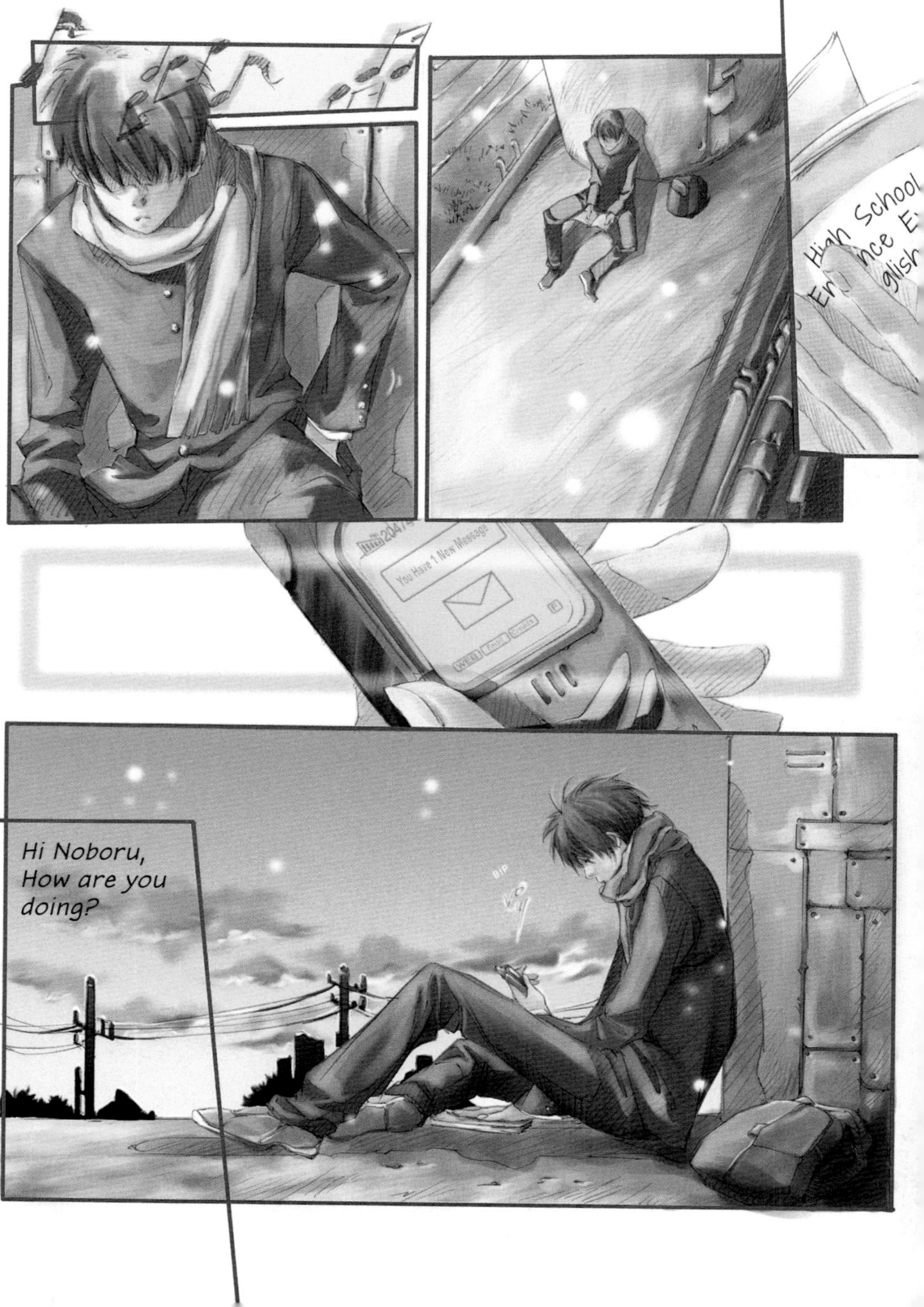
High School
You Have 1 New Message
BIP
Hi Noboru,
How are you
doing?

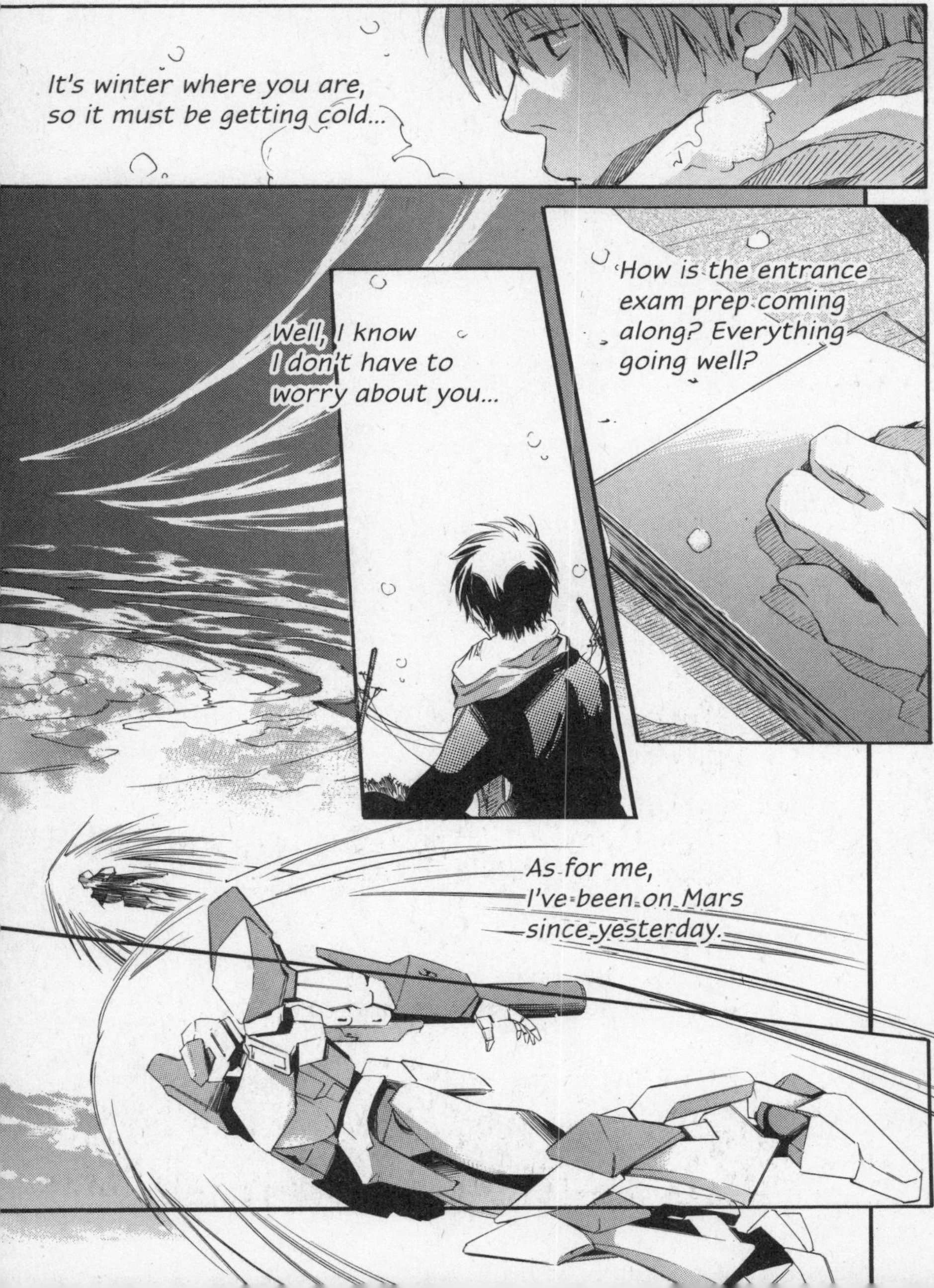
It's winter where you are, so it must be getting cold...
How is the entrance exam prep coming along? Everything going well?
Well, I know I don't have to worry about you...
As for me, I've been on Mars since yesterday.

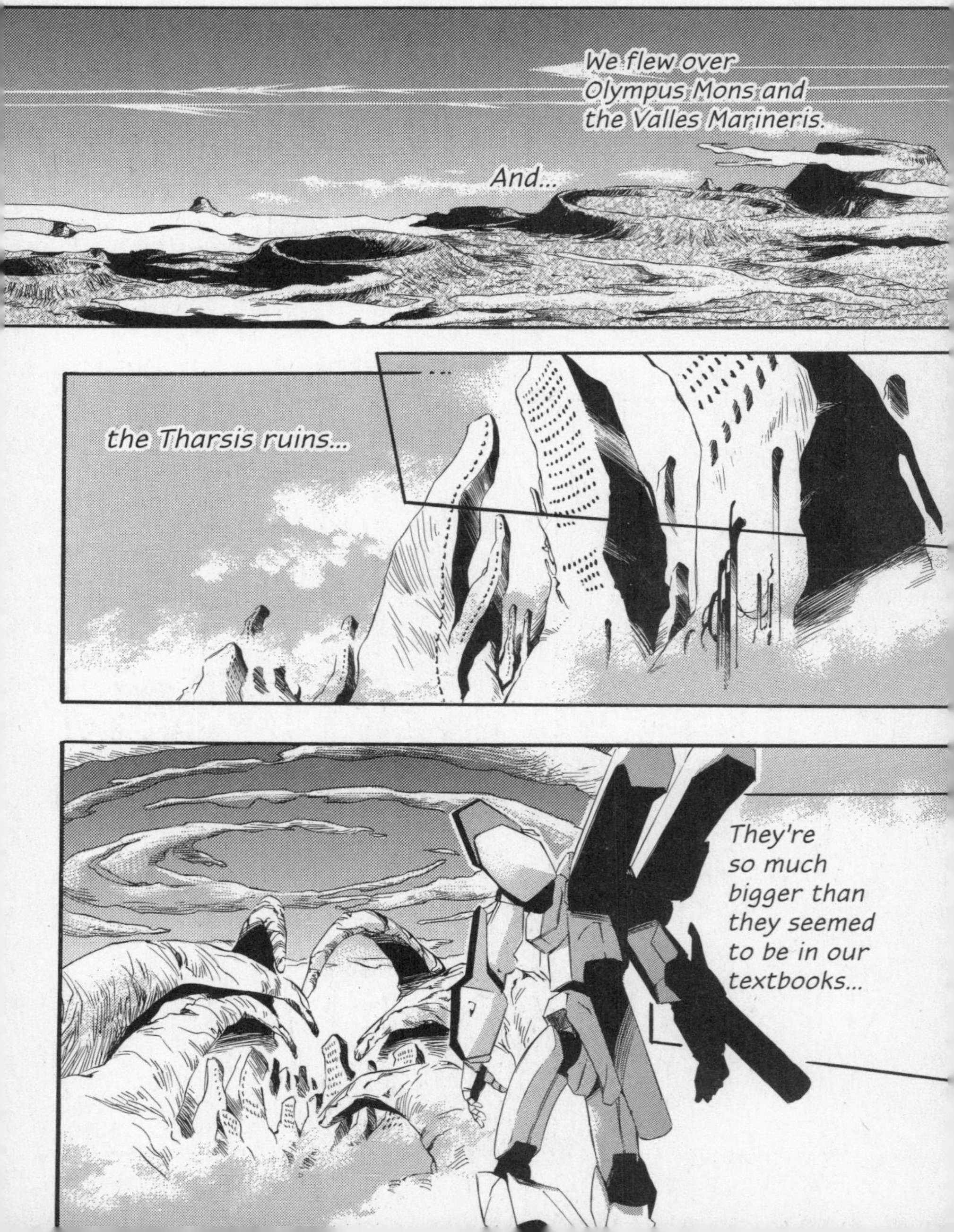
We flew over Olympus Mons and the Valles Marineris.
And...
the Tharsis ruins...
They're so much bigger than they seemed to be in our textbooks...

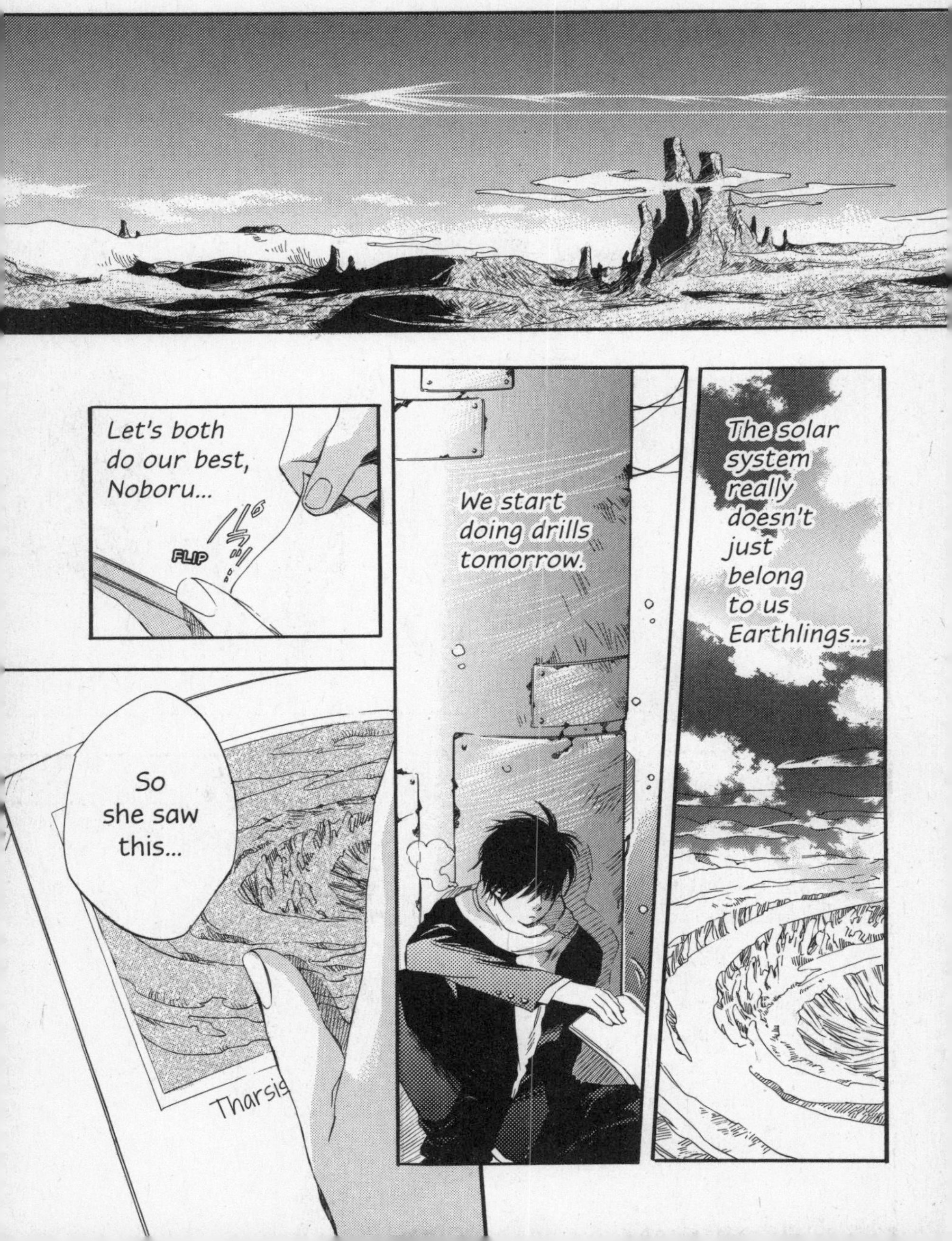

The solar system really doesn't just belong to us Earthlings...
We start doing drills tomorrow.
Let's both do our best, Noboru...
FLIP
So she saw this...
Tharsis

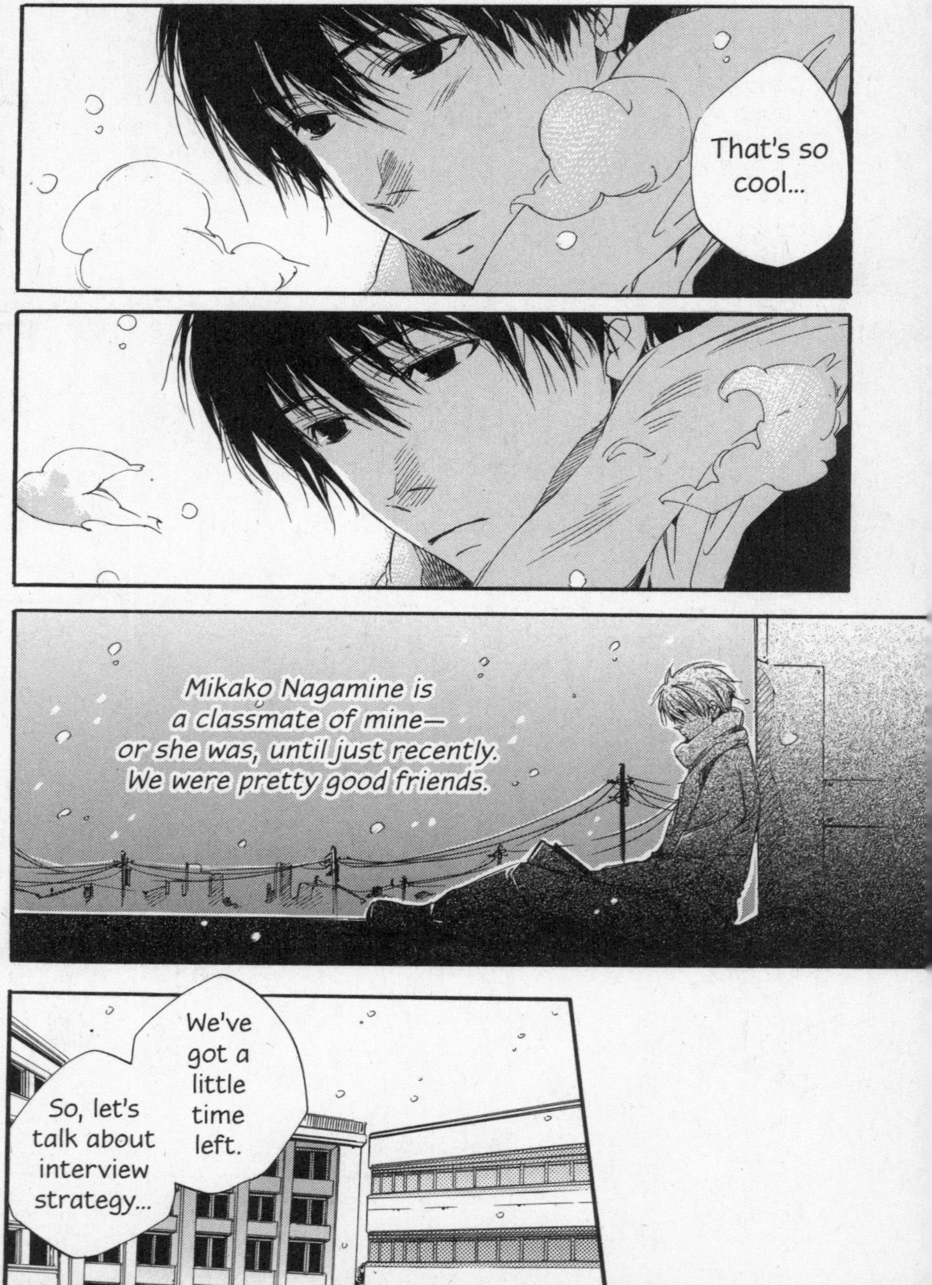
That's so cool...
Mikako Nagamine is a classmate of mine— or she was, until just recently. We were pretty good friends.
We've got a little time left.
So, let's talk about interview strategy...

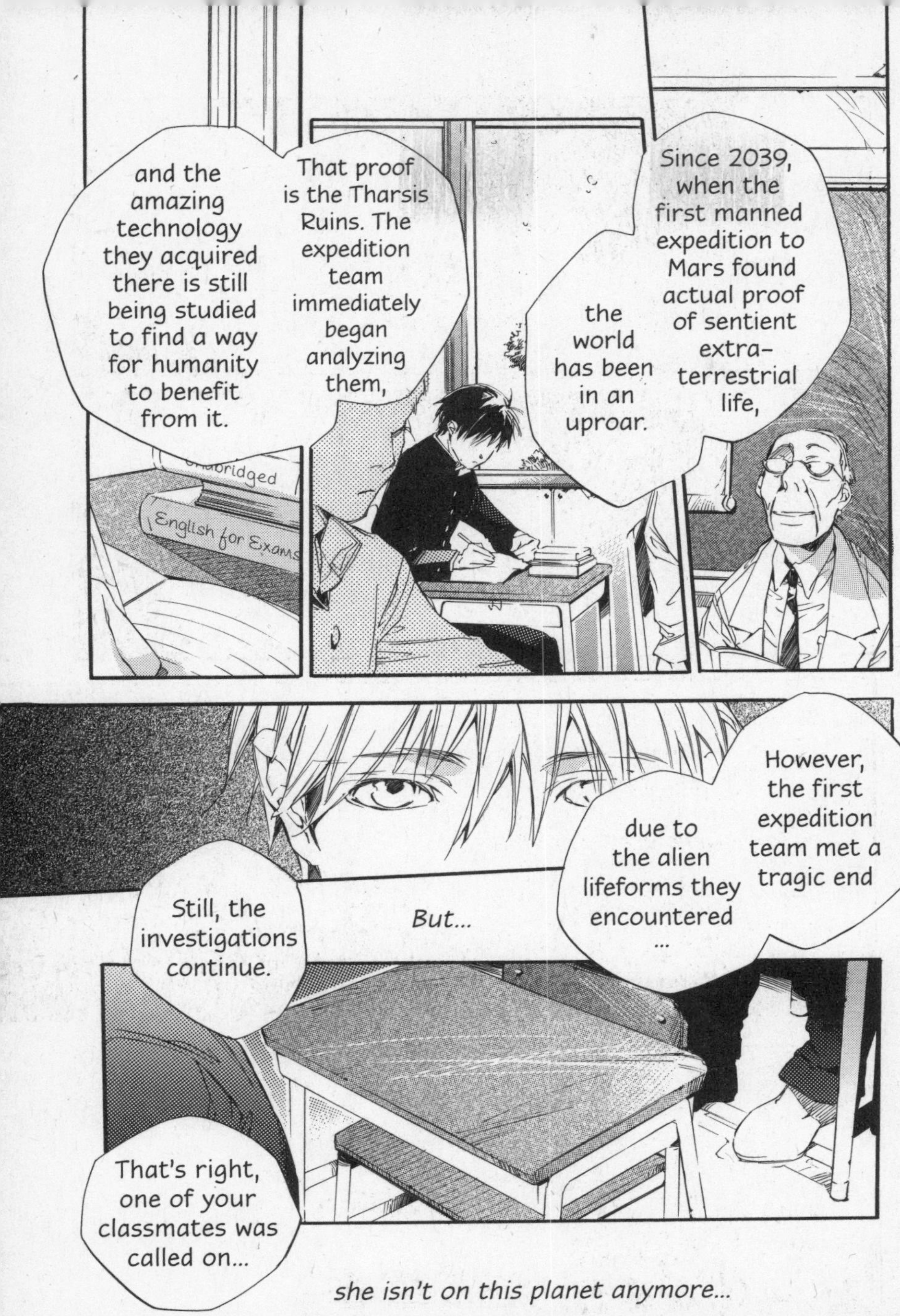
Since 2039, when the first manned expedition to Mars found actual proof of sentient extra-terrestrial life,
the world has been in an uproar.
That proof is the Tharsis Ruins. The expedition team immediately began analyzing them,
and the amazing technology they acquired there is still being studied to find a way for humanity to benefit from it.
Unabridged
English for Exams
However, the first expedition team met a tragic end
due to the alien lifeforms they encountered...
But...
Still, the investigations continue.
That's right, one of your classmates was called on...
she isn't on this planet anymore...

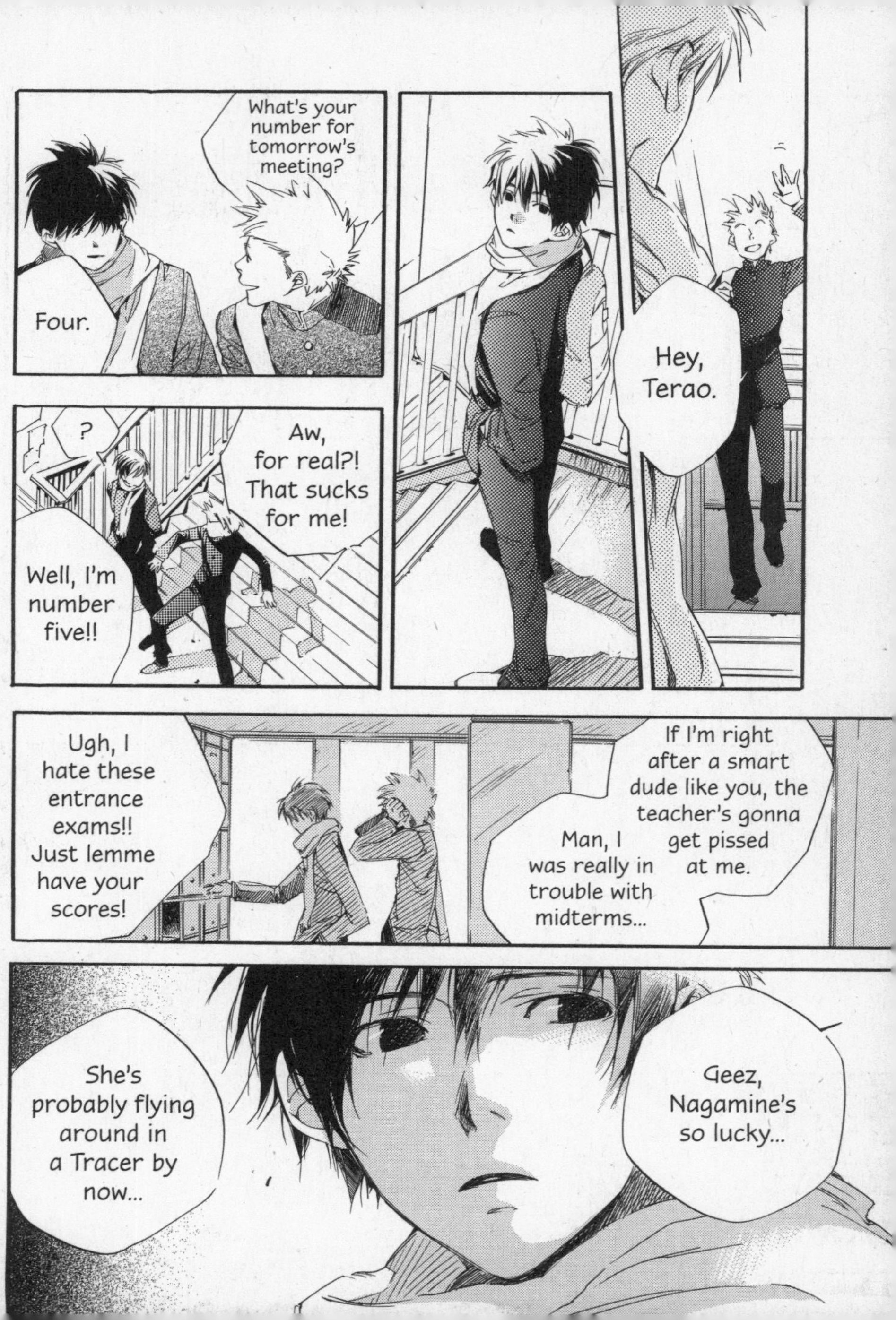
Hey, Terao.
What's your number for tomorrow's meeting?
Four.
Aw, for real?! That sucks for me!
?
Well, I'm number five!!
If I'm right after a smart dude like you, the teacher's gonna get pissed at me.
Man, I was really in trouble with midterms...
Ugh, I hate these entrance exams!! Just lemme have your scores!
Geez, Nagamine's so lucky...
She's probably flying around in a Tracer by now...

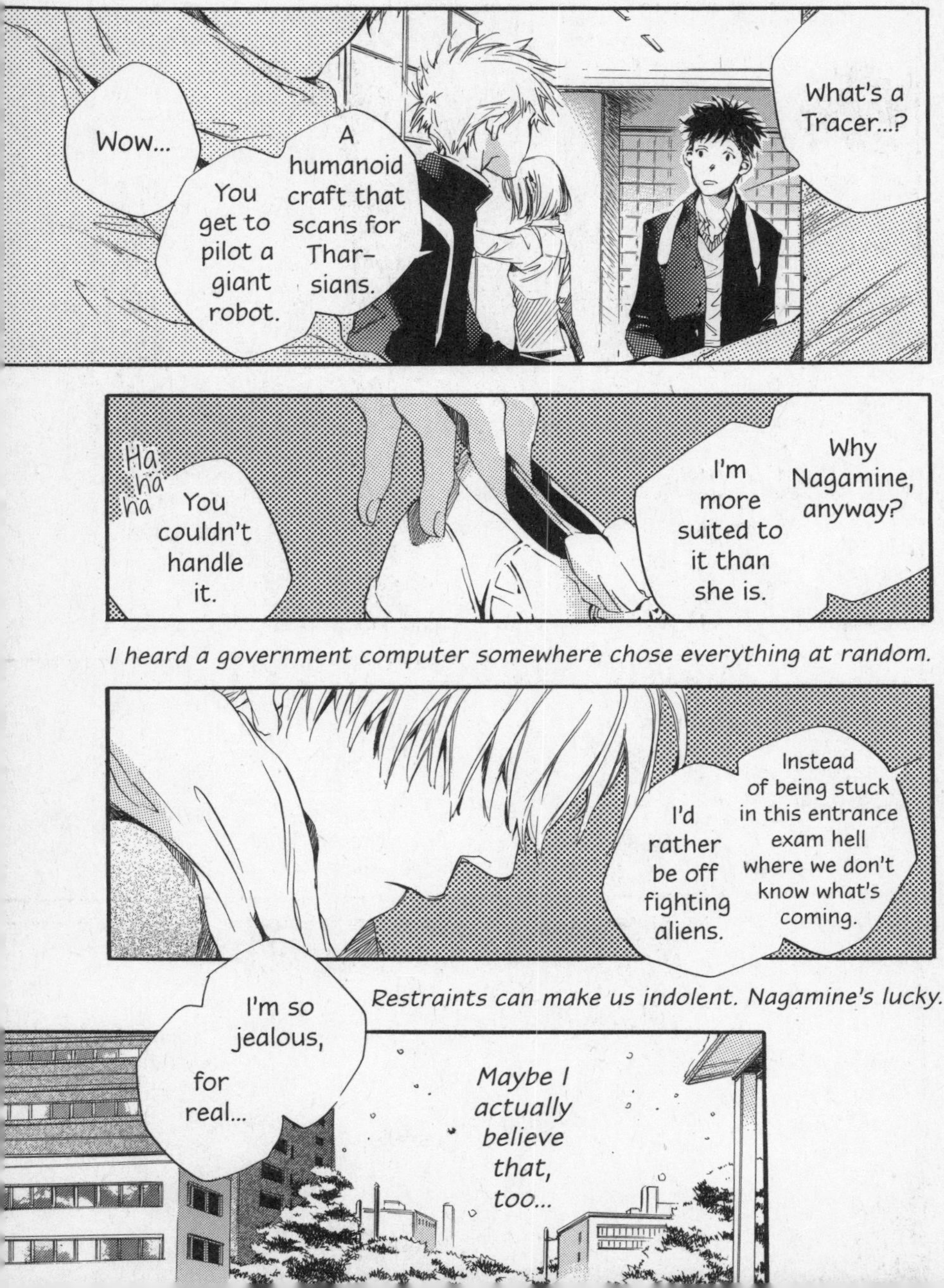
What's a Tracer...?
A humanoid craft that scans for Thar-sians.
Wow...
You get to pilot a giant robot.
Why Nagamine, anyway?
I'm more suited to it than she is.
Ha ha ha
You couldn't handle it.
I heard a government computer somewhere chose everything at random.
Instead of being stuck in this entrance exam hell where we don't know what's coming.
I'd rather be off fighting aliens.
Restraints can make us indolent. Nagamine's lucky.
Maybe I actually believe that, too...
I'm so jealous,
for real...

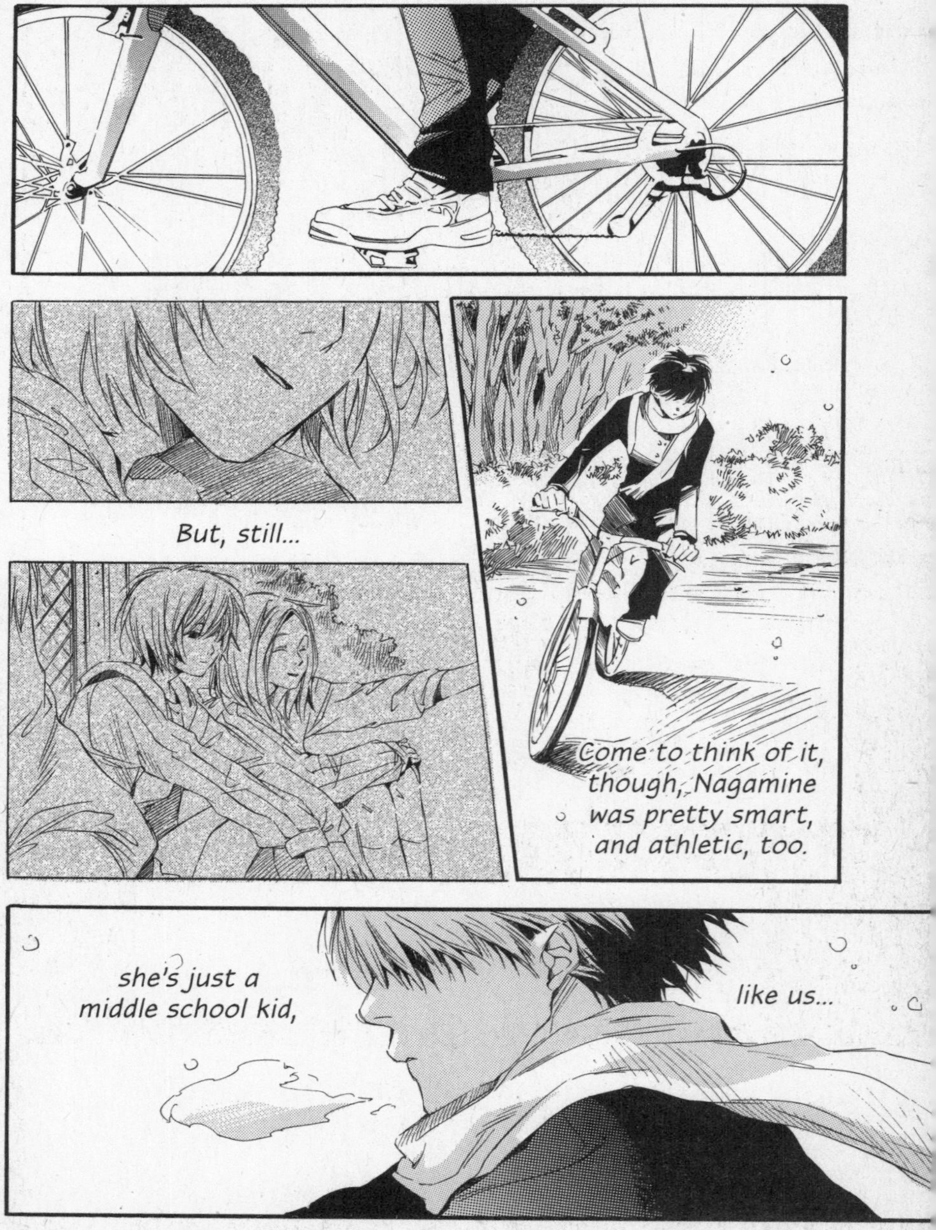
Come to think of it, though, Nagamine was pretty smart, and athletic, too.
But, still...
she's just a middle school kid,
like us...

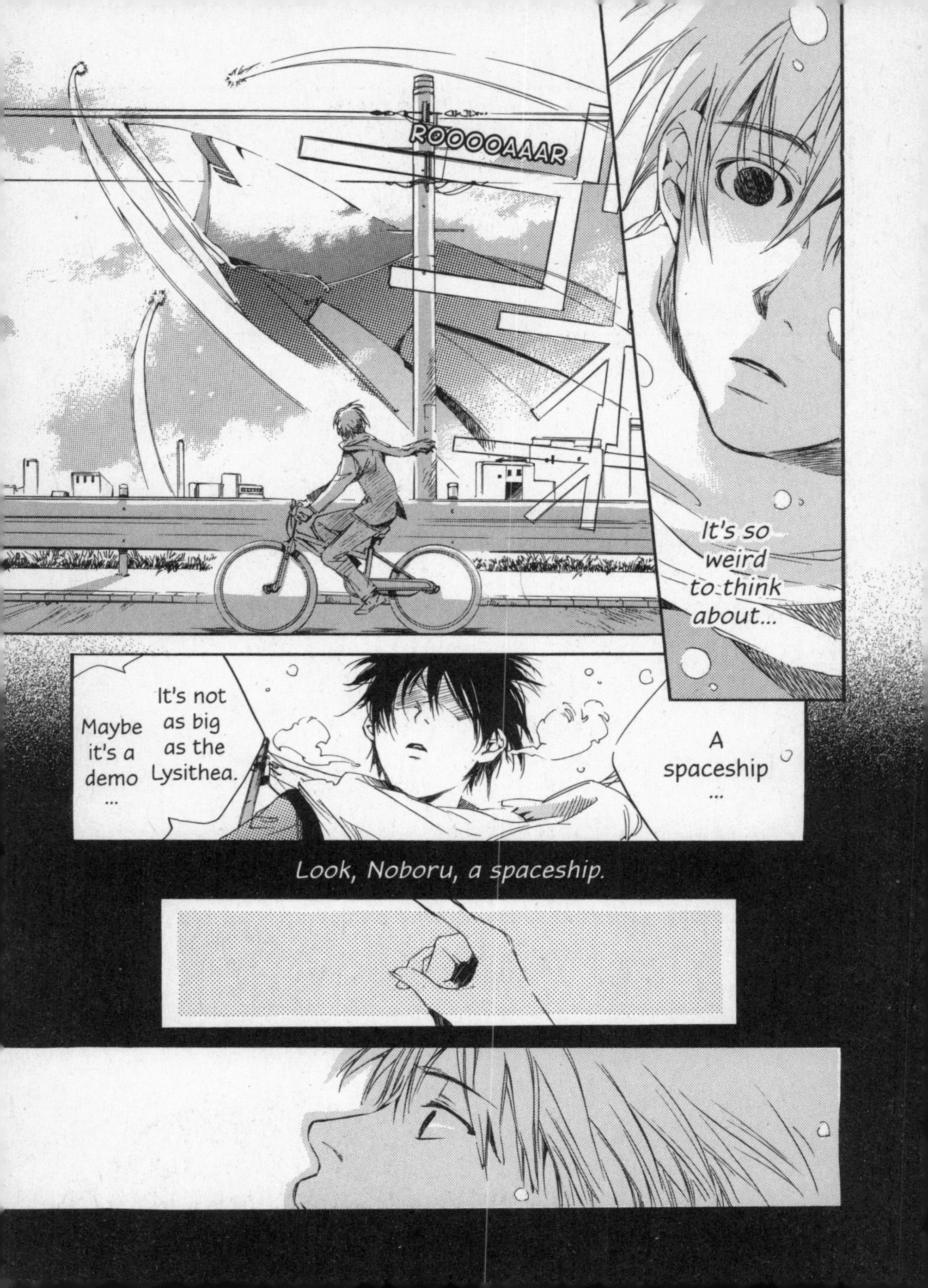
It's so weird to think about...
ROOOOAAAR
A spaceship ...
It's not as big as the Lysithea.
Maybe it's a demo ...
Look, Noboru, a spaceship.

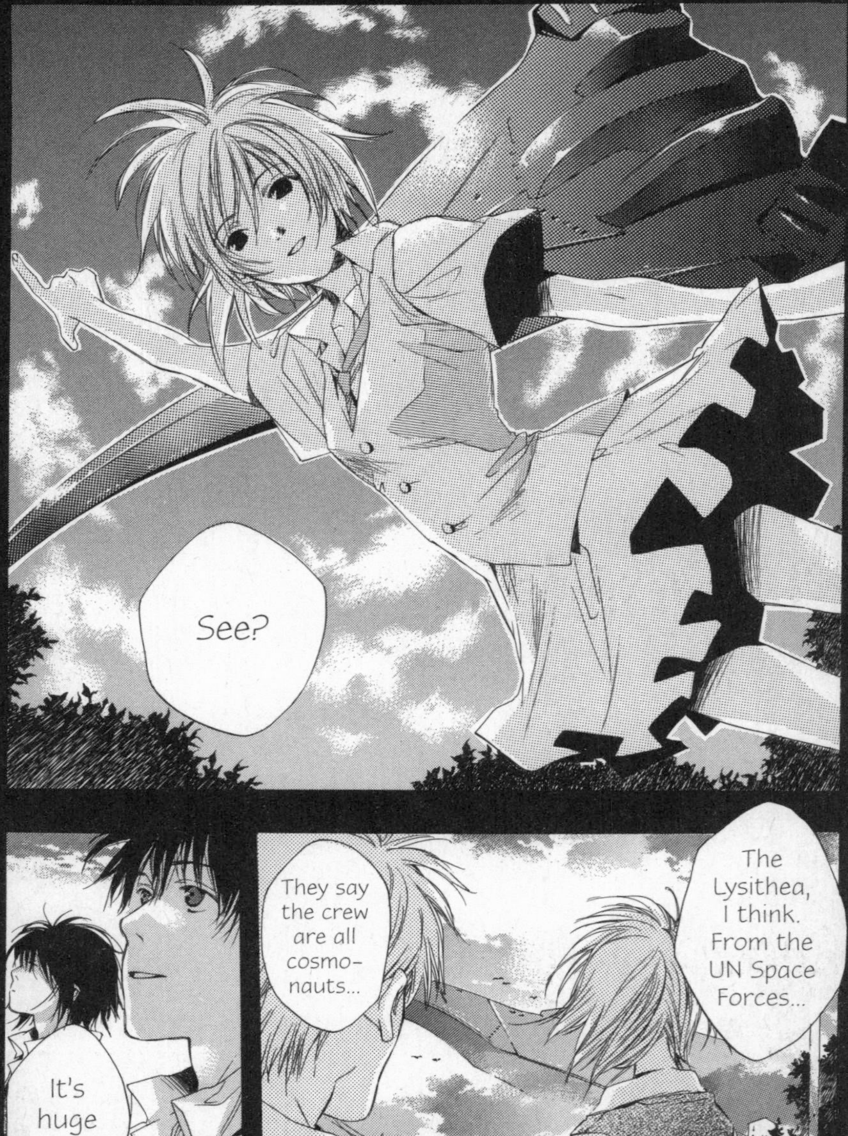
See?
The Lysithea, I think. From the UN Space Forces...
They say the crew are all cosmo-nauts...
It's huge ...

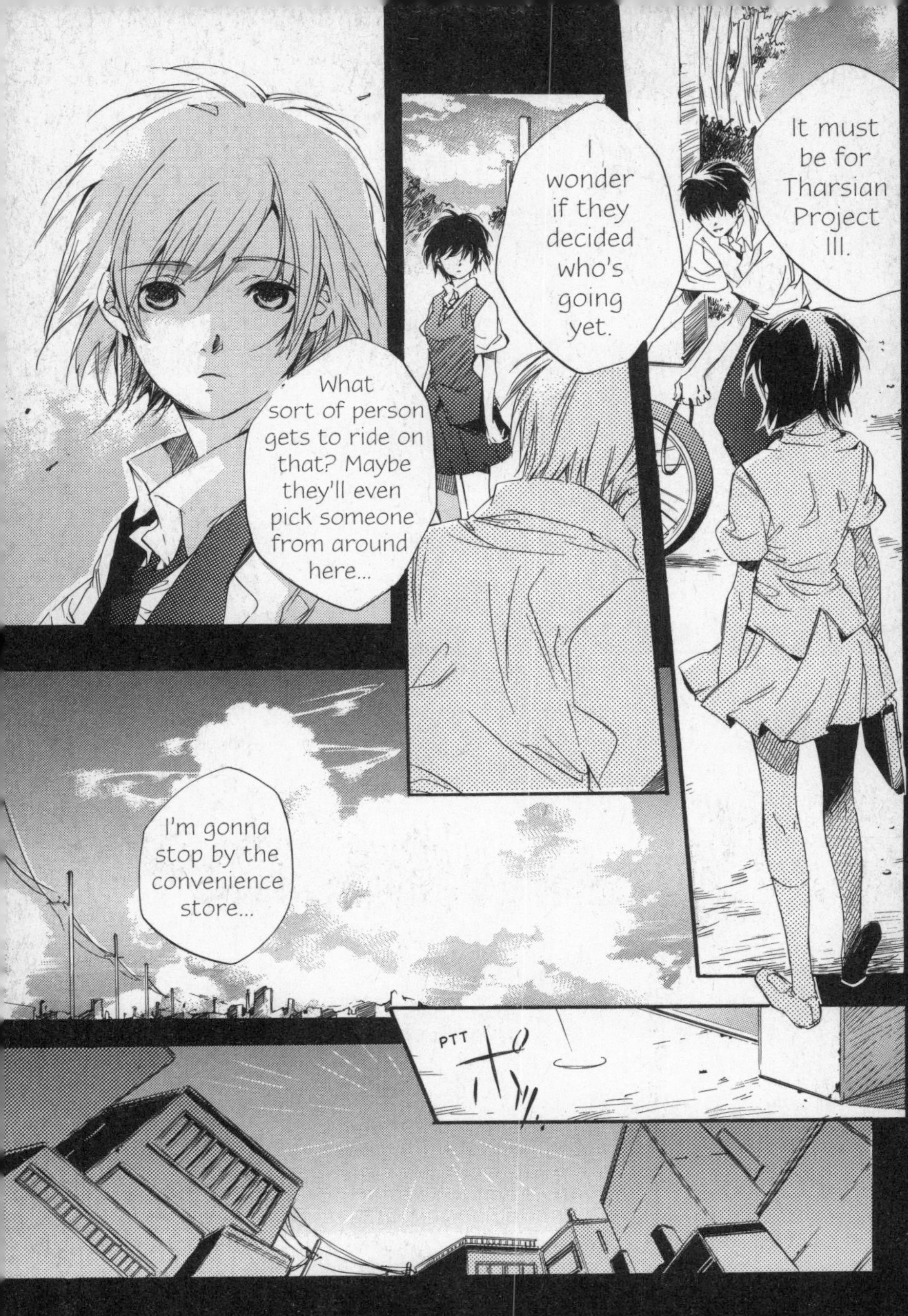
It must be for Tharsian Project III.
I wonder if they decided who's going yet.
What sort of person gets to ride on that? Maybe they'll even pick someone from around here...
I'm gonna stop by the convenience store...
PTT

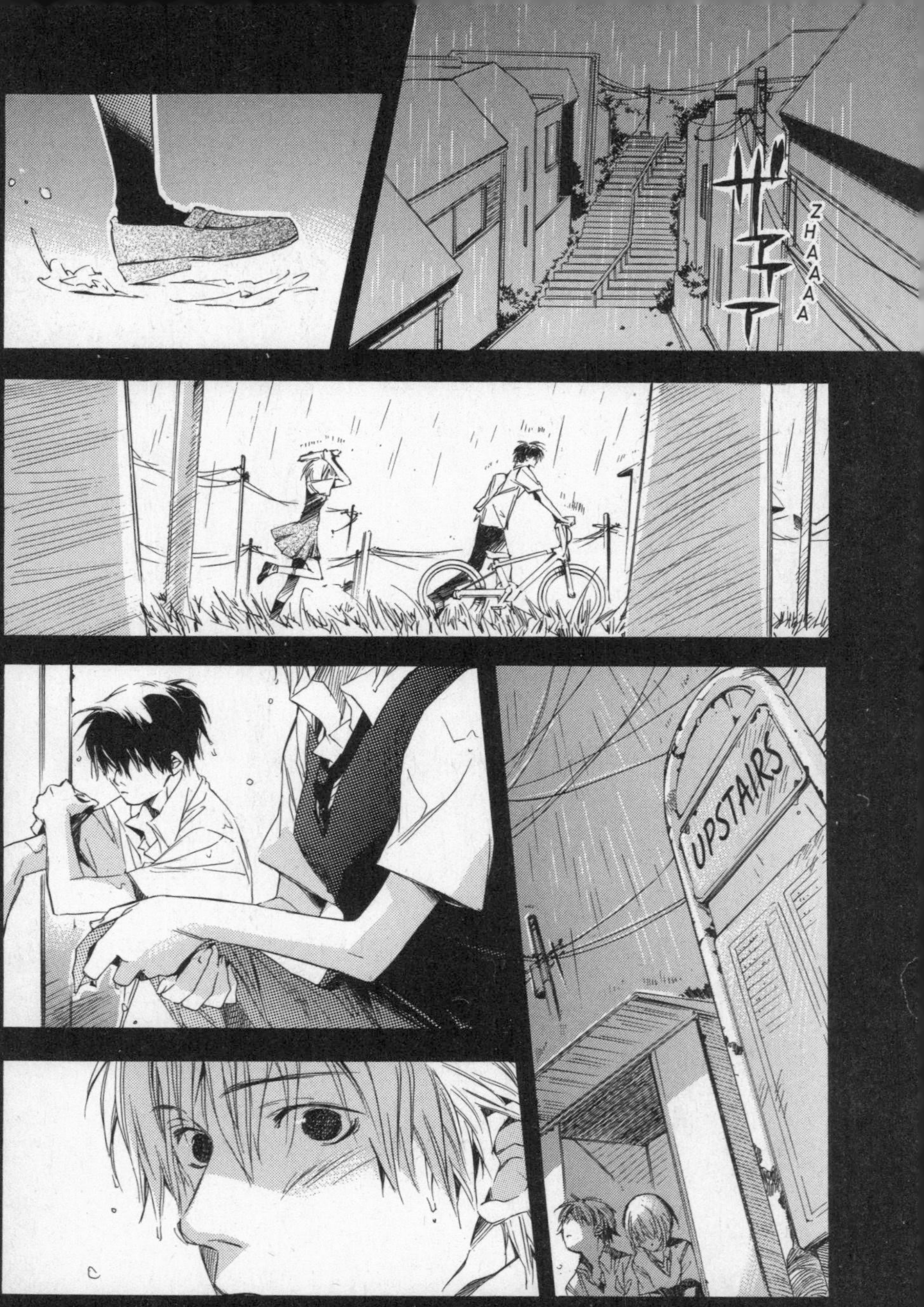
ZHAAAA
UPSTAIRS

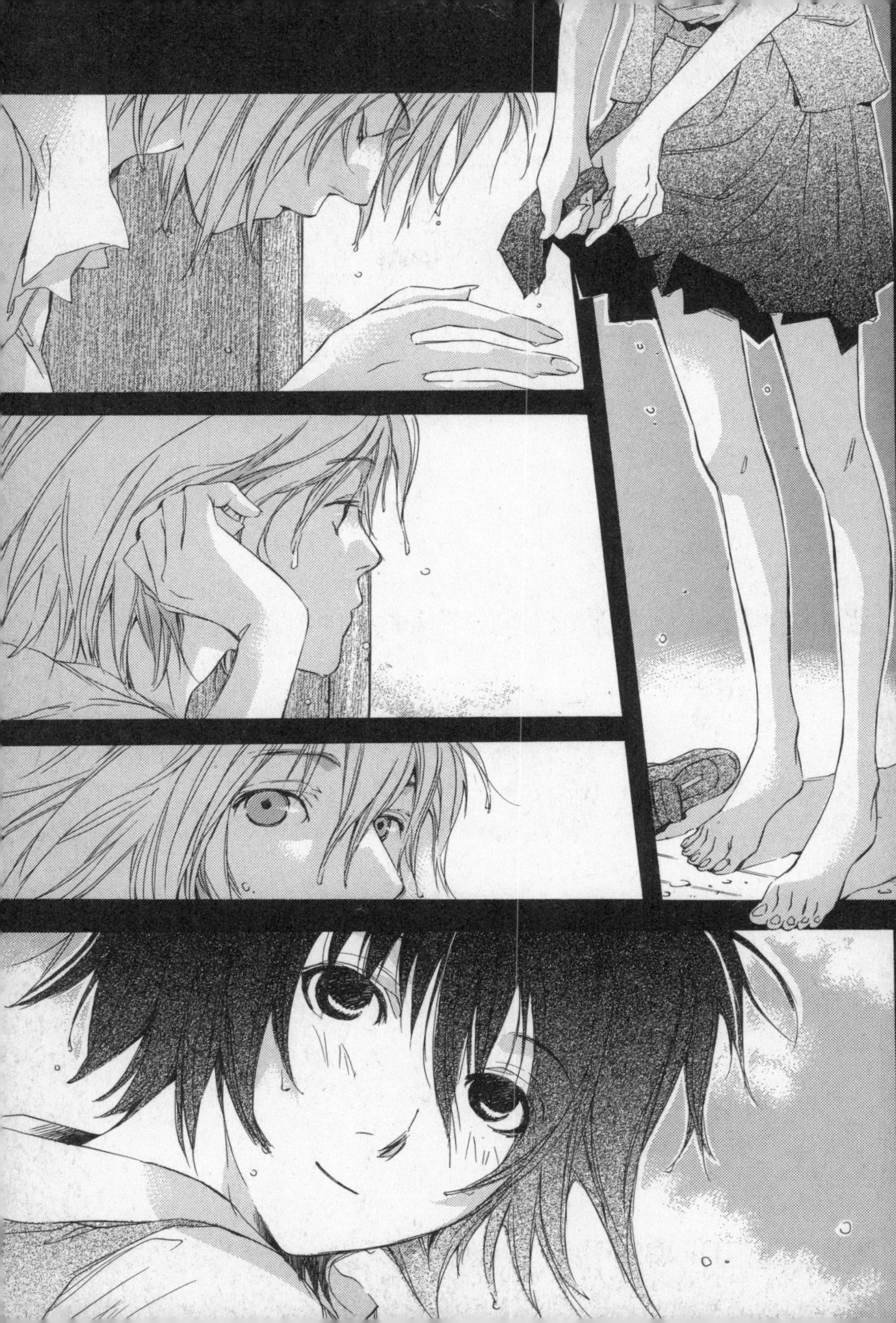

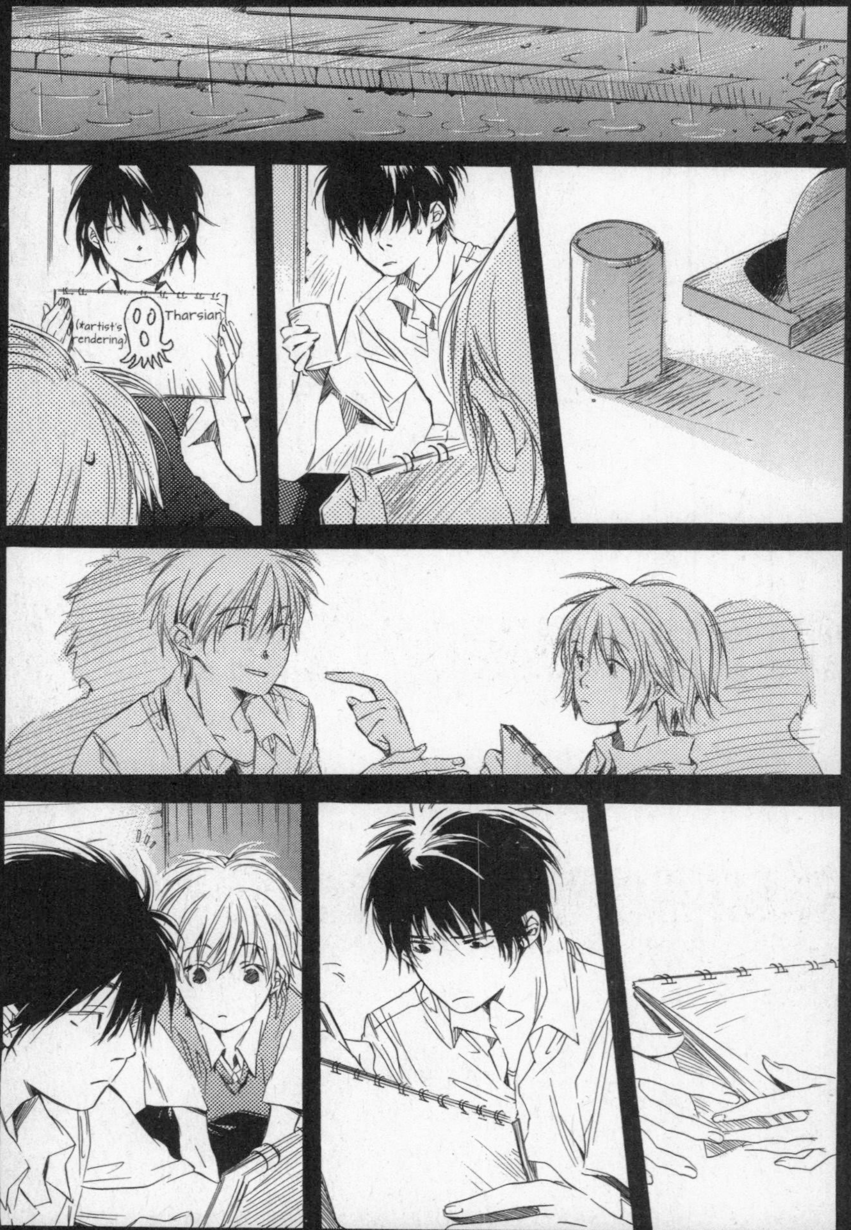
Tharsian
(*artist's rendering)

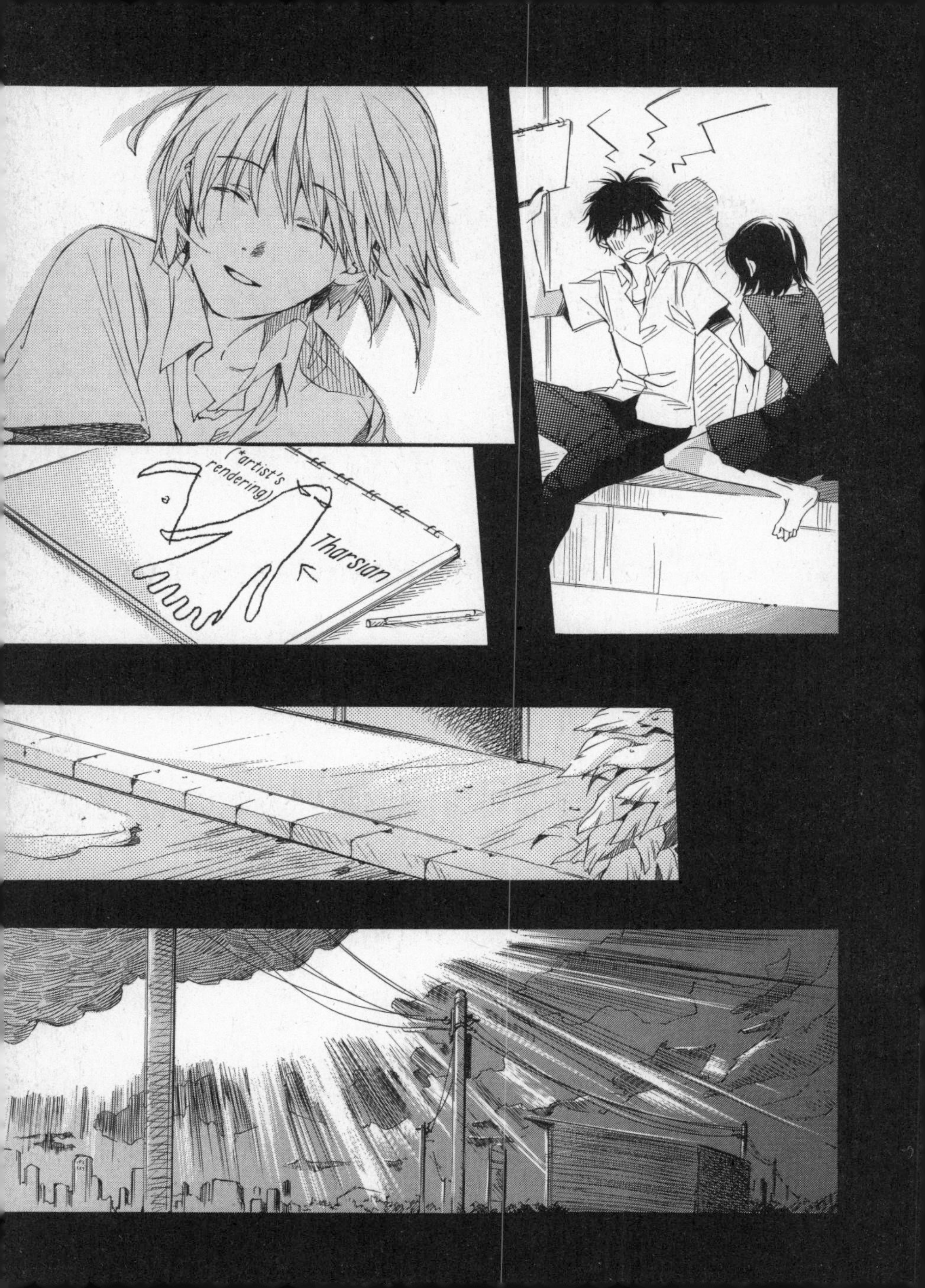
(*artist's rendering)
Tharsian

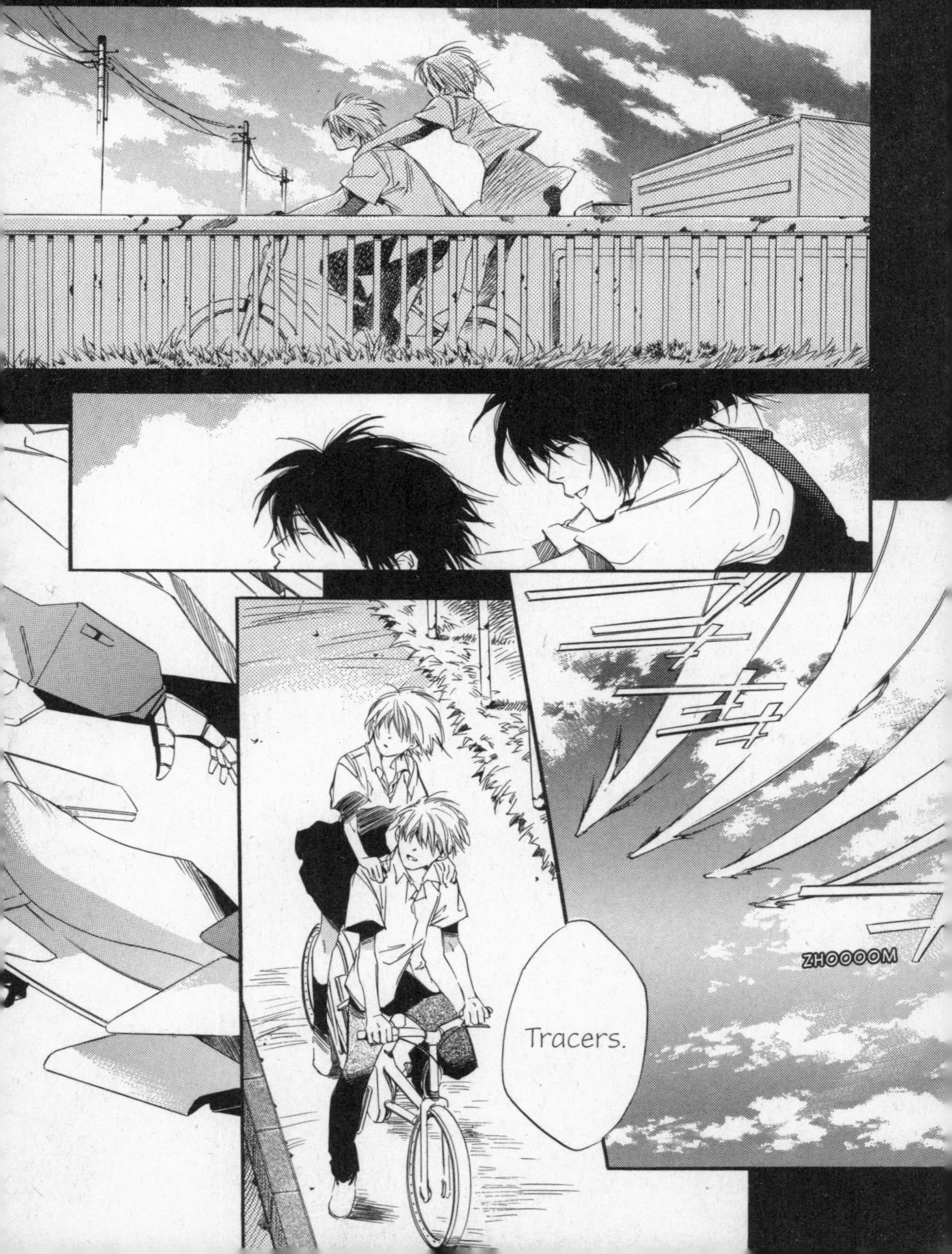
ZHOOOOM
Tracers.

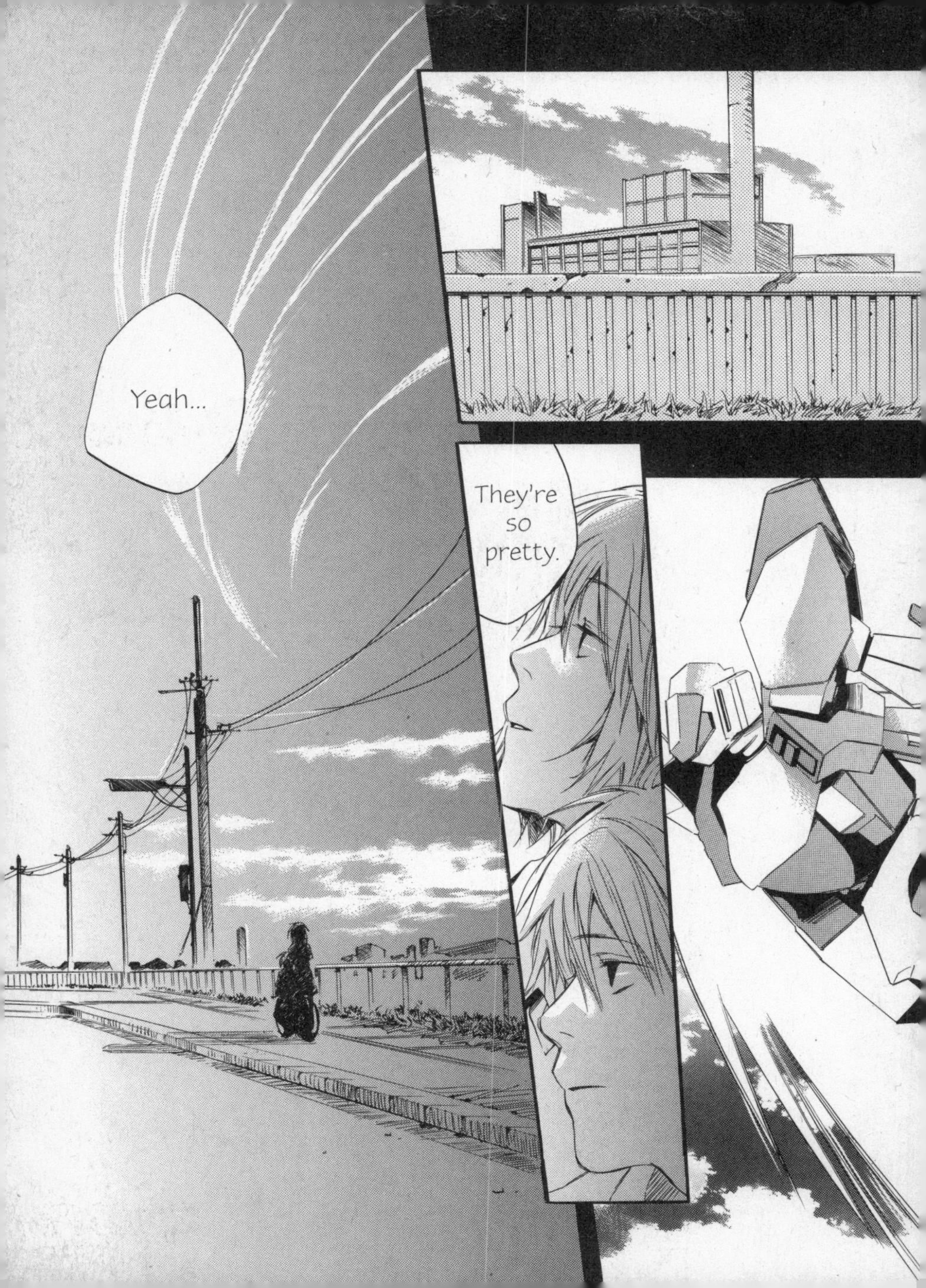
They're so pretty.
Yeah...

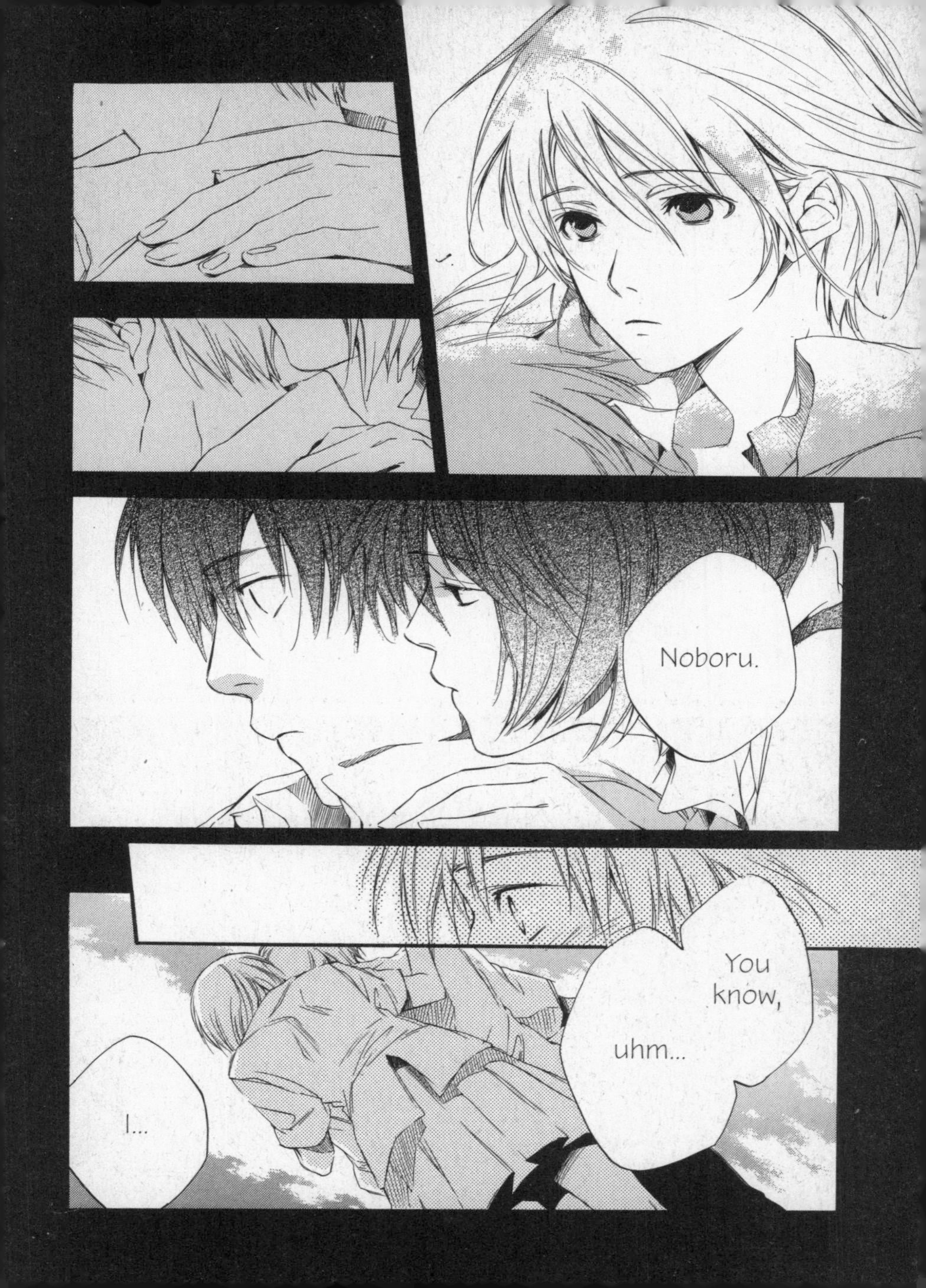
Noboru.
You know, uhm...
I...

I'm going to pilot one of those...

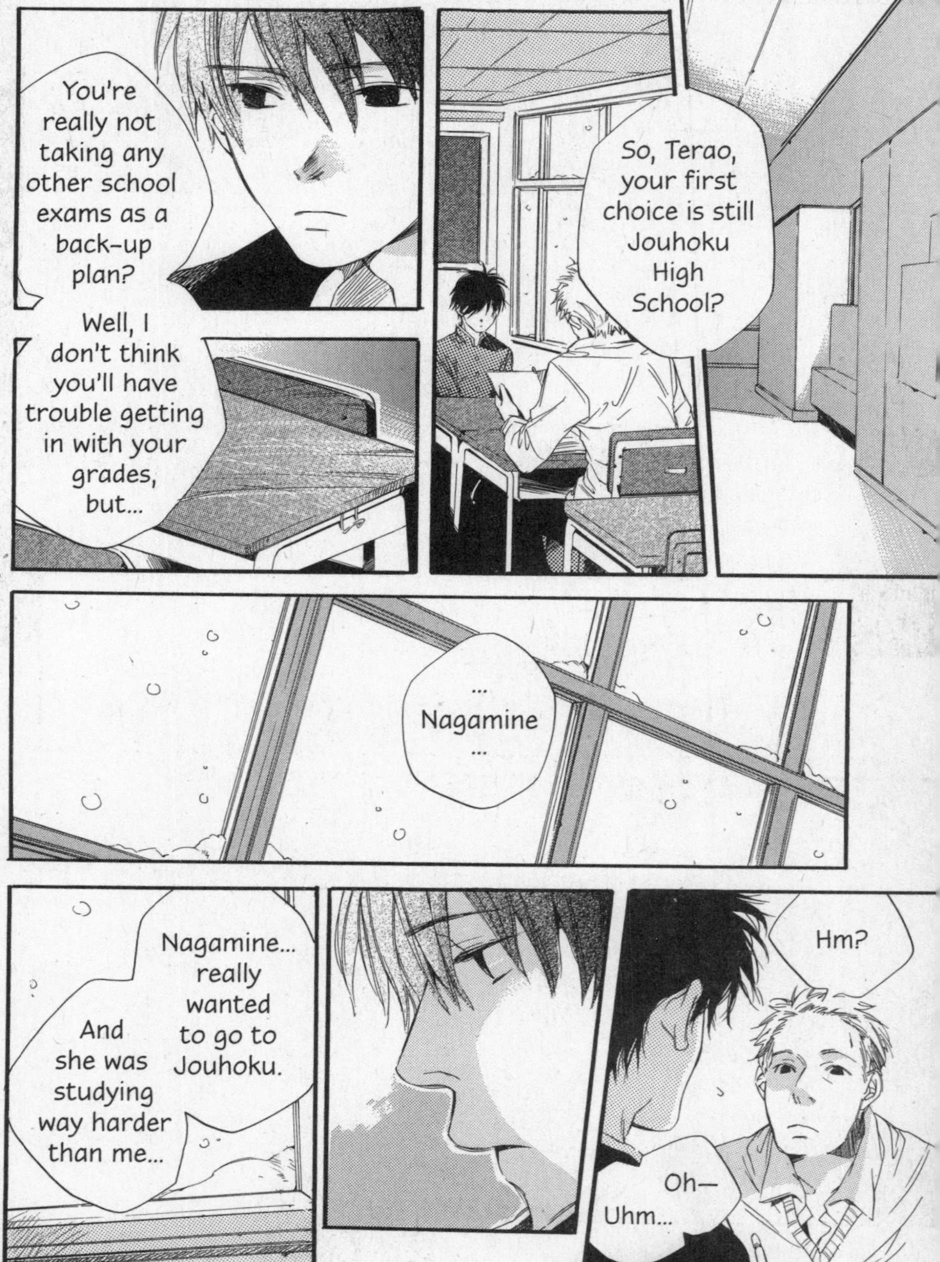
So, Terao, your first choice is still Jouhoku High School?
You're really not taking any other school exams as a back-up plan?
Well, I don't think you'll have trouble getting in with your grades, but...
... Nagamine ...
Hm?
Oh— Uhm...
Nagamine... really wanted to go to Jouhoku.
And she was studying way harder than me...

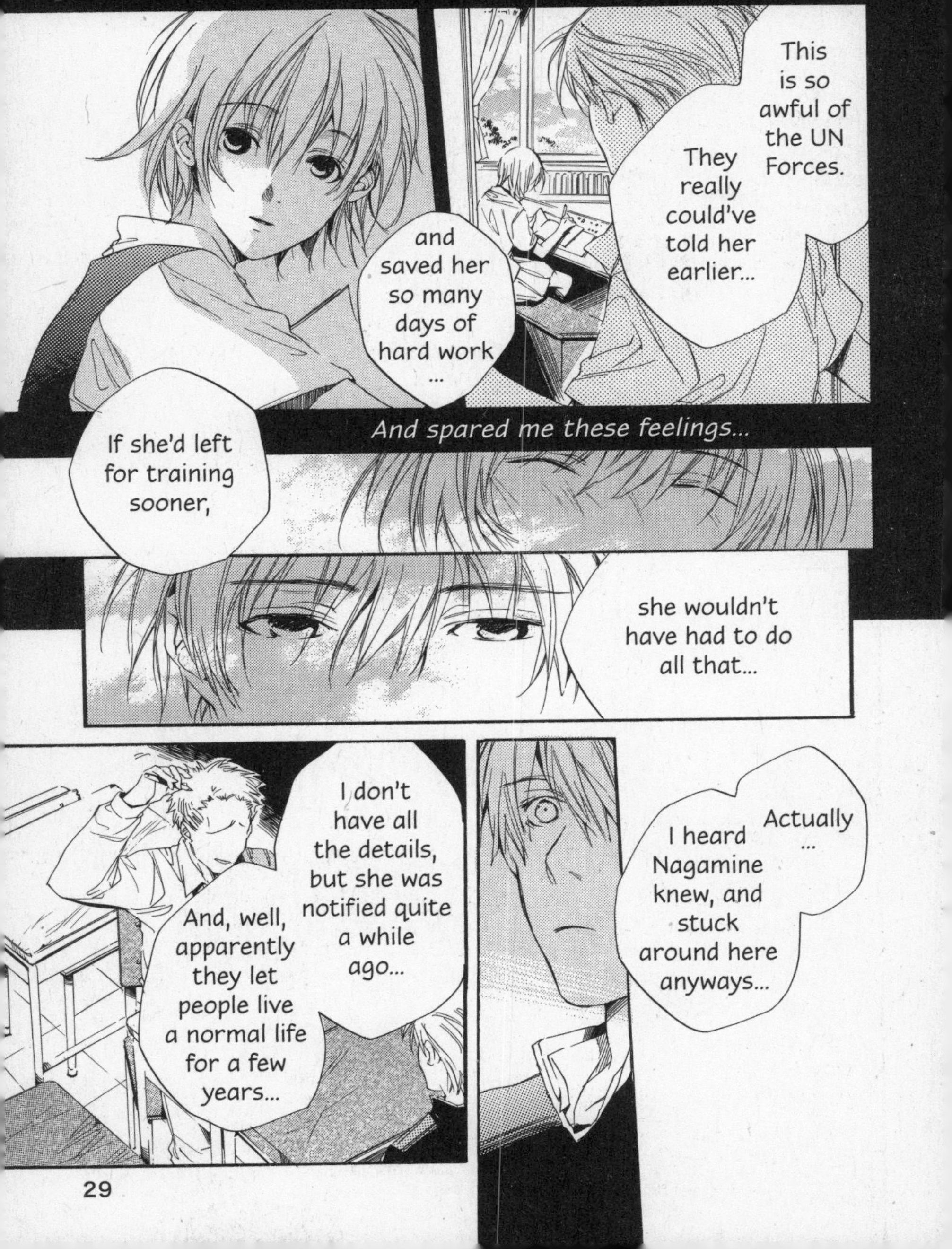
This is so awful of the UN Forces.
They really could've told her earlier...
and saved her so many days of hard work ...
And spared me these feelings...
If she'd left for training sooner,
she wouldn't have had to do all that...
Actually ...
I heard Nagamine knew, and stuck around here anyways...
I don't have all the details, but she was notified quite a while ago...
And, well, apparently they let people live a normal life for a few years...

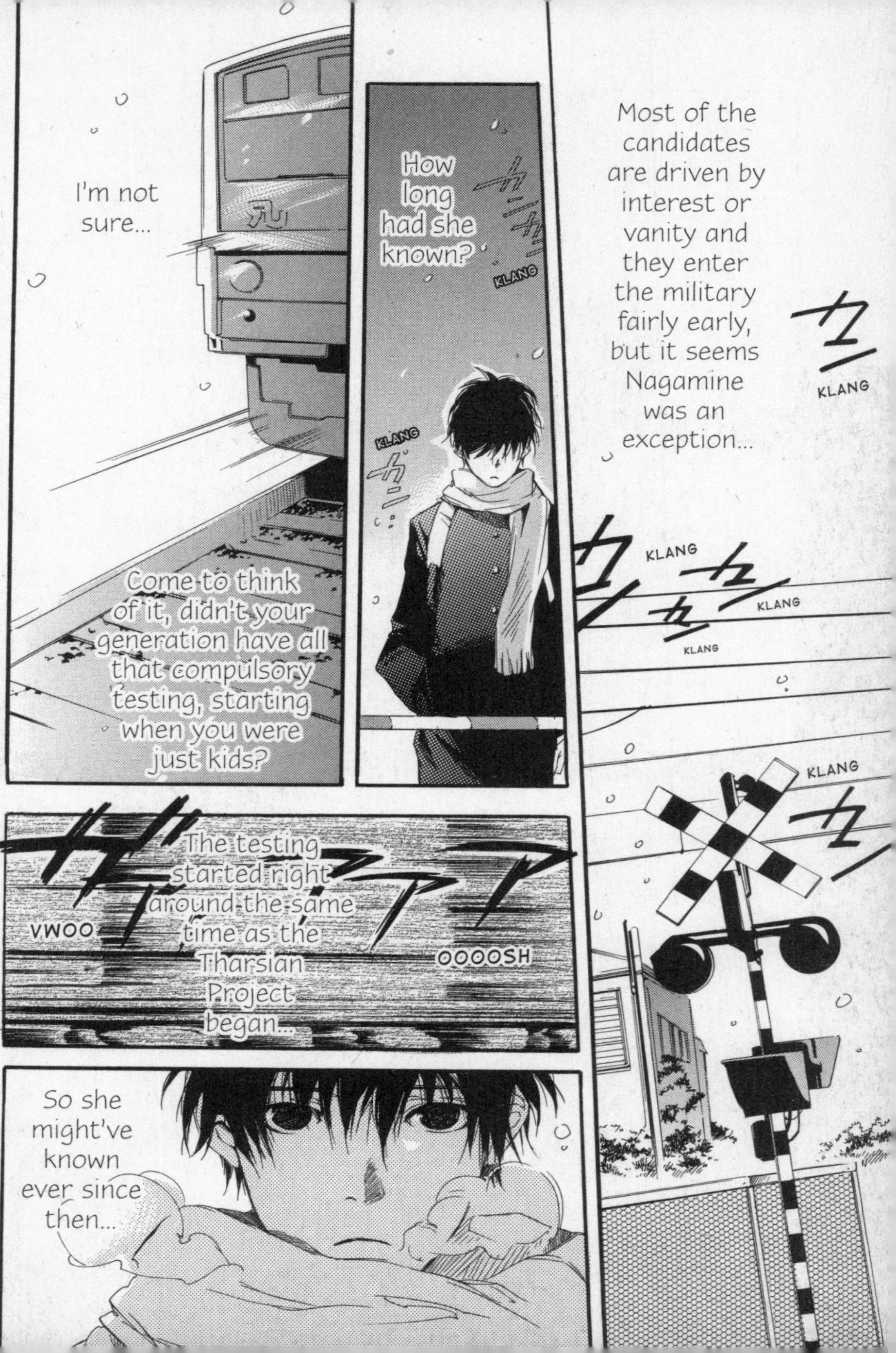
Most of the candidates are driven by interest or vanity and they enter the military fairly early, but it seems Nagamine was an exception...
KLANG
KLANG
KLANG
KLANG
KLANG
How long had she known?
KLANG
KLANG
I'm not sure...
Come to think of it, didn't your generation have all that compulsory testing, starting when you were just kids?
OOOOSH
The testing started right around the same time as the Tharsian Project began...
VWOO
So she might've known ever since then...

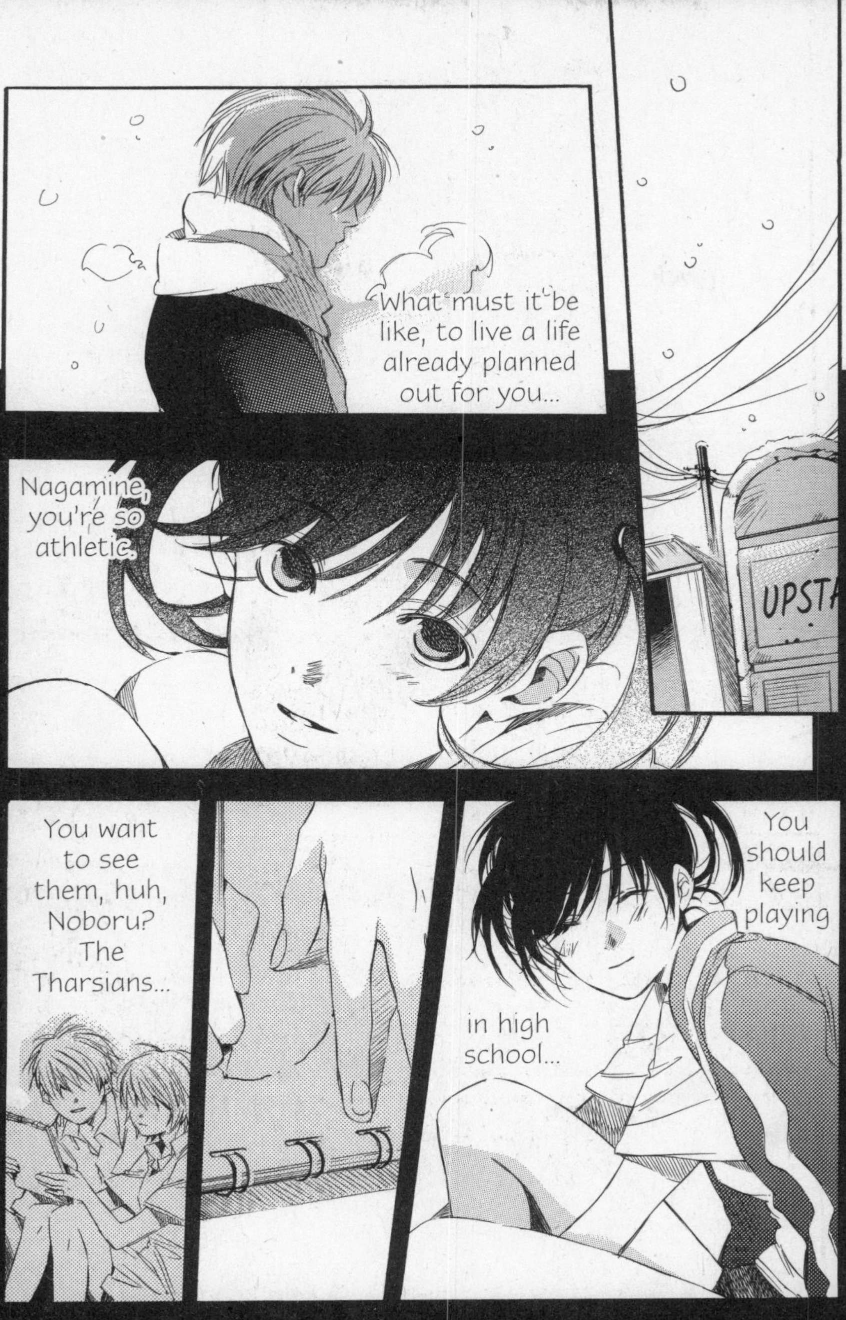
UPSTA
What must it be like, to live a life already planned out for you...
Nagamine, you're so athletic.
You should keep playing
in high school...
You want to see them, huh, Noboru? The Tharsians...

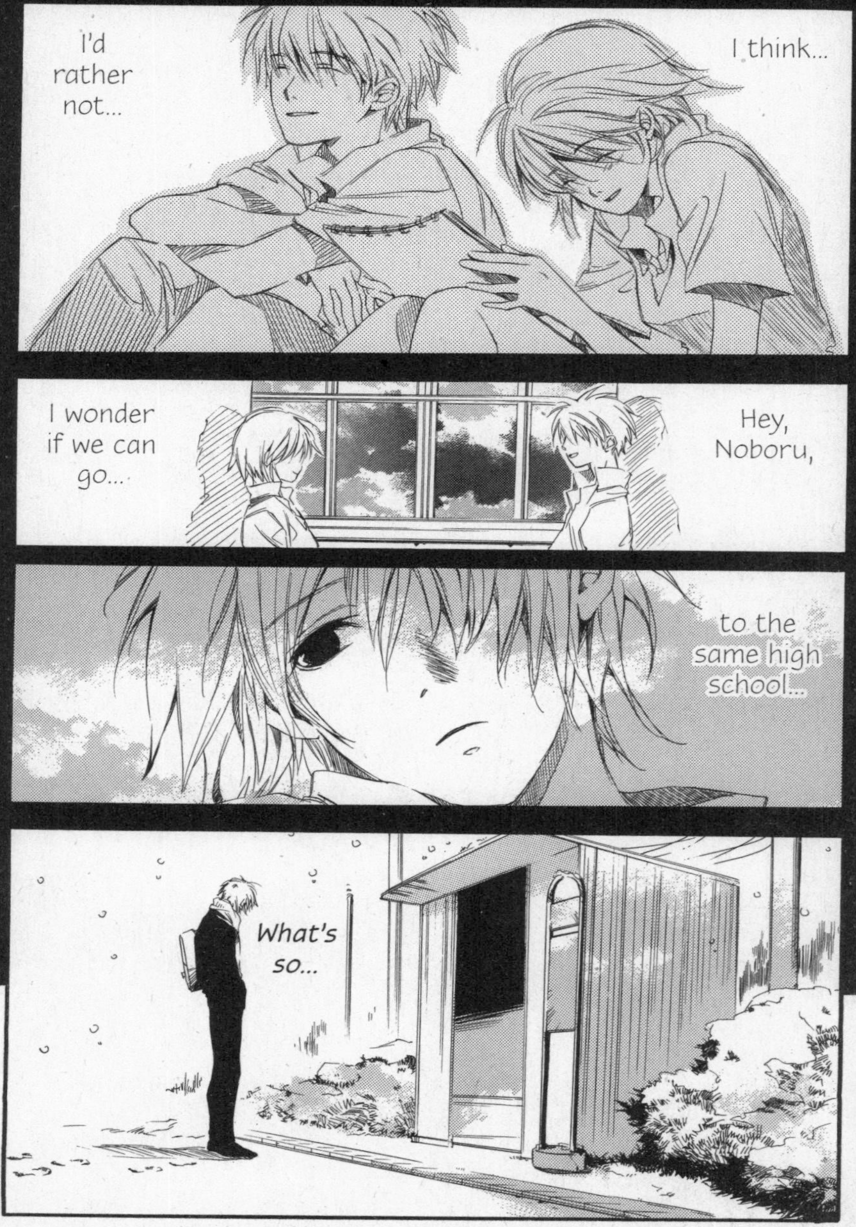
I think...
I'd rather not...
Hey, Noboru,
I wonder if we can go...
to the same high school...
What's so...

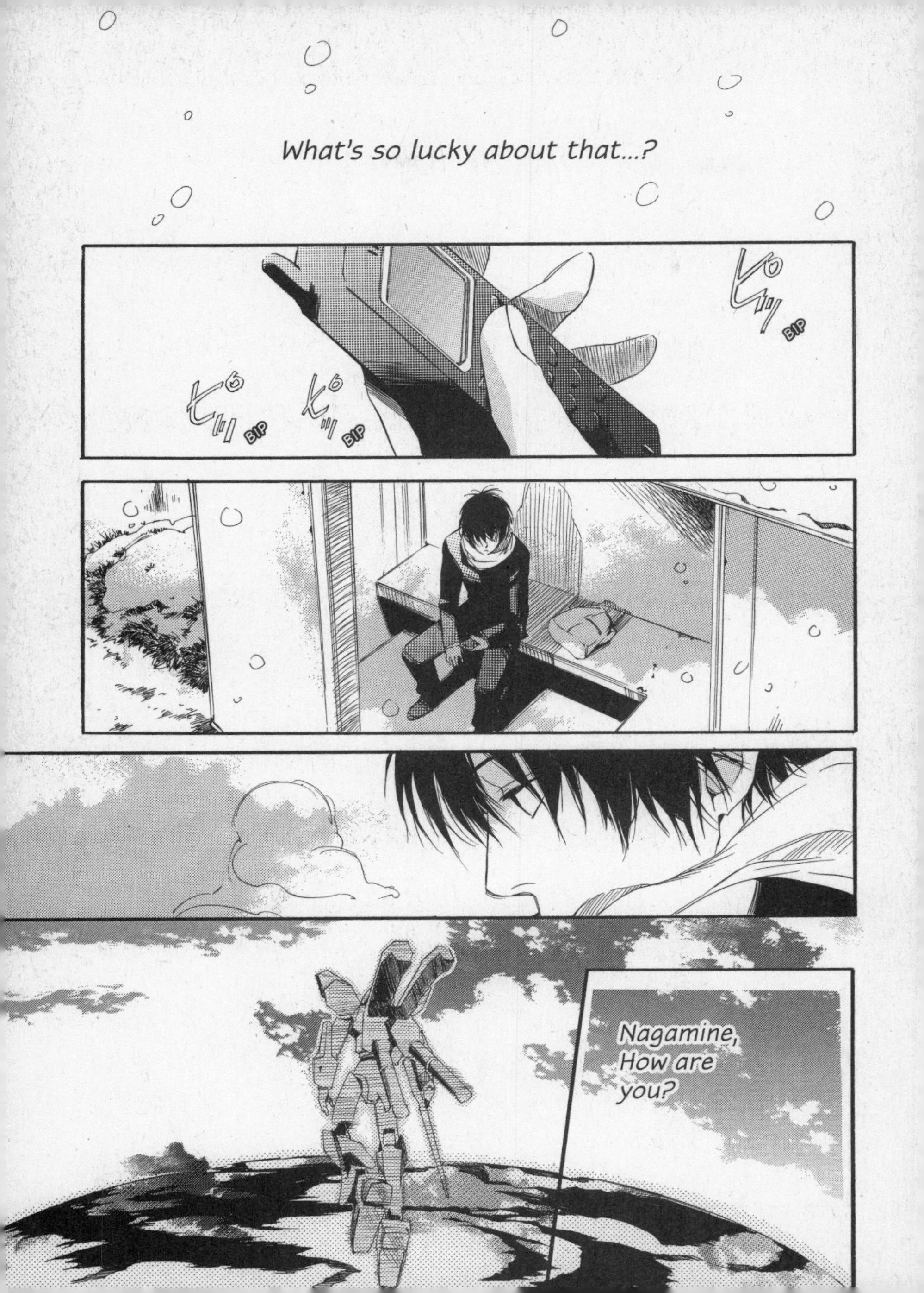

What's so lucky about that...?
ピッ BIP
ピッ BIP
ピッ BIP
Nagamine,
How are
you?

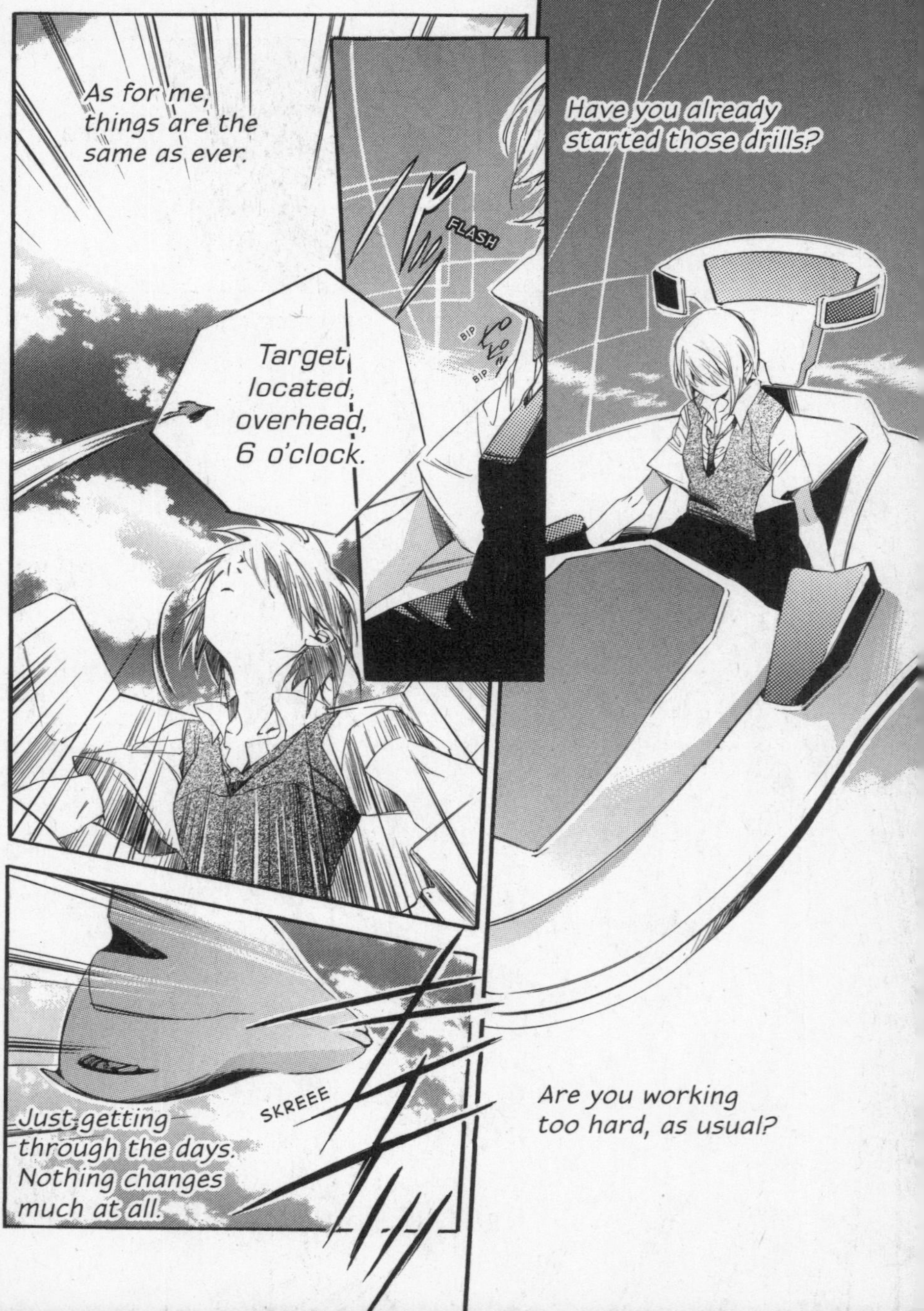
Have you already started those drills?
Are you working too hard, as usual?
FLASH
BIP
BIP
As for me, things are the same as ever.
Target located, overhead, 6 o'clock.
SKREEE
Just getting through the days. Nothing changes much at all.

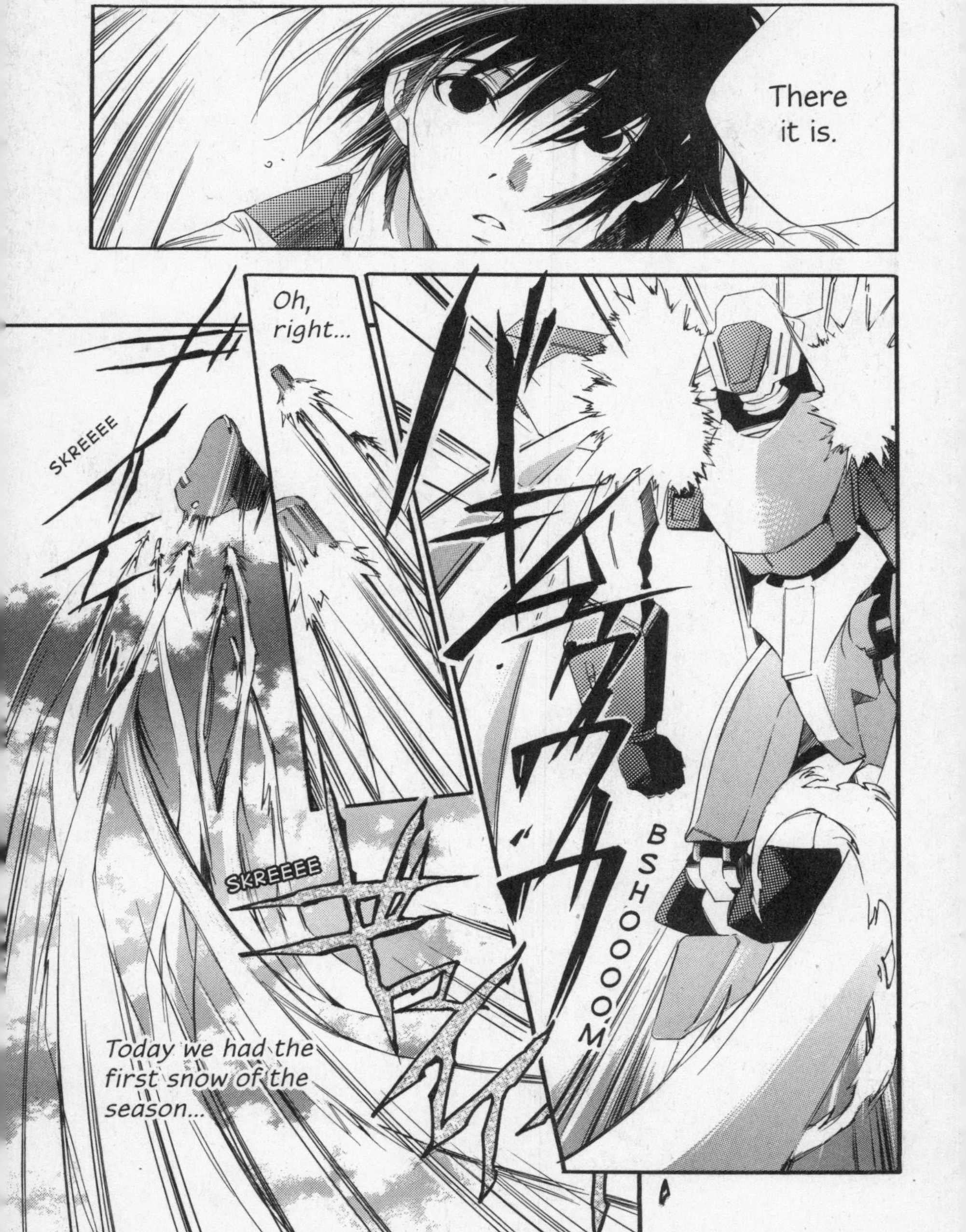

There it is.
BSHOOOOOOM
Oh, right...
SKREEEE
SKREEEEE
Today we had the first snow of the season...

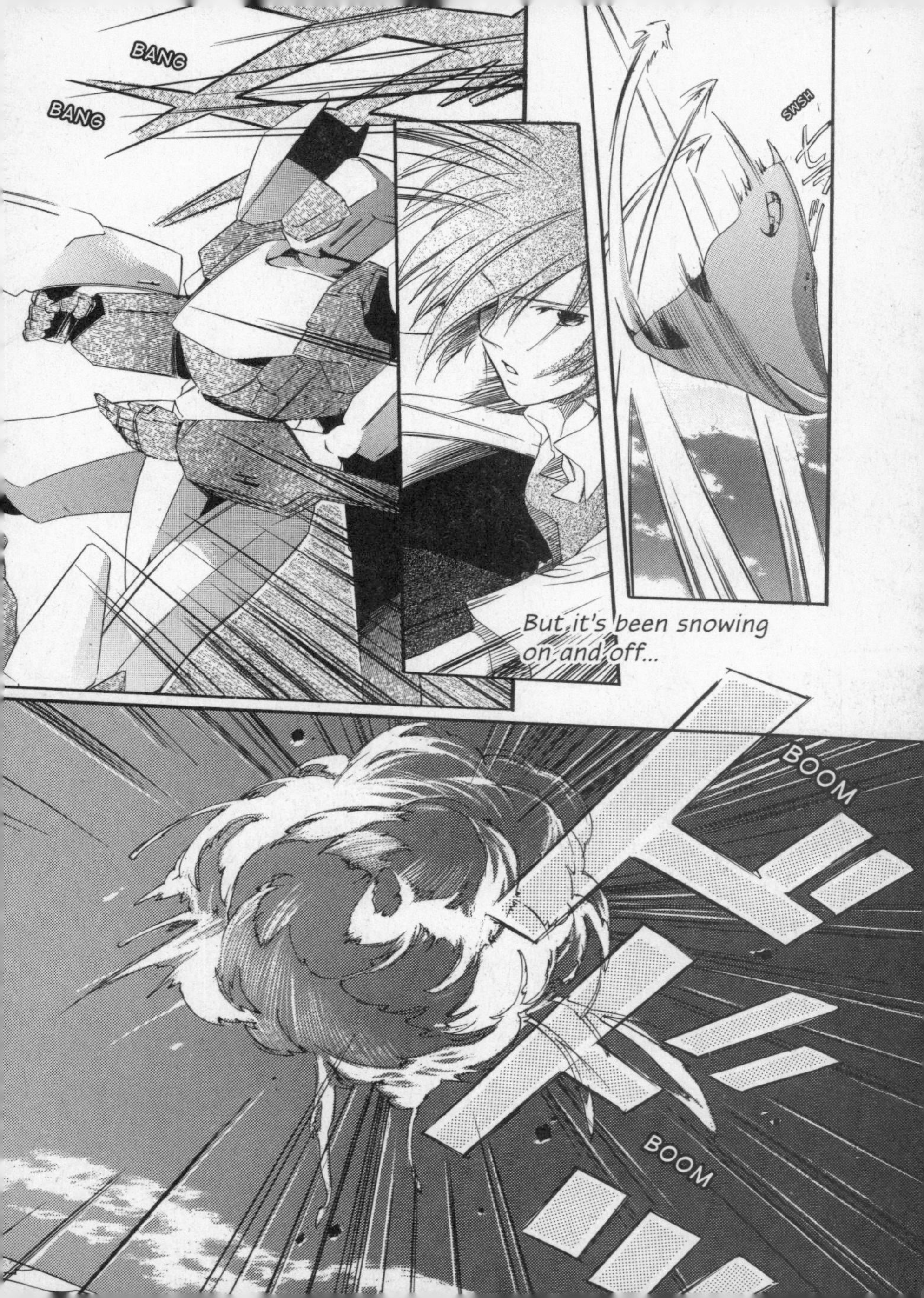
SWSH
But it's been snowing on and off...
BANG
BANG
BOOM
BOOM

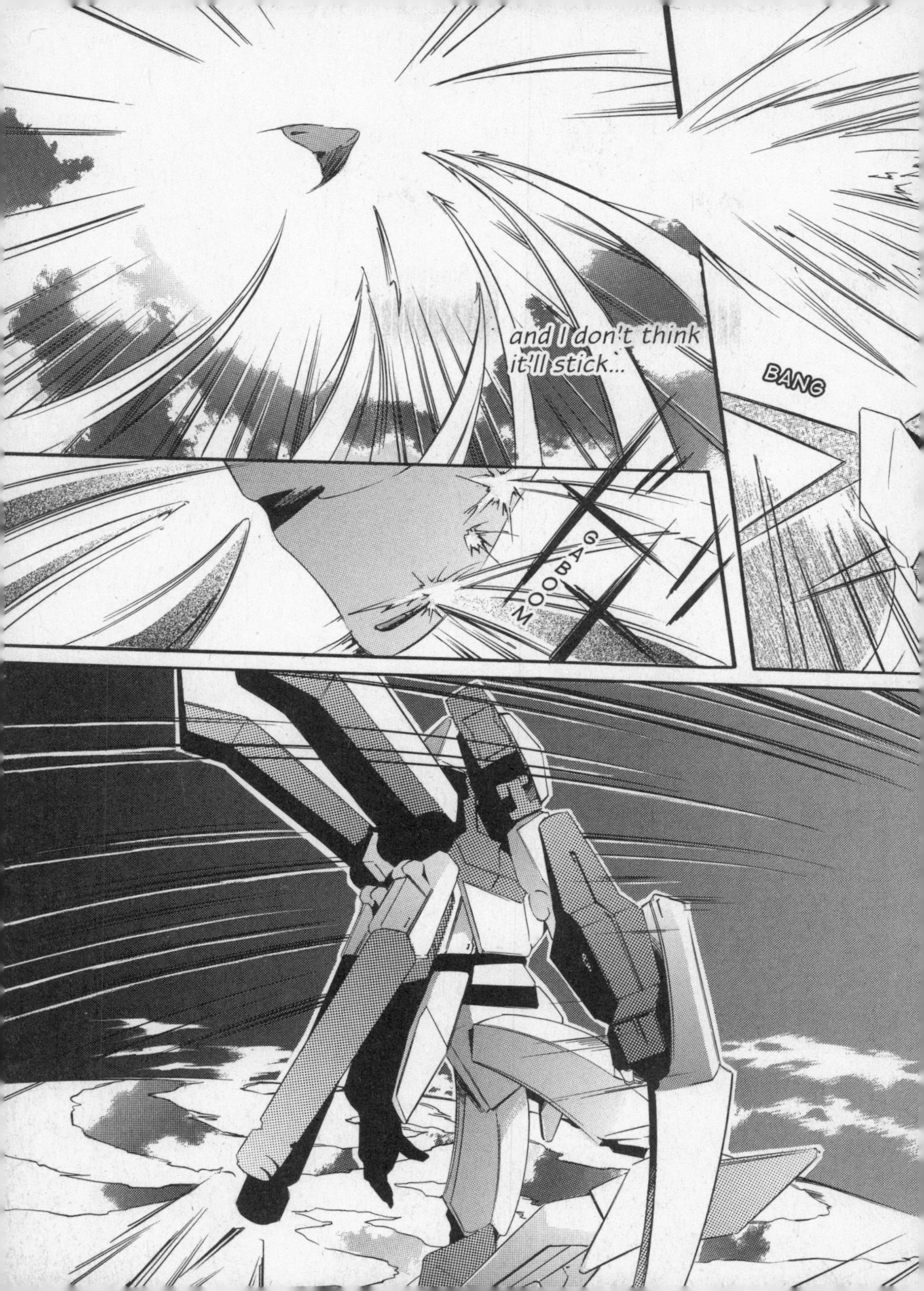
and I don't think it'll stick...
BANG
GABOOM

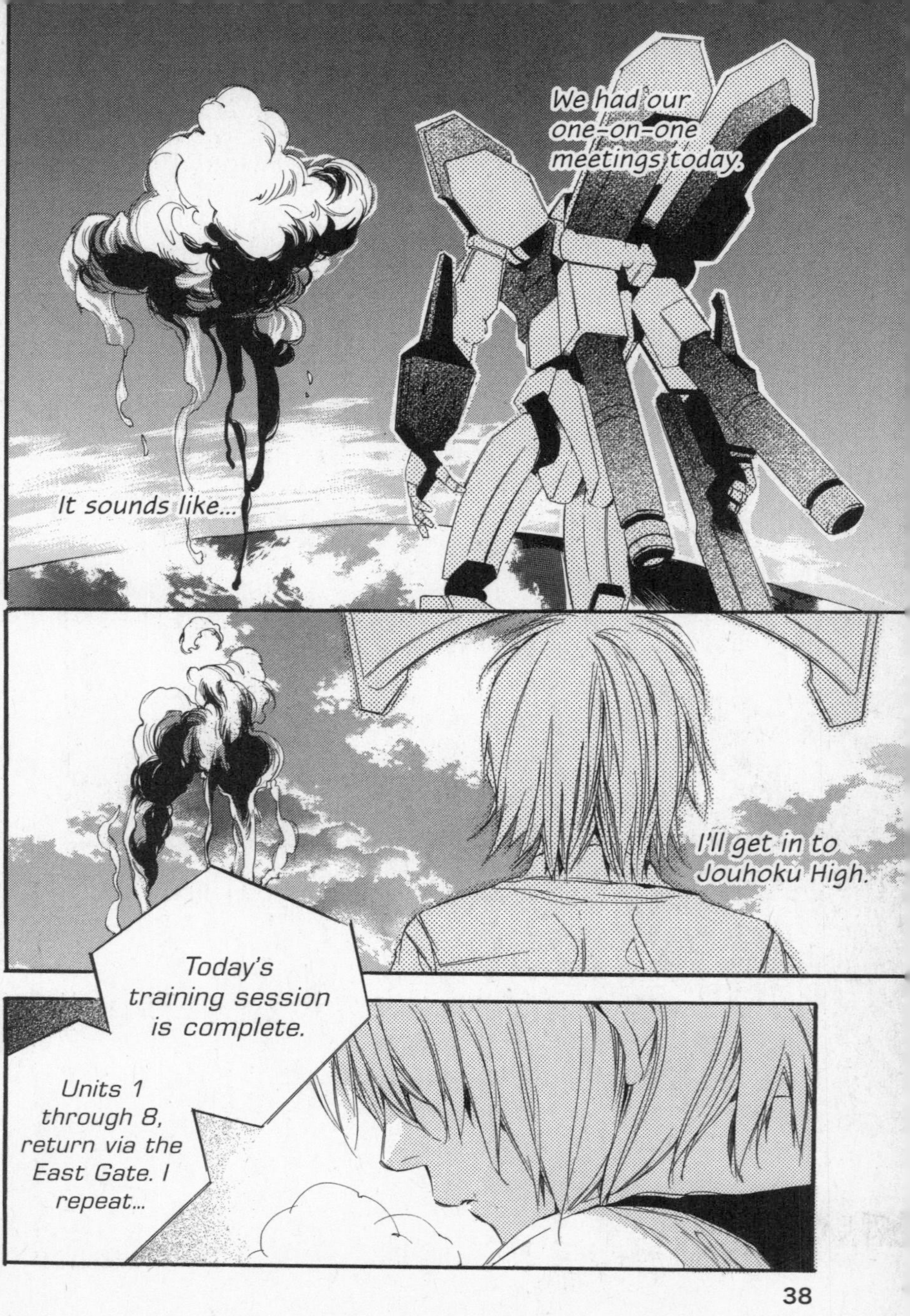
We had our one-on-one meetings today.
It sounds like...
I'll get in to Jouhoku High.
Today's training session is complete.
Units 1 through 8, return via the East Gate. I repeat...

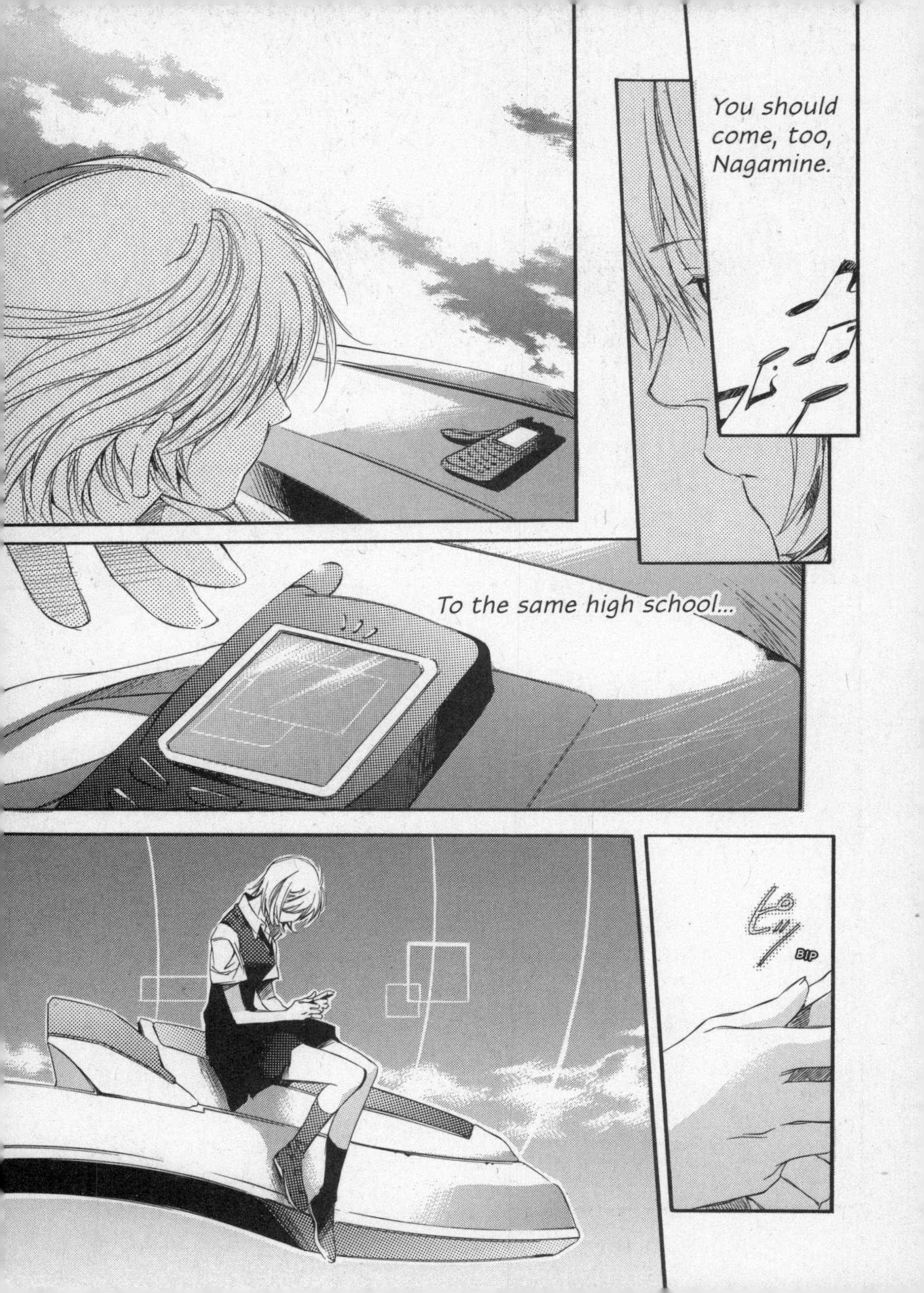
You should come, too, Nagamine.
To the same high school...
BIP

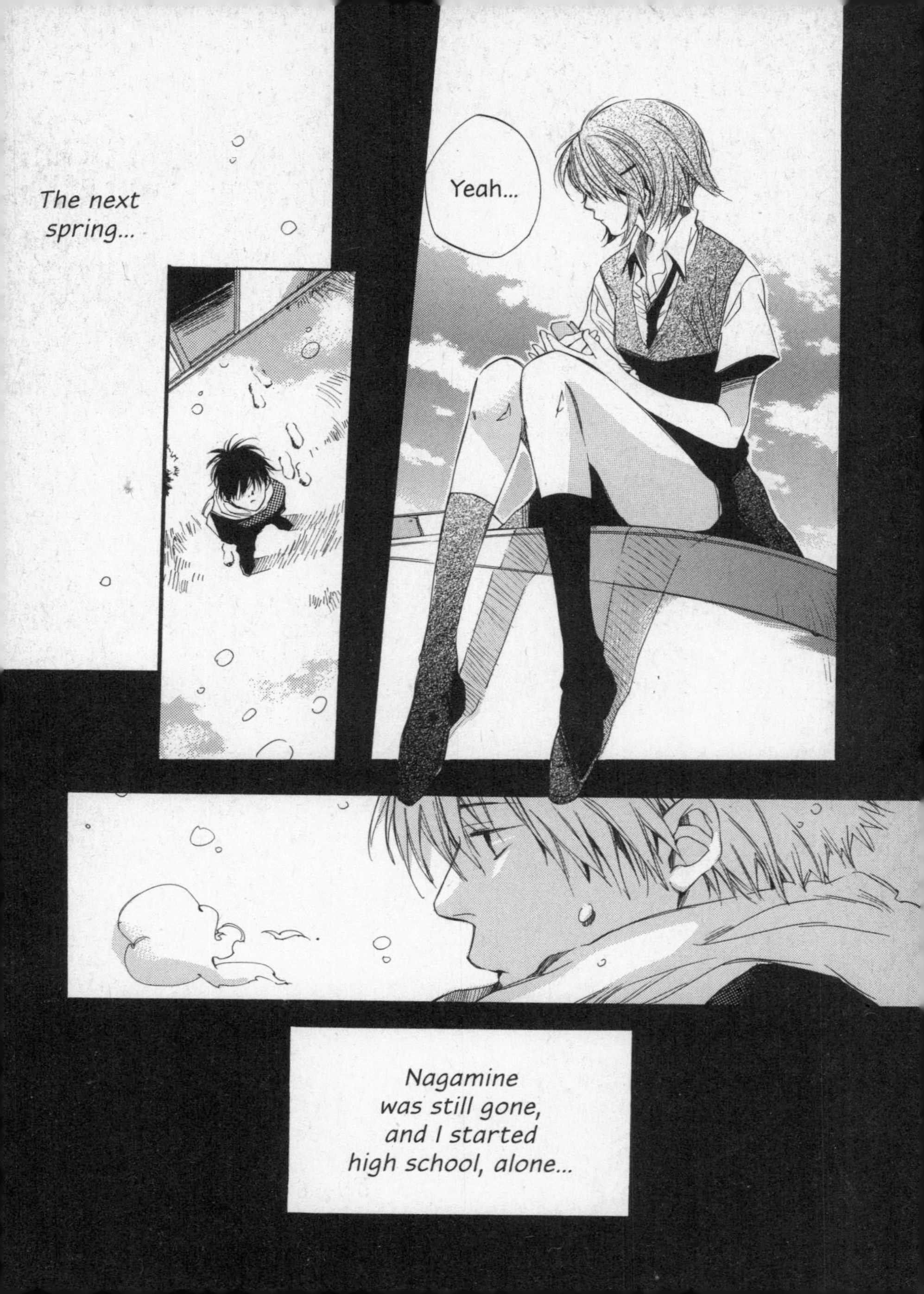
Yeah...
The next spring...
Nagamine was still gone, and I started high school, alone...

Voices of a Distant Star

Chapter 2

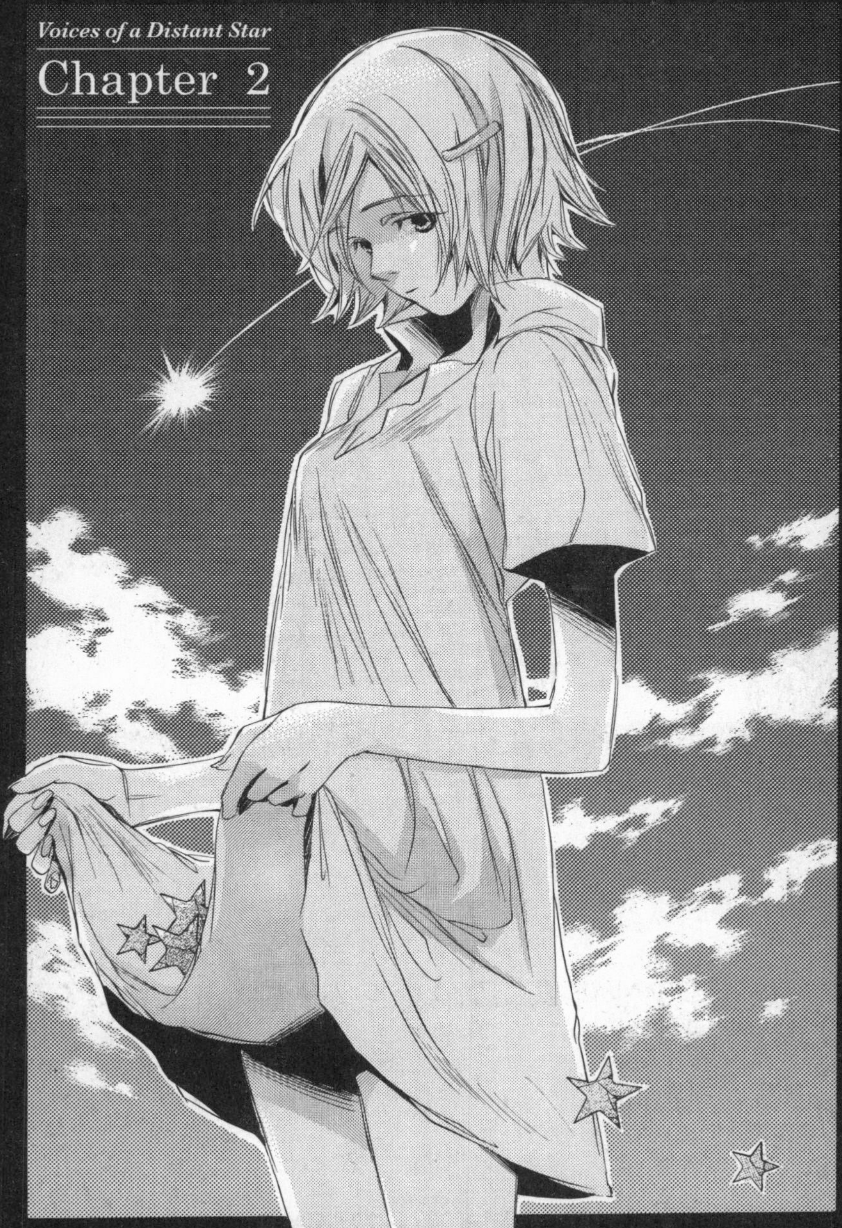

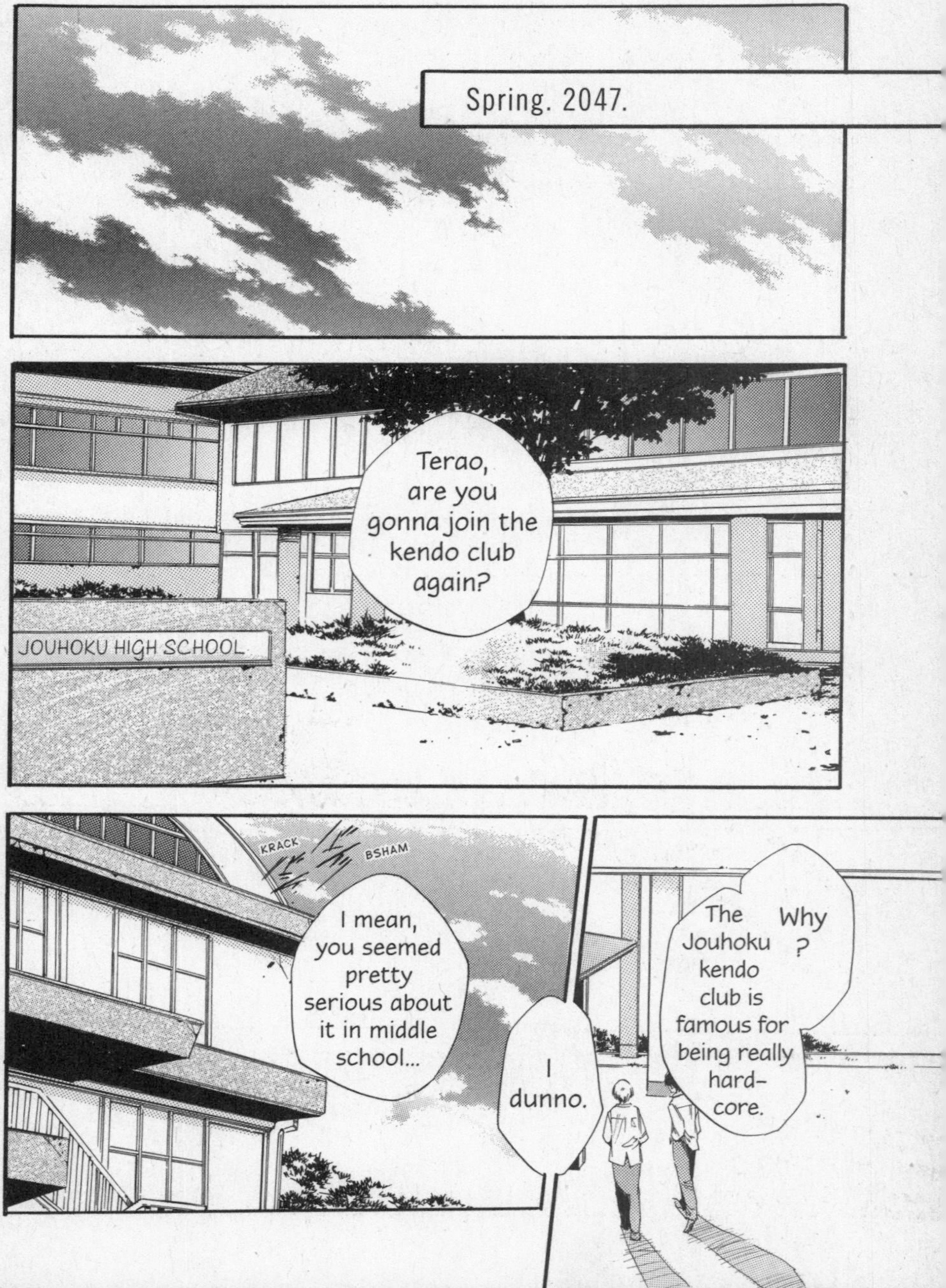
Spring. 2047.
Terao, are you gonna join the kendo club again?
JOUHOKU HIGH SCHOOL
Why?
The Jouhoku kendo club is famous for being really hard-core.
I dunno.
KRACK
BSHAM
I mean, you seemed pretty serious about it in middle school...

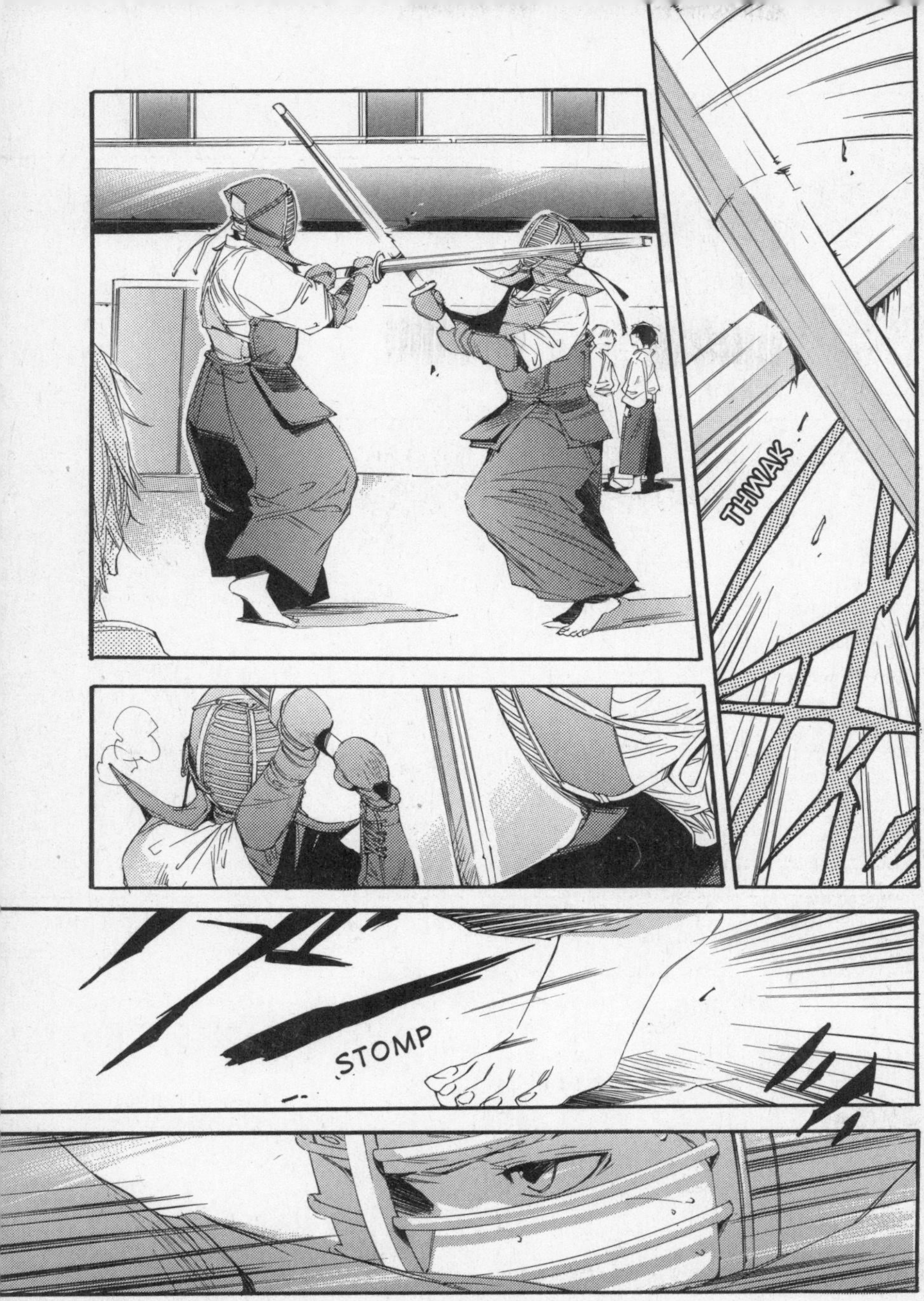
THWAK
STOMP

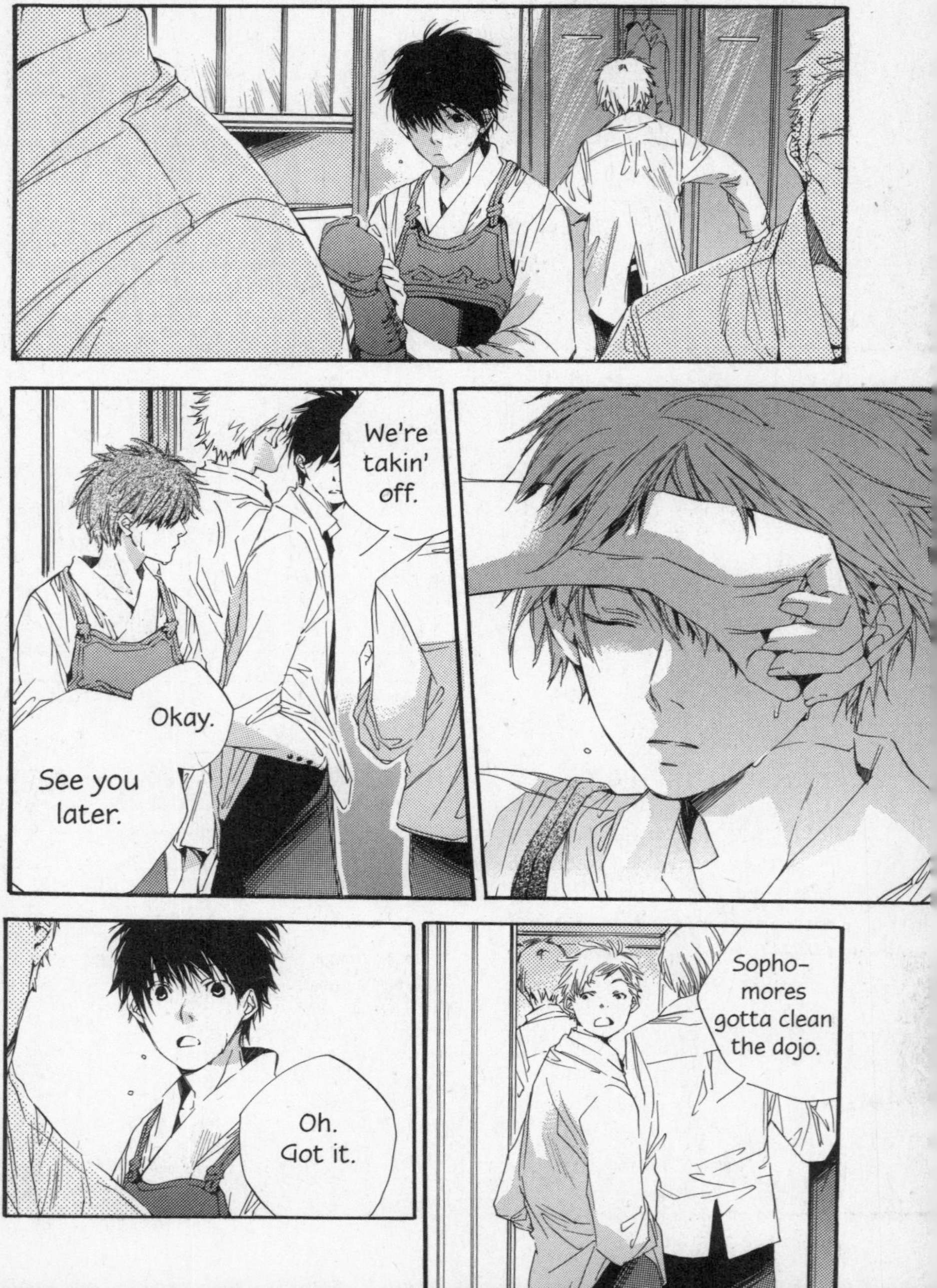
We're takin' off.
Okay.
See you later.
Sopho- mores gotta clean the dojo.
Oh. Got it.

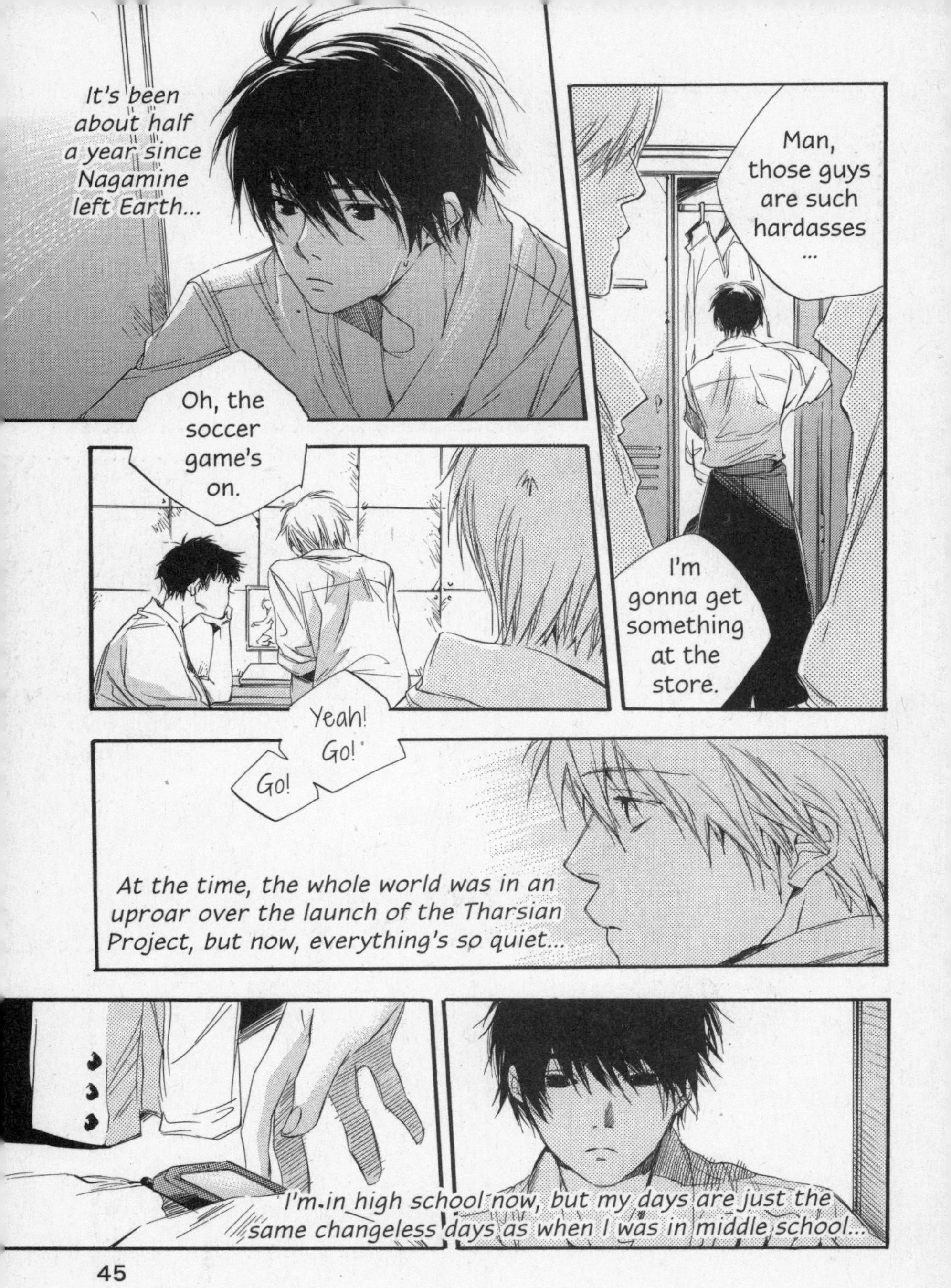
Man, those guys are such hardasses ...
I'm gonna get something at the store.
It's been about half a year since Nagamine left Earth...
Oh, the soccer game's on.
Yeah! Go!
Go!
At the time, the whole world was in an uproar over the launch of the Tharsian Project, but now, everything's so quiet...
I'm in high school now, but my days are just the same changeless days as when I was in middle school...

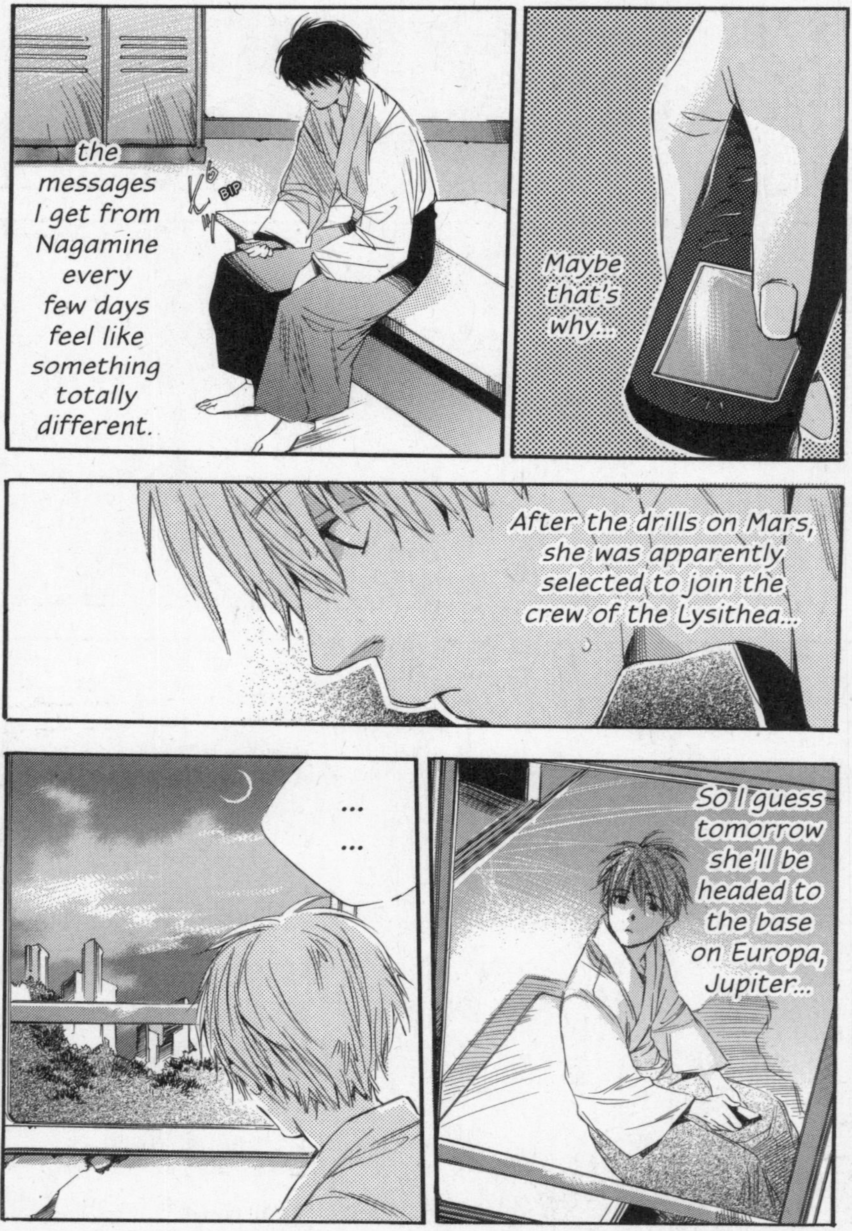
Maybe that's why...
the messages I get from Nagamine every few days feel like something totally different.
BIP
After the drills on Mars, she was apparently selected to join the crew of the Lysithea...
So I guess tomorrow she'll be headed to the base on Europa, Jupiter...
...
...

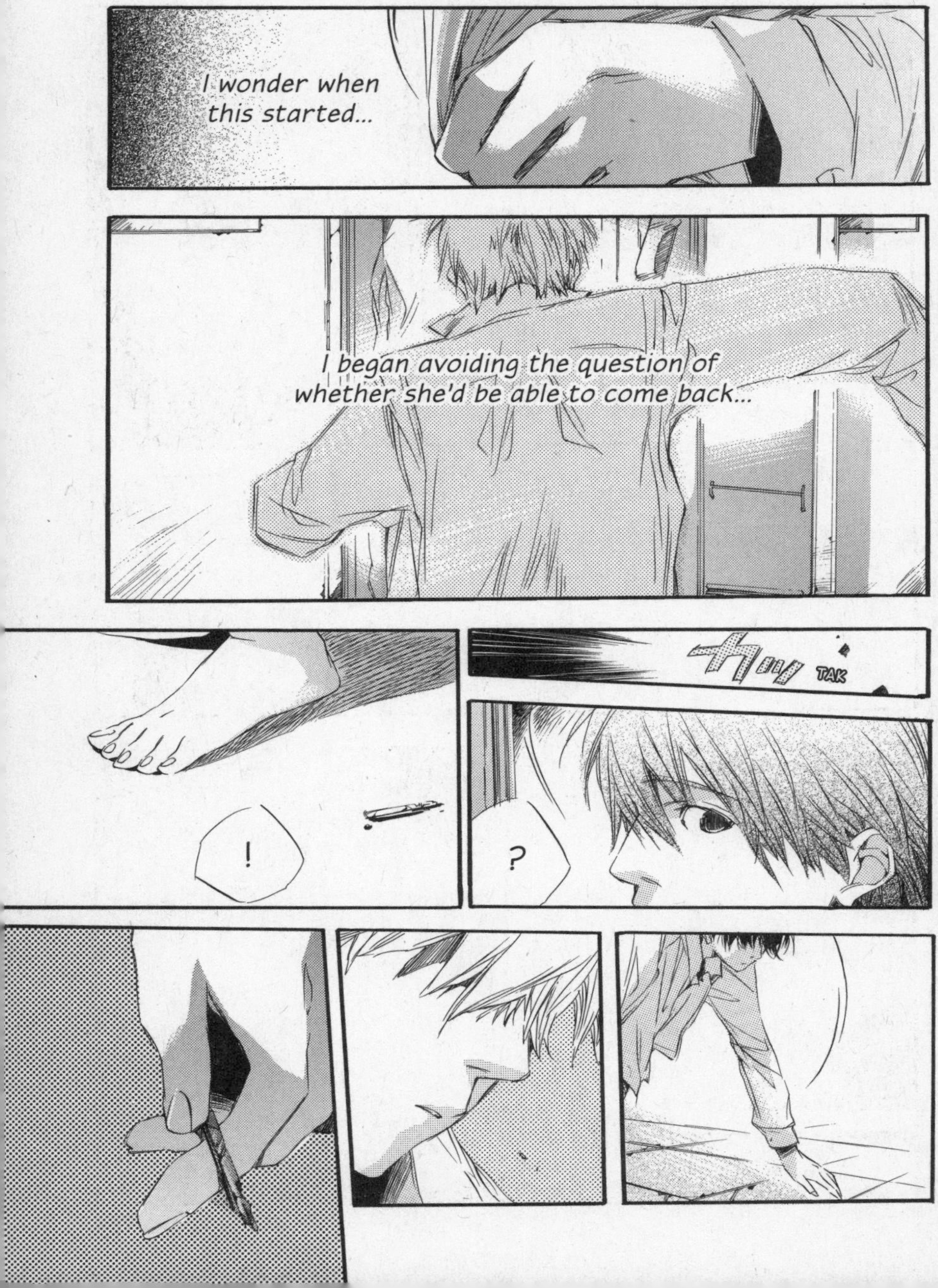
I wonder when this started...
I began avoiding the question of whether she'd be able to come back...
TAK
?
!

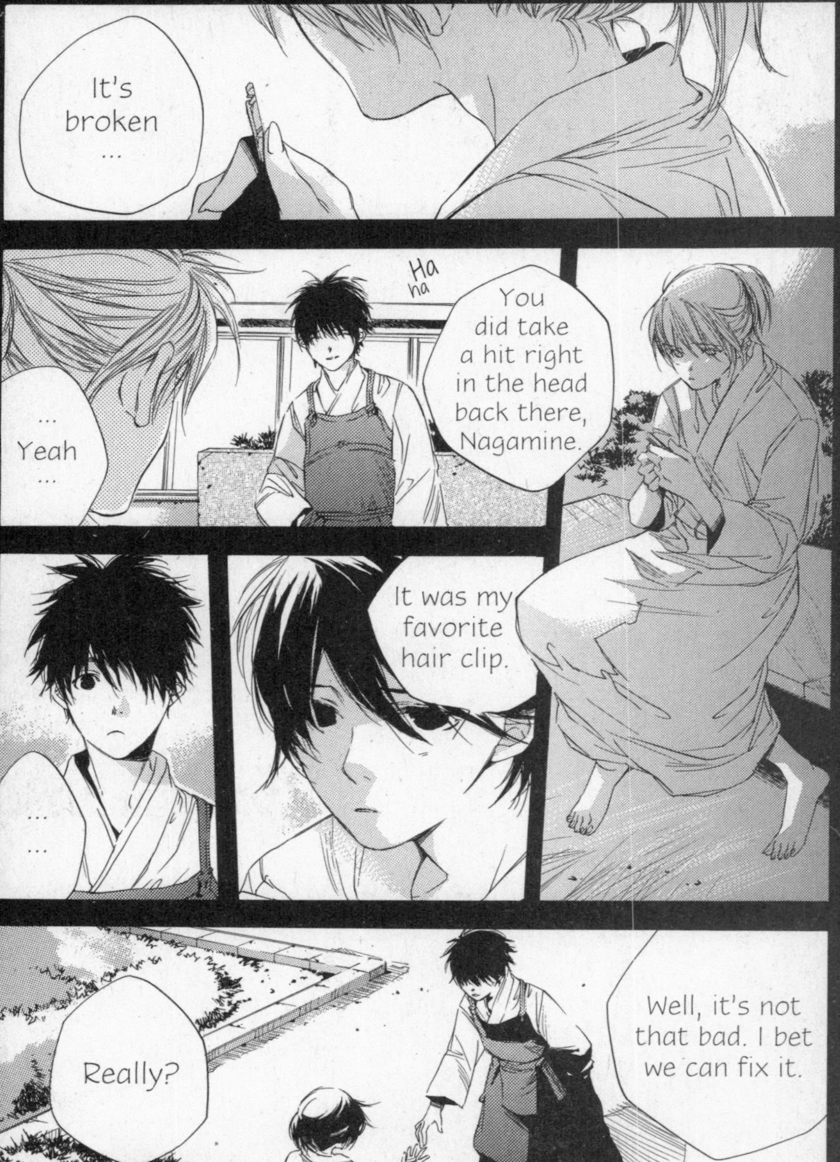
It's broken ...
Ha ha
You did take a hit right in the head back there, Nagamine.
... Yeah ...
It was my favorite hair clip.
... ...
Well, it's not that bad. I bet we can fix it.
Really?

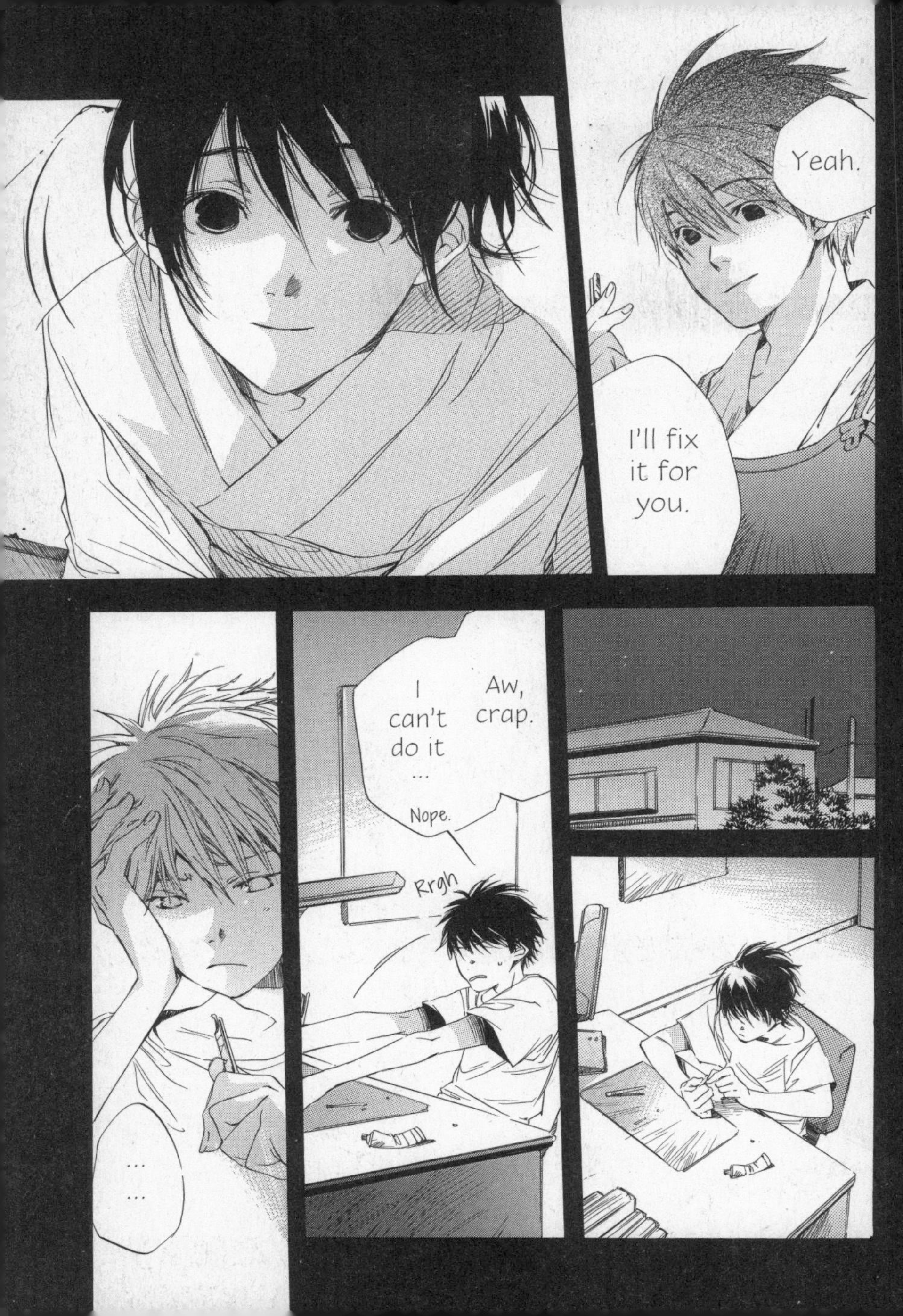
Yeah.
I'll fix it for you.
Aw, crap.
I can't do it …
Nope.
Rrgh
… …

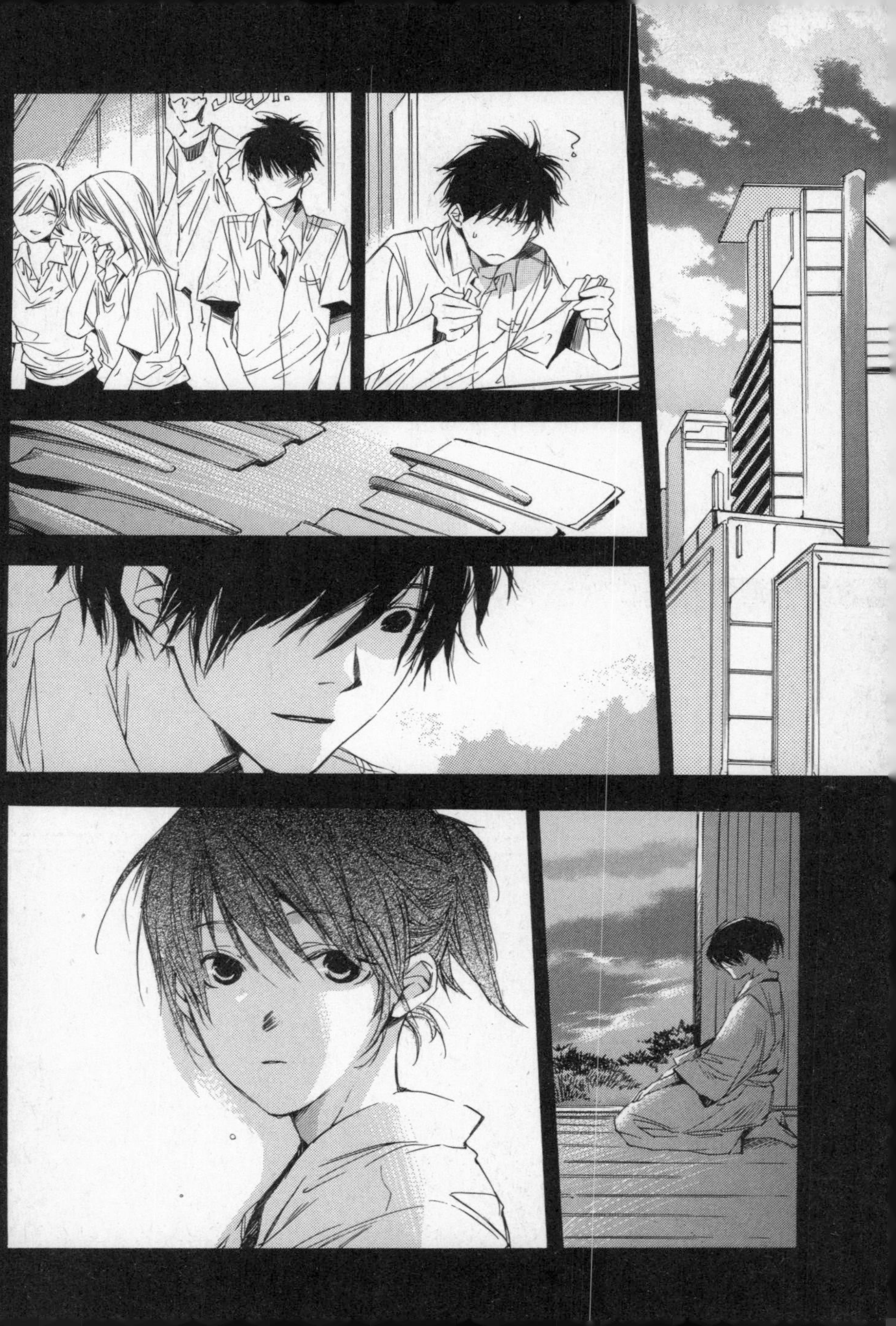

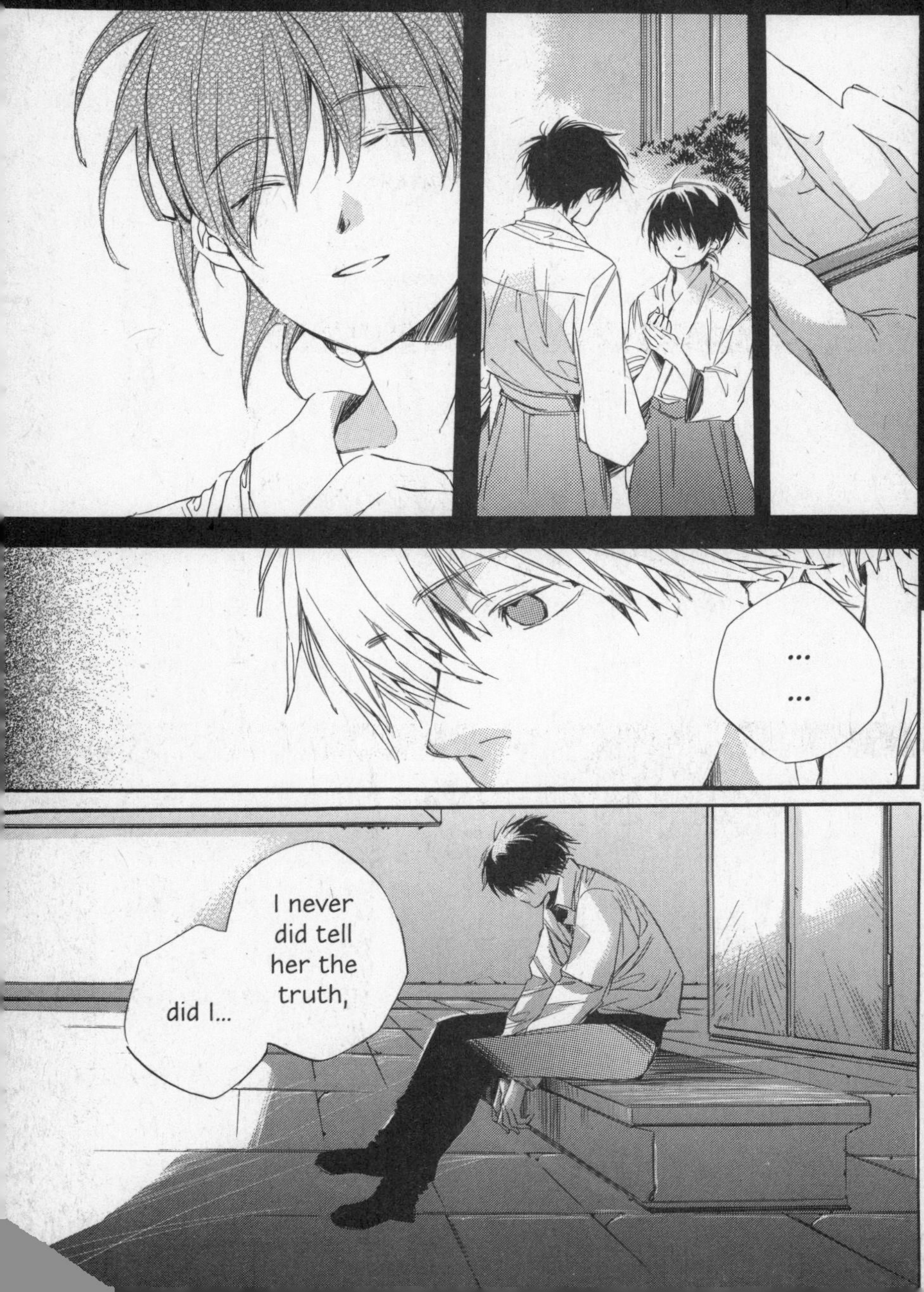
…
…
I never did tell her the truth,
did I…

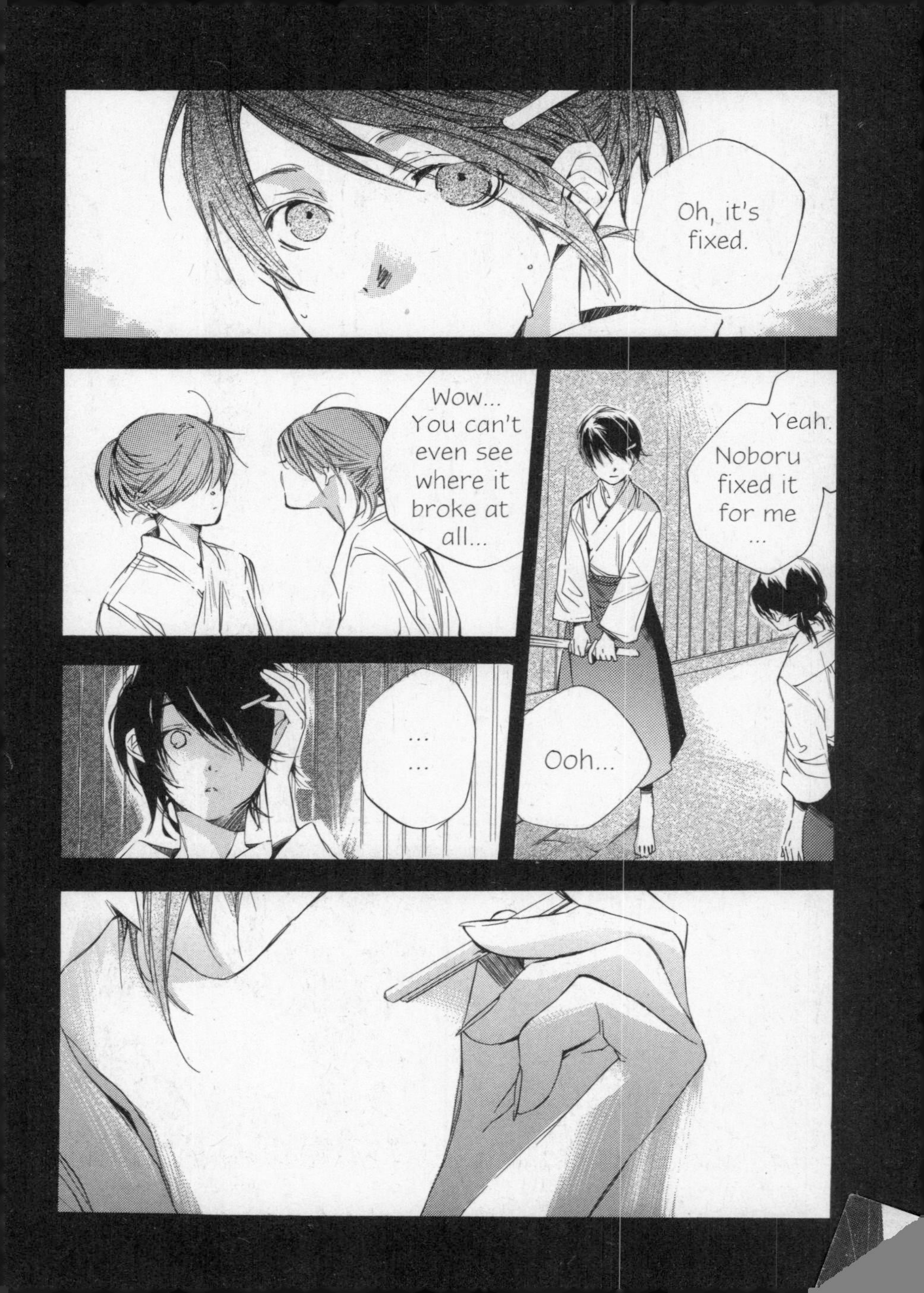
Oh, it's fixed.
Yeah. Noboru fixed it for me ...
Ooh...
Wow... You can't even see where it broke at all...
... ...

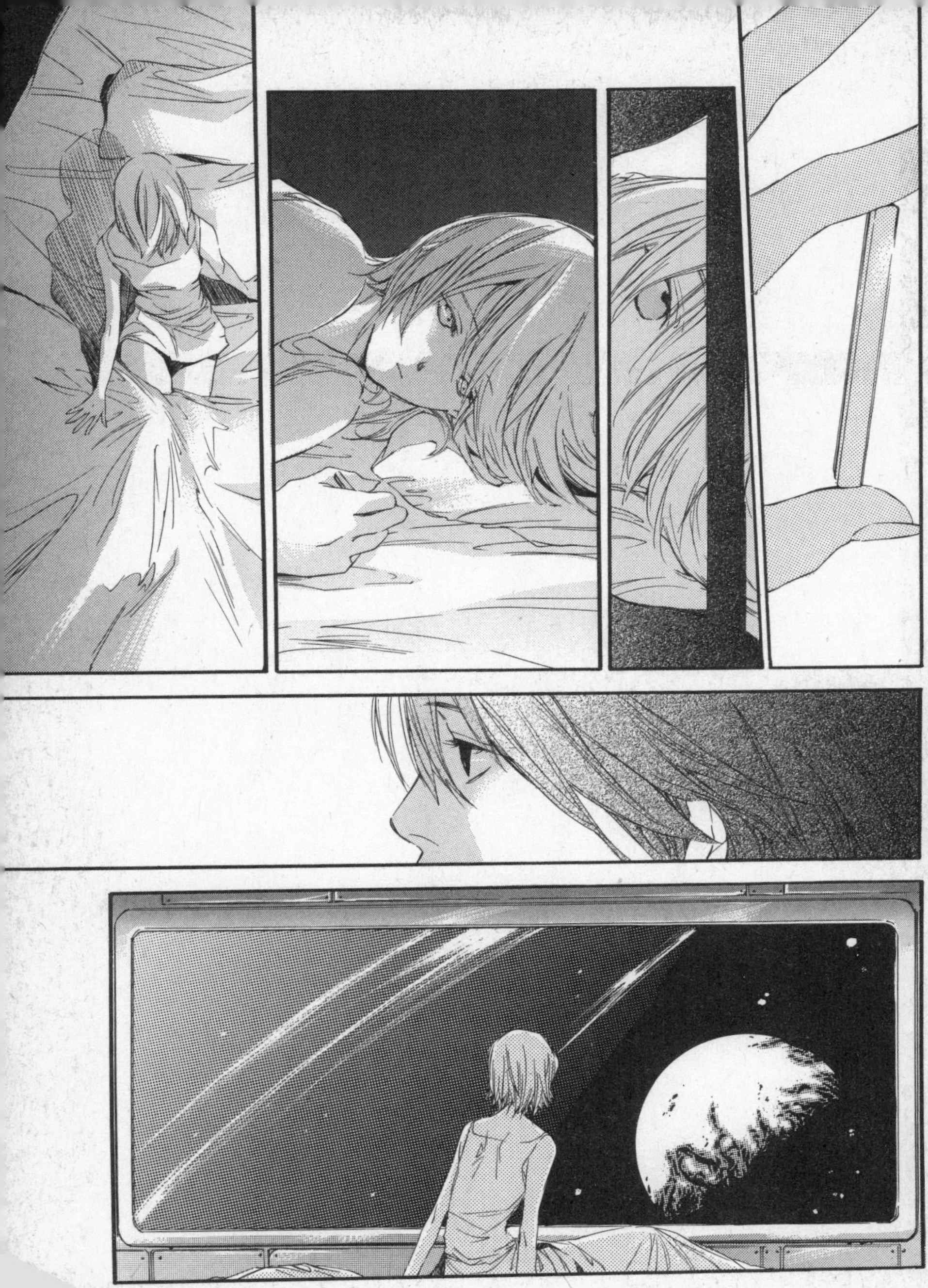

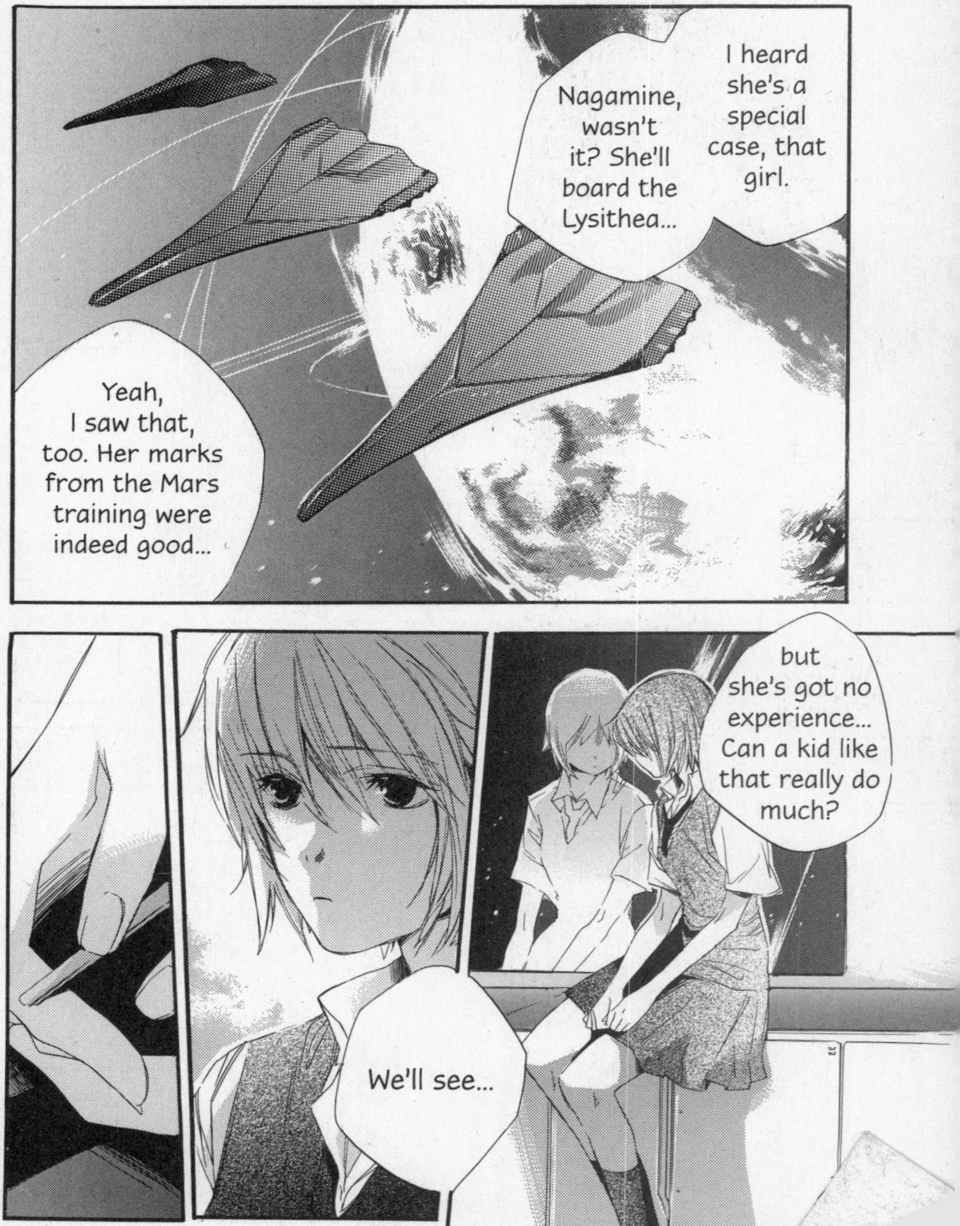
I heard she's a special case, that girl.
Nagamine, wasn't it? She'll board the Lysithea...
Yeah, I saw that, too. Her marks from the Mars training were indeed good...
but she's got no experience... Can a kid like that really do much?
We'll see...

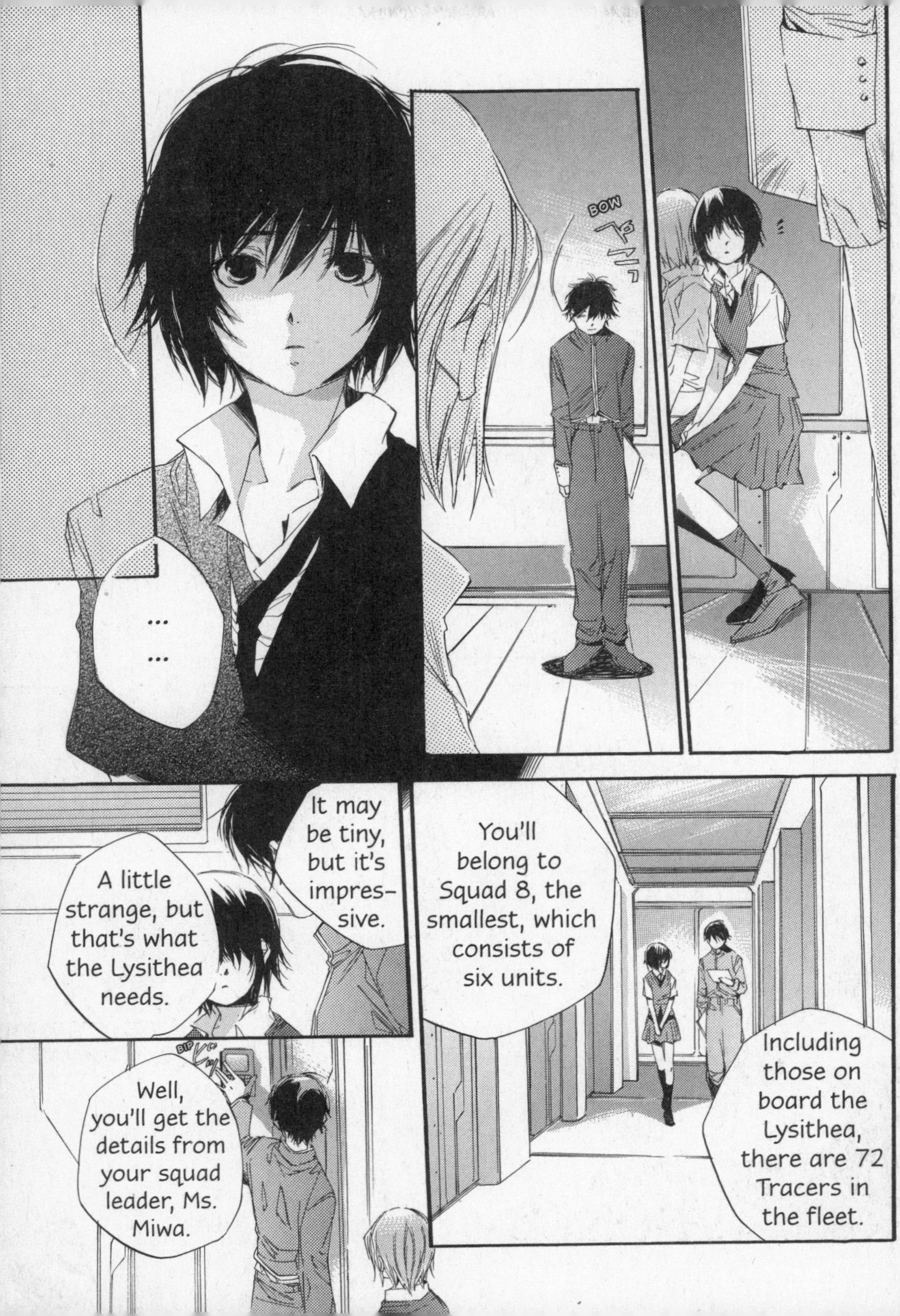
BOW
...
...
You'll belong to Squad 8, the smallest, which consists of six units.
Including those on board the Lysithea, there are 72 Tracers in the fleet.
It may be tiny, but it's impressive.
A little strange, but that's what the Lysithea needs.
BIP
Well, you'll get the details from your squad leader, Ms. Miwa.

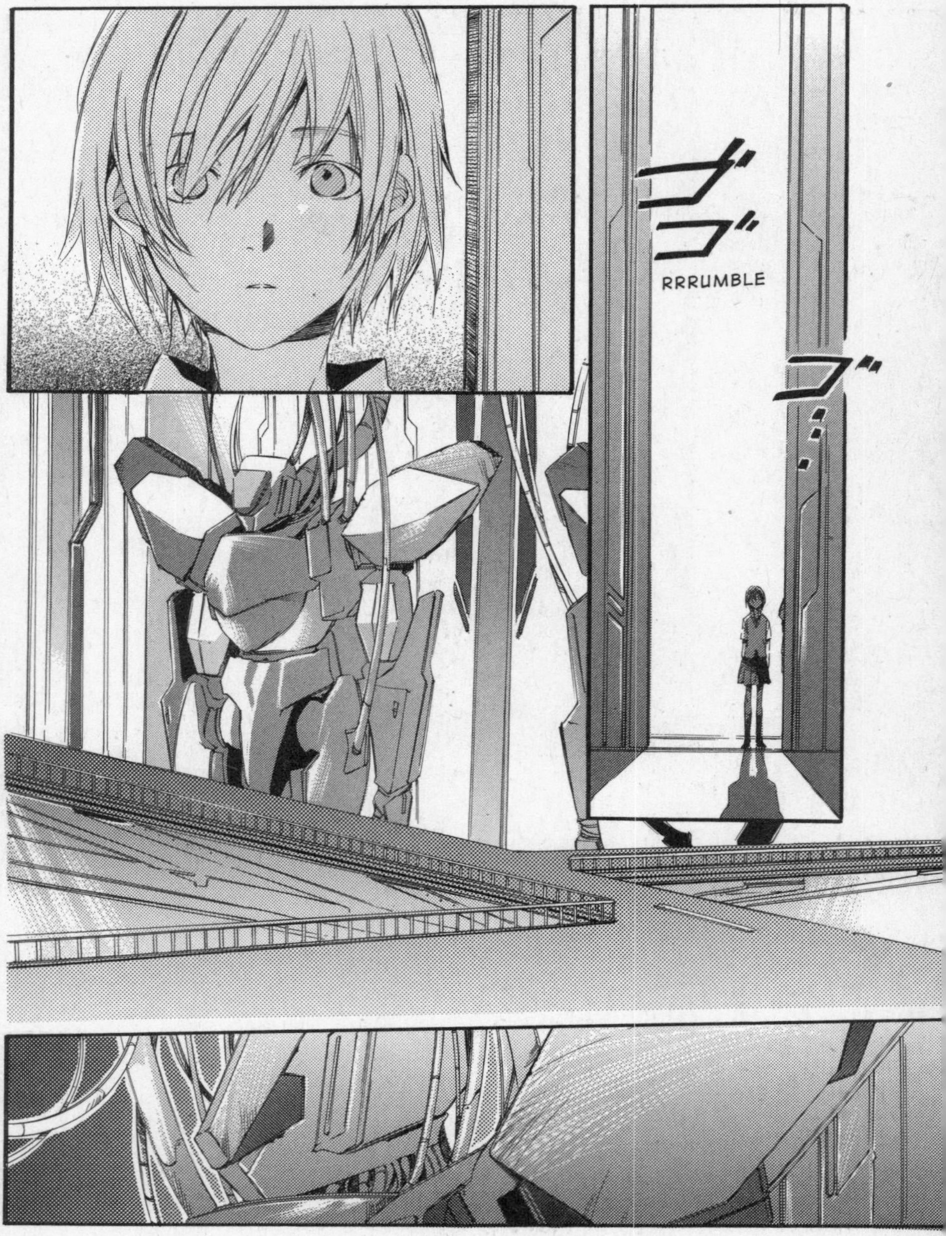
ゴゴ
RRRUMBLE
ゴ...

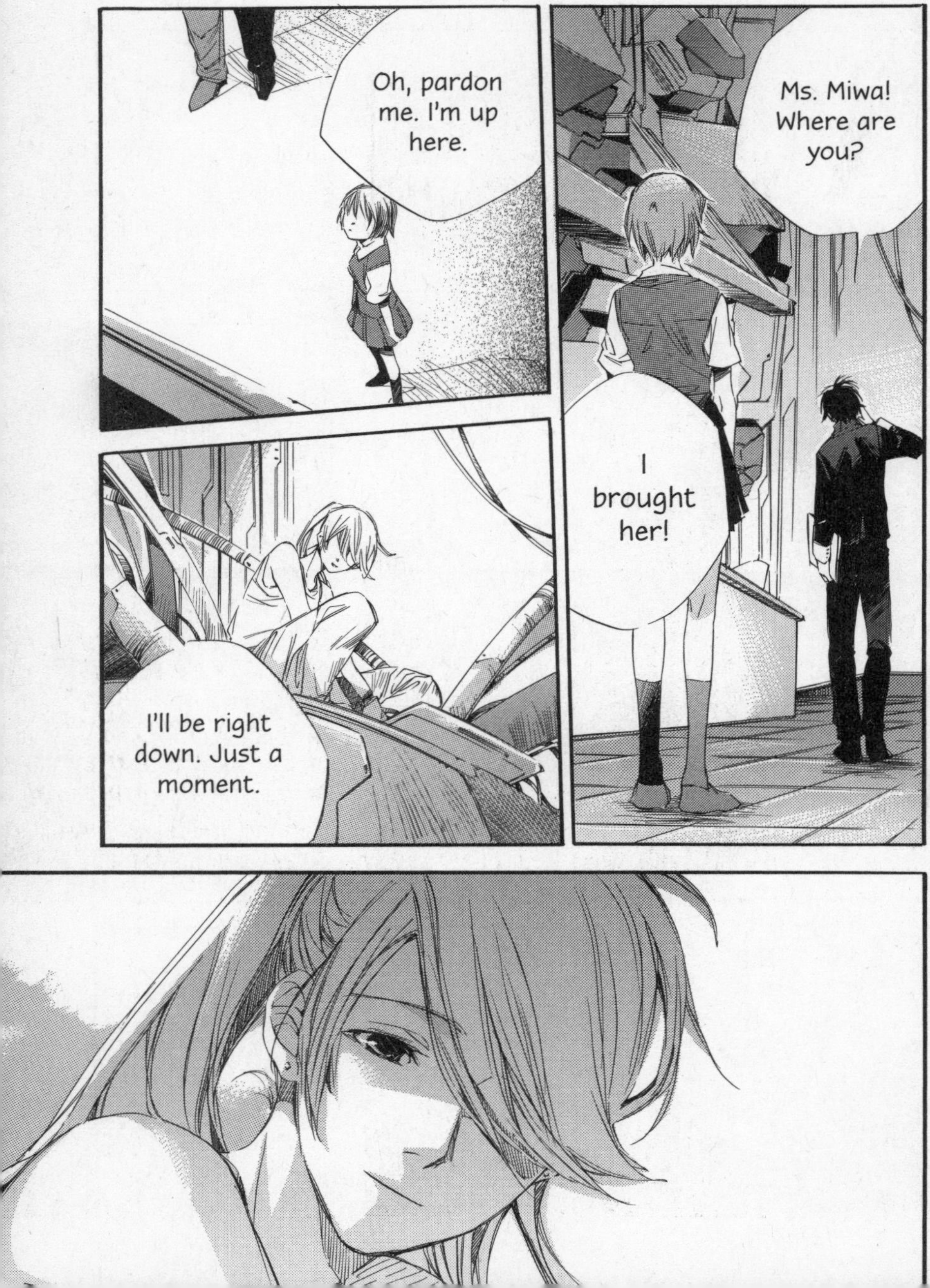
Ms. Miwa! Where are you?
I brought her!
Oh, pardon me. I'm up here.
I'll be right down. Just a moment.

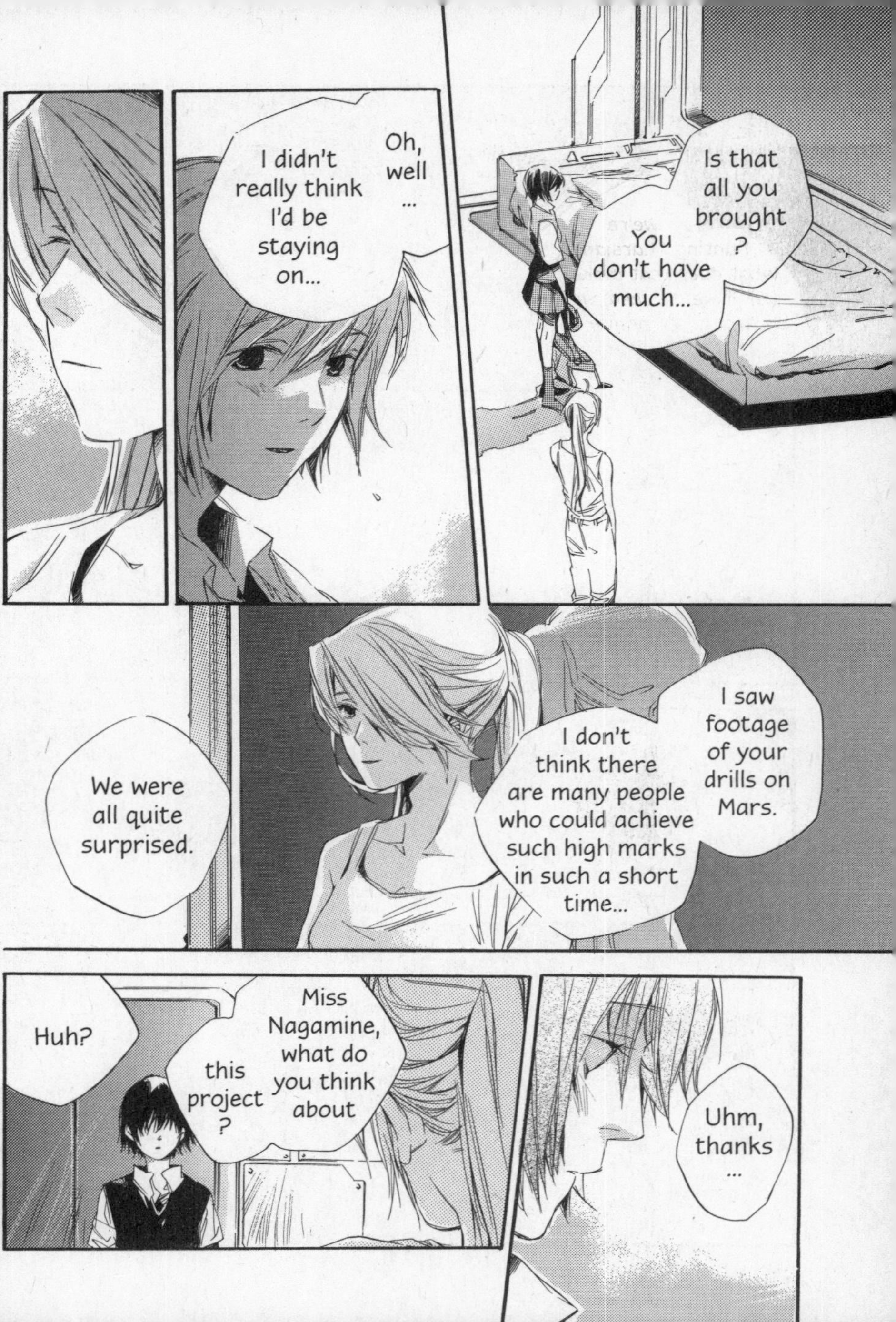
Is that all you brought?
You don't have much...
Oh, well ...
I didn't really think I'd be staying on...
I saw footage of your drills on Mars.
I don't think there are many people who could achieve such high marks in such a short time...
We were all quite surprised.
Uhm, thanks ...
Miss Nagamine, what do you think about this project?
Huh?

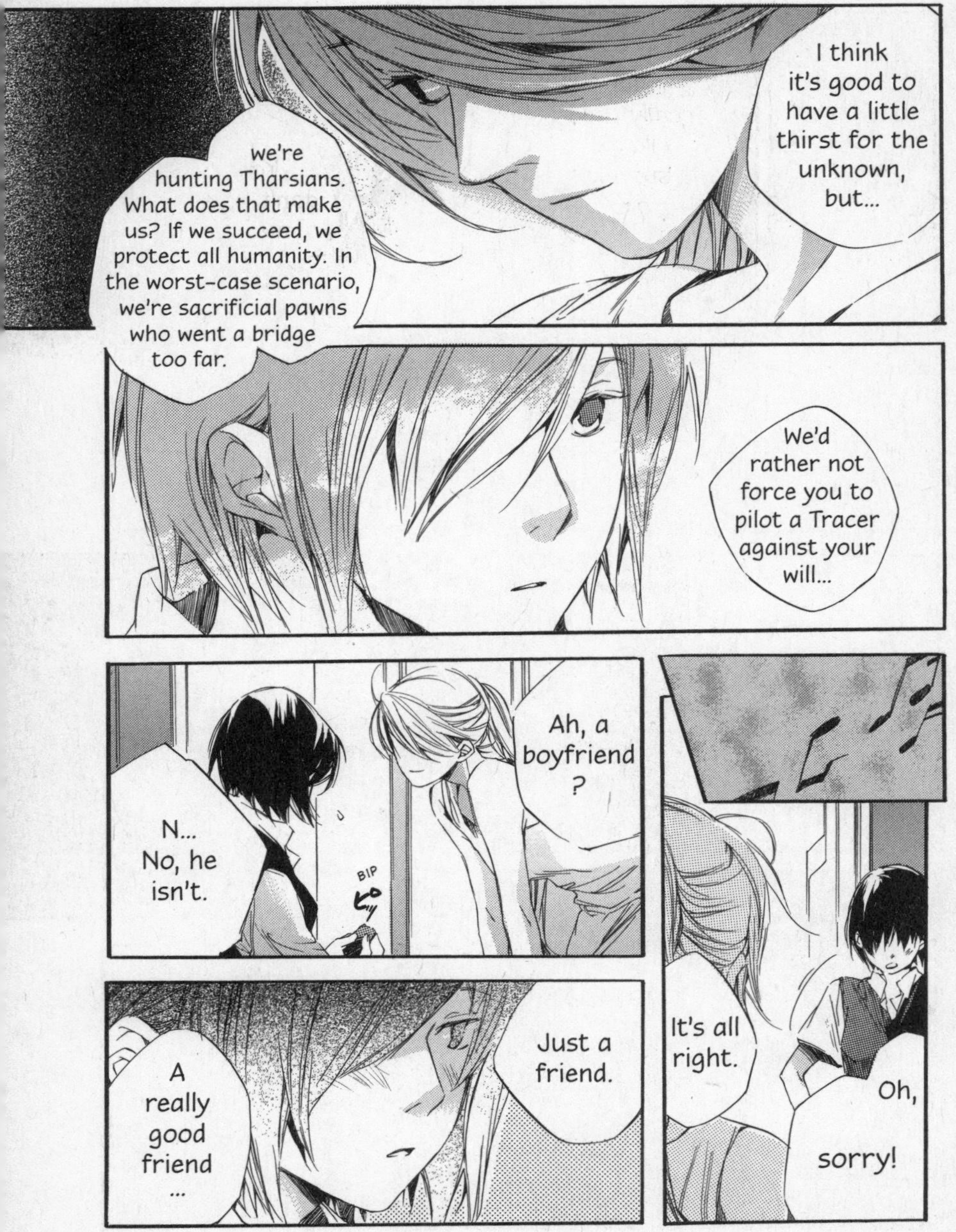
I think it's good to have a little thirst for the unknown, but...
we're hunting Tharsians. What does that make us? If we succeed, we protect all humanity. In the worst-case scenario, we're sacrificial pawns who went a bridge too far.
We'd rather not force you to pilot a Tracer against your will...
Oh, sorry!
It's all right.
Ah, a boyfriend?
N... No, he isn't.
BIP
Just a friend.
A really good friend ...

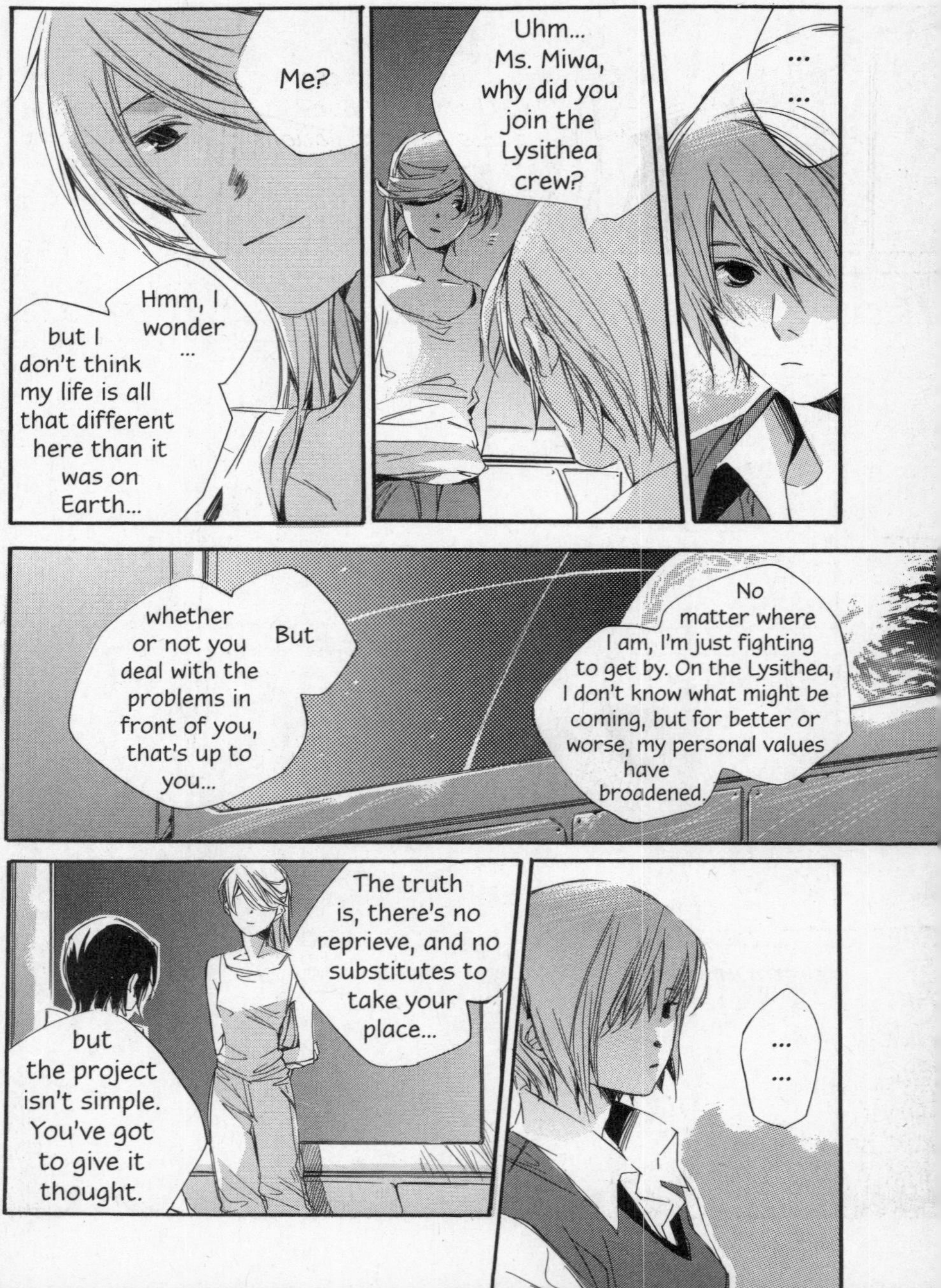
... ...
Uhm... Ms. Miwa, why did you join the Lysithea crew?
Me?
Hmm, I wonder ...
but I don't think my life is all that different here than it was on Earth...
No matter where I am, I'm just fighting to get by. On the Lysithea, I don't know what might be coming, but for better or worse, my personal values have broadened.
But
whether or not you deal with the problems in front of you, that's up to you...
... ...
The truth is, there's no reprieve, and no substitutes to take your place...
but the project isn't simple. You've got to give it thought.

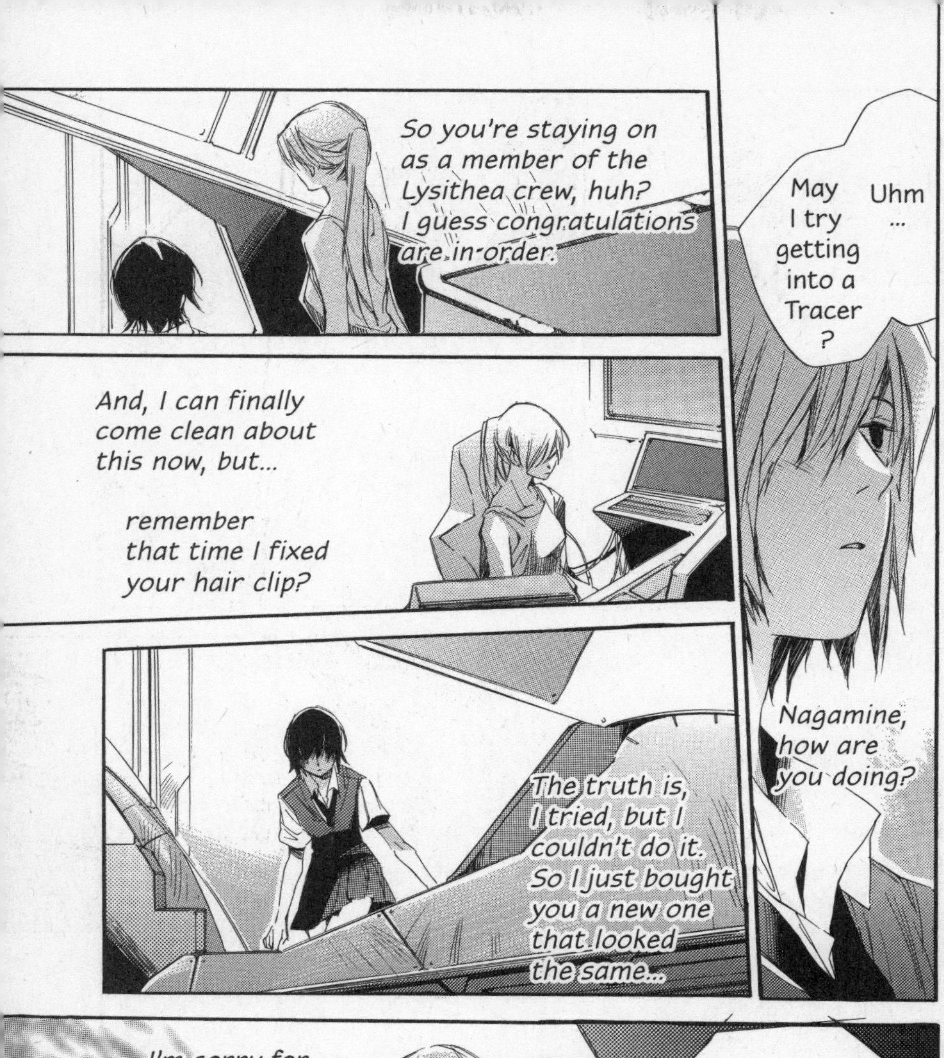

Uhm ...
May I try getting into a Tracer ?
Nagamine, how are you doing?
So you're staying on as a member of the Lysithea crew, huh? I guess congratulations are in order.
And, I can finally come clean about this now, but...
remember that time I fixed your hair clip?
The truth is, I tried, but I couldn't do it. So I just bought you a new one that looked the same...
The settings are the same as for your drills.
You shouldn't have any trouble operating it...
I'm sorry for lying to you...
Roger.

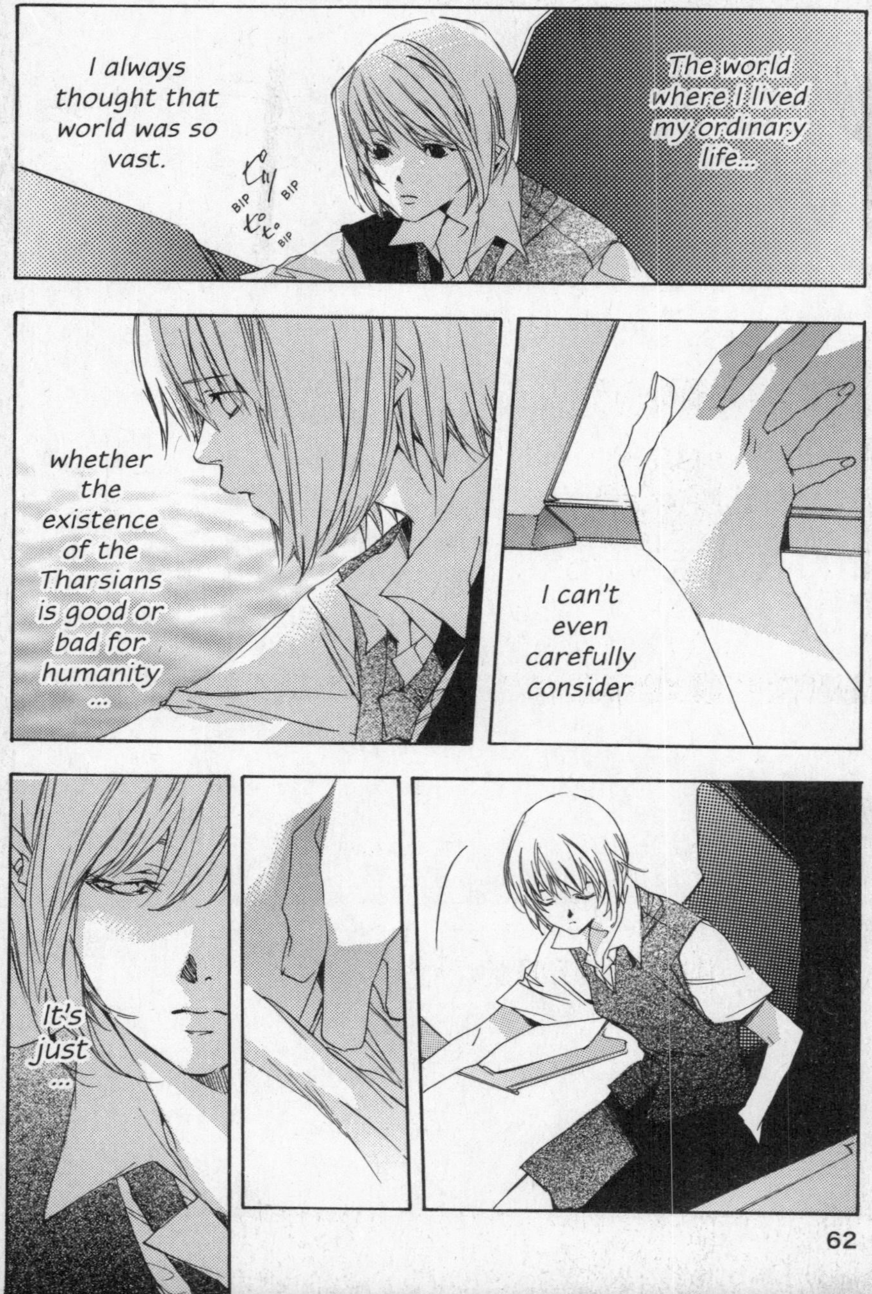
The world where I lived my ordinary life...
I always thought that world was so vast.
BIP BIP
BIP BIP
I can't even carefully consider
whether the existence of the Tharsians is good or bad for humanity ...
It's just ...

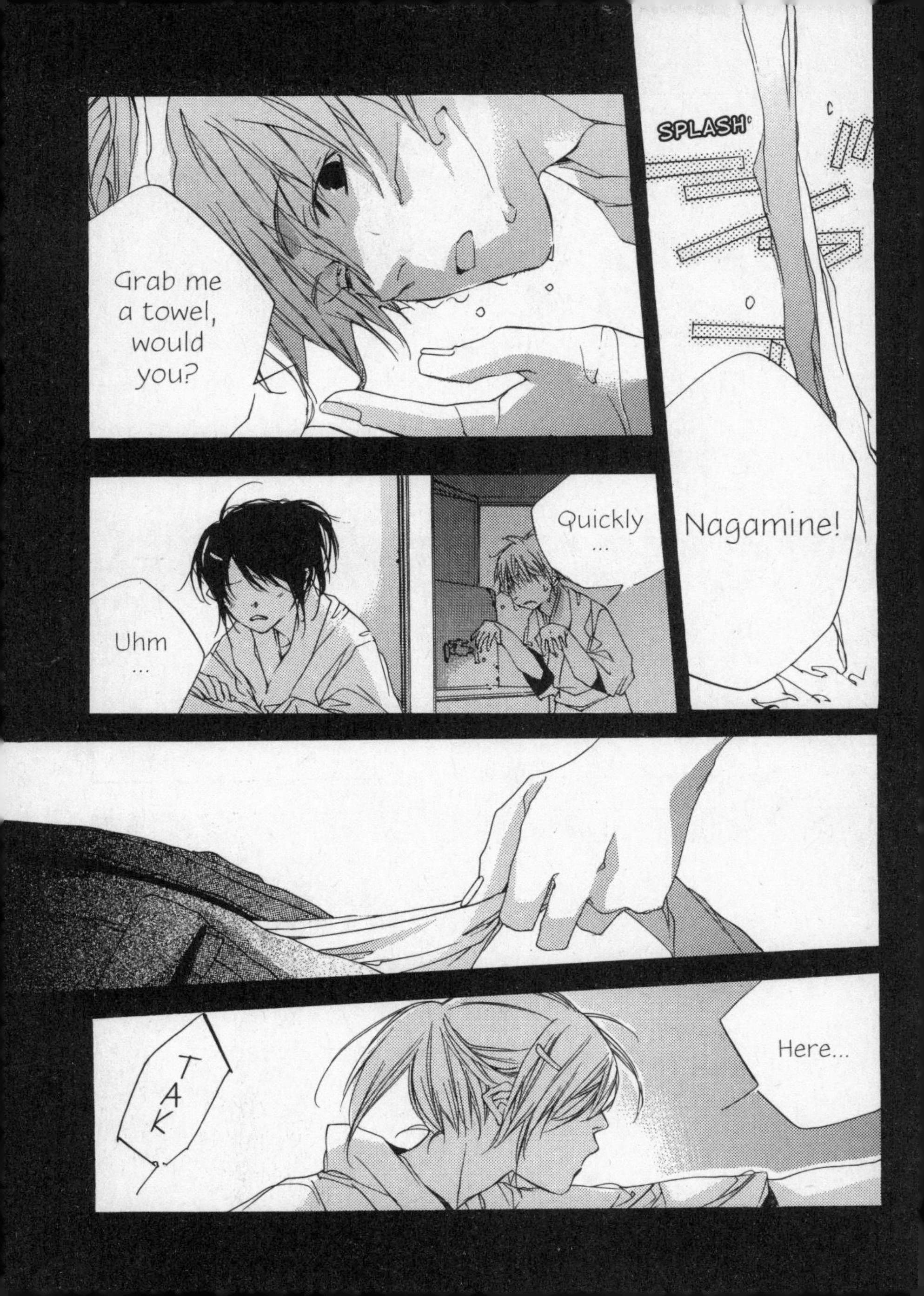
SPLASH
Nagamine!
Grab me a towel, would you?
Quickly ...
Uhm ...
Here...
TAK

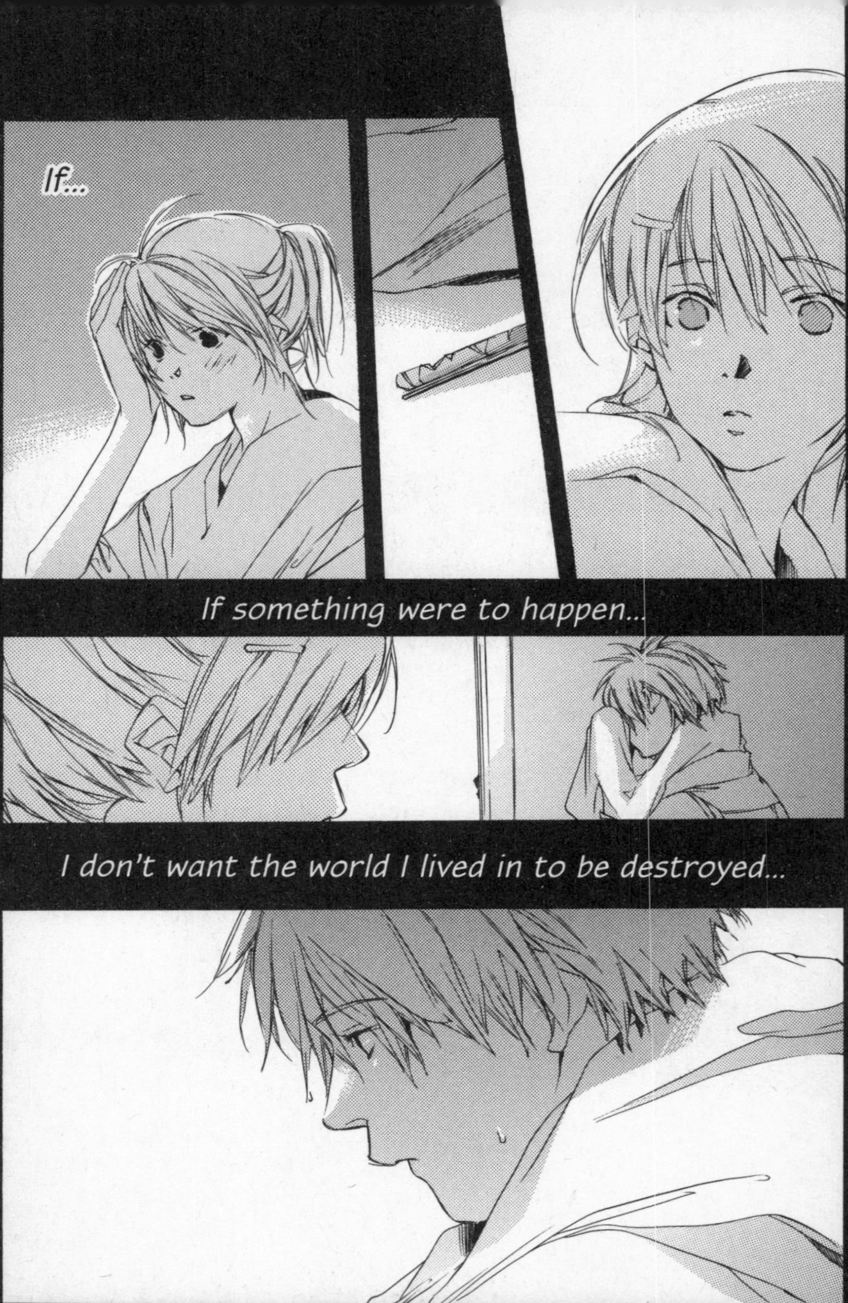
If...
If something were to happen...
I don't want the world I lived in to be destroyed...

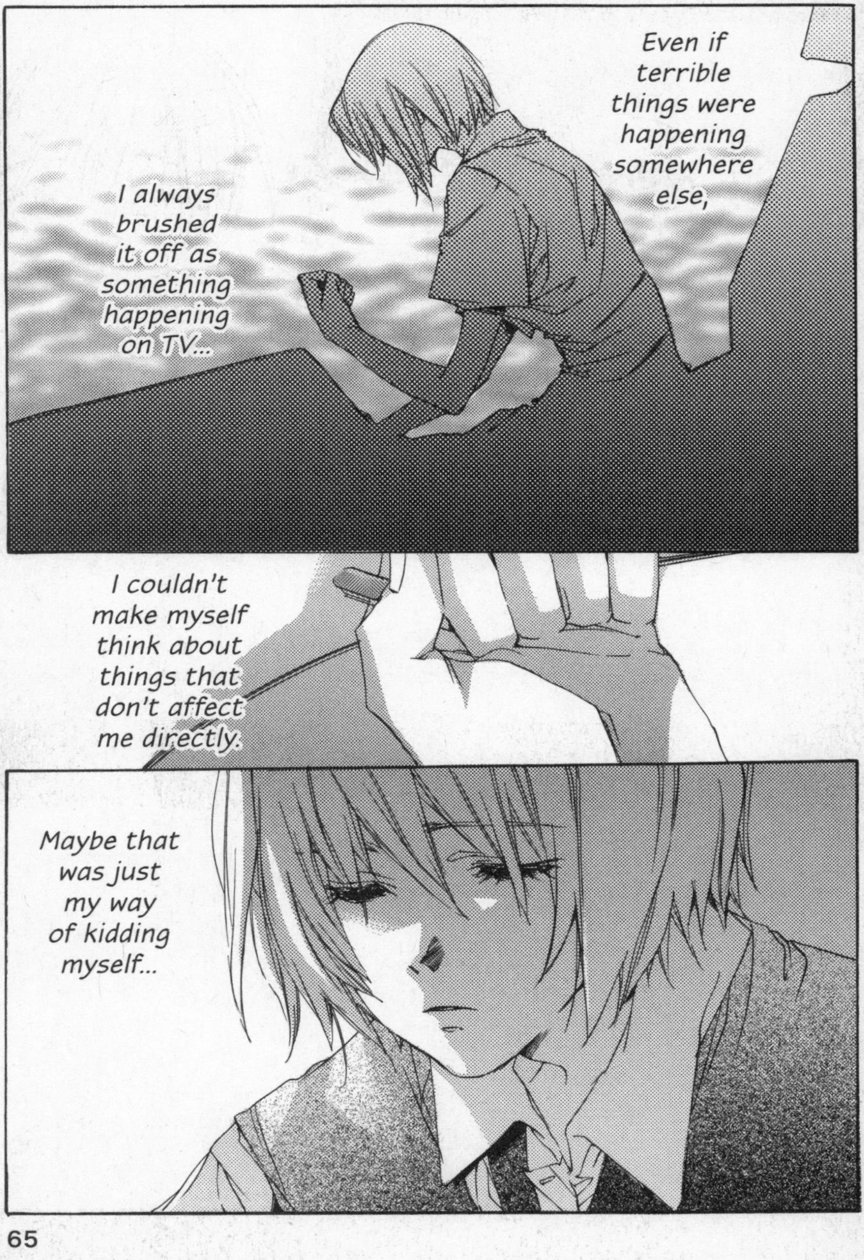
Even if terrible things were happening somewhere else,
I always brushed it off as something happening on TV...
I couldn't make myself think about things that don't affect me directly.
Maybe that was just my way of kidding myself...

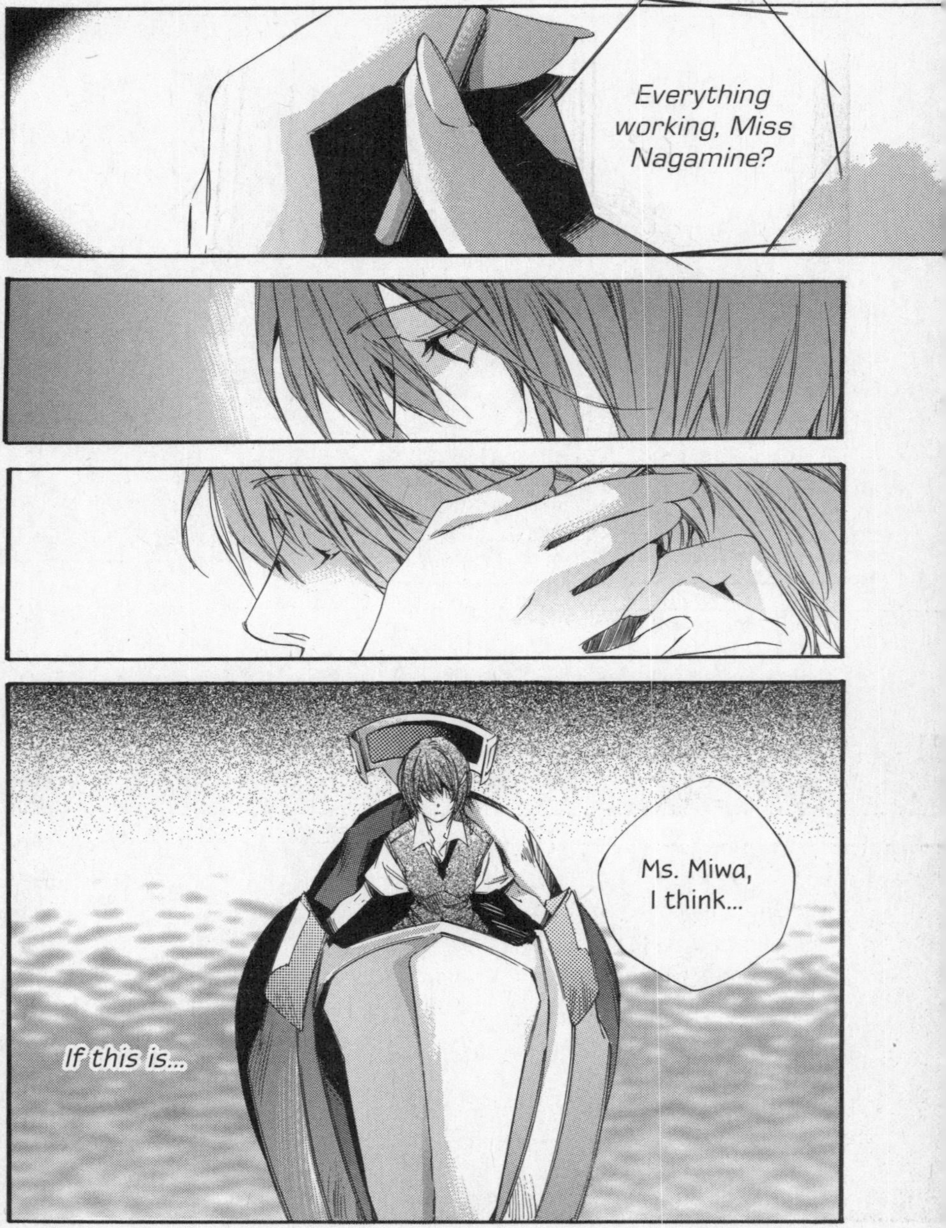
Everything working, Miss Nagamine?
Ms. Miwa, I think...
If this is...

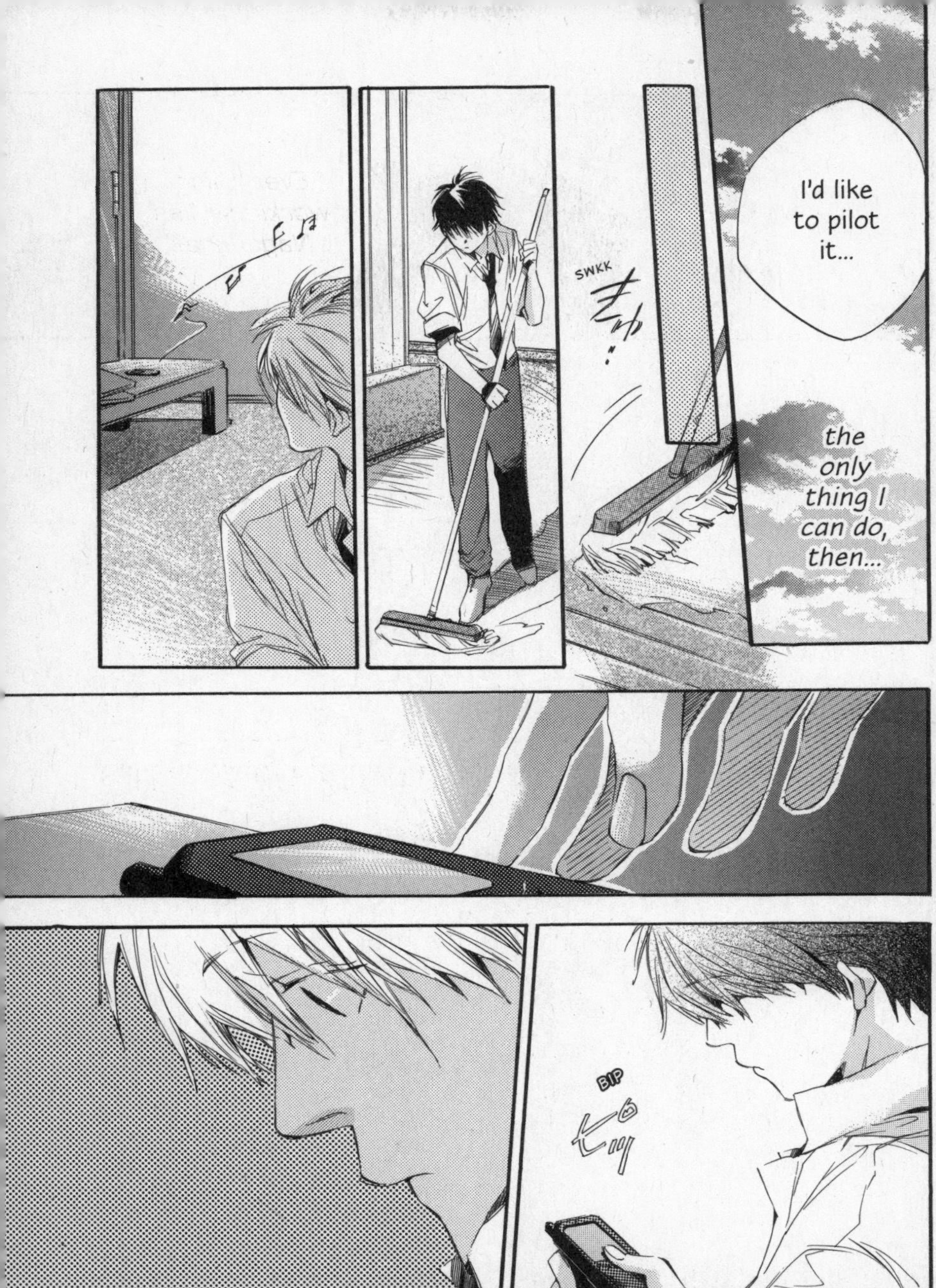
I'd like to pilot it...
the only thing I can do, then...
SWKK
BIP

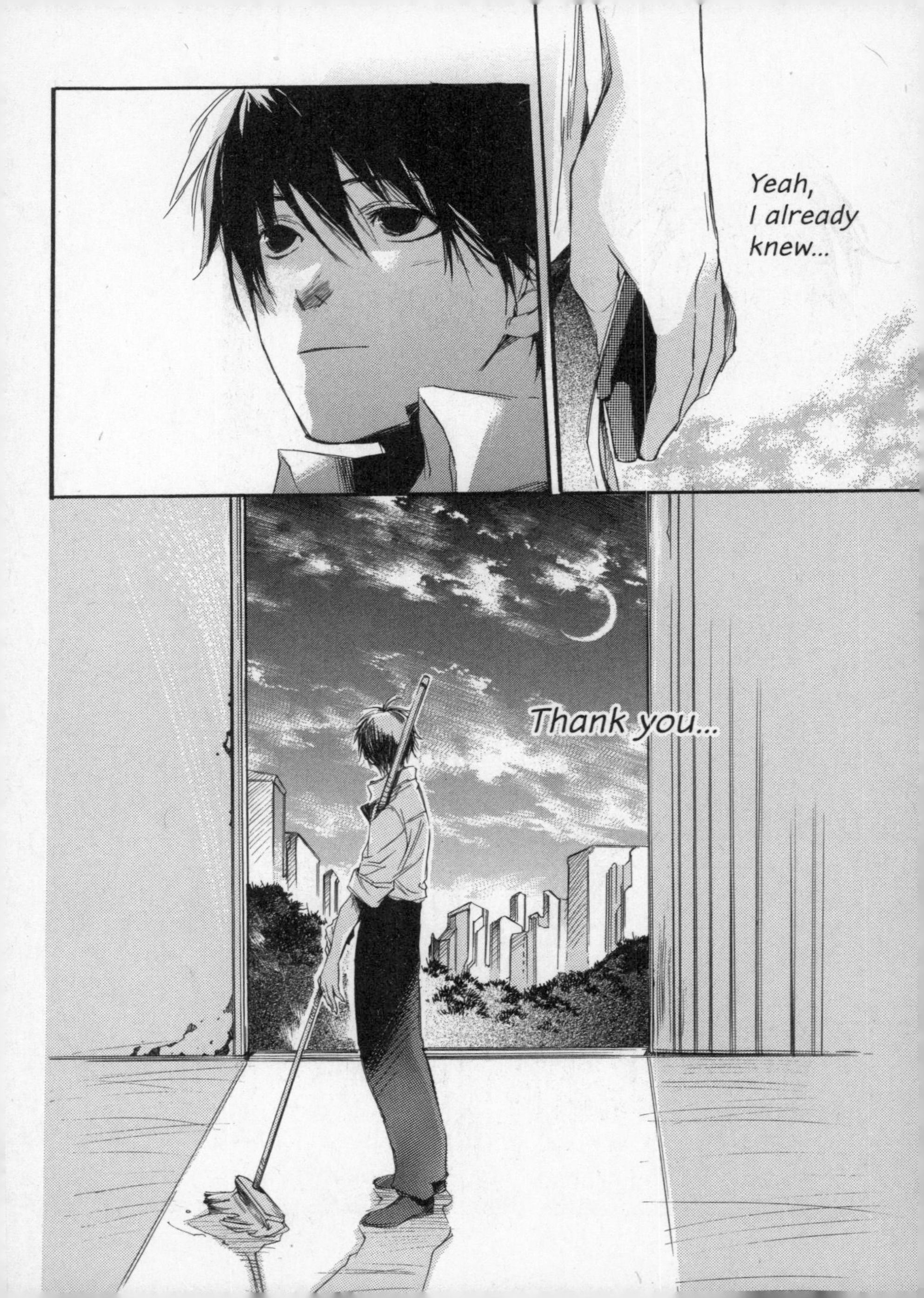
Yeah,
I already
knew...
Thank you...

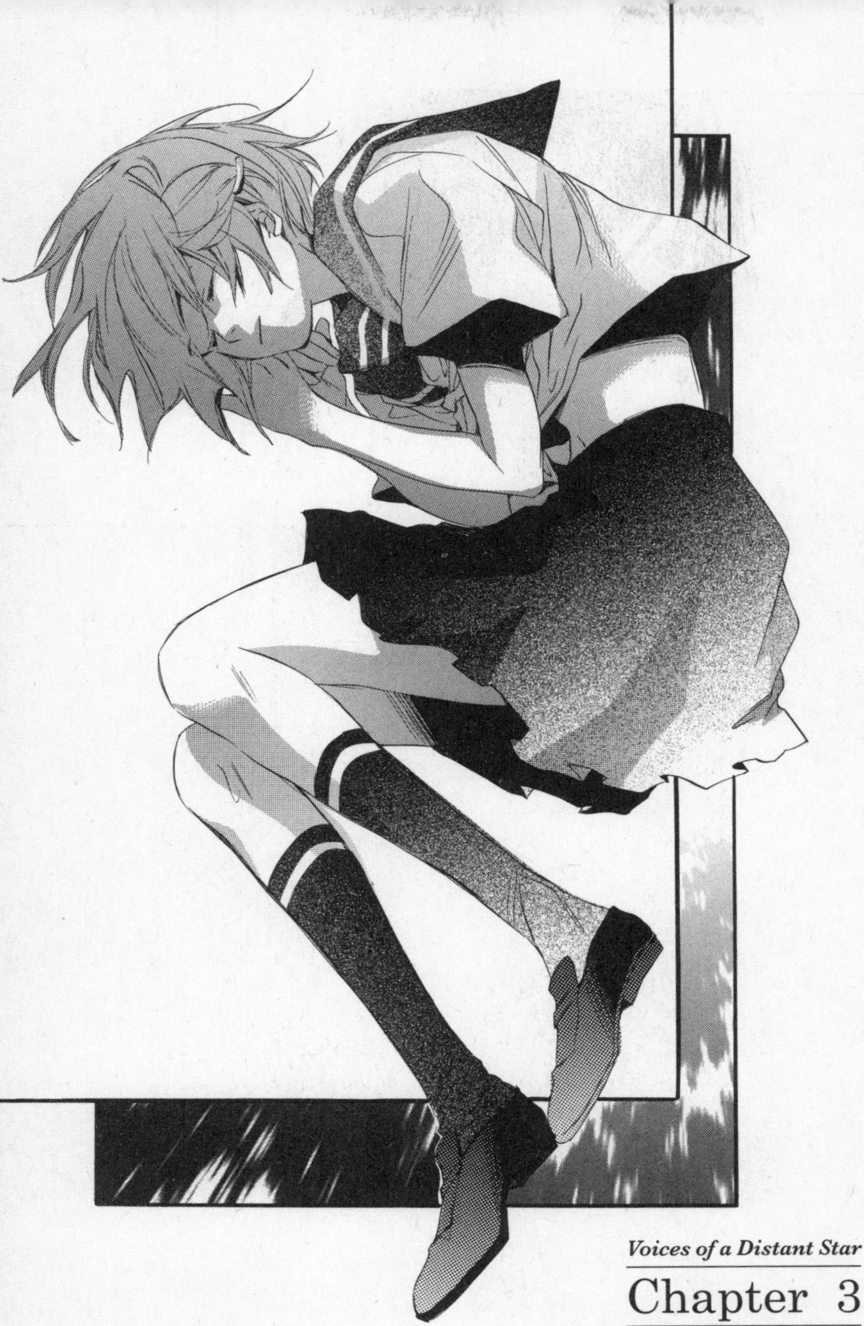

Voices of a Distant Star

Chapter 3

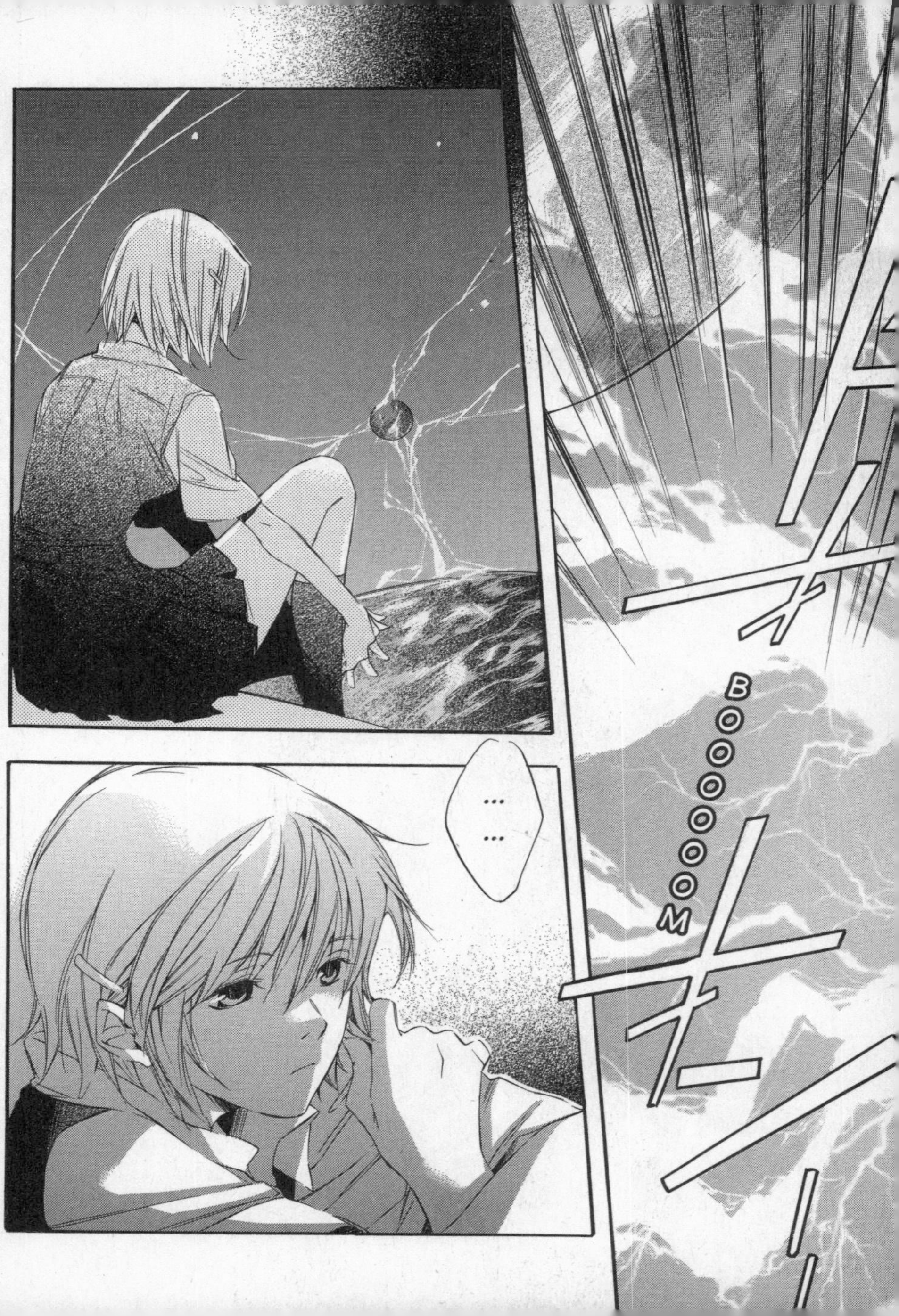
BOOOOOOOM
...
...

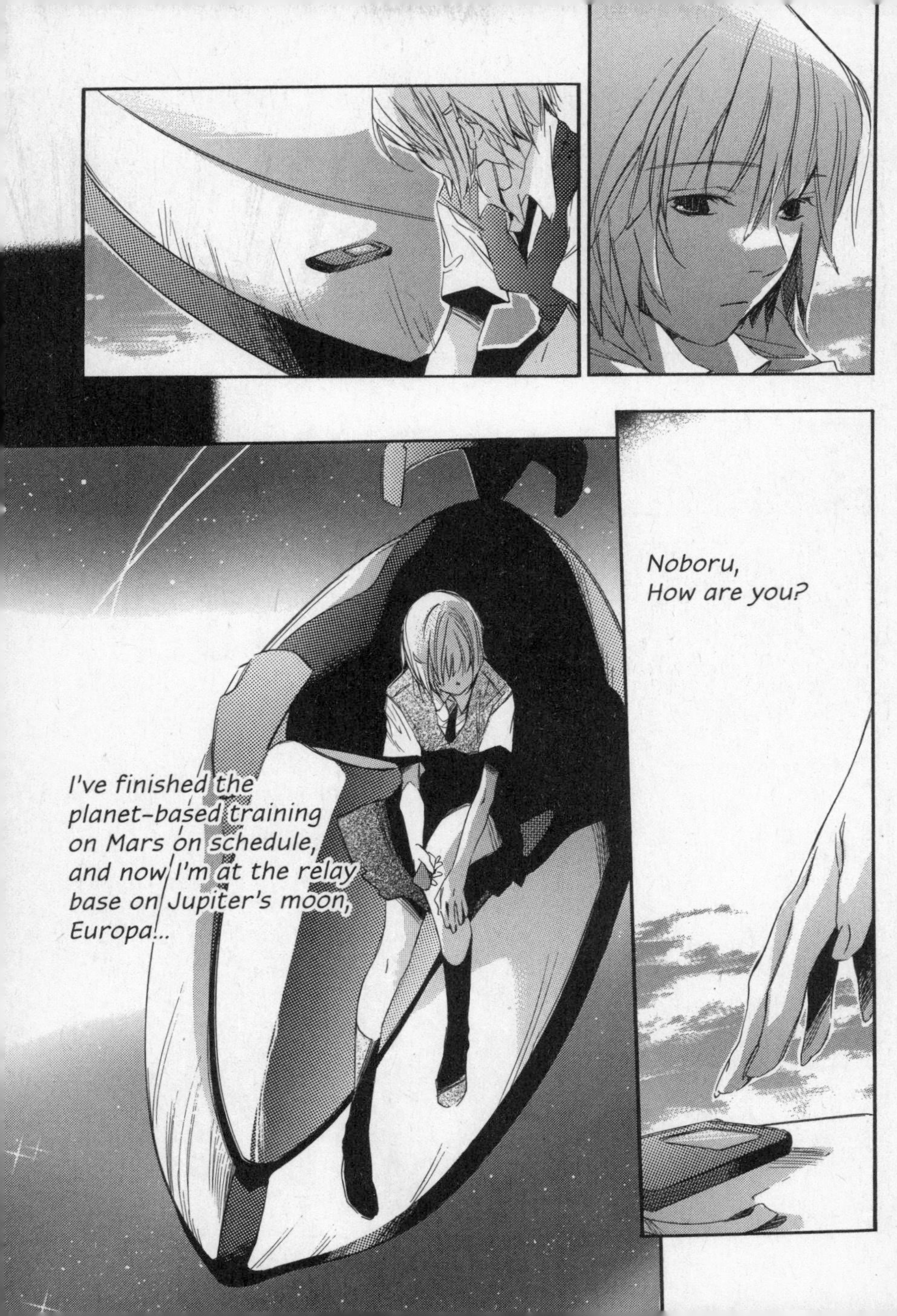
Noboru,
How are you?
I've finished the planet-based training on Mars on schedule, and now I'm at the relay base on Jupiter's moon, Europa...

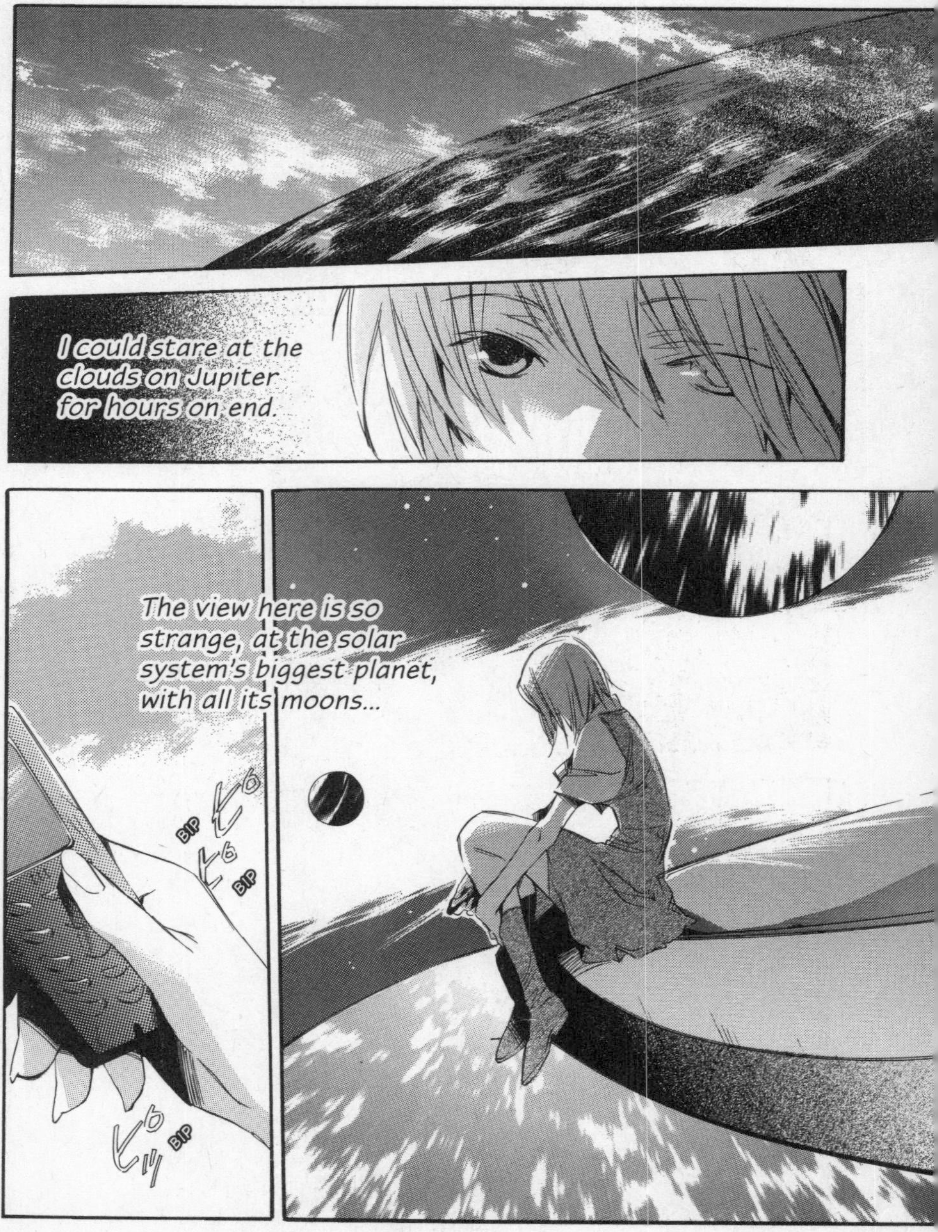
I could stare at the clouds on Jupiter for hours on end.
The view here is so strange, at the solar system's biggest planet, with all its moons...
BIP
BIP
BIP

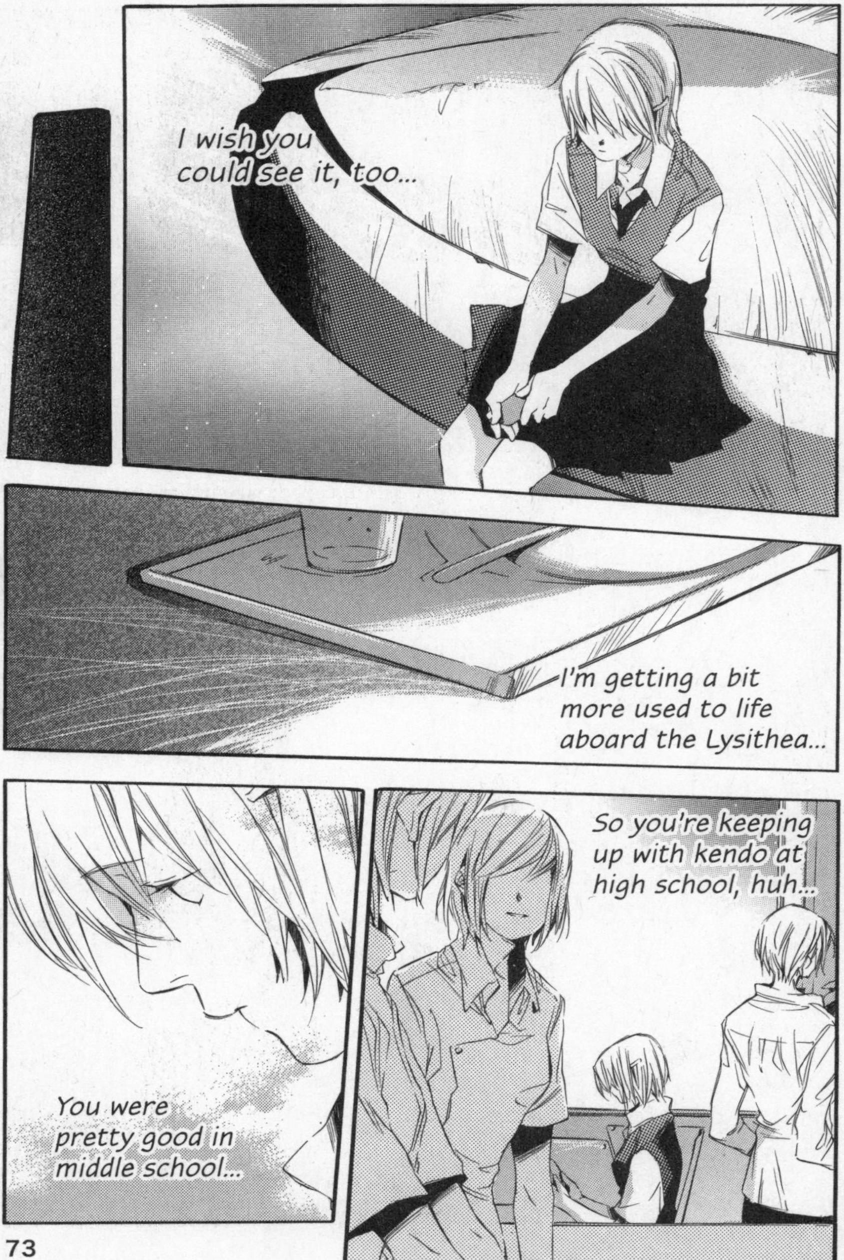
I wish you could see it, too...
I'm getting a bit more used to life aboard the Lysithea...
So you're keeping up with kendo at high school, huh...
You were pretty good in middle school...

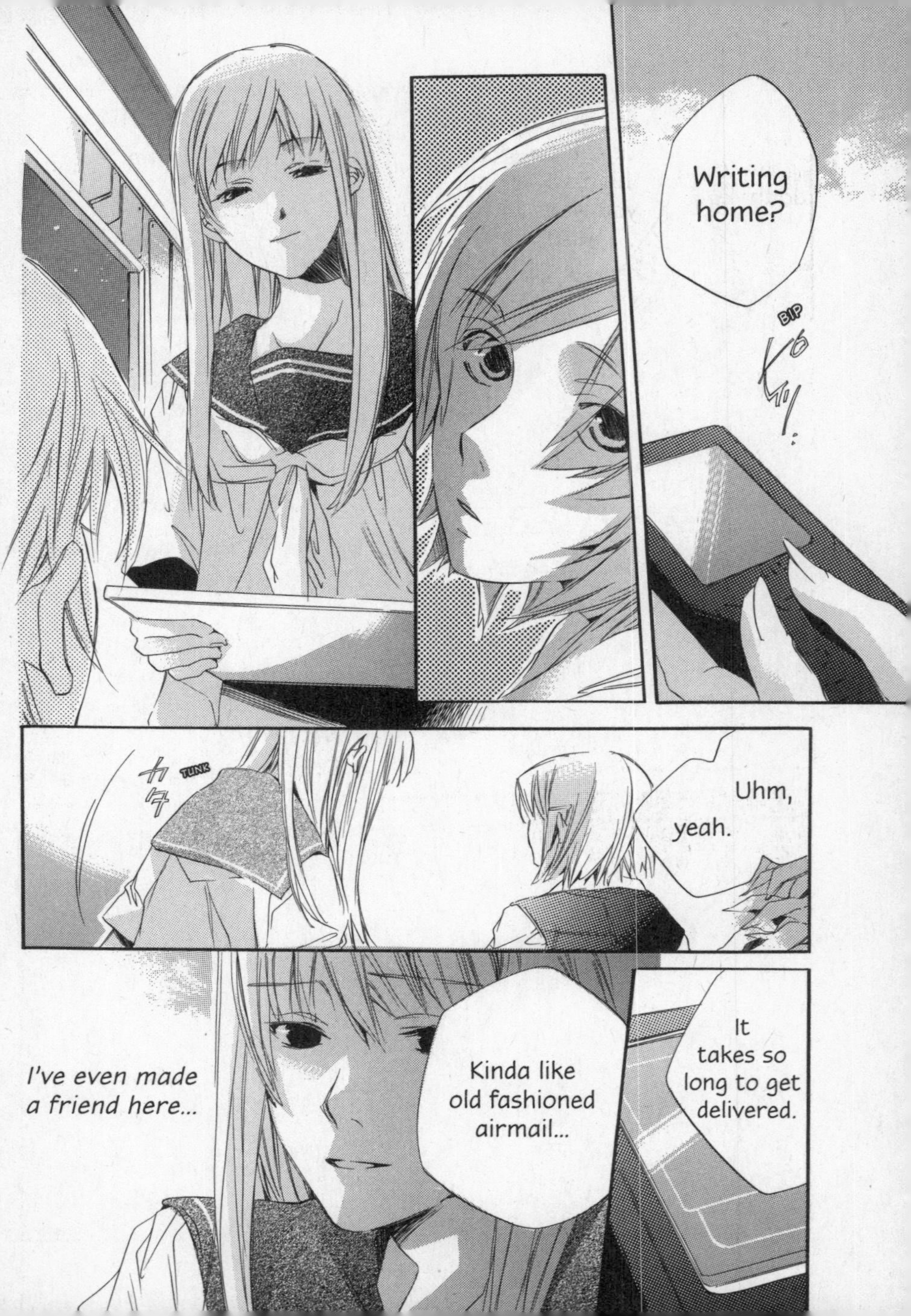
Writing home?
BIP
Uhm, yeah.
TUNK
It takes so long to get delivered.
Kinda like old fashioned airmail...
I've even made a friend here...

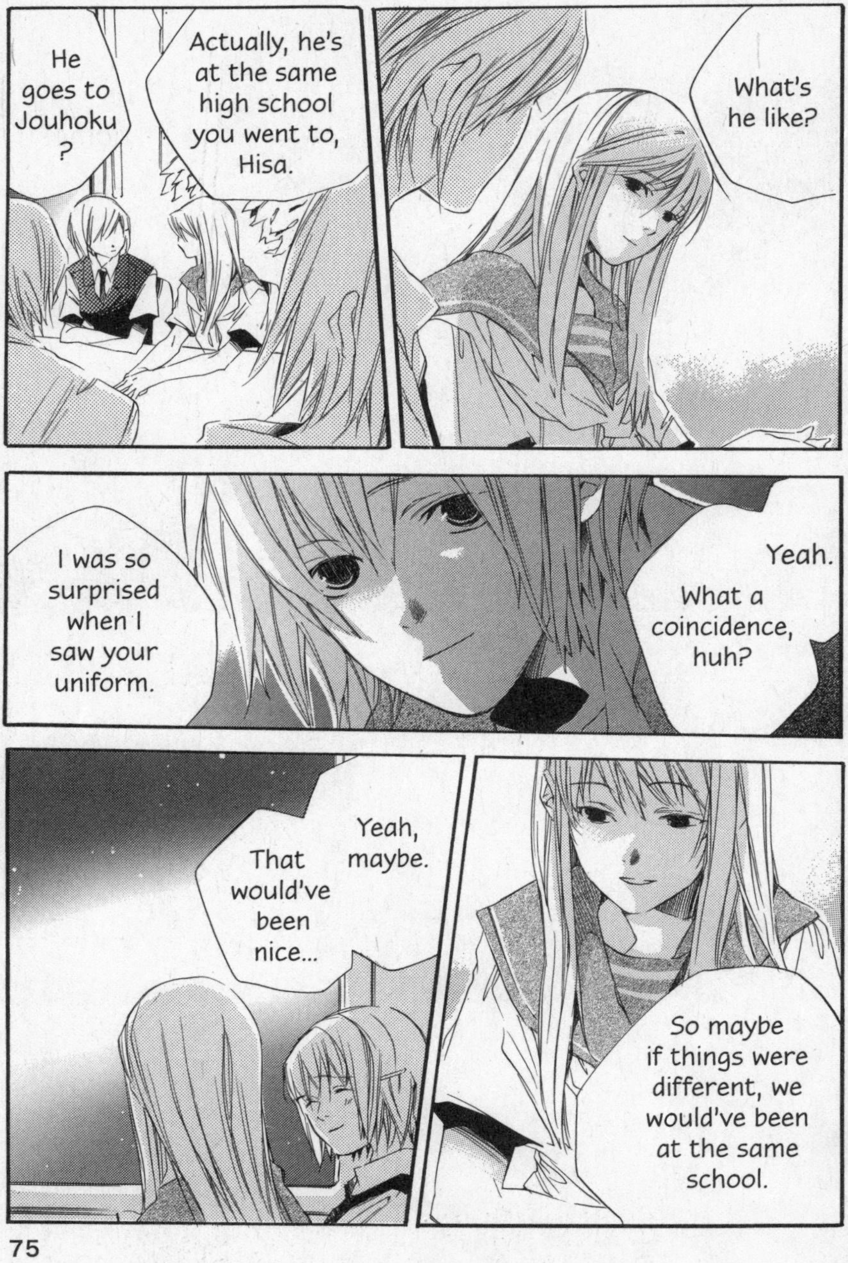
What's he like?
Actually, he's at the same high school you went to, Hisa.
He goes to Jouhoku?
Yeah.
What a coincidence, huh?
I was so surprised when I saw your uniform.
So maybe if things were different, we would've been at the same school.
Yeah, maybe.
That would've been nice...

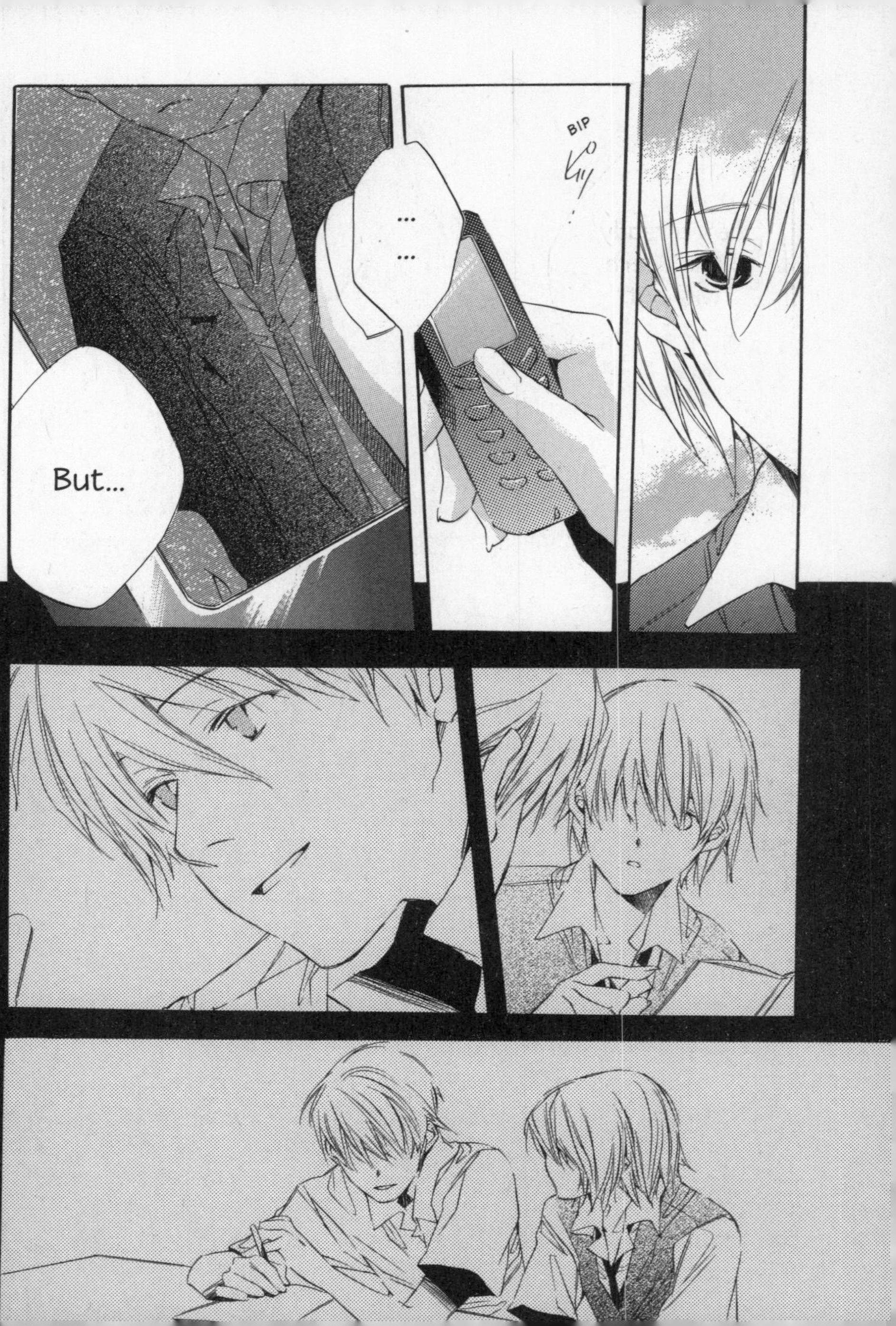
BIP
...
...
But...

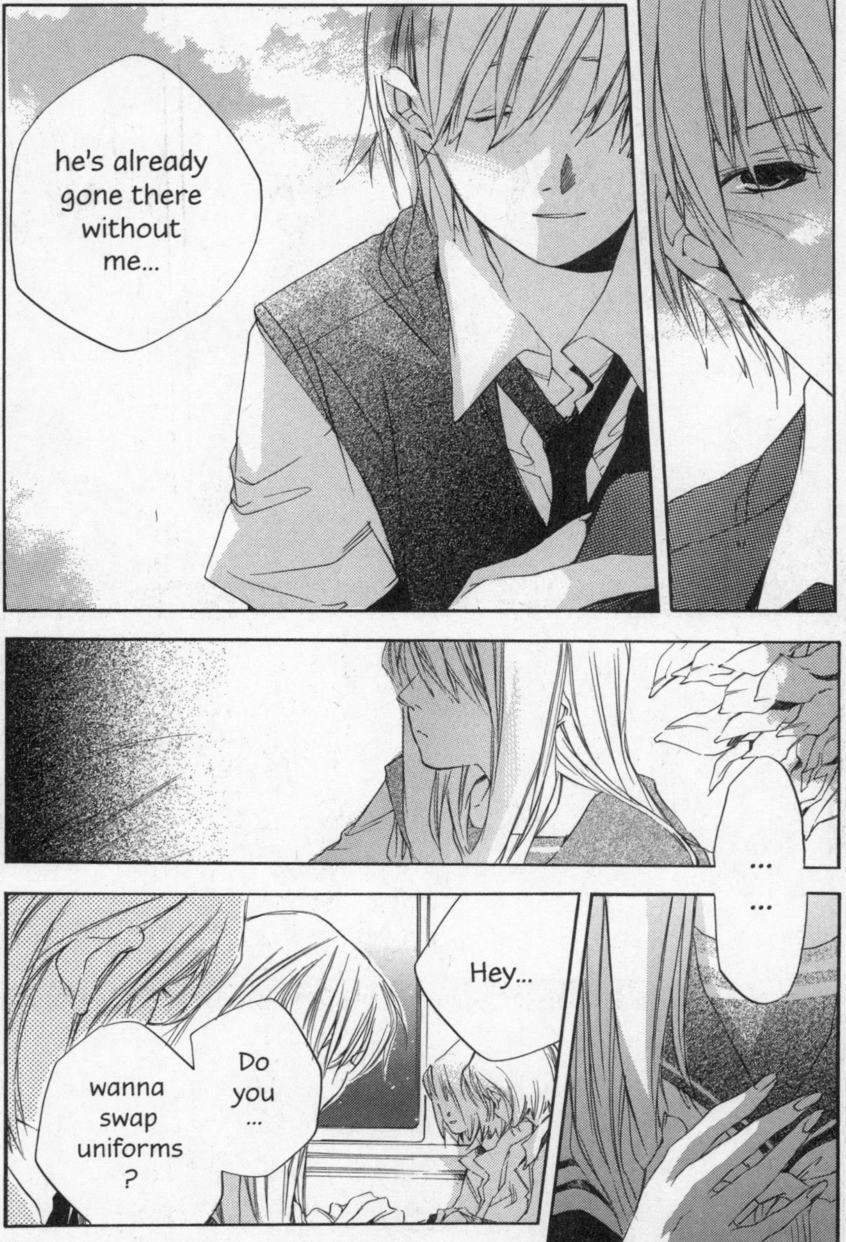
he's already gone there without me...
...
...
Hey...
Do you ...
wanna swap uniforms ?

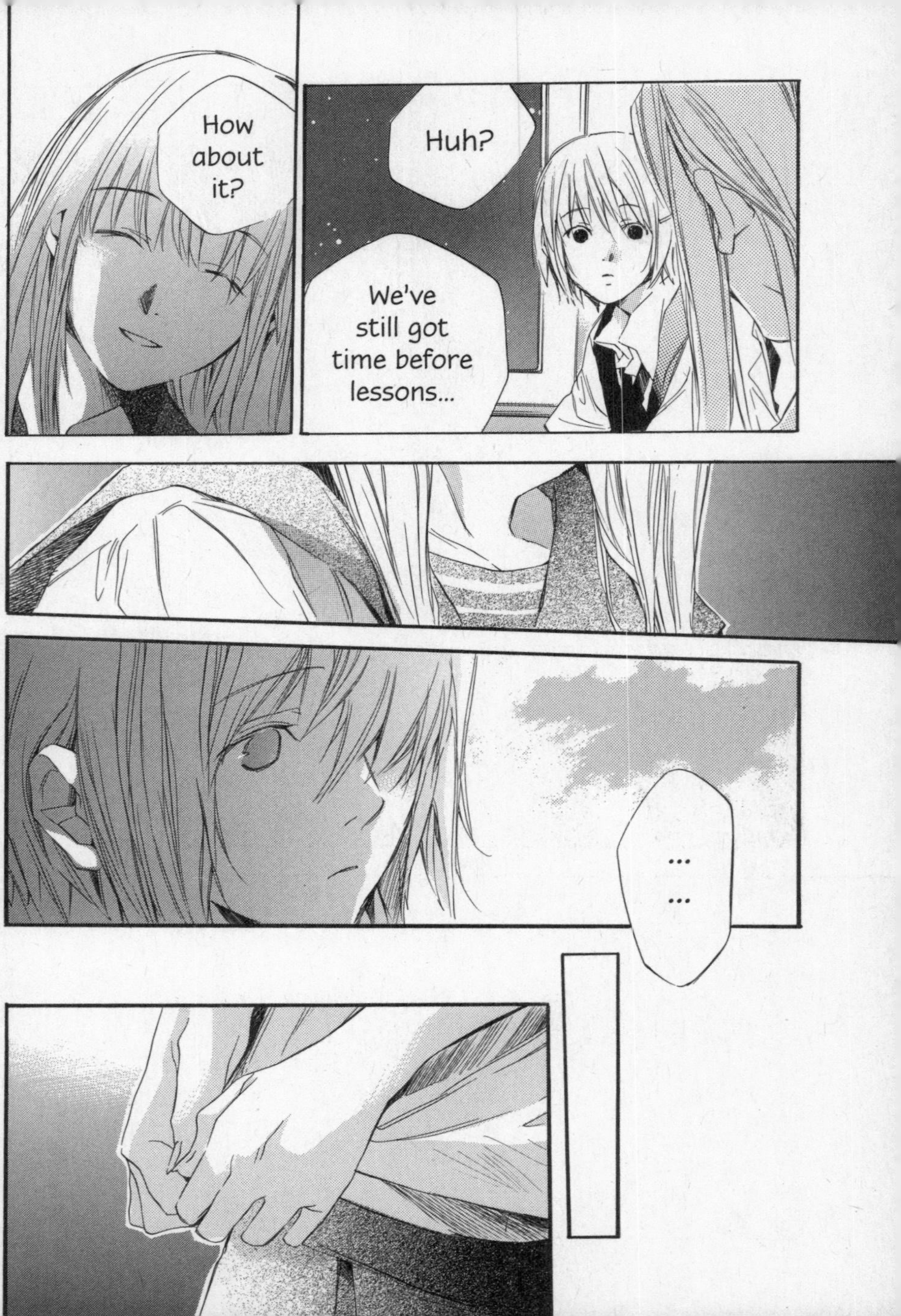

Huh?
We've still got time before lessons...
How about it?
... ...

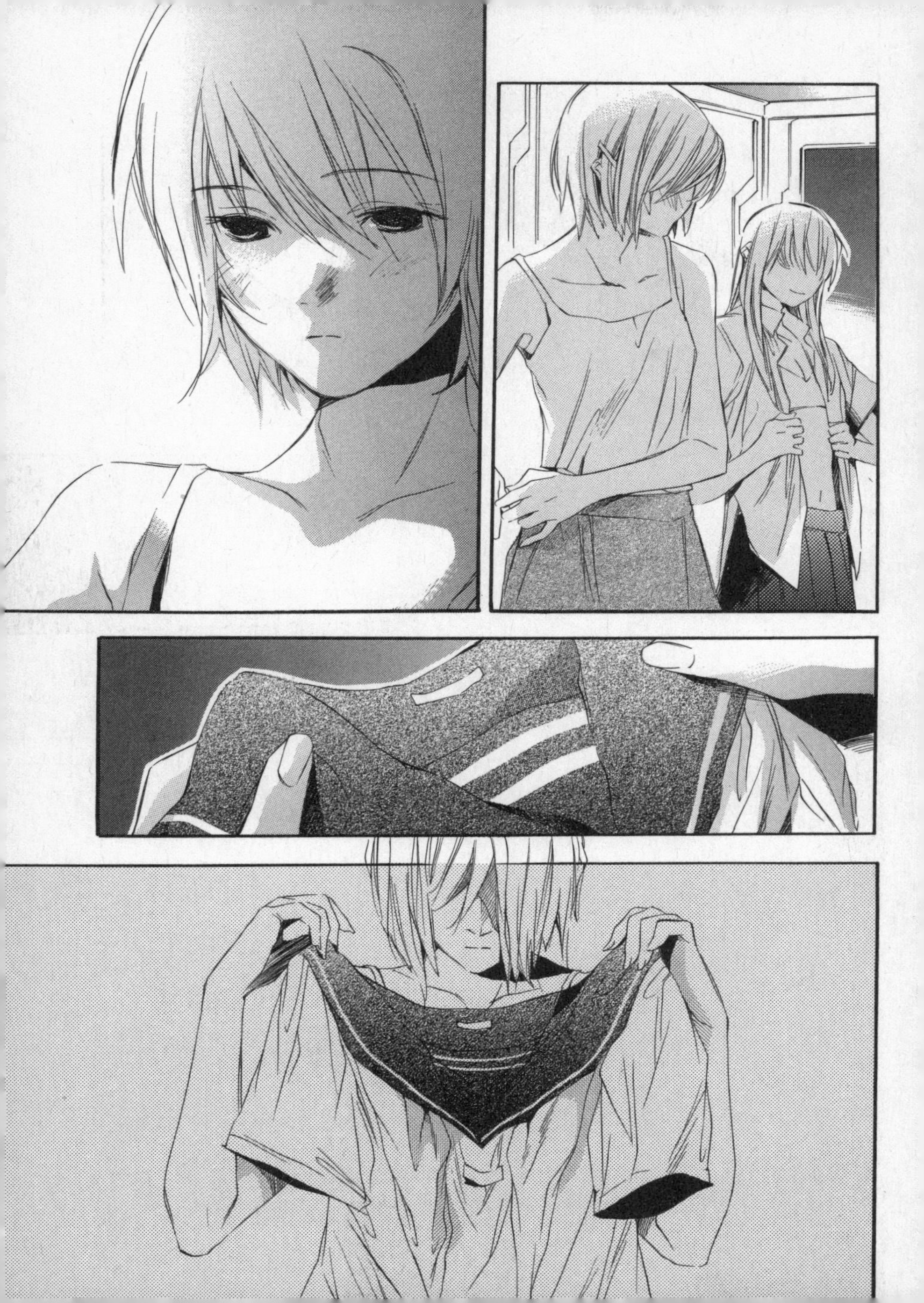

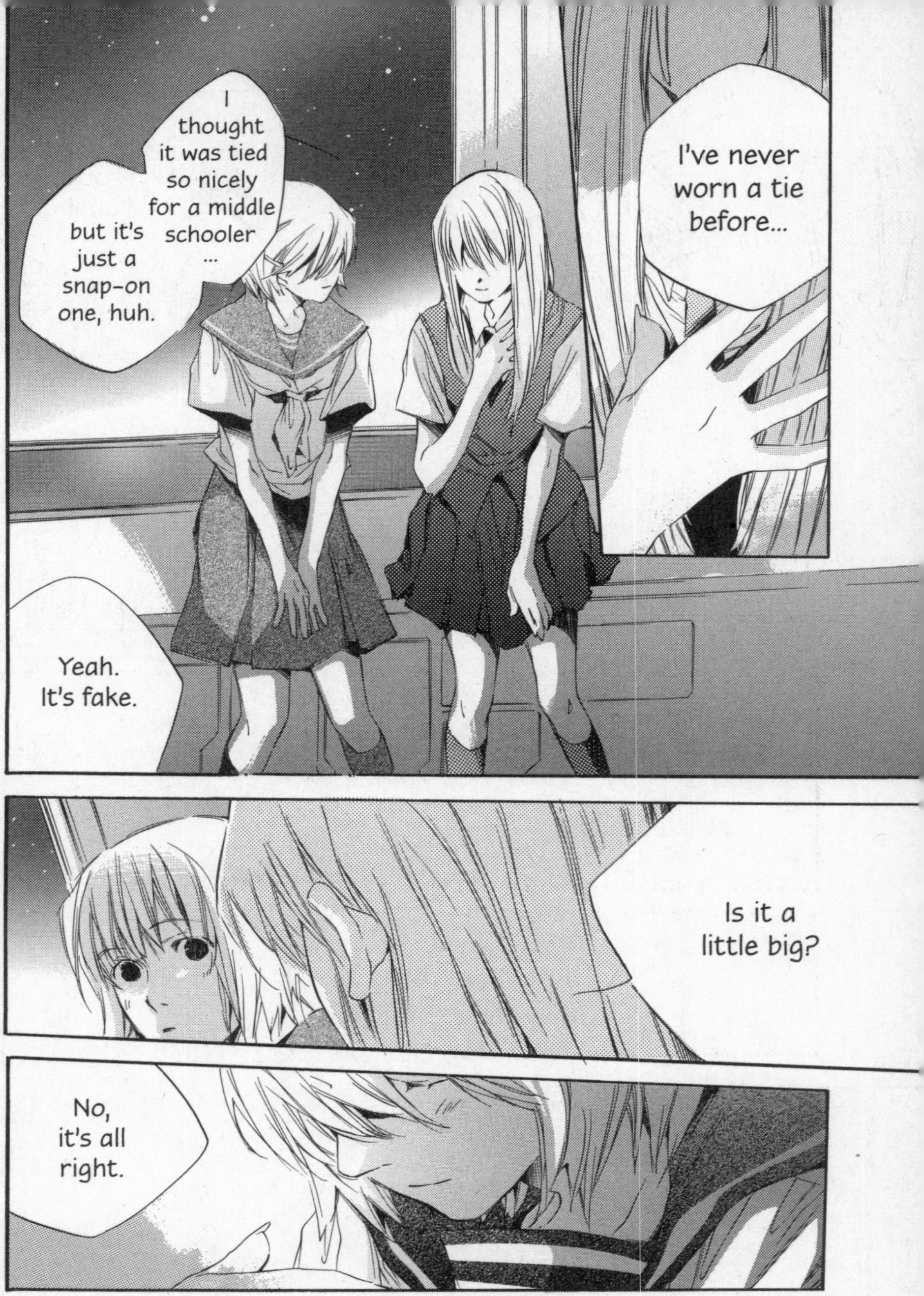
I've never worn a tie before...
I thought it was tied so nicely for a middle schooler ...
but it's just a snap-on one, huh.
Yeah. It's fake.
Is it a little big?
No, it's all right.

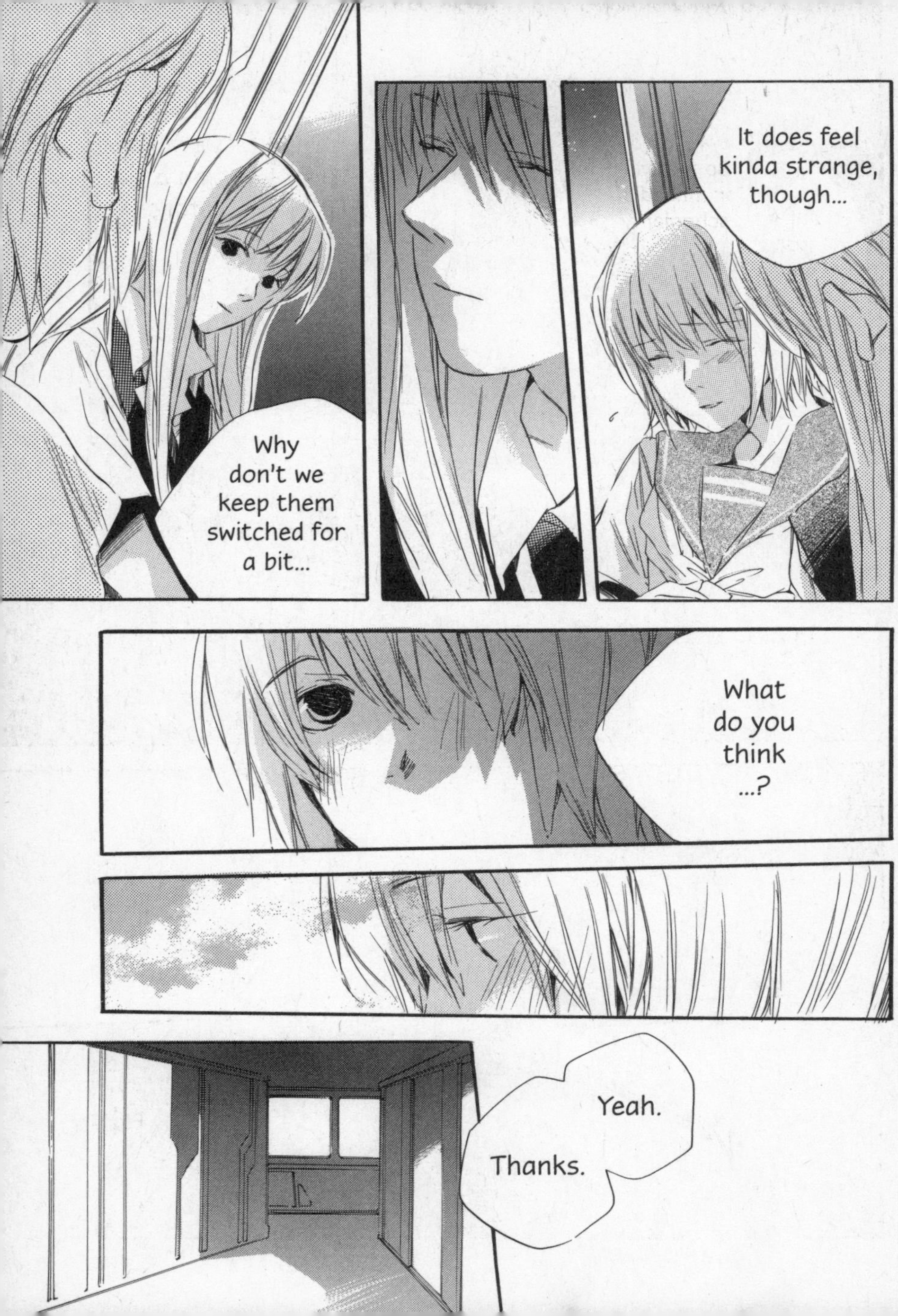
It does feel kinda strange, though...
Why don't we keep them switched for a bit...
What do you think ...?
Yeah.
Thanks.

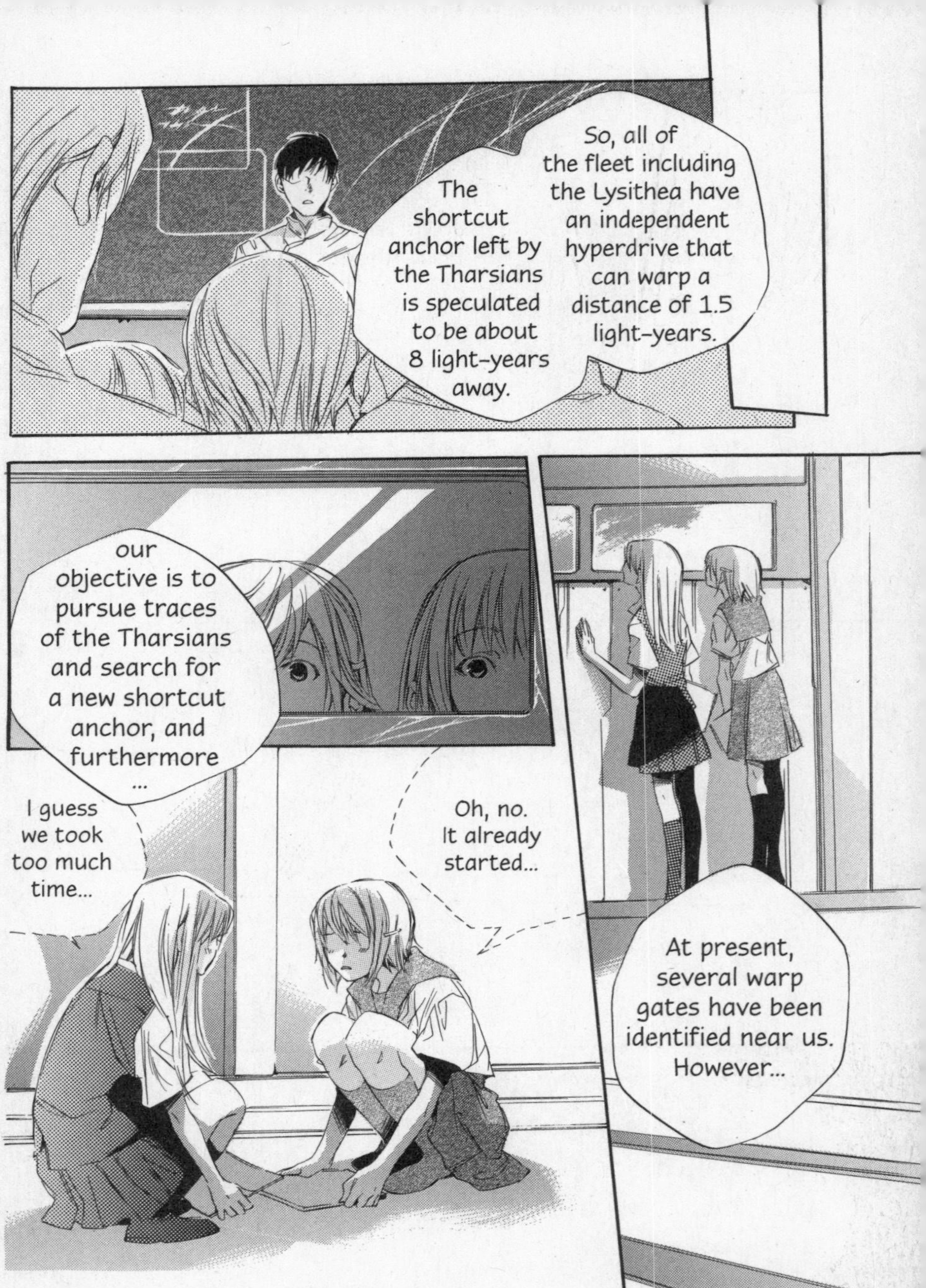
So, all of the fleet including the Lysithea have an independent hyperdrive that can warp a distance of 1.5 light-years.
The shortcut anchor left by the Tharsians is speculated to be about 8 light-years away.
At present, several warp gates have been identified near us. However...
our objective is to pursue traces of the Tharsians and search for a new shortcut anchor, and furthermore ...
Oh, no. It already started...
I guess we took too much time...

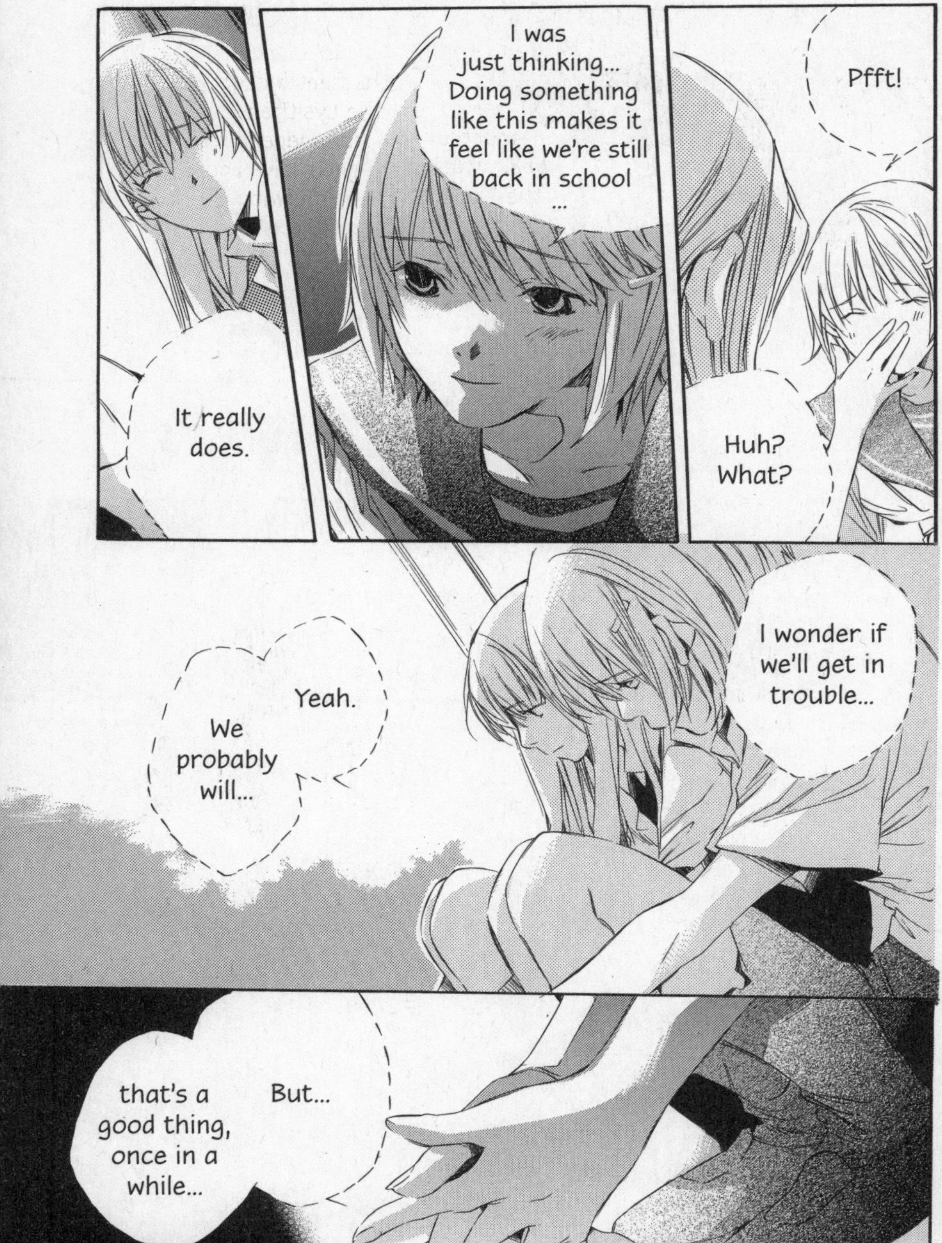
Pfft!
Huh? What?
I was just thinking... Doing something like this makes it feel like we're still back in school ...
It really does.
I wonder if we'll get in trouble...
Yeah. We probably will...
But...
that's a good thing, once in a while...

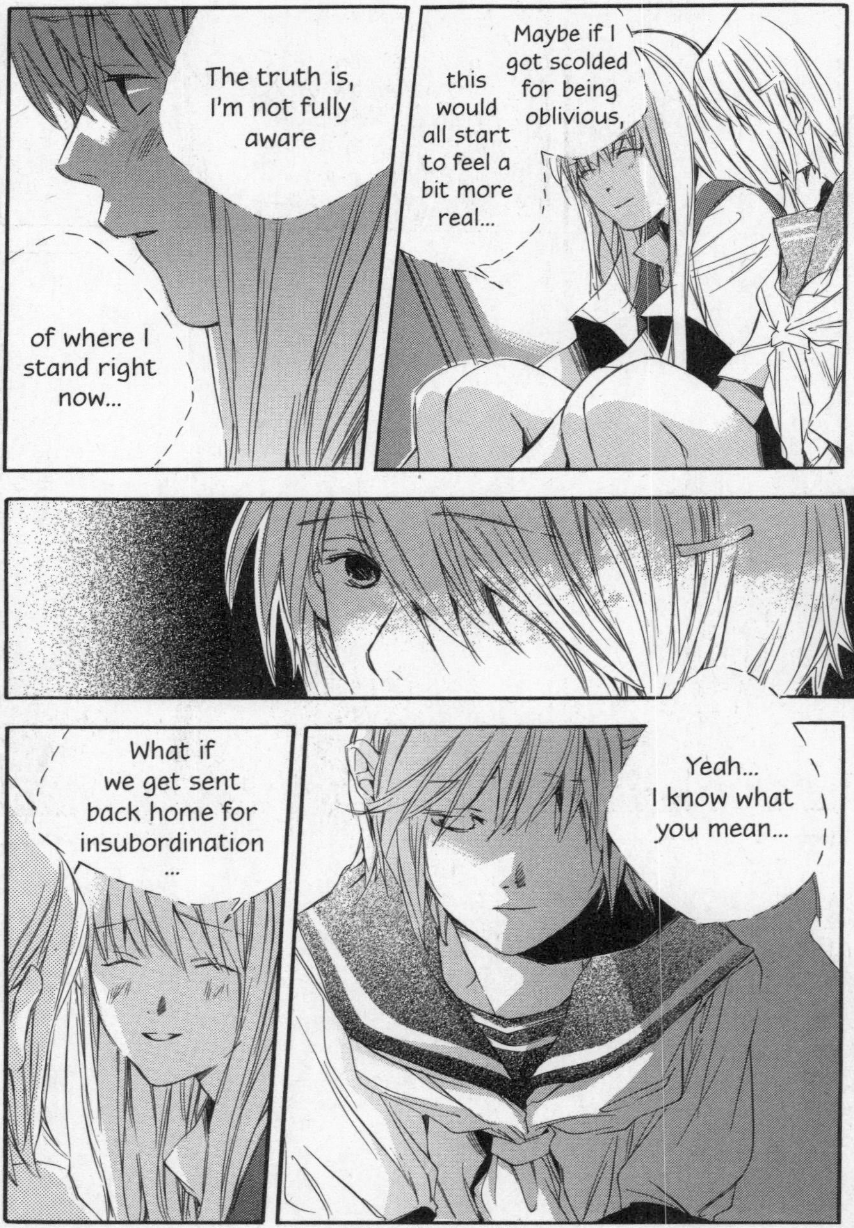
Maybe if I got scolded for being oblivious, this would all start to feel a bit more real...
The truth is, I'm not fully aware
of where I stand right now...
Yeah... I know what you mean...
What if we get sent back home for insubordination ...

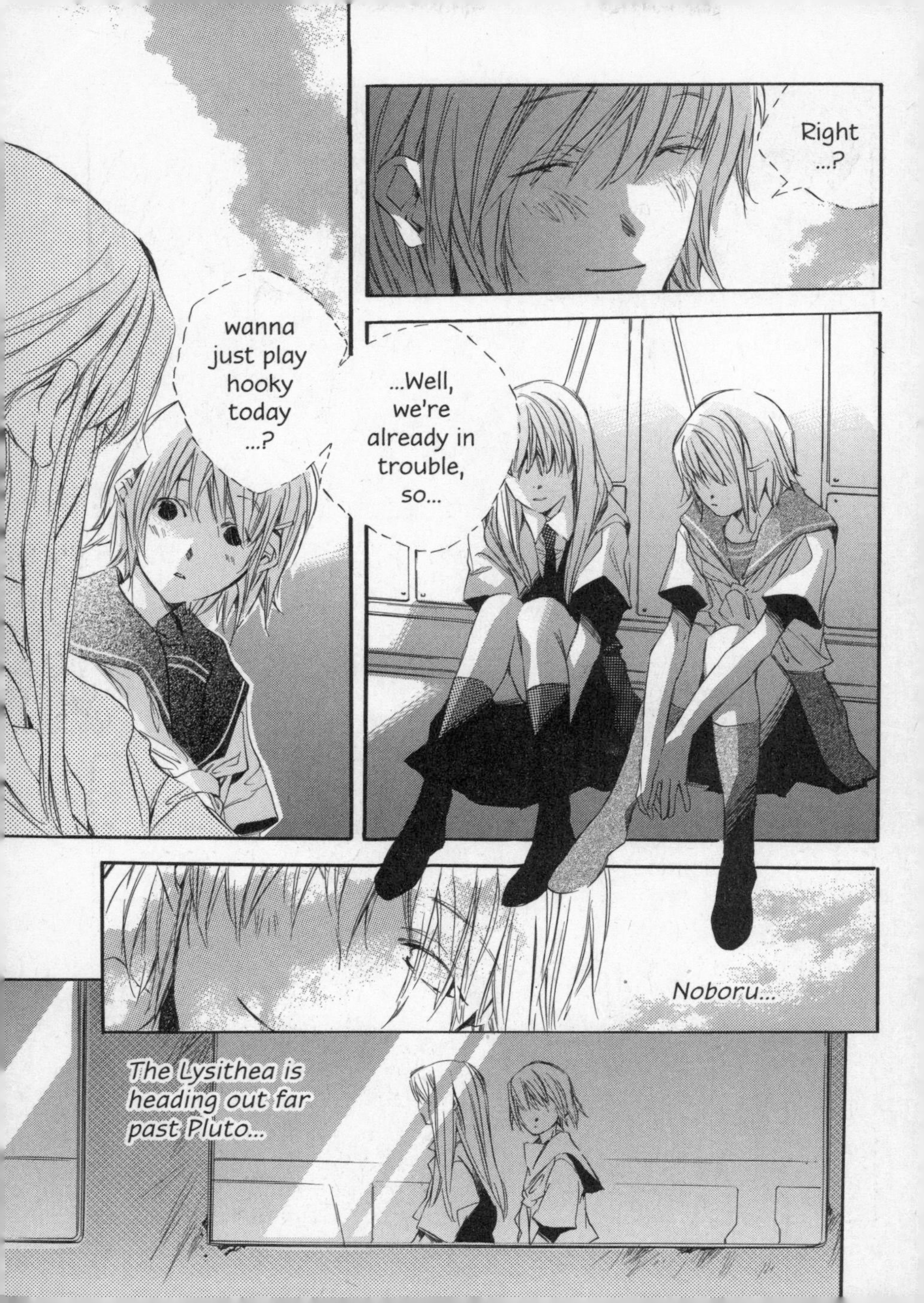
Right ...?
...Well, we're already in trouble, so...
wanna just play hooky today ...?
Noboru...
The Lysithea is heading out far past Pluto...

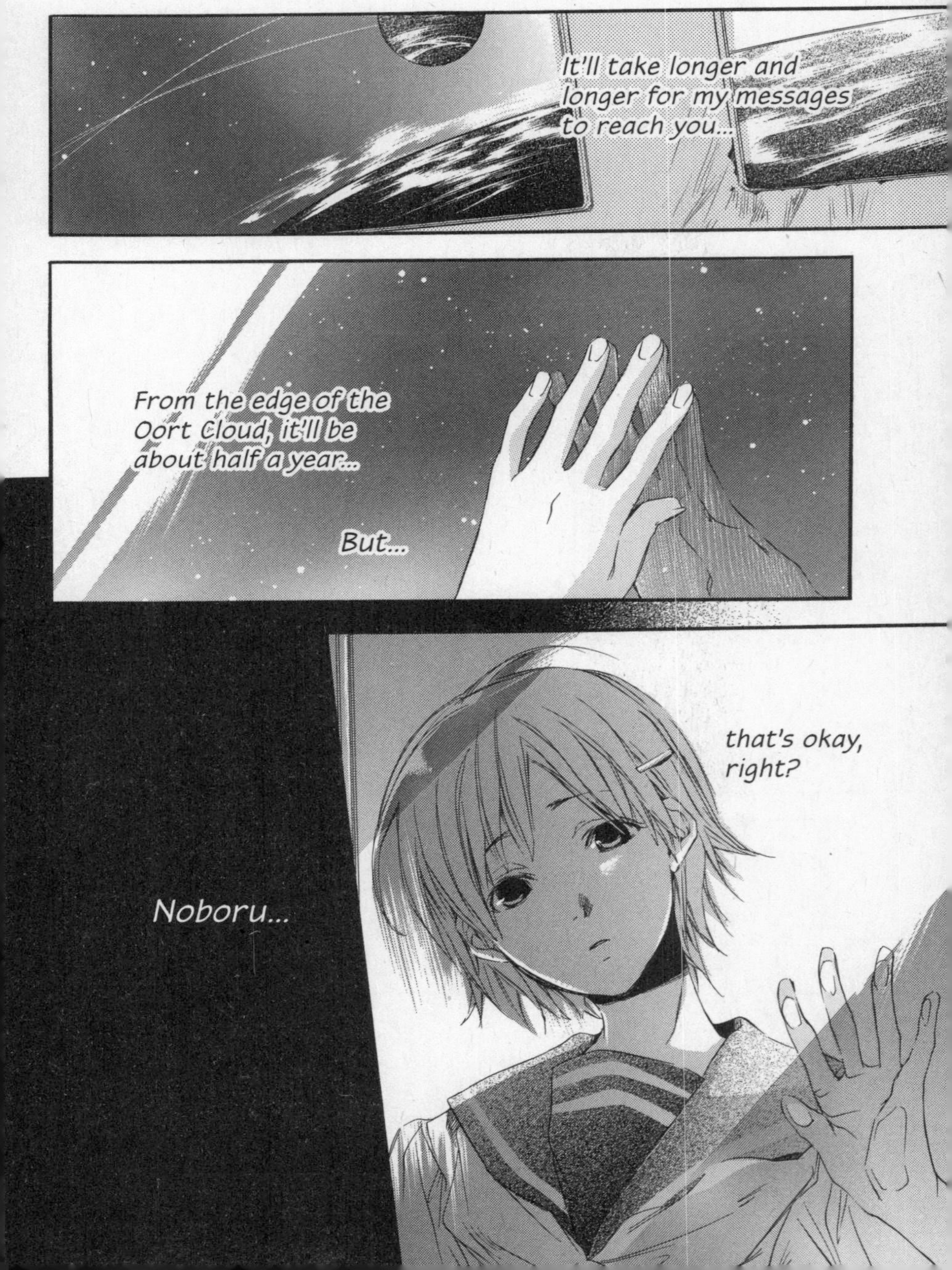
It'll take longer and longer for my messages to reach you...
From the edge of the Oort Cloud, it'll be about half a year...
But...
that's okay, right?
Noboru...

Voices of a Distant Star

Chapter 4

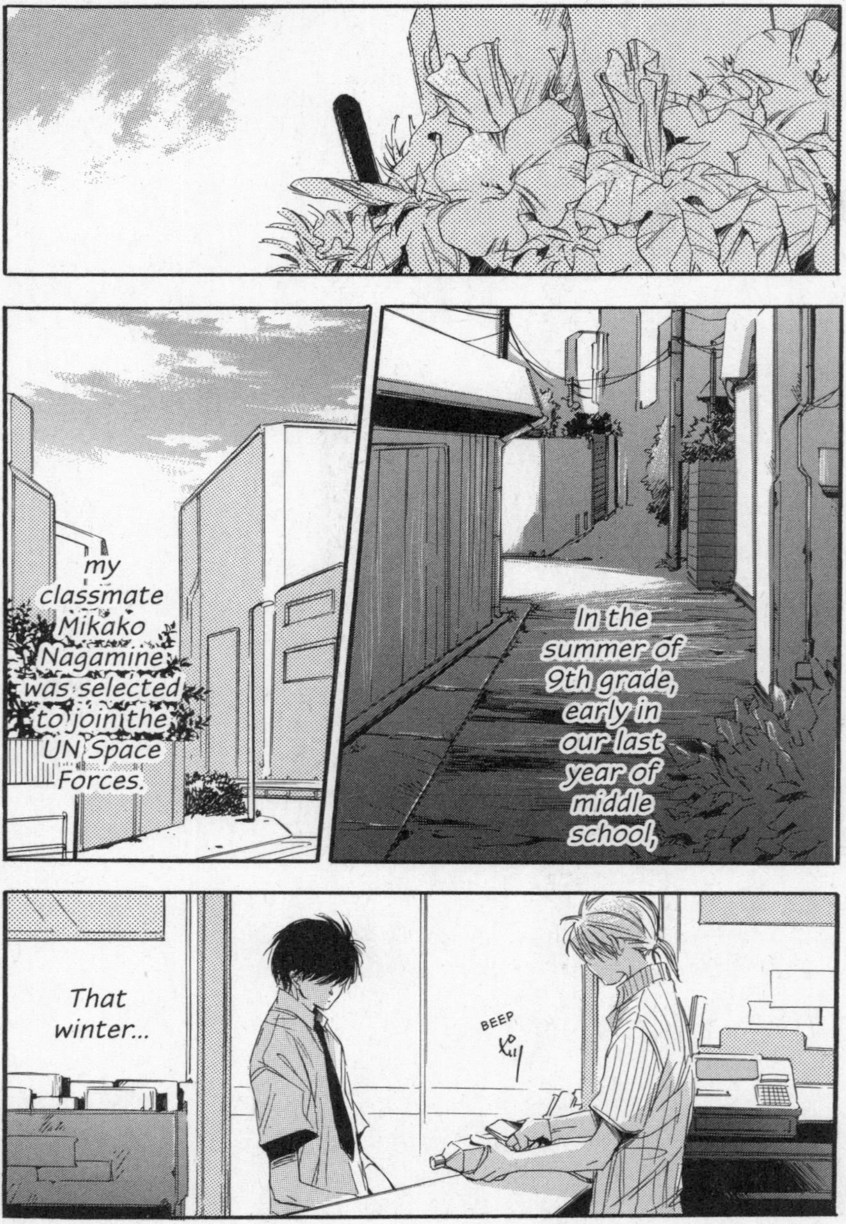
In the summer of 9th grade, early in our last year of middle school,
my classmate Mikako Nagamine was selected to join the UN Space Forces.
BEEP
That winter...

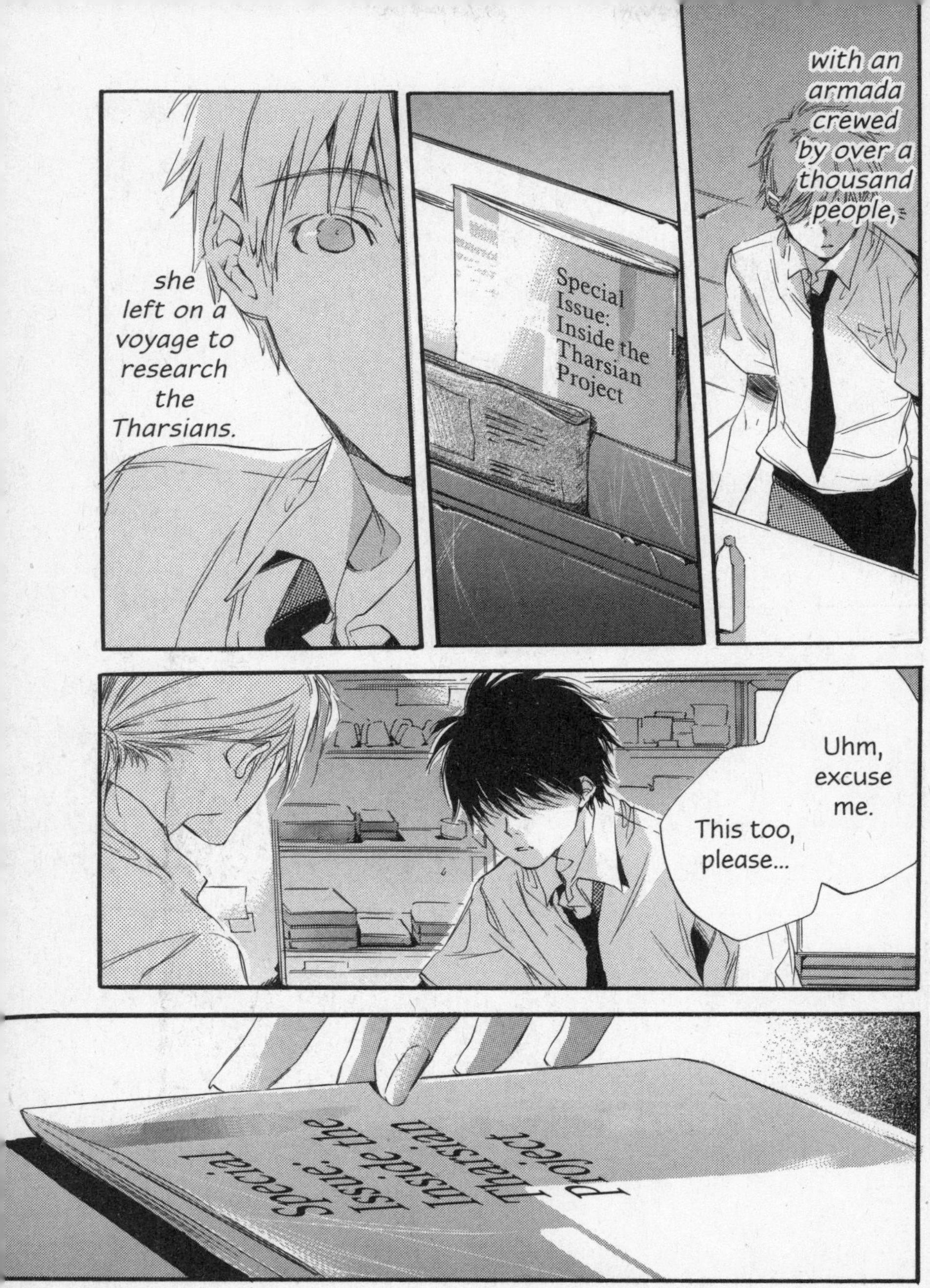
with an armada crewed by over a thousand people,
Special Issue: Inside the Tharsian Project
she left on a voyage to research the Tharsians.
Uhm, excuse me.
This too, please...
Special Issue: Inside the Tharsian Project

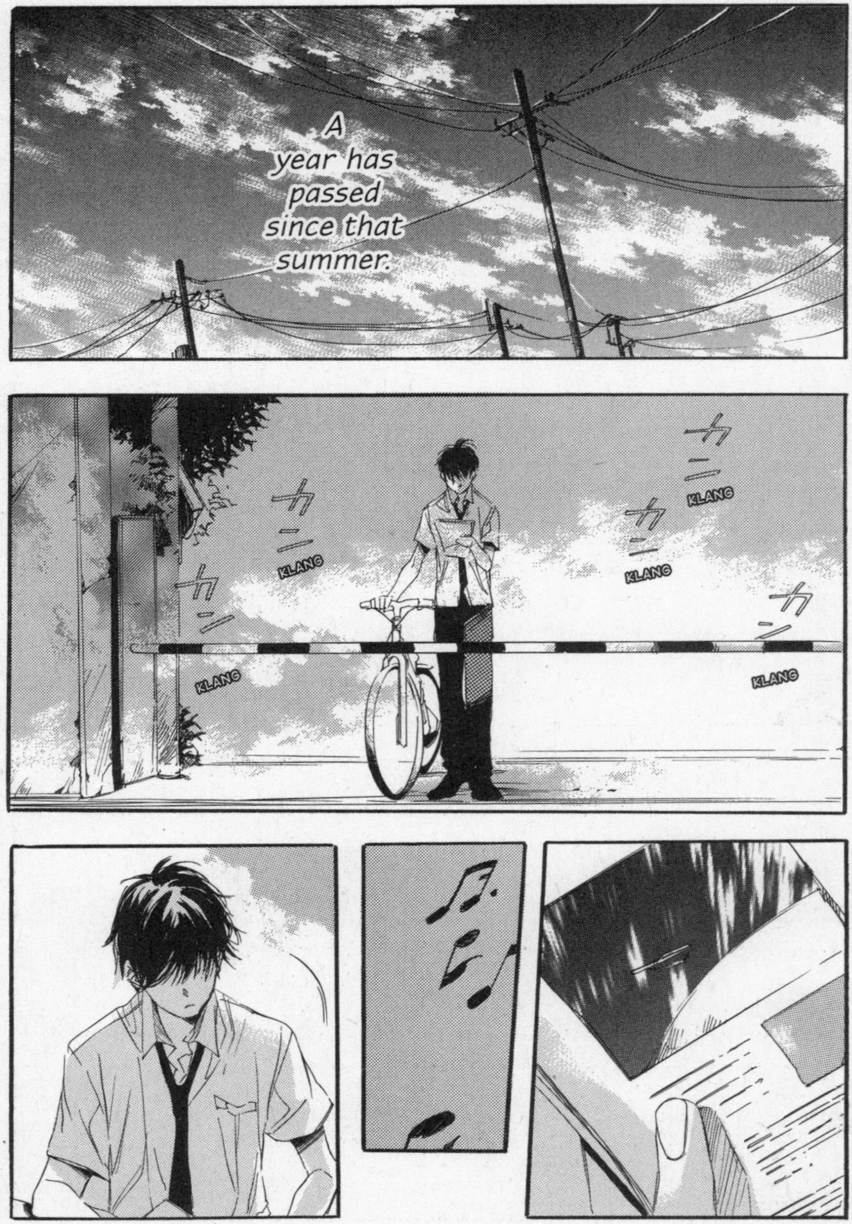
A year has passed since that summer.
カン
KLANG
カン
KLANG
カン
KLANG
カン
KLANG
カン
KLANG

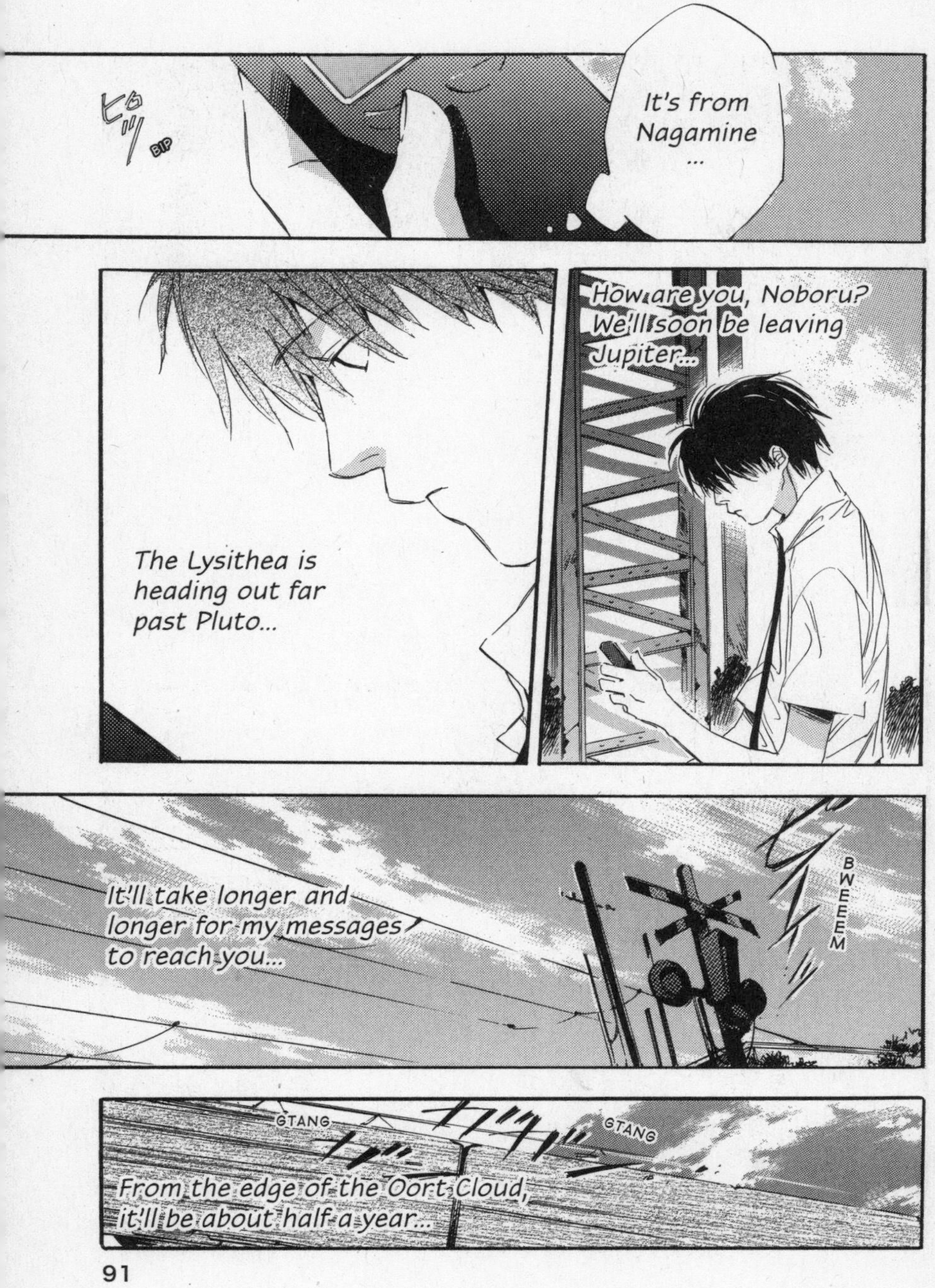
ピッ
BIP
It's from Nagamine ...
How are you, Noboru? We'll soon be leaving Jupiter...
The Lysithea is heading out far past Pluto...
BWEEEEM
It'll take longer and longer for my messages to reach you...
GTANG
GTANG
From the edge of the Oort Cloud, it'll be about half a year...

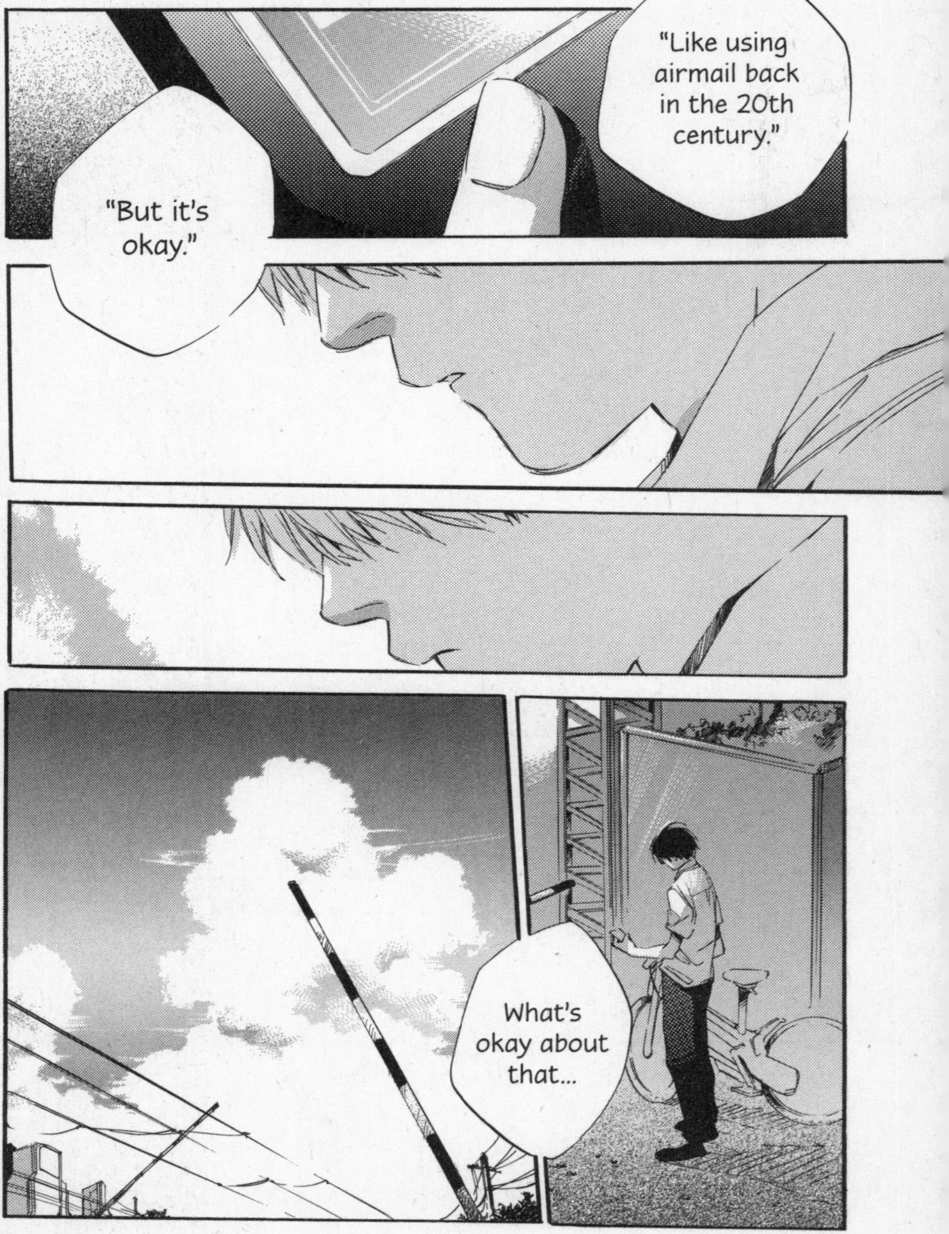
"Like using airmail back in the 20th century."
"But it's okay."
What's okay about that...

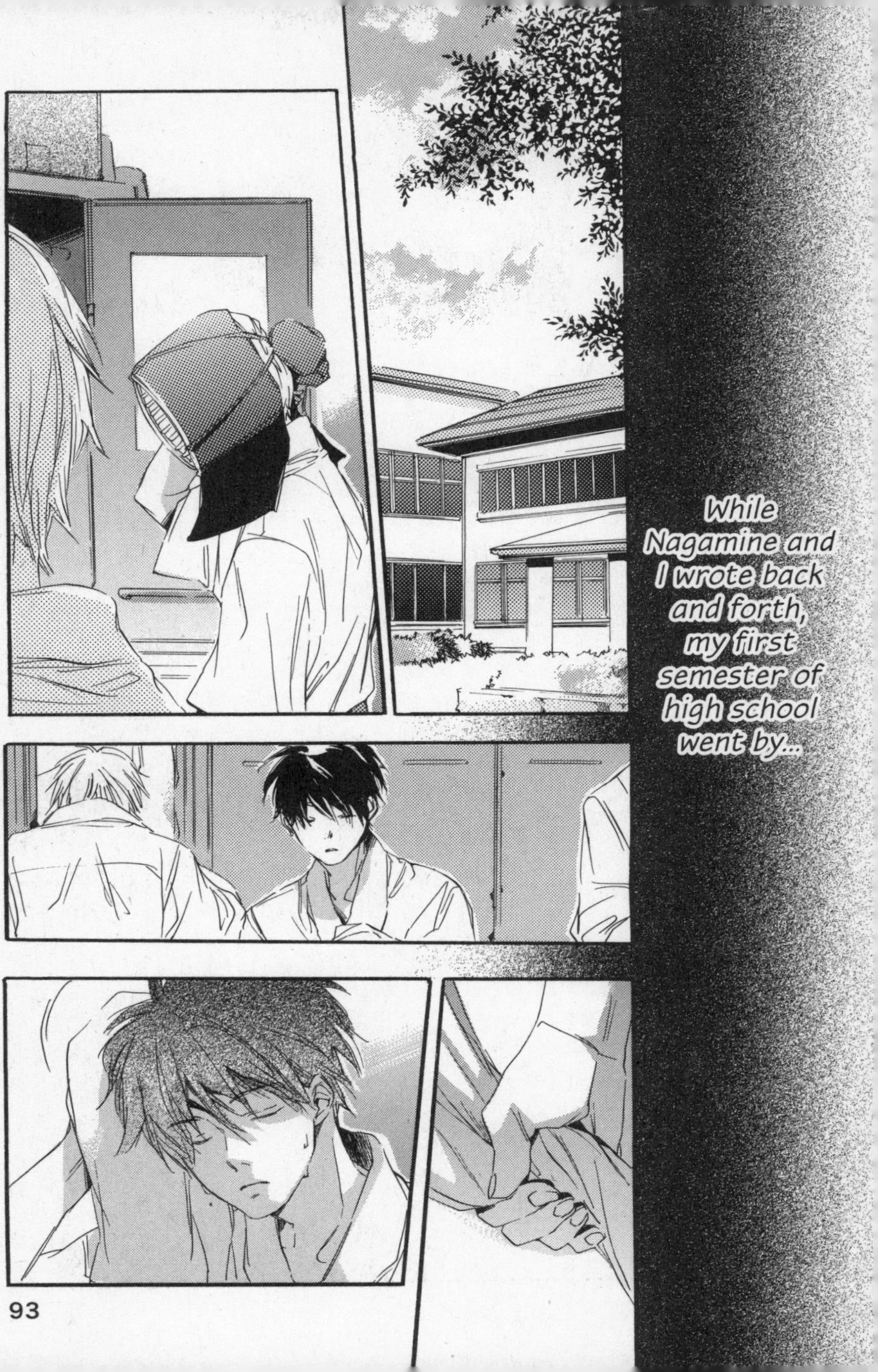
While Nagamine and I wrote back and forth, my first semester of high school went by...

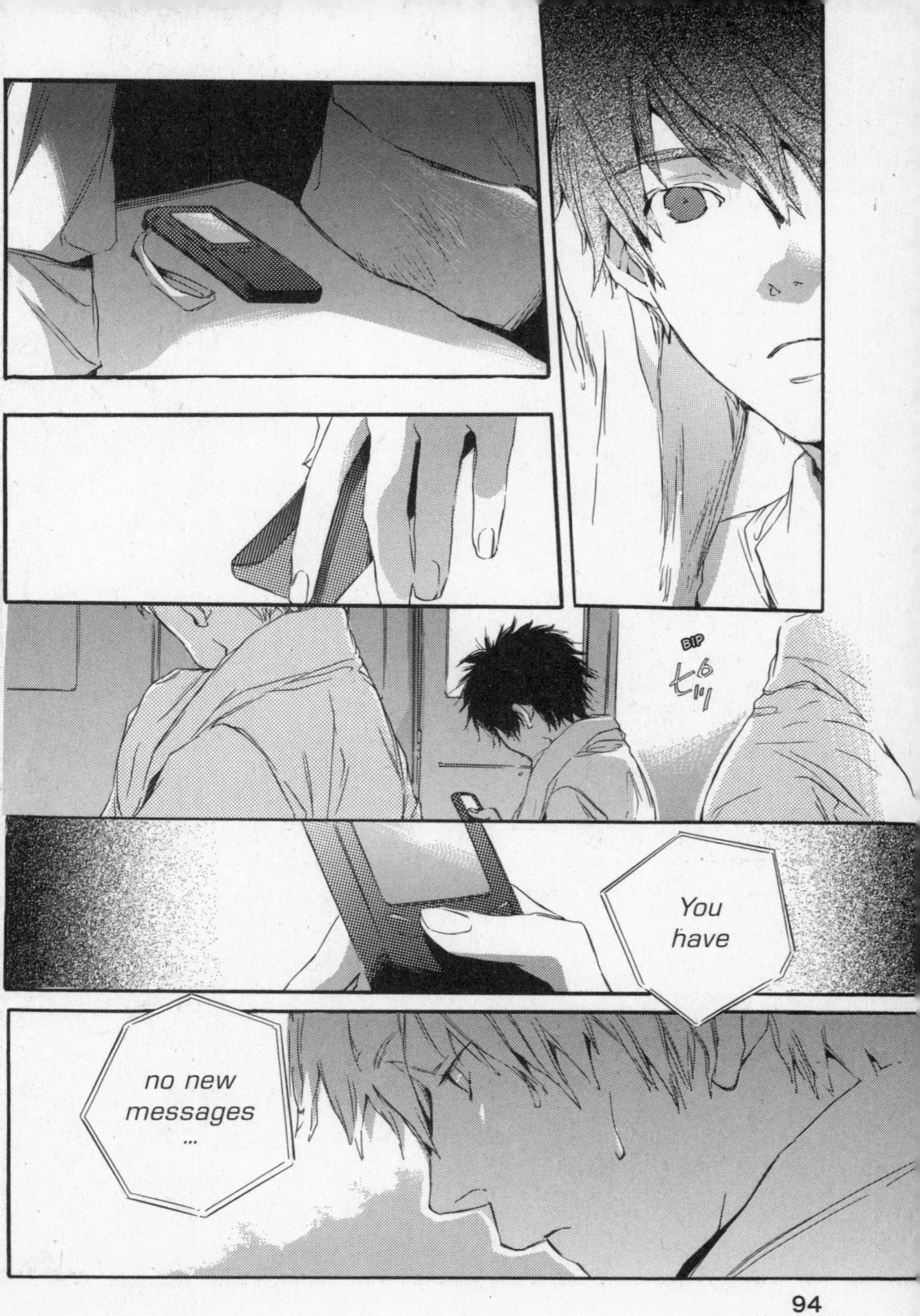
BIP
ピッ
You have
no new messages ...

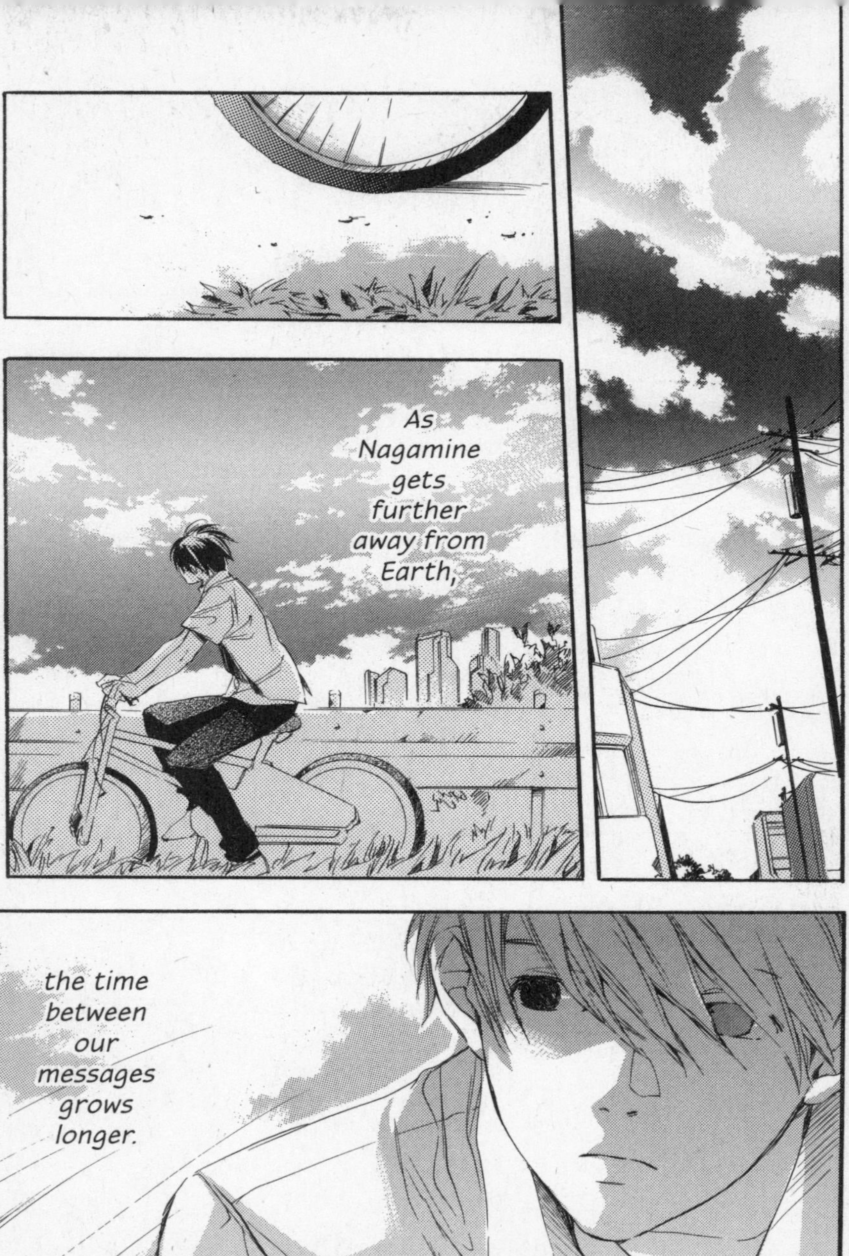
As Nagamine gets further away from Earth,
the time between our messages grows longer.

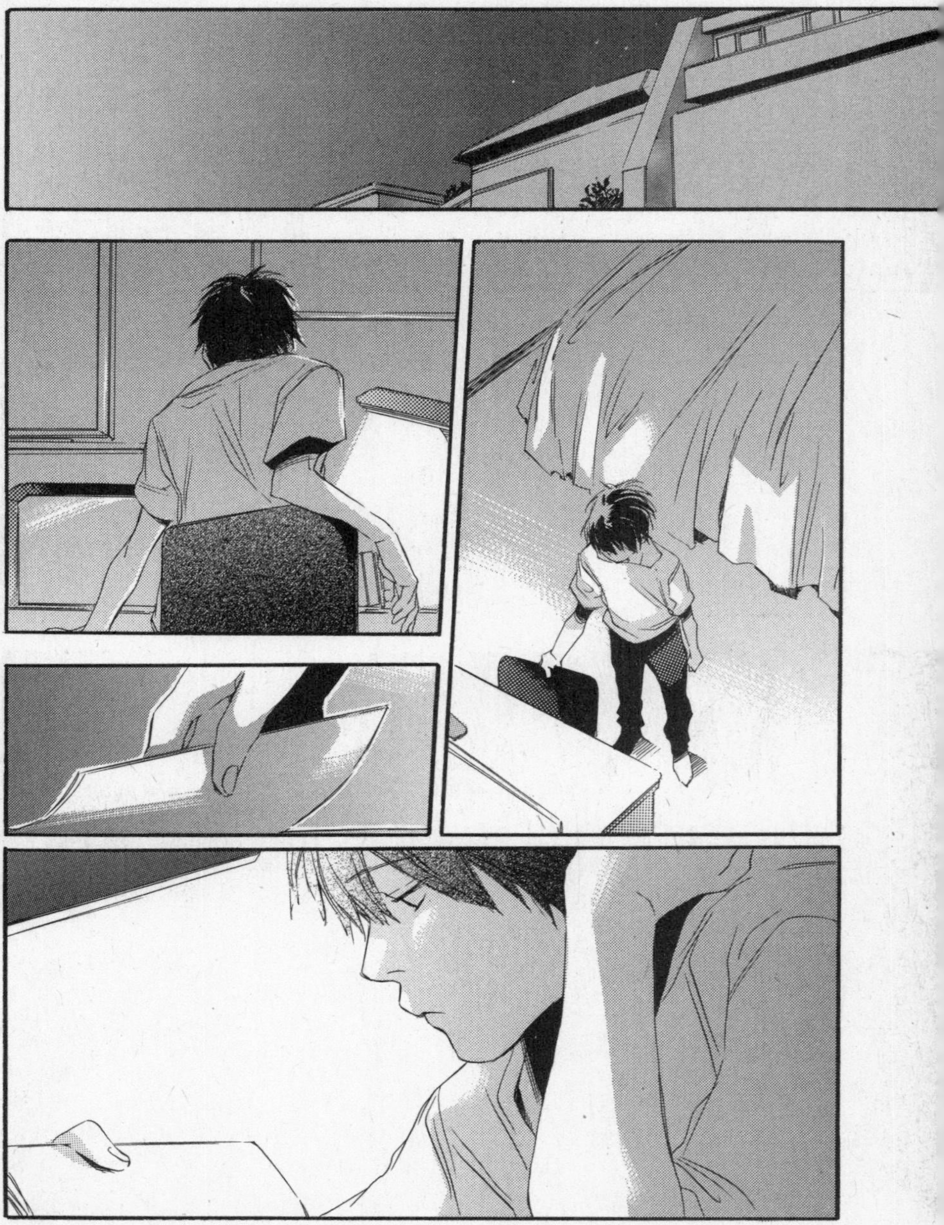

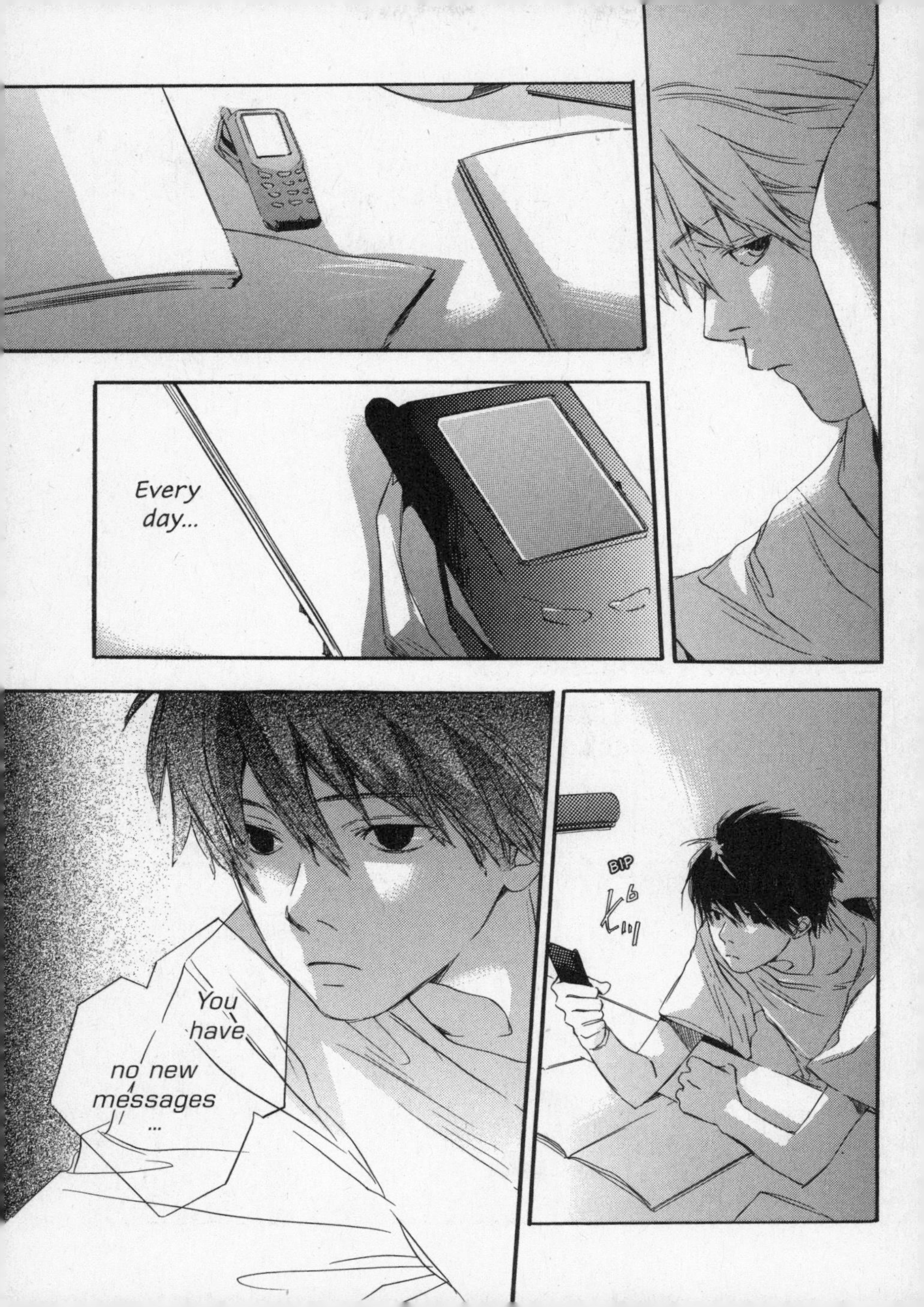
Every day...
BIP
You have no new messages ...

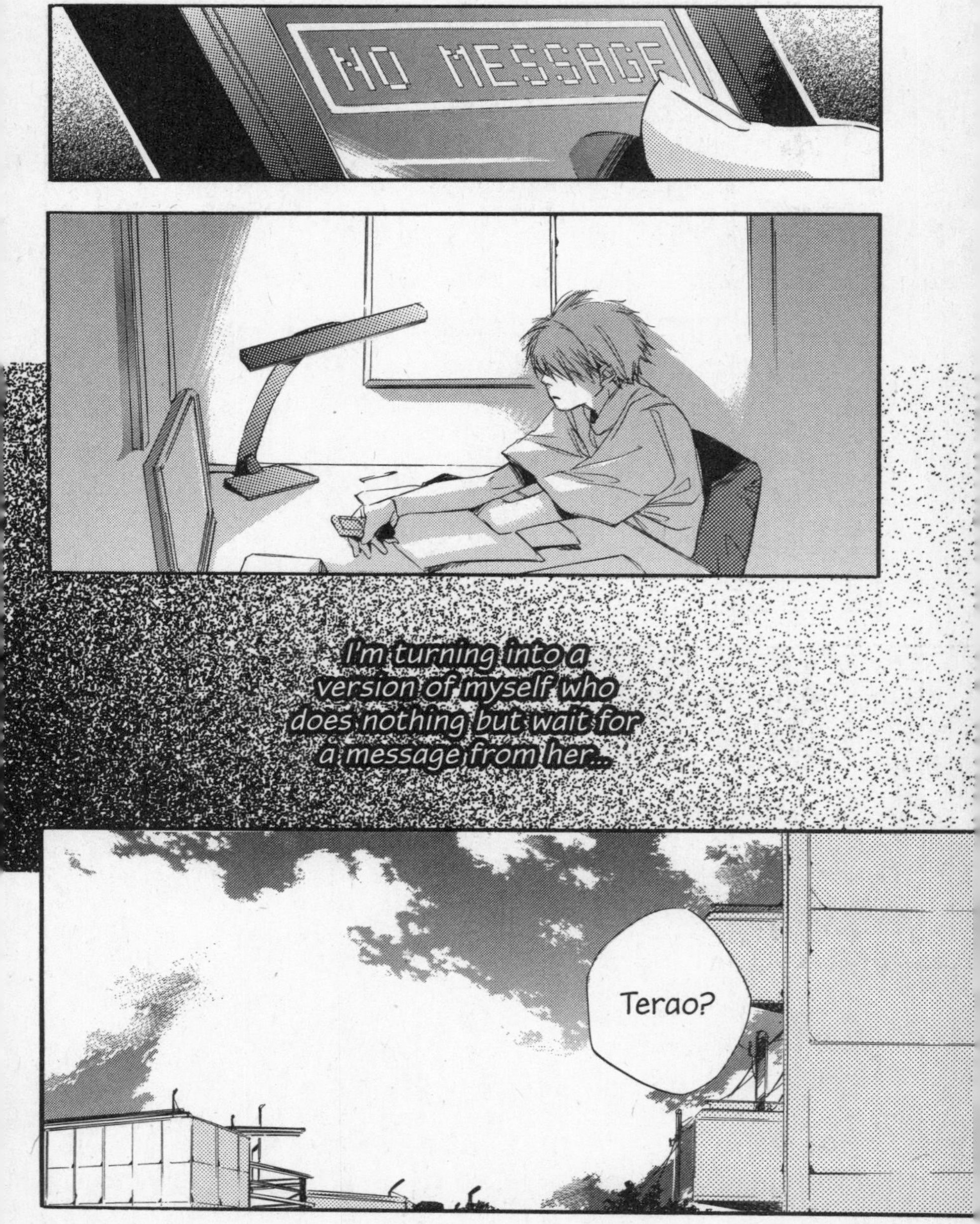
NO MESSAGE
I'm turning into a version of myself who does nothing but wait for a message from her...
Terao?

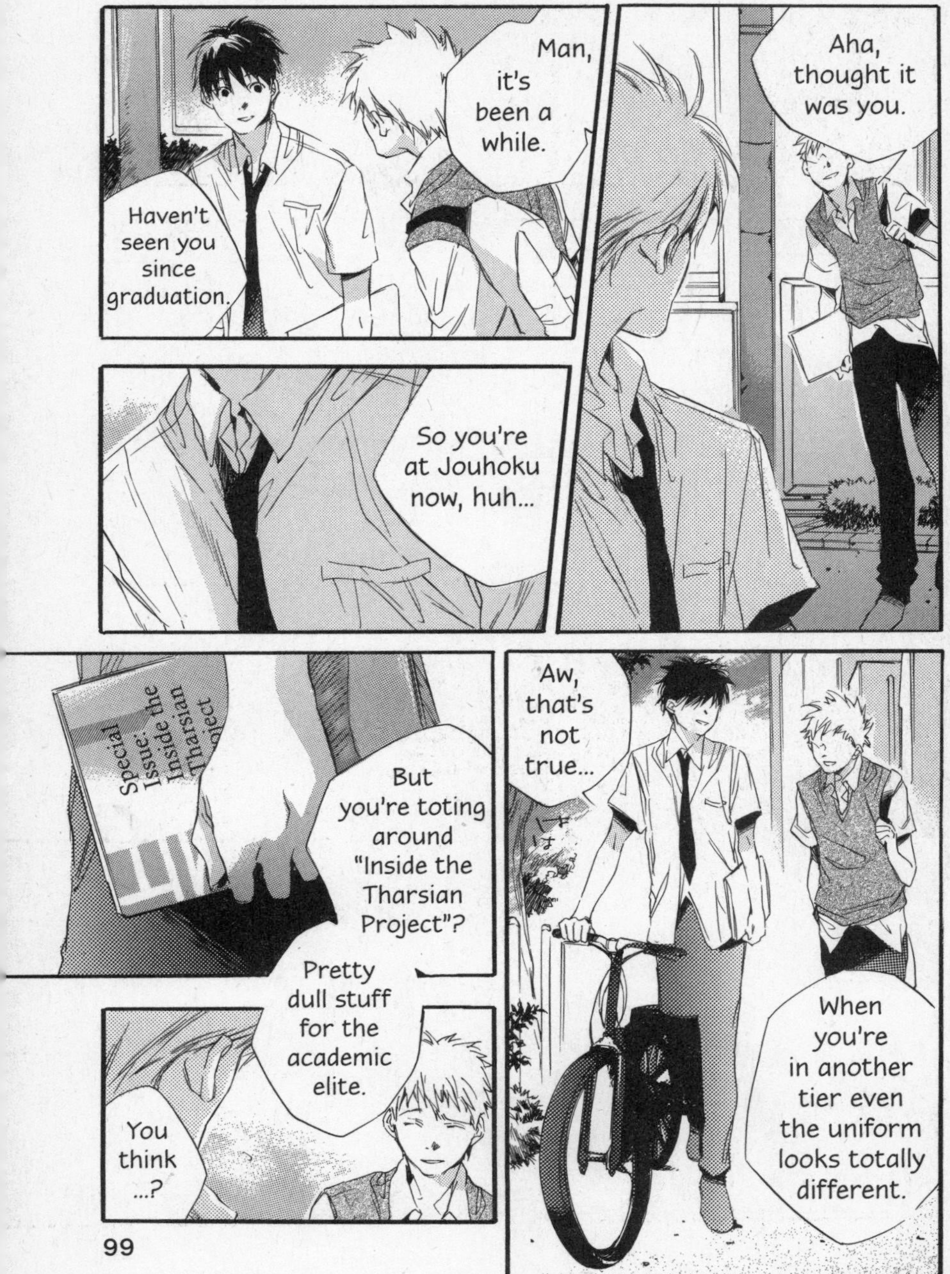

Aha, thought it was you.
Man, it's been a while.
Haven't seen you since graduation.
So you're at Jouhoku now, huh...
Aw, that's not true...
When you're in another tier even the uniform looks totally different.
Special Issue: Inside the Tharsian Project
But you're toting around "Inside the Tharsian Project"?
Pretty dull stuff for the academic elite.
You think ...?

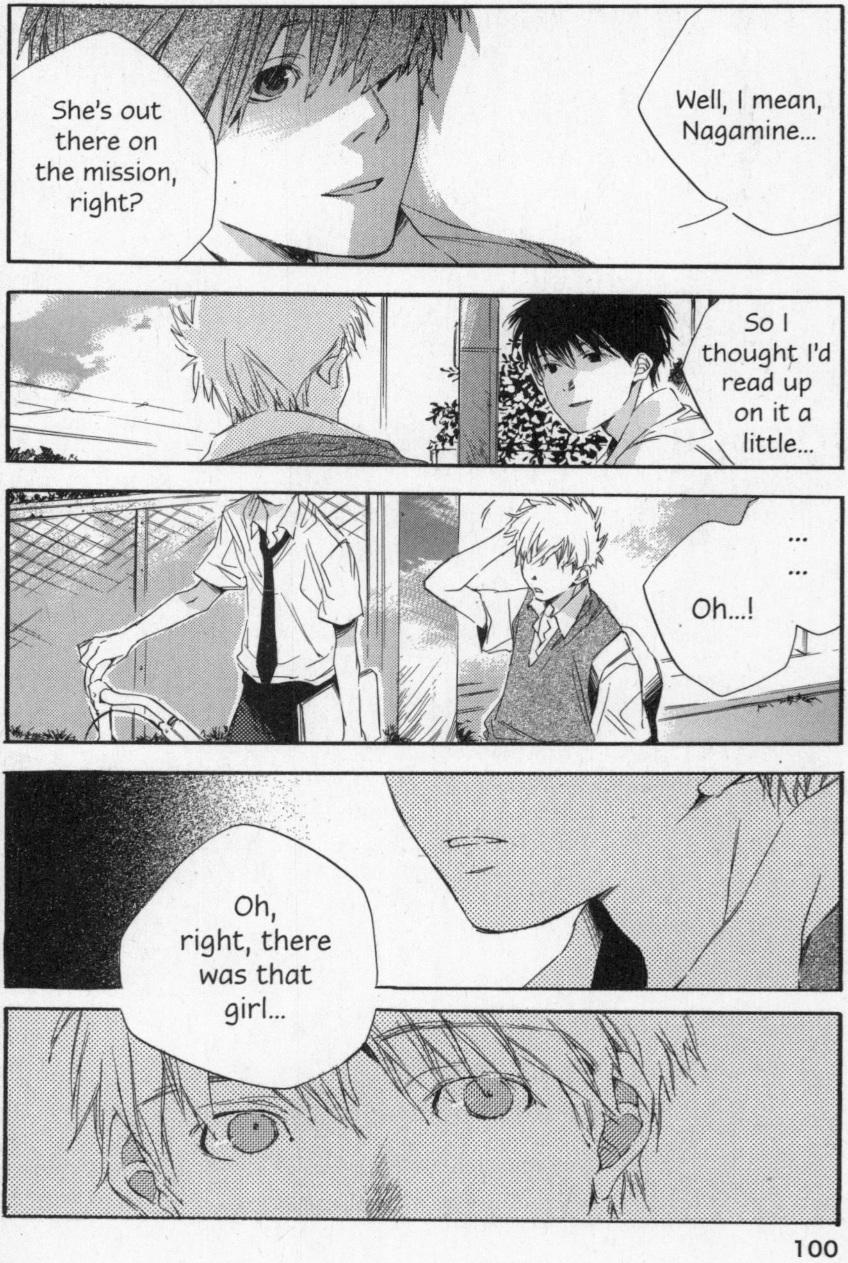
Well, I mean, Nagamine...
She's out there on the mission, right?
So I thought I'd read up on it a little...
...
...
Oh...!
Oh, right, there was that girl...

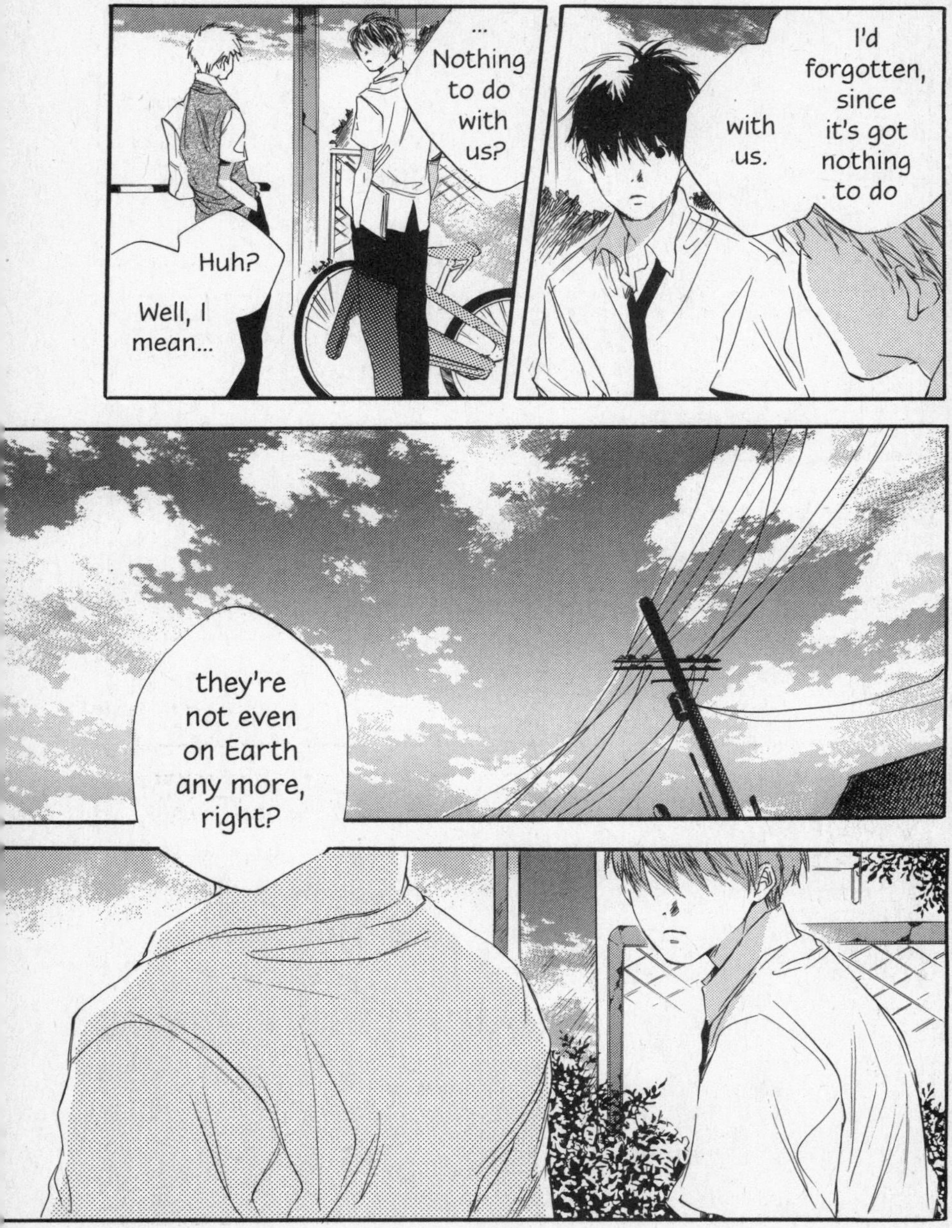
I'd forgotten, since it's got nothing to do
with us.
... Nothing to do with us?
Huh?
Well, I mean...
they're not even on Earth any more, right?

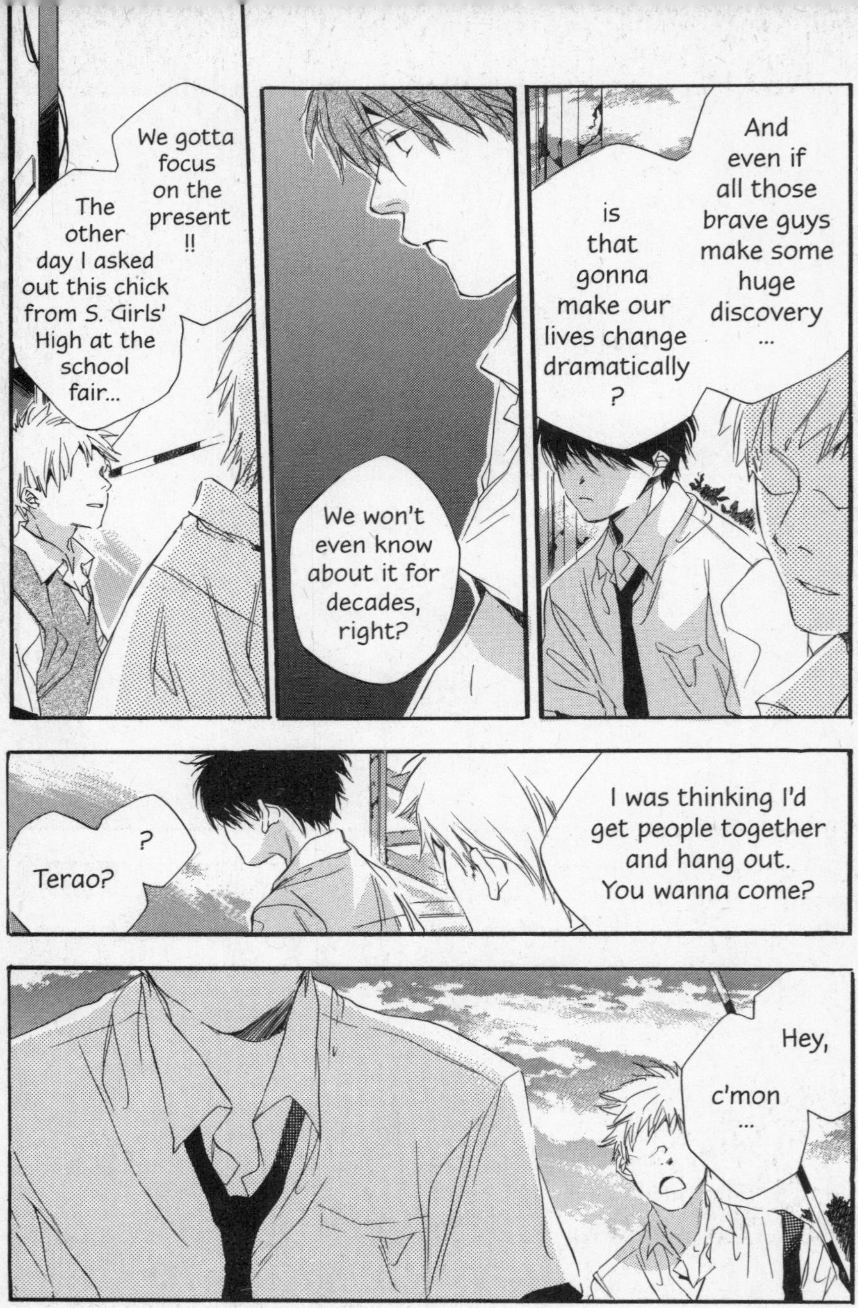
And even if all those brave guys make some huge discovery ...
is that gonna make our lives change dramatically ?
We won't even know about it for decades, right?
We gotta focus on the present !!
The other day I asked out this chick from S. Girls' High at the school fair...
I was thinking I'd get people together and hang out. You wanna come?
? Terao?
Hey, c'mon ...

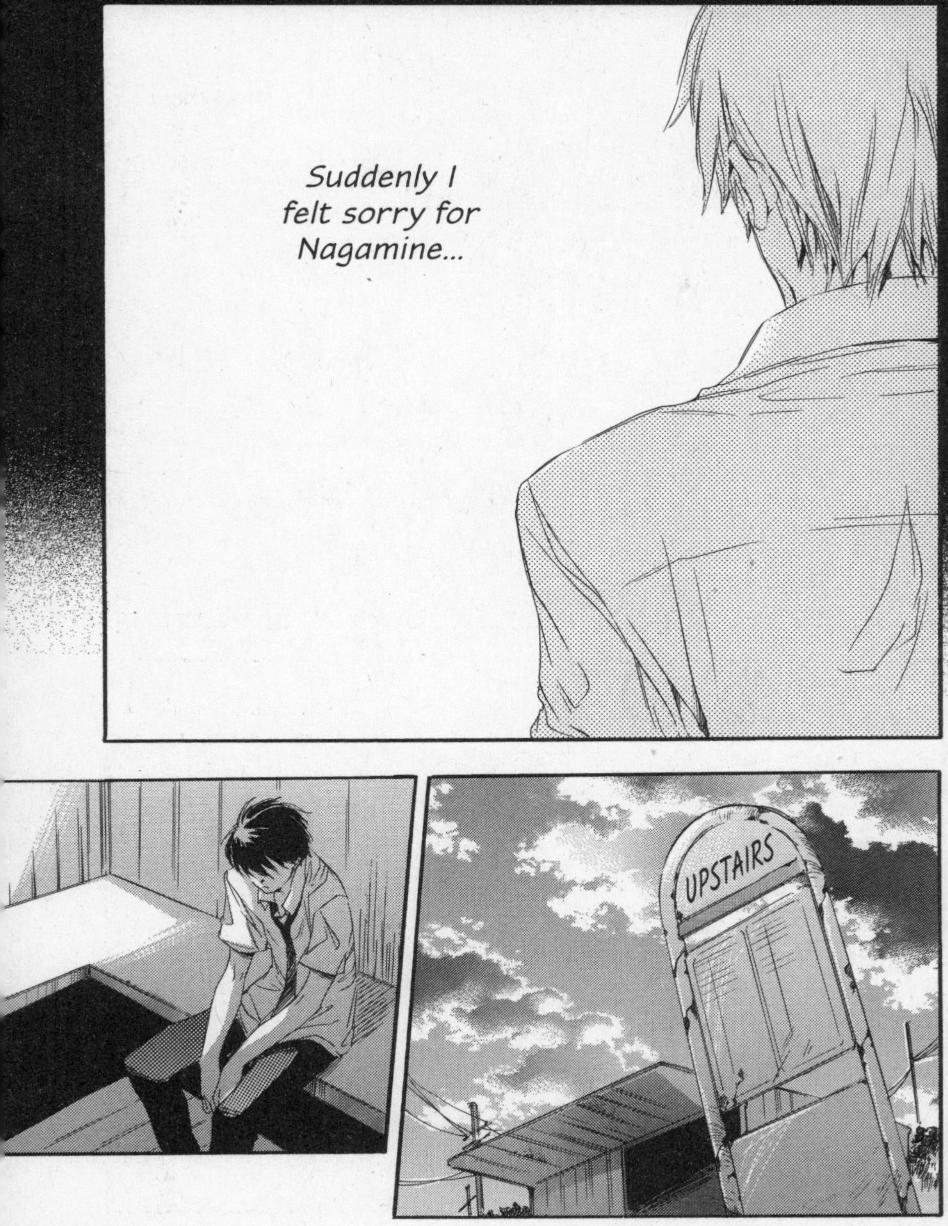
Suddenly I felt sorry for Nagamine...
UPSTAIRS

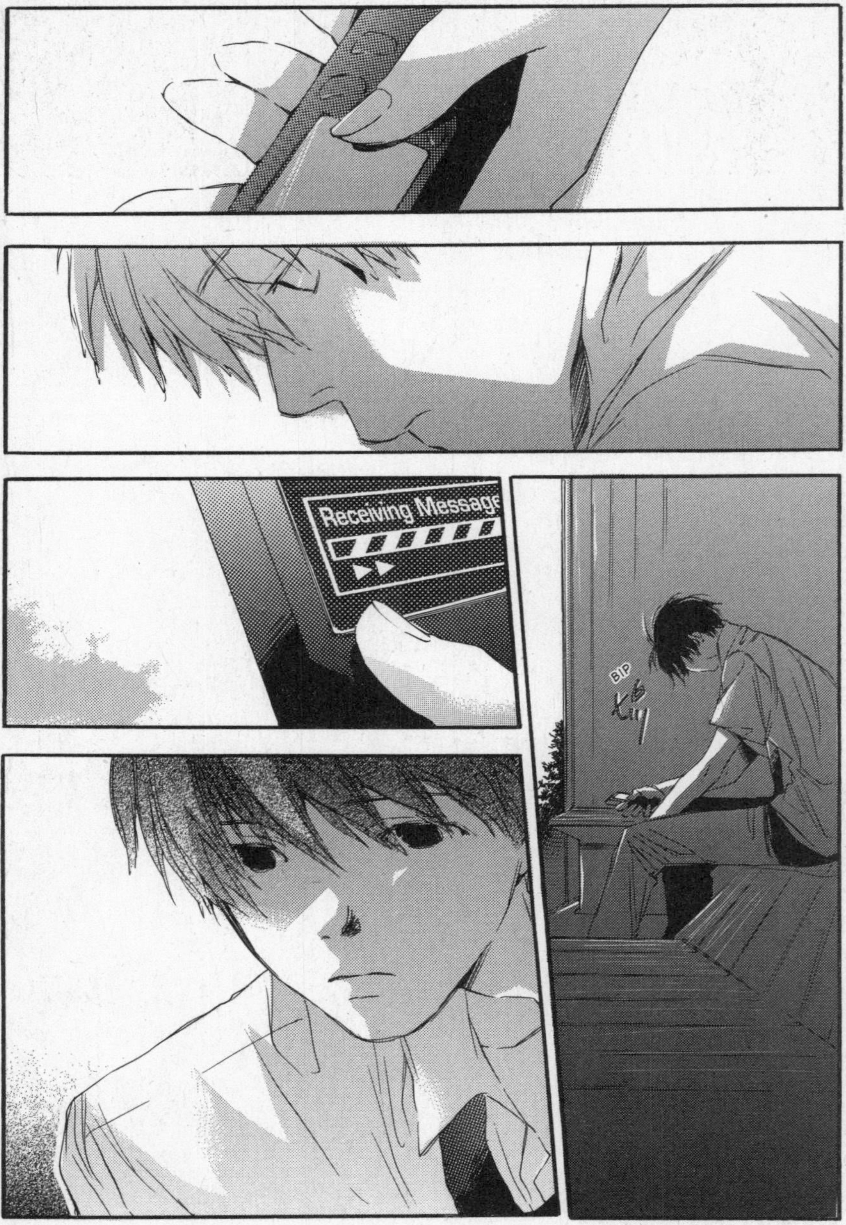
Receiving Message
BIP

You have no new messages.

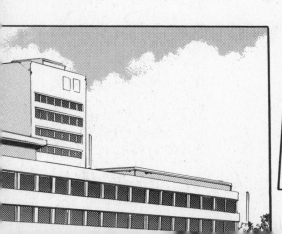

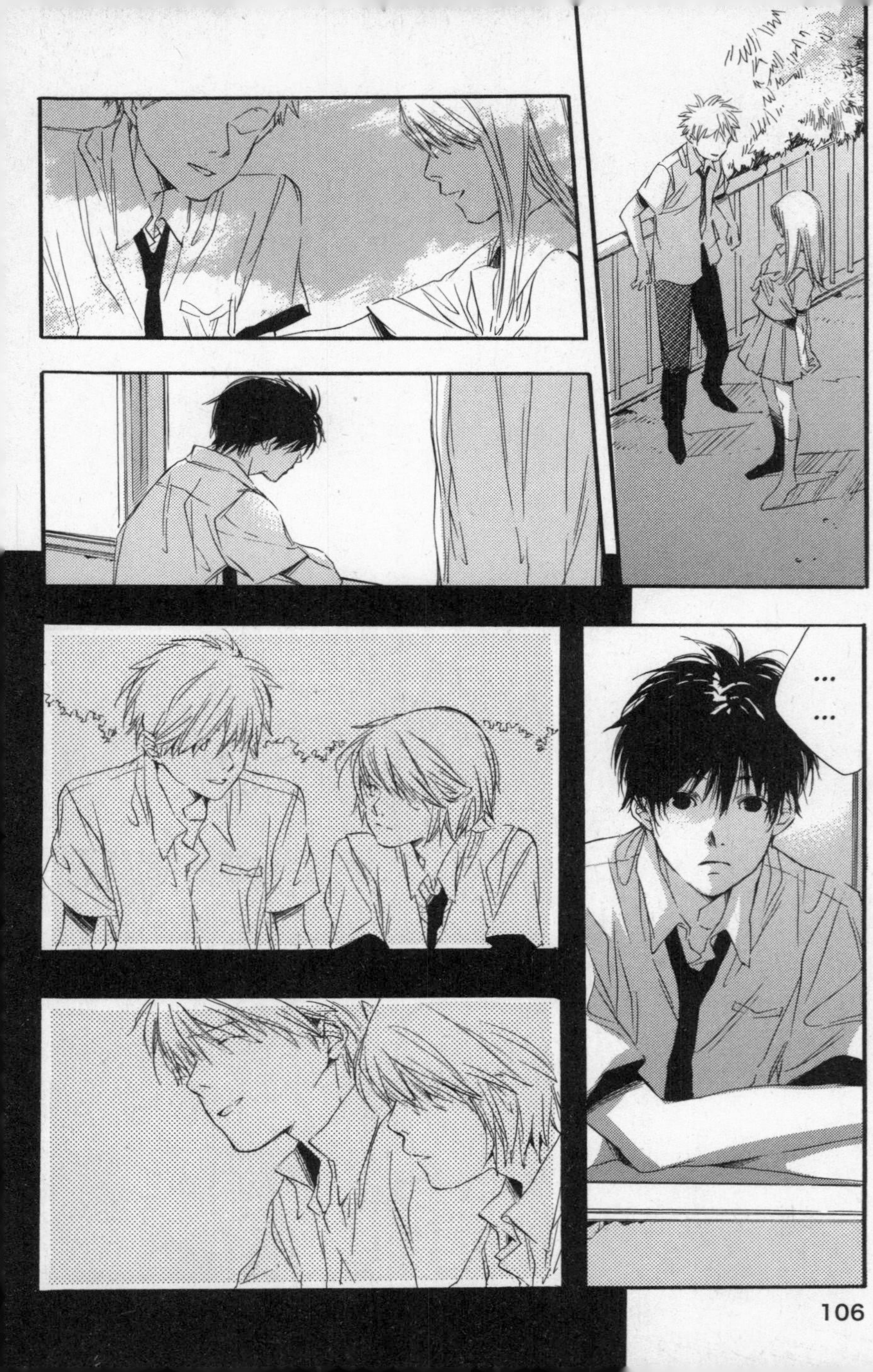
...
...

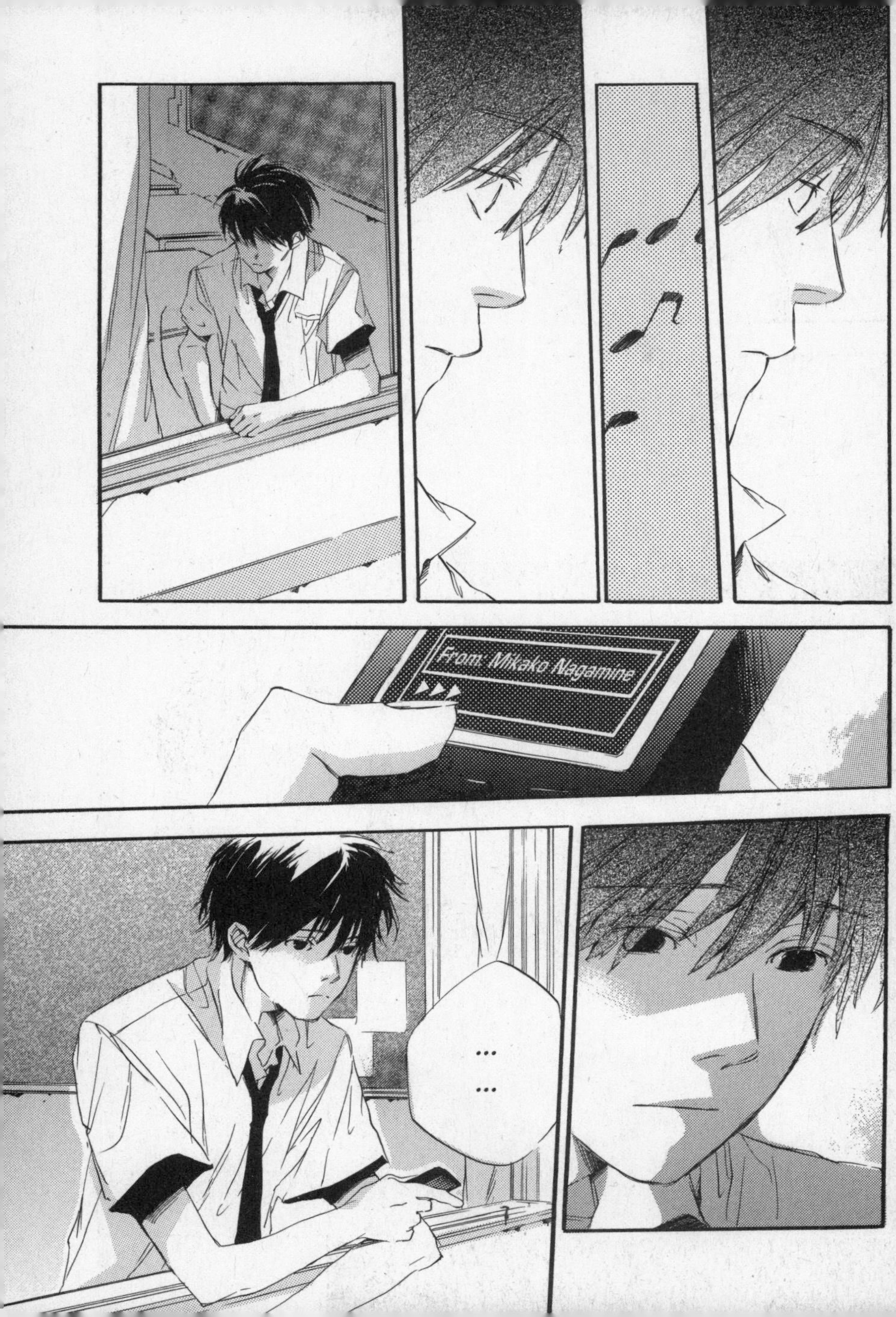

From: Mikako Nagamine
...
...

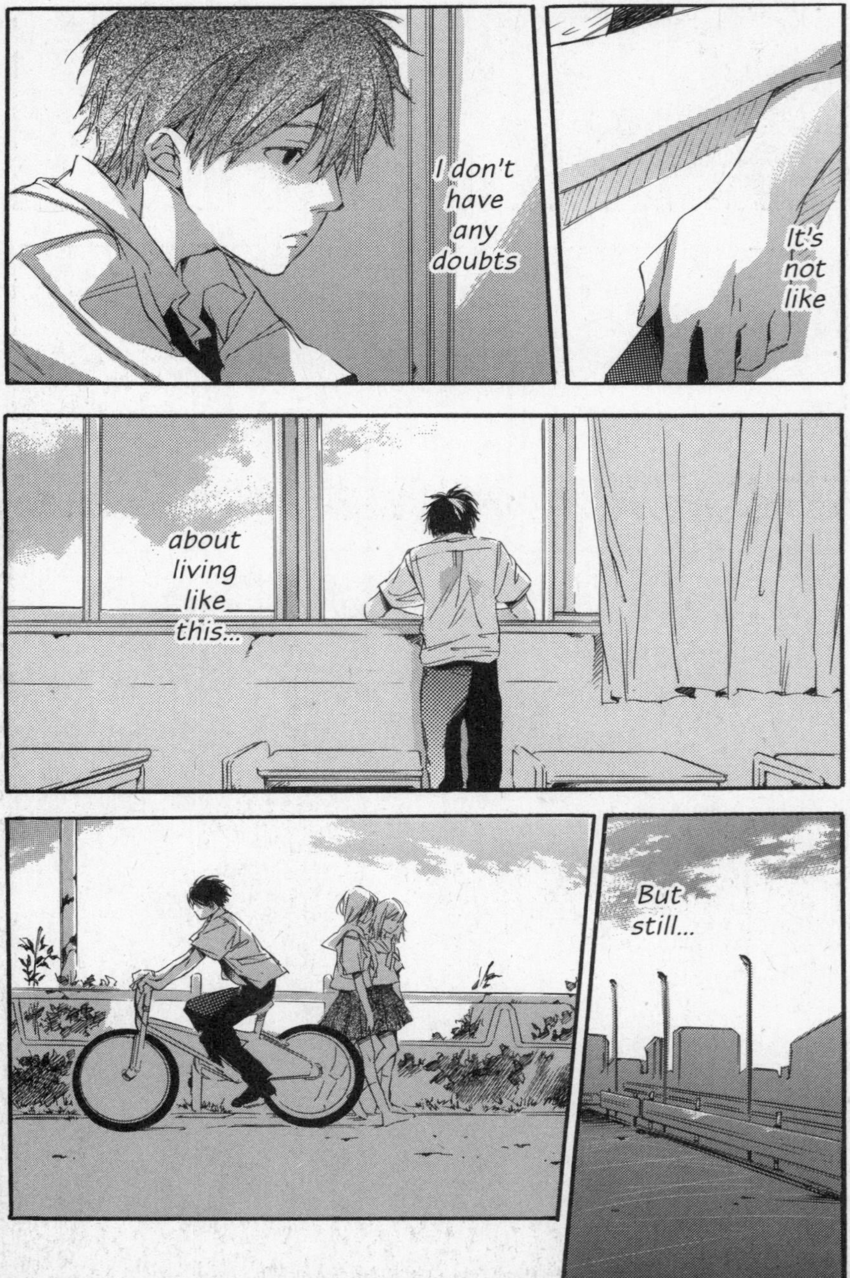
It's not like
I don't have any doubts
about living like this...
But still...

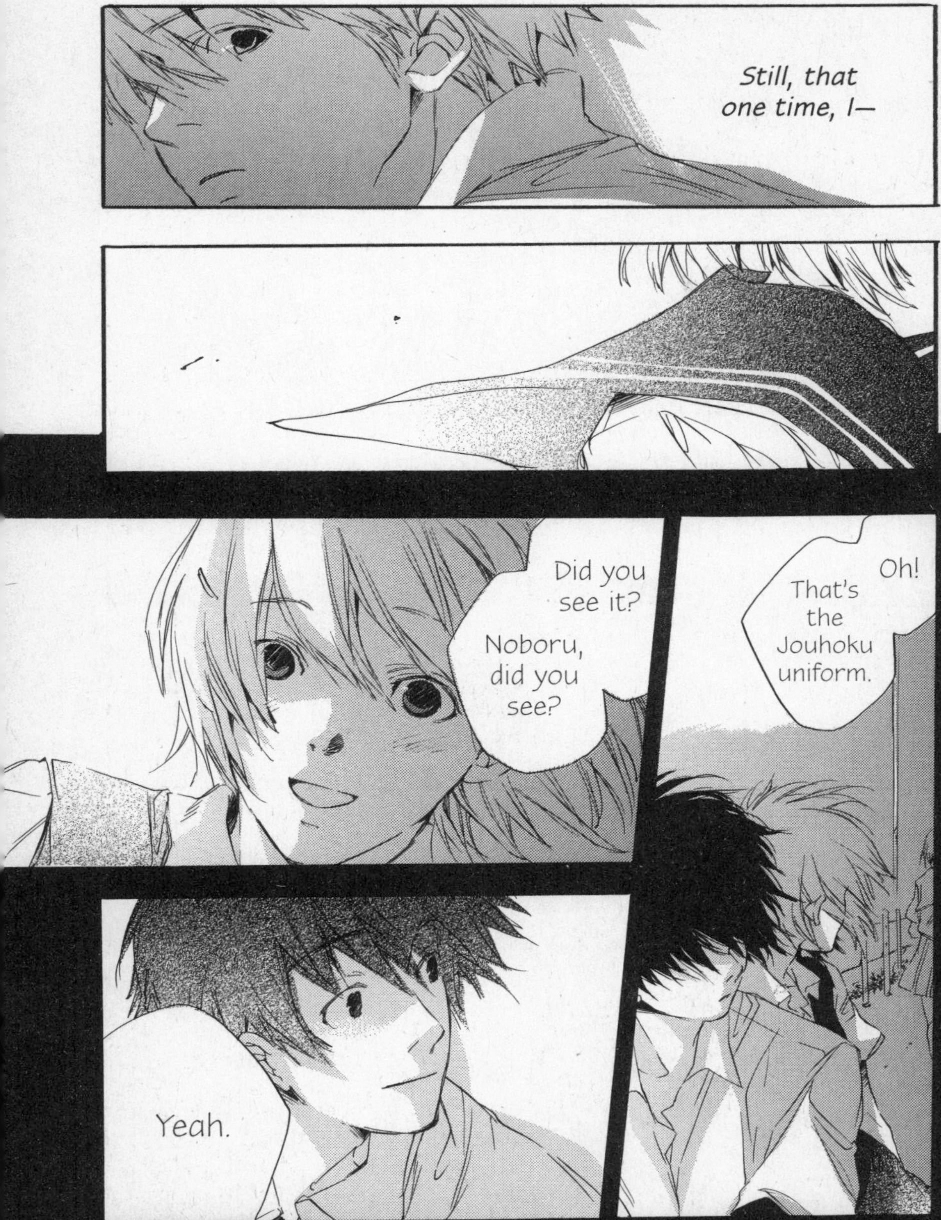
Still, that one time, I—
Oh!
That's the Jouhoku uniform.
Did you see it?
Noboru, did you see?
Yeah.

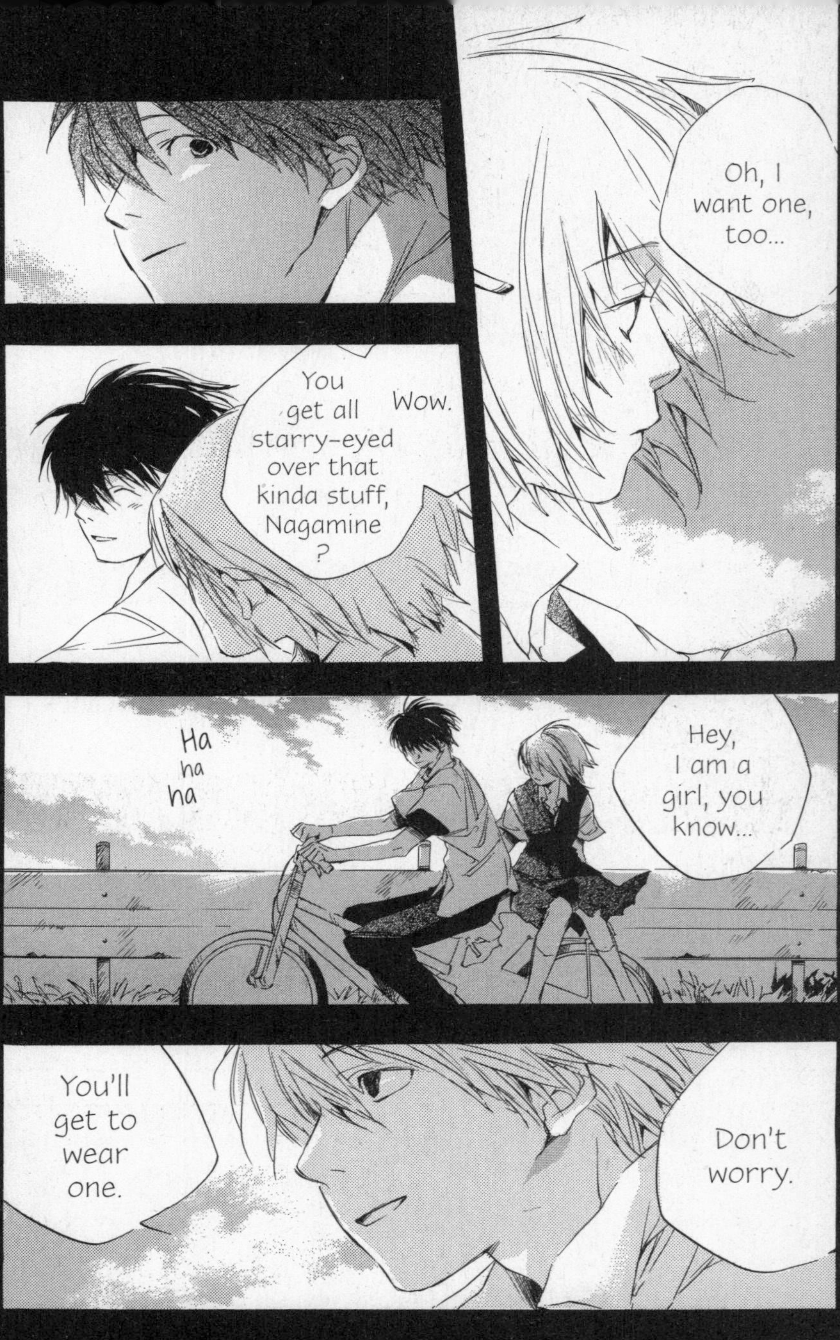
Oh, I want one, too...
Wow.
You get all starry-eyed over that kinda stuff, Nagamine?
Hey, I am a girl, you know...
Ha ha ha
Don't worry.
You'll get to wear one.

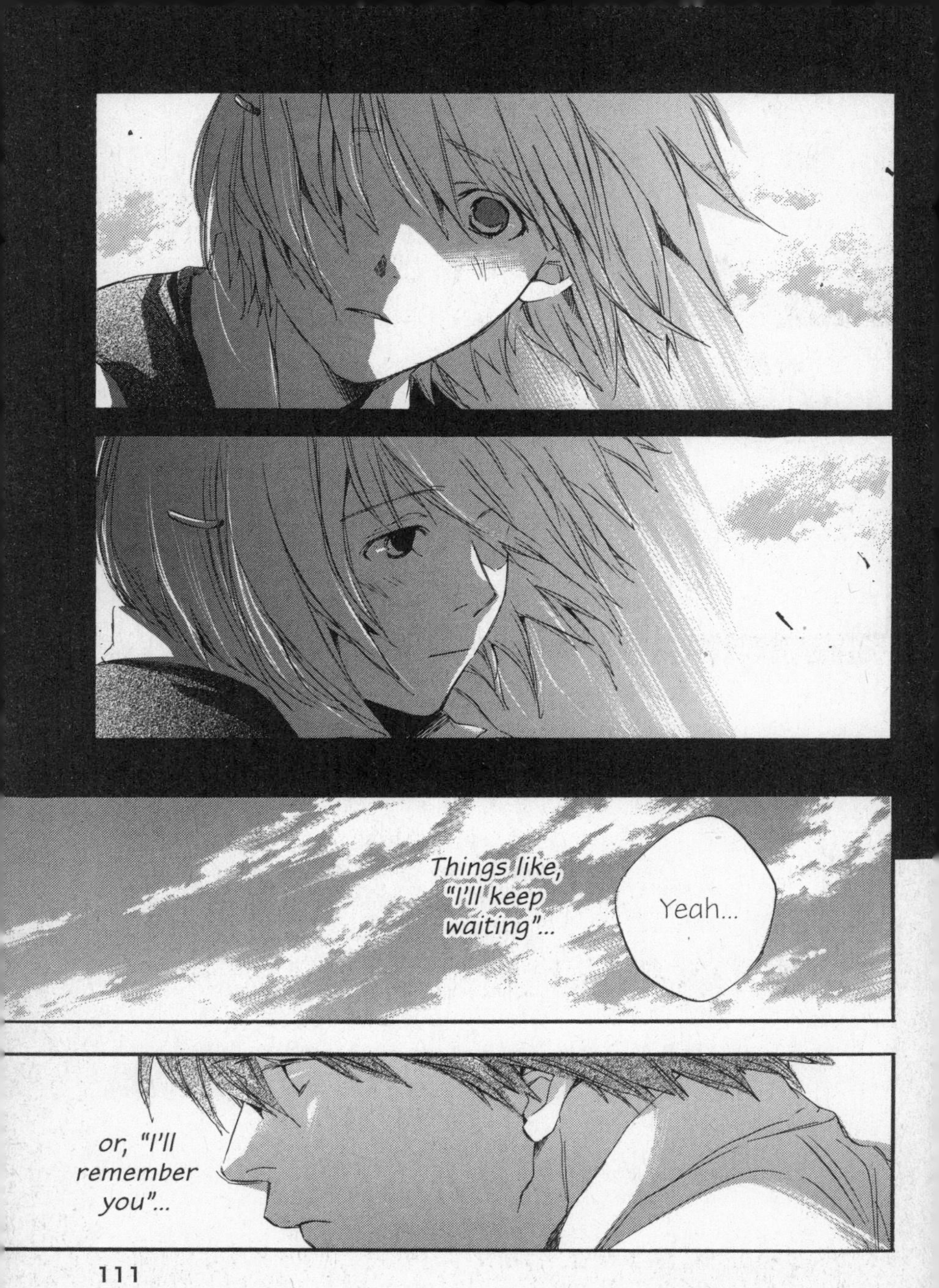
Yeah...
Things like, "I'll keep waiting"...
or, "I'll remember you"...

All those...

trite, shallow phrases...

I really did believe them...

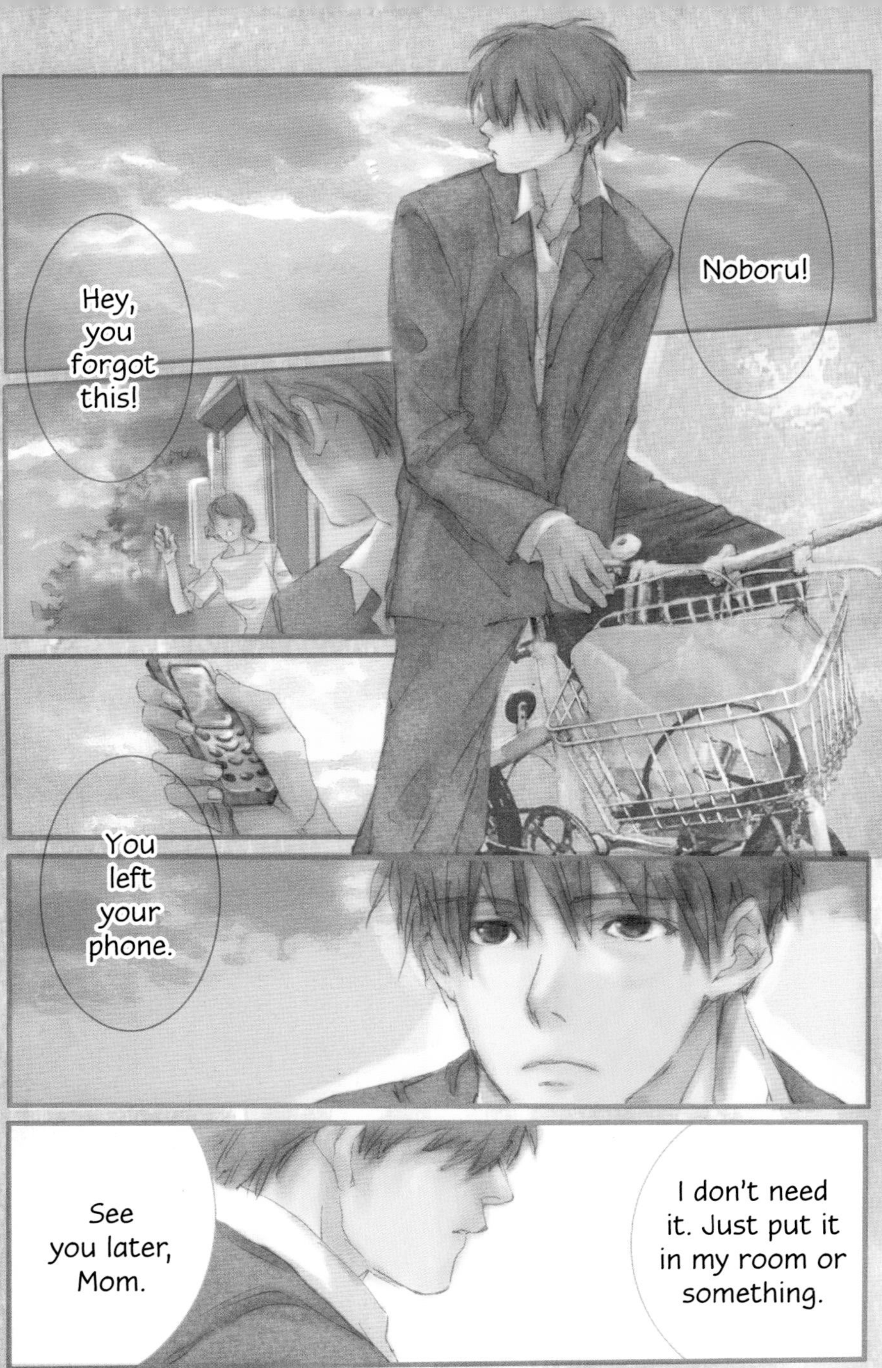
Noboru!
Hey, you forgot this!
You left your phone.
I don't need it. Just put it in my room or something.
See you later, Mom.

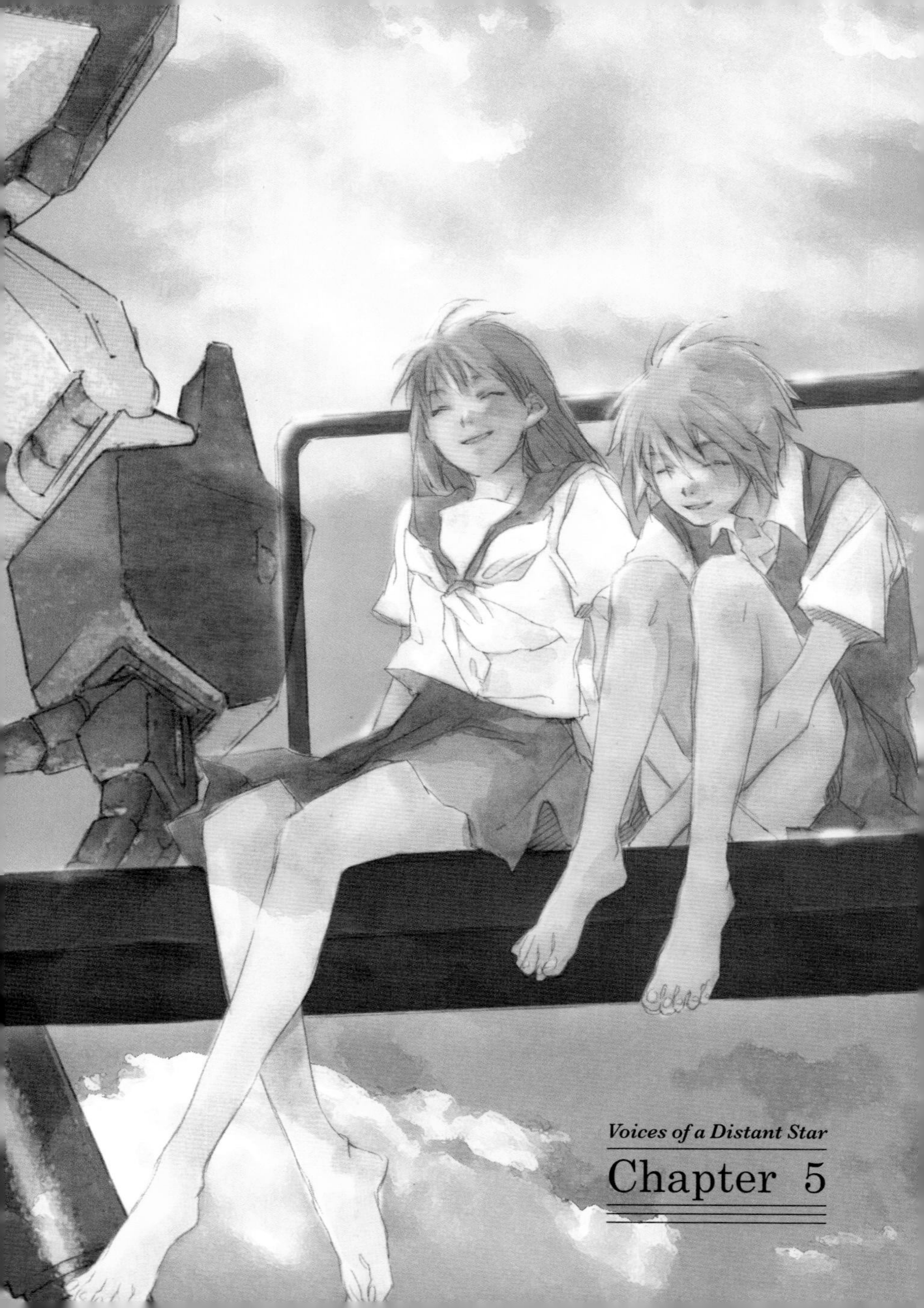

Voices of a Distant Star

Chapter 5

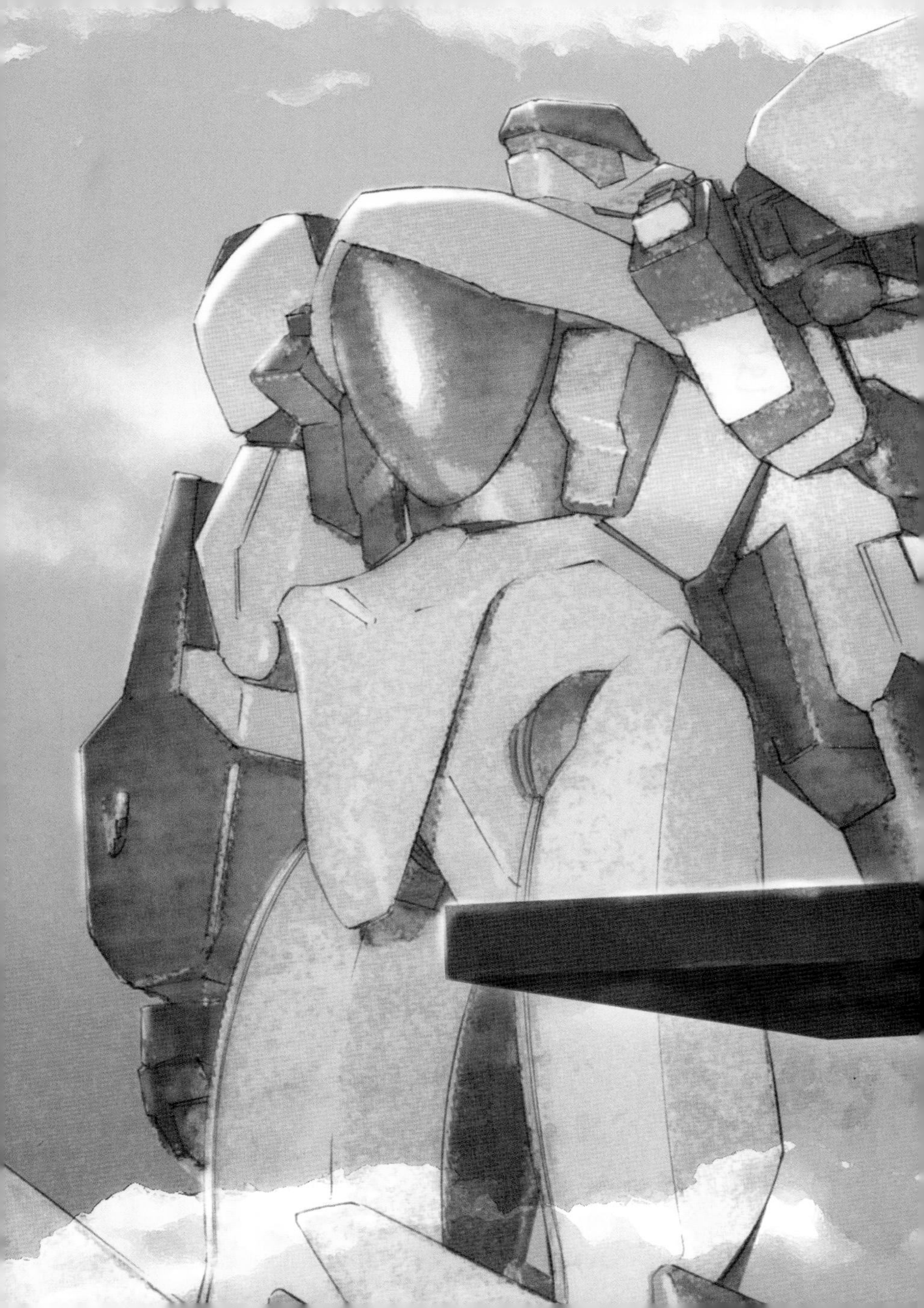

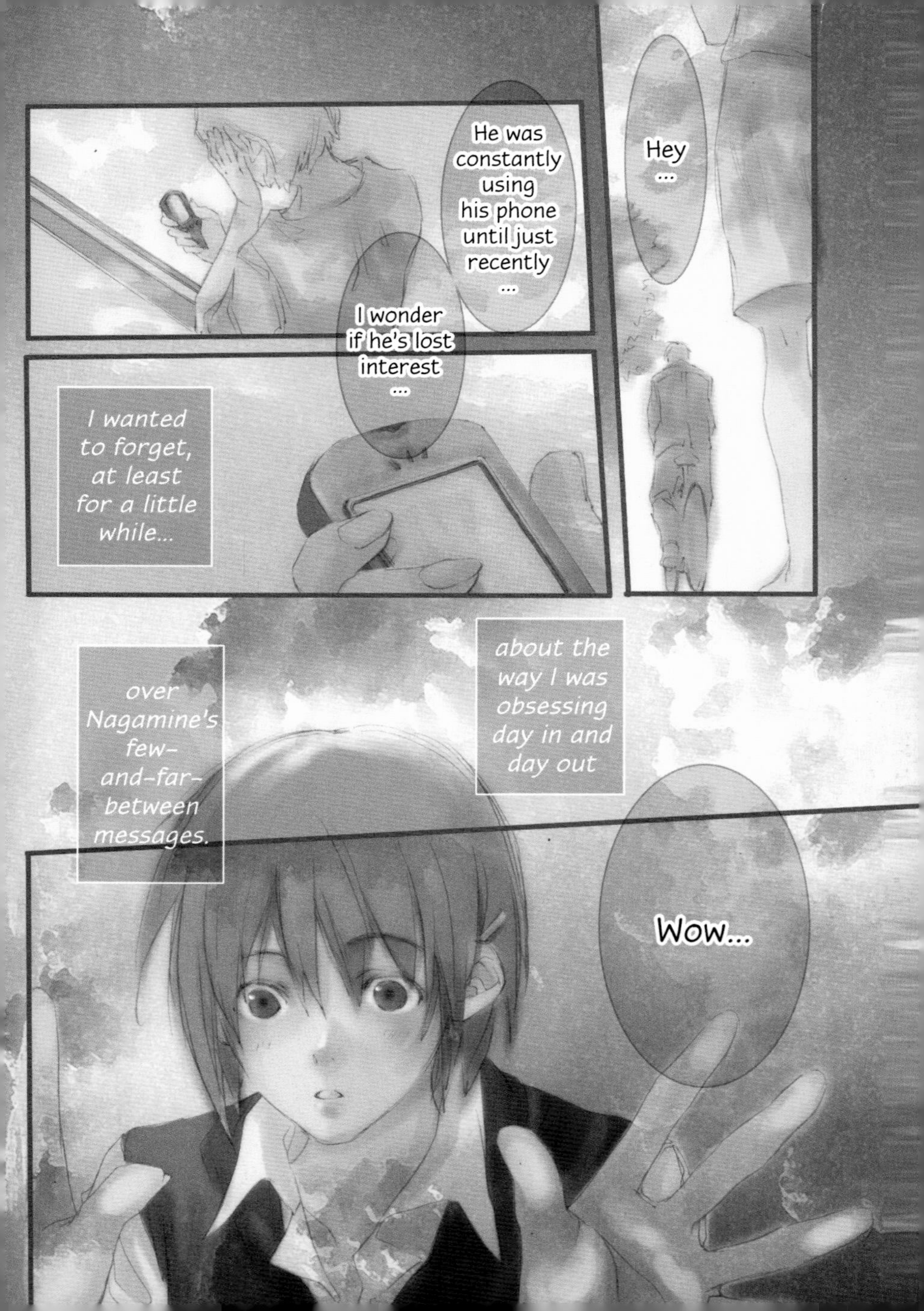
Hey ...
He was constantly using his phone until just recently ...
I wonder if he's lost interest ...
I wanted to forget, at least for a little while...
about the way I was obsessing day in and day out
over Nagamine's few-and-far-between messages.
Wow...

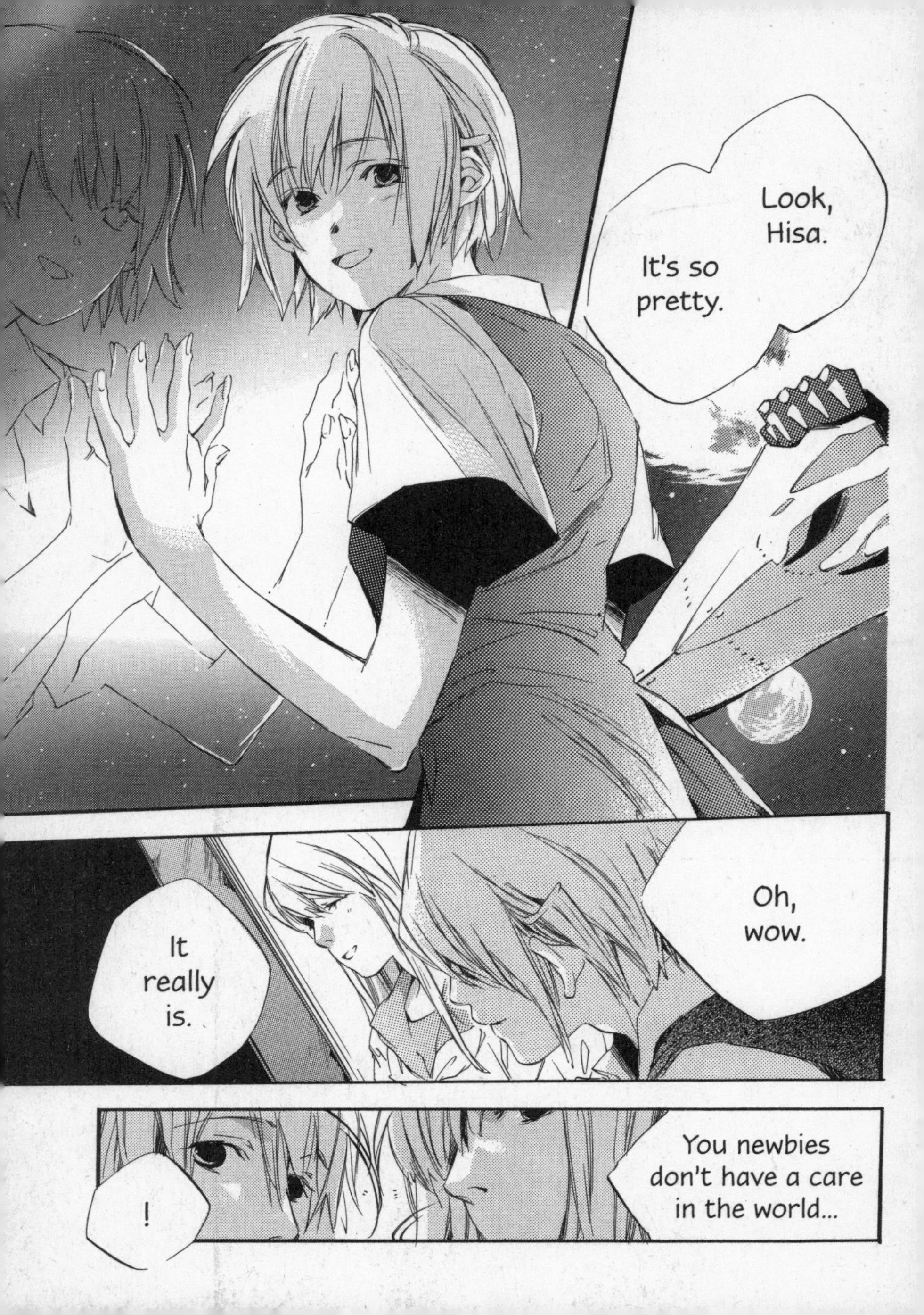
Look, Hisa.
It's so pretty.
Oh, wow.
It really is.
You newbies don't have a care in the world...
!

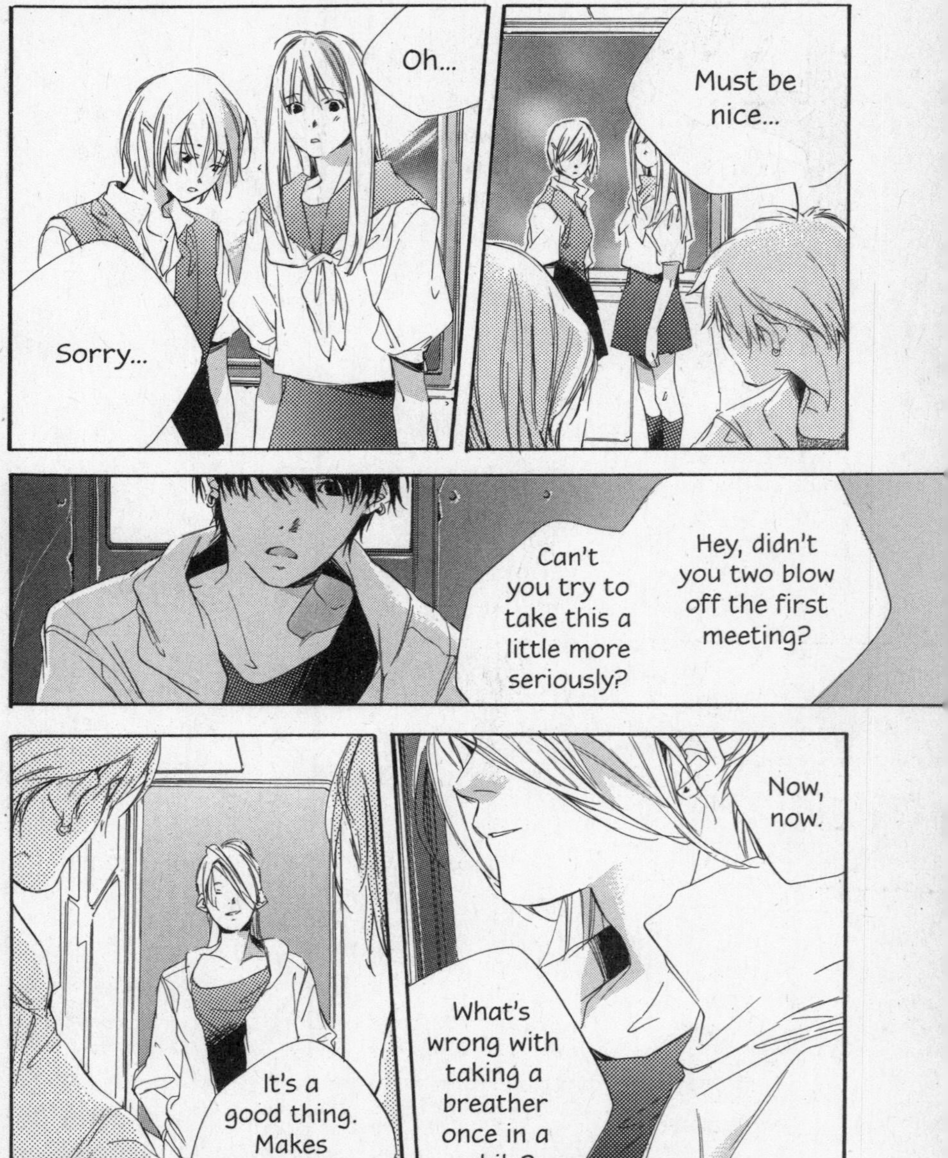
Must be nice...
Oh...
Sorry...
Hey, didn't you two blow off the first meeting?
Can't you try to take this a little more seriously?
Now, now.
What's wrong with taking a breather once in a while?
It's a good thing. Makes you more likeable.

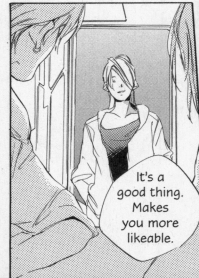

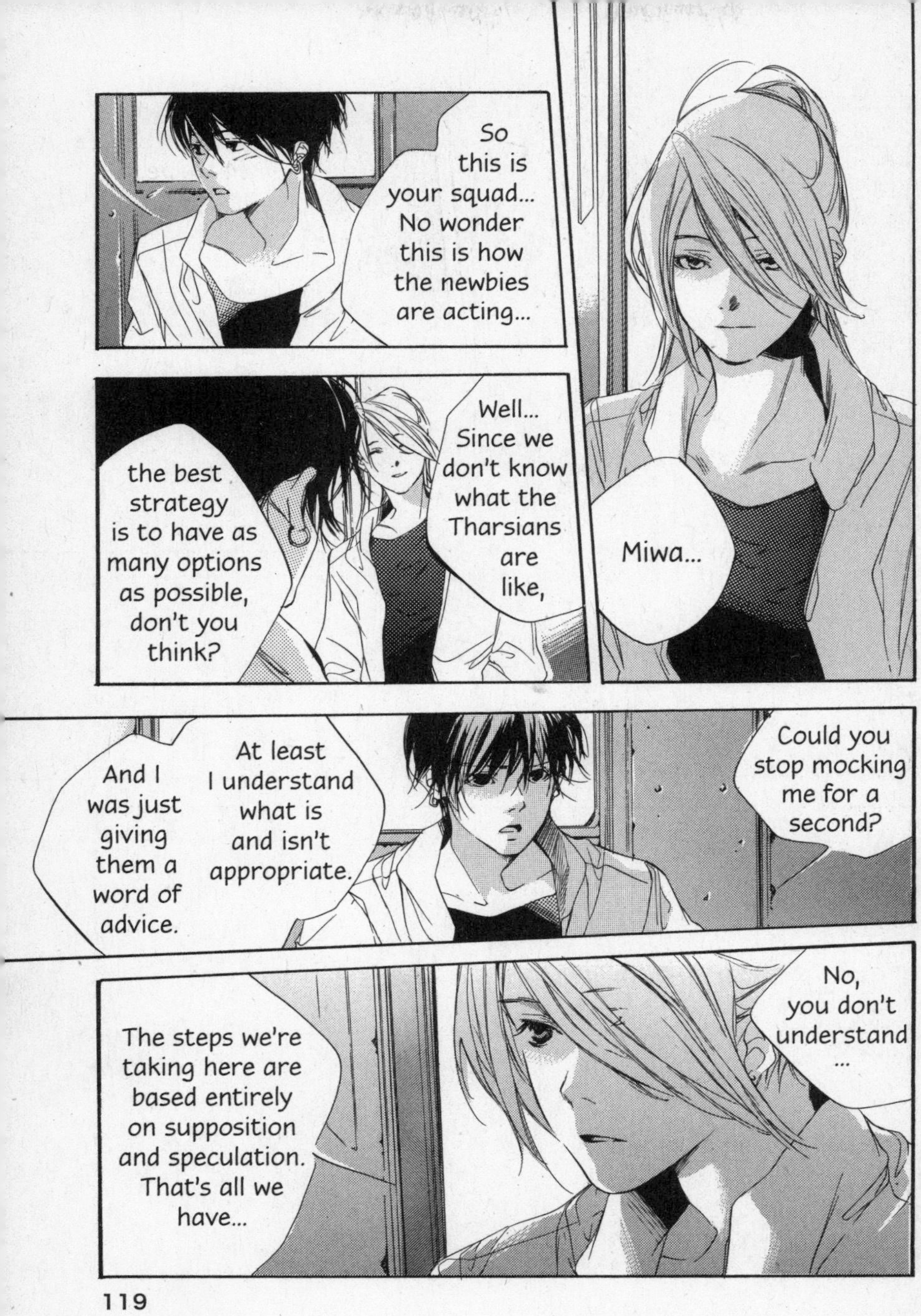
Miwa...
So this is your squad... No wonder this is how the newbies are acting...
Well... Since we don't know what the Tharsians are like,
the best strategy is to have as many options as possible, don't you think?
Could you stop mocking me for a second?
At least I understand what is and isn't appropriate.
And I was just giving them a word of advice.
No, you don't understand...
The steps we're taking here are based entirely on supposition and speculation. That's all we have...

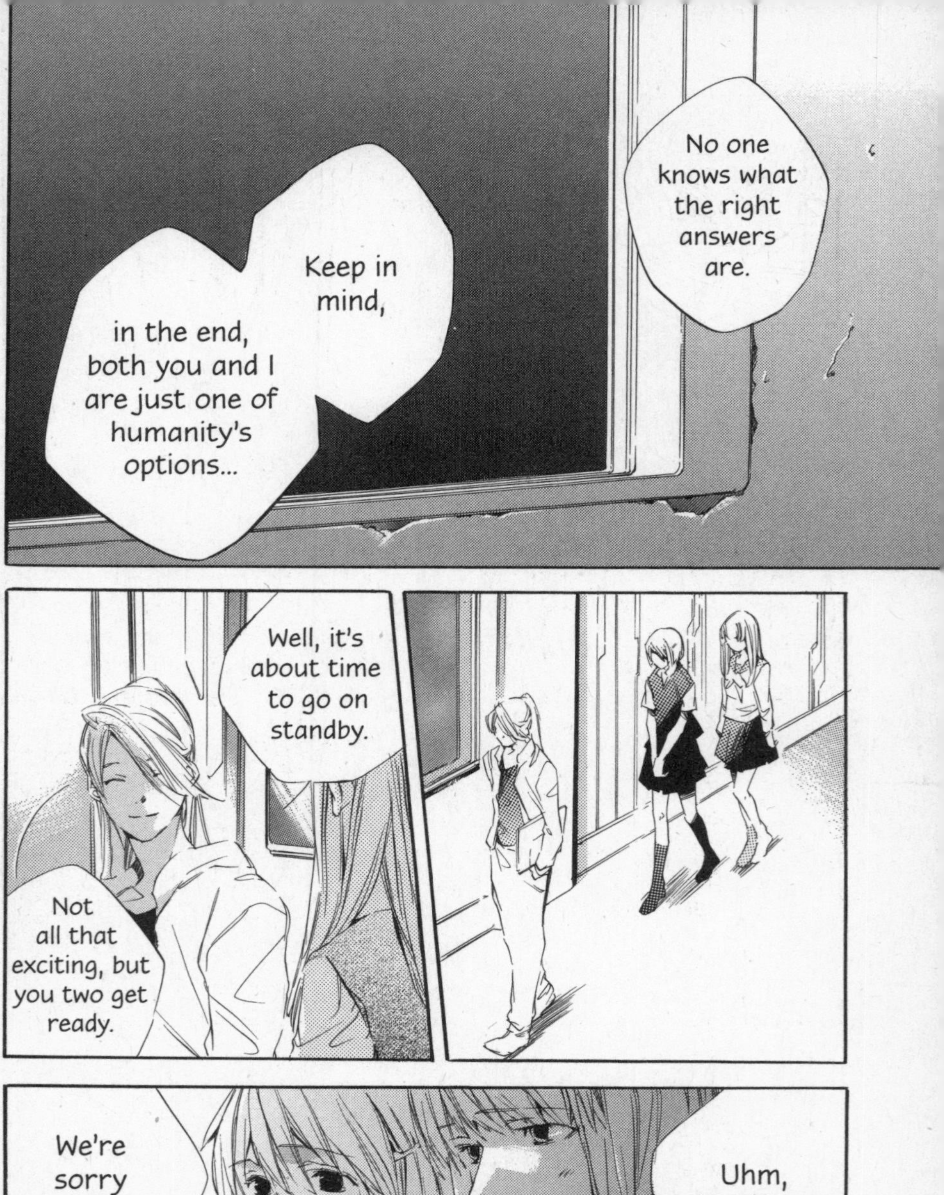
No one knows what the right answers are.
Keep in mind,
in the end, both you and I are just one of humanity's options...
Well, it's about time to go on standby.
Not all that exciting, but you two get ready.
Uhm, Ms. Miwa ...
We're sorry about all that.

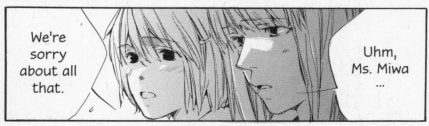

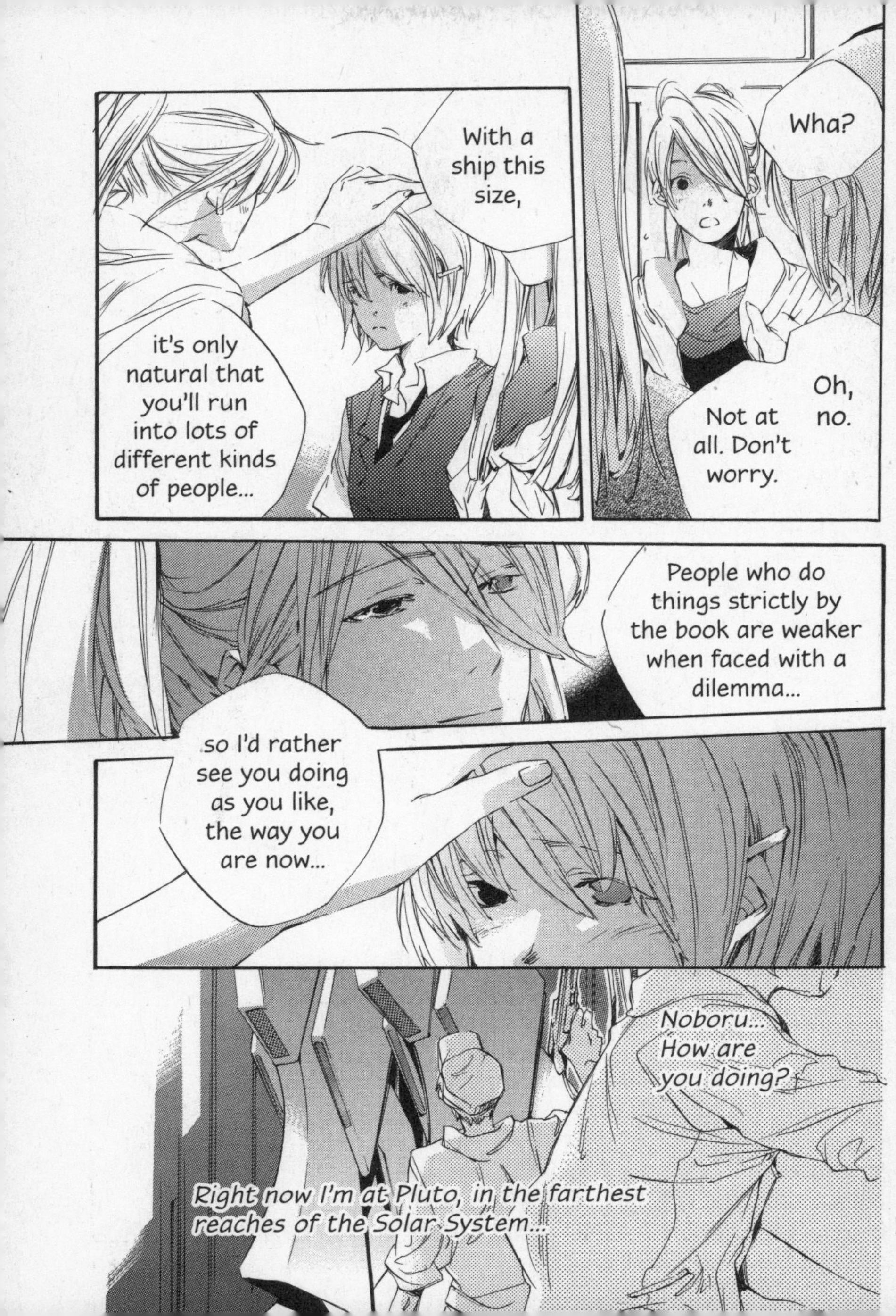

Wha?
Oh, no.
Not at all. Don't worry.
With a ship this size,
it's only natural that you'll run into lots of different kinds of people...
People who do things strictly by the book are weaker when faced with a dilemma...
so I'd rather see you doing as you like, the way you are now...
Noboru... How are you doing?
Right now I'm at Pluto, in the farthest reaches of the Solar System...

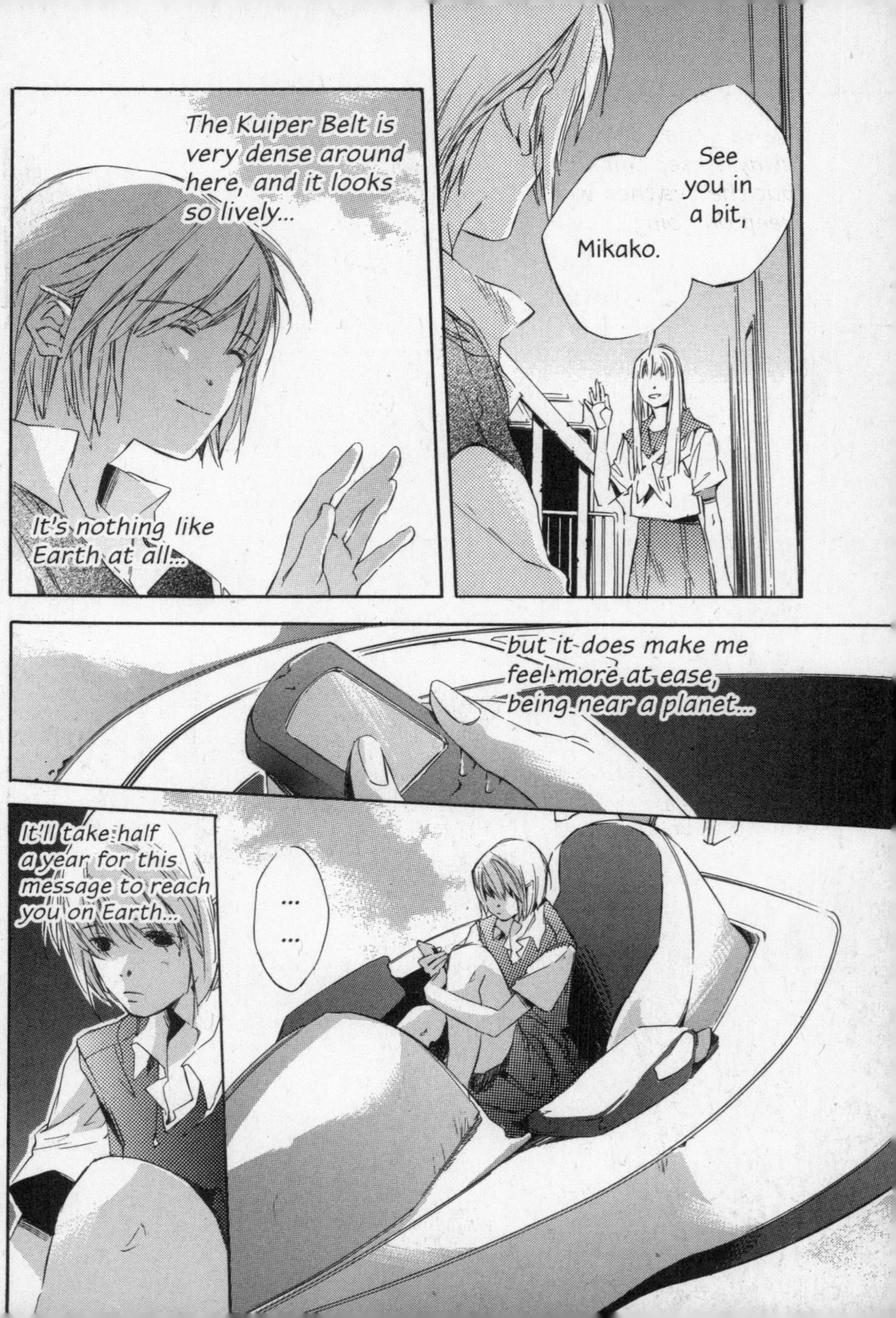

See you in a bit, Mikako.
The Kuiper Belt is very dense around here, and it looks so lively...
It's nothing like Earth at all...
but it does make me feel more at ease, being near a planet...
... ...
It'll take half a year for this message to reach you on Earth...

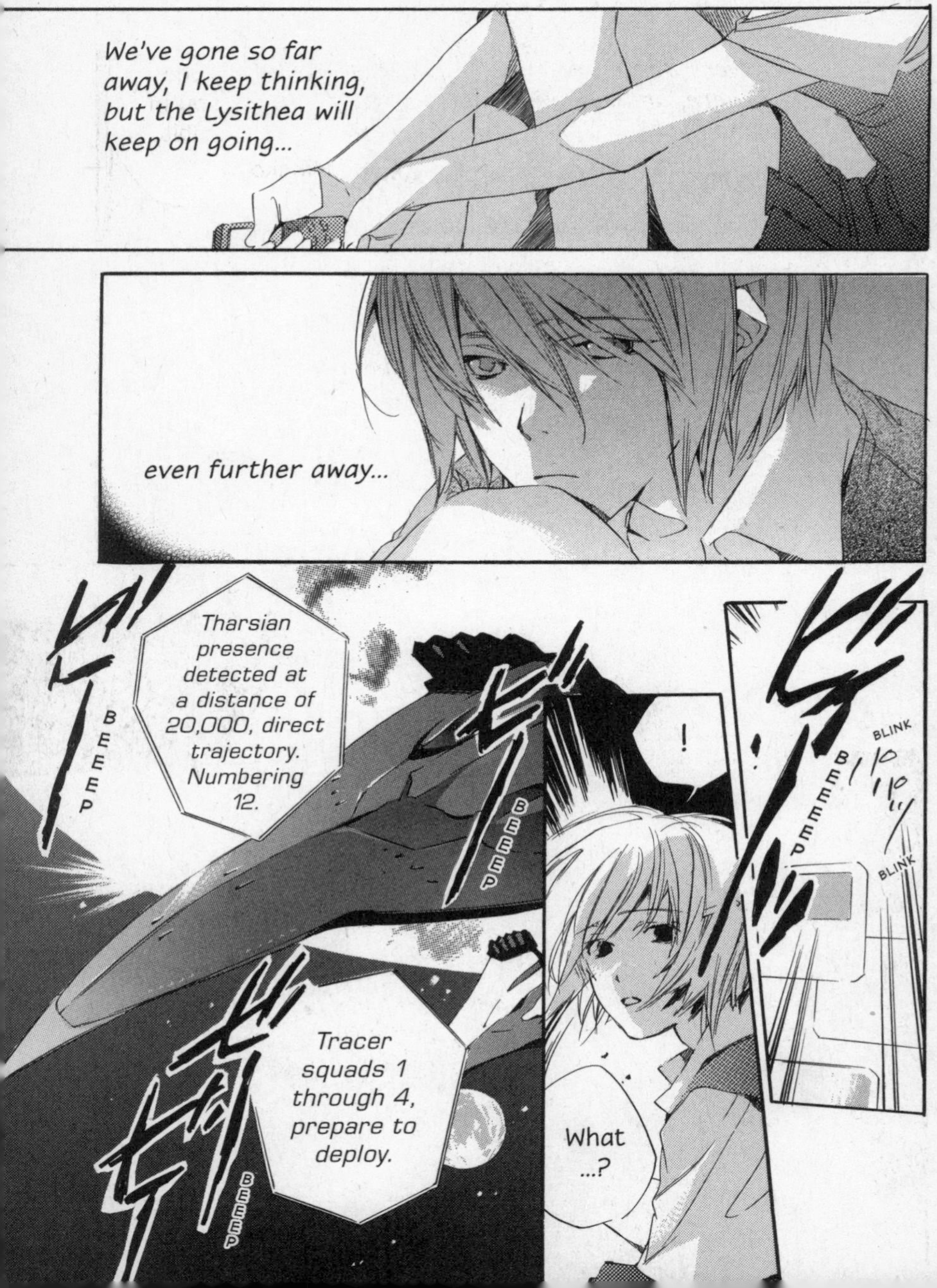
We've gone so far away, I keep thinking, but the Lysithea will keep on going...
even further away...
!
BEEEEP
BLINK
BLINK
What ...?
Tharsian presence detected at a distance of 20,000, direct trajectory. Numbering 12.
BEEEP
BEEEEP
Tracer squads 1 through 4, prepare to deploy.
BEEEEP
BEEEP

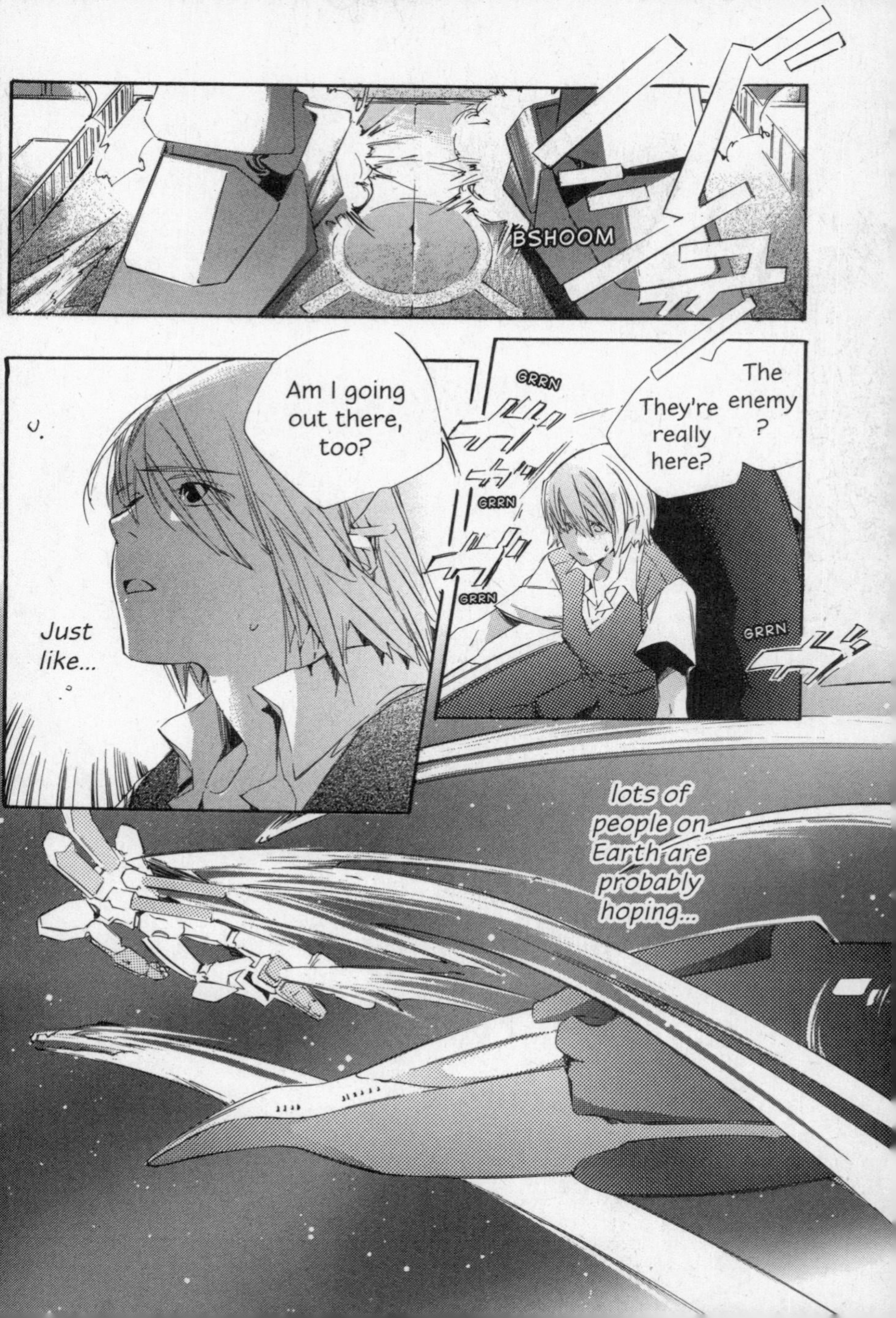

BSHOOM
GRRN
The enemy?
They're really here?
GRRN
GRRN
GRRN
Am I going out there, too?
Just like...
lots of people on Earth are probably hoping...

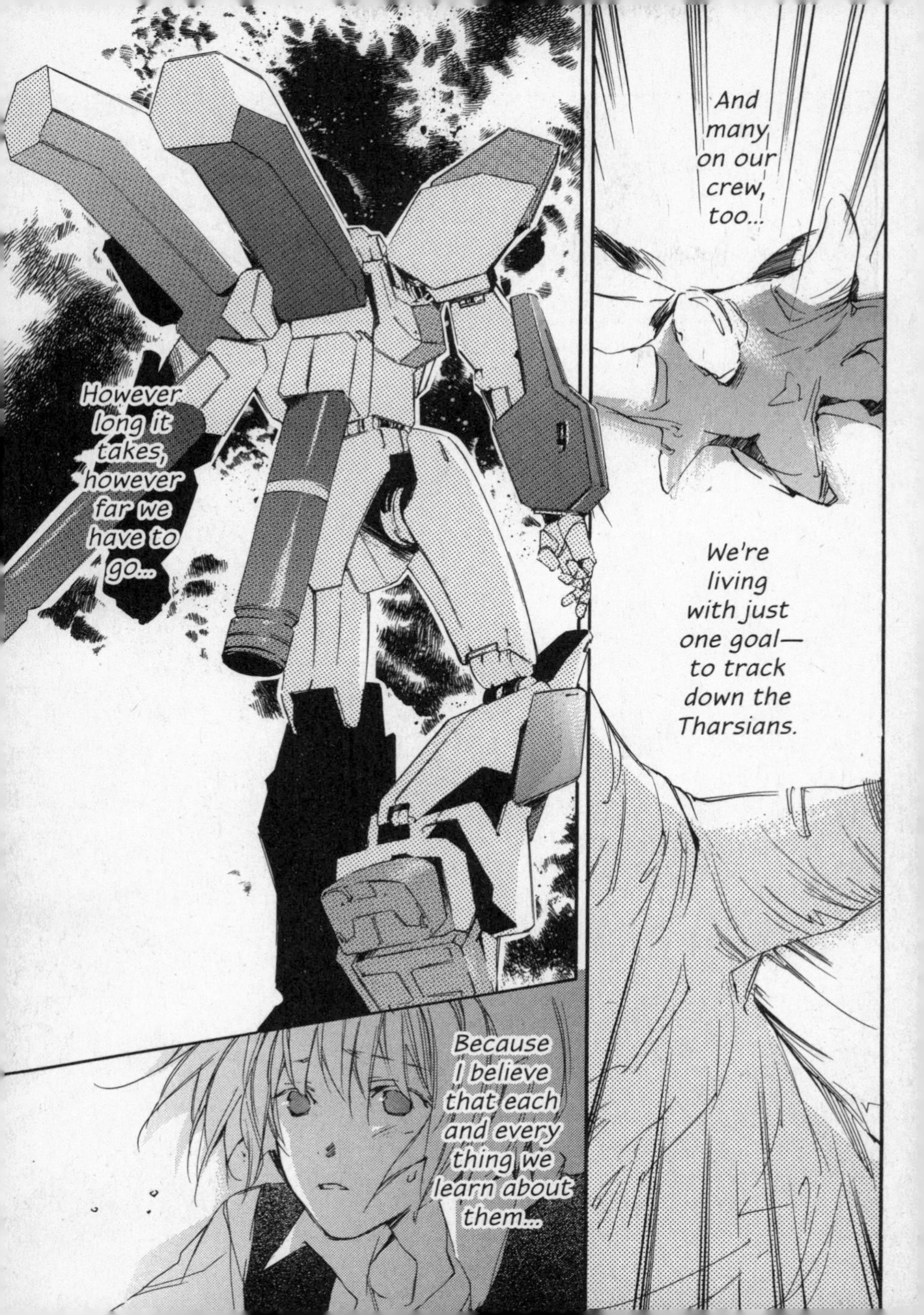
And many on our crew, too...
We're living with just one goal—to track down the Tharsians.
However long it takes, however far we have to go...
Because I believe that each and every thing we learn about them...

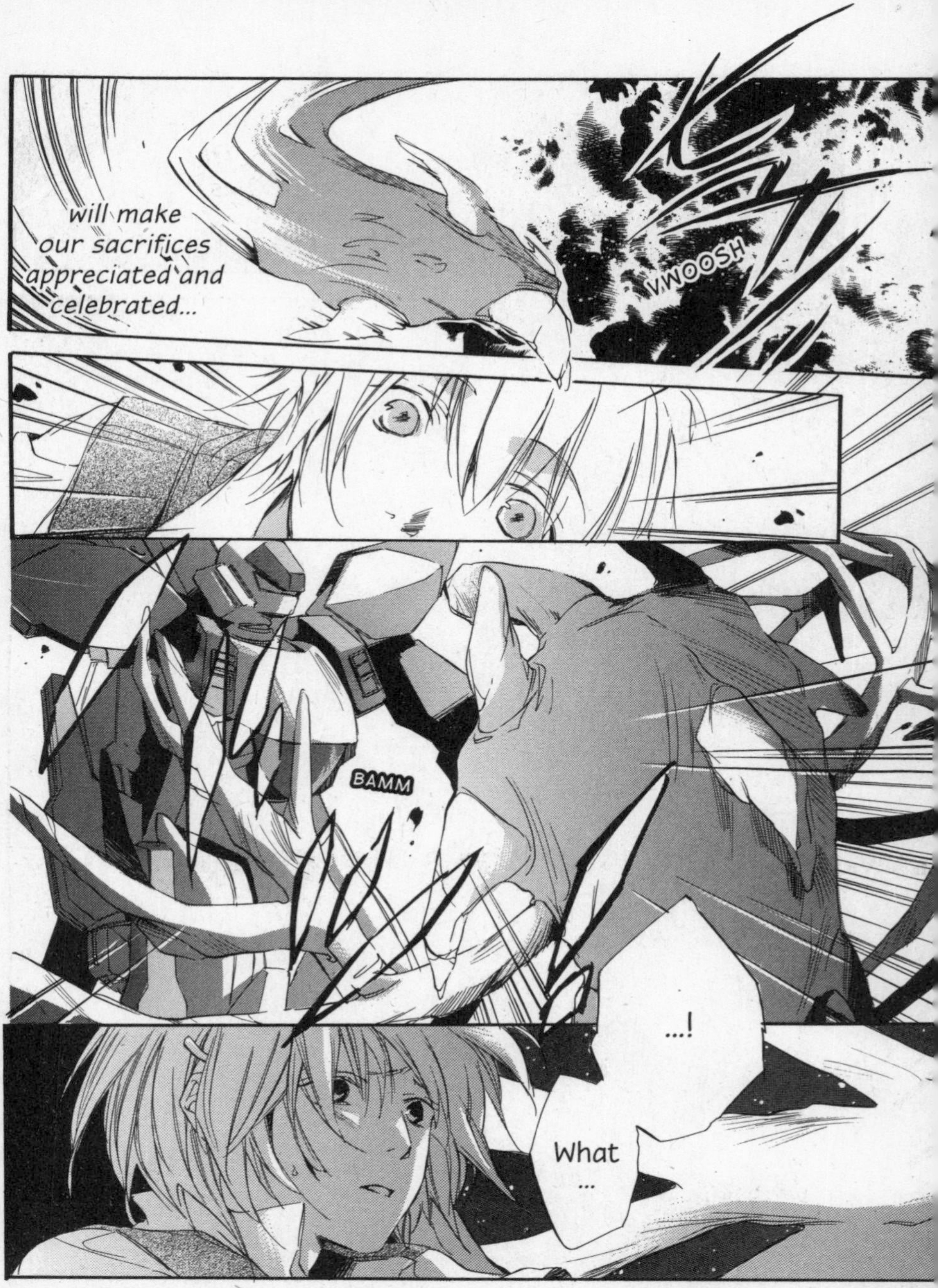

will make our sacrifices appreciated and celebrated...
VWOOSH
BAMM
...!
What ...

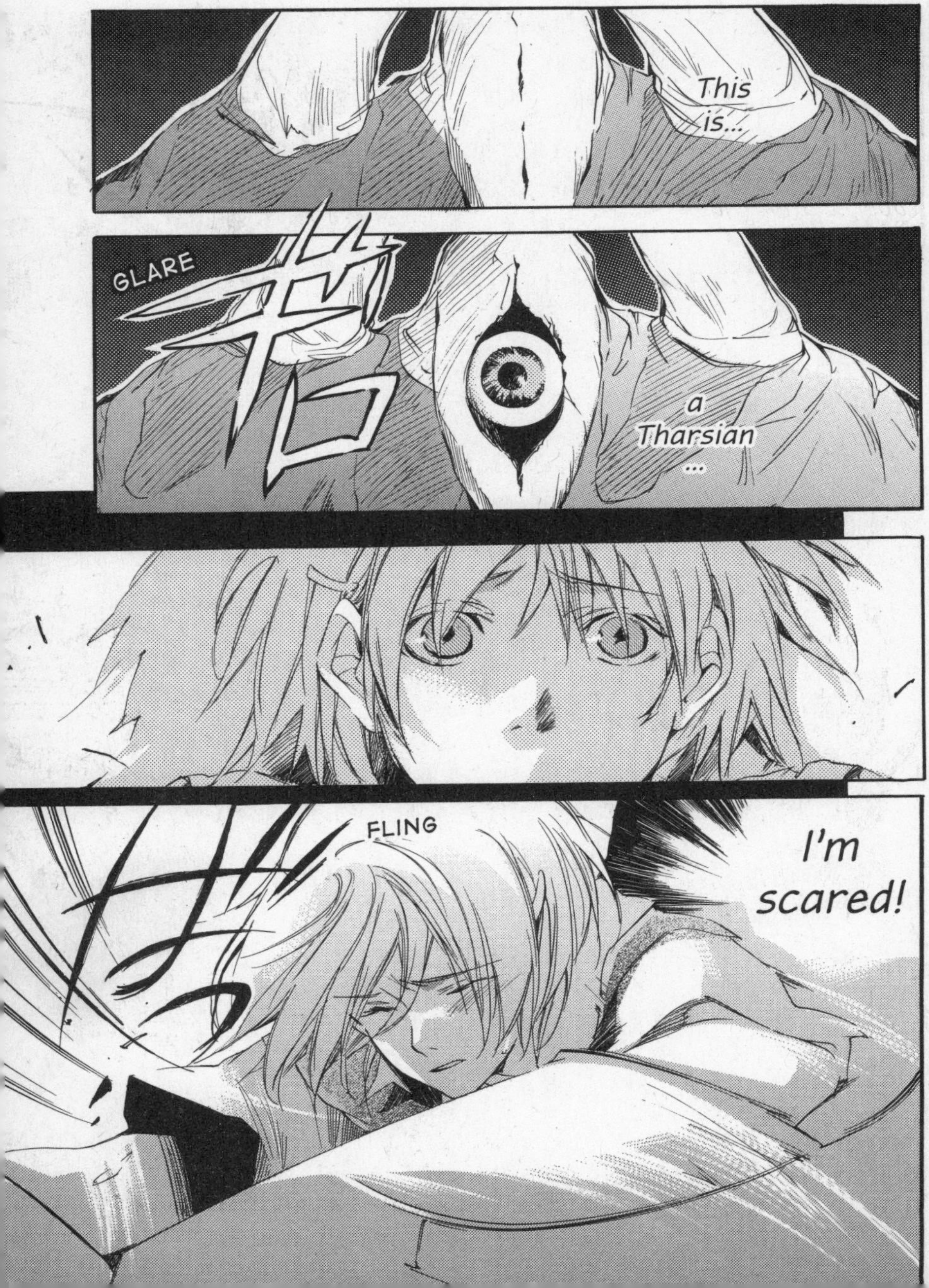
This is...
GLARE
a Tharsian ...
FLING
I'm scared!

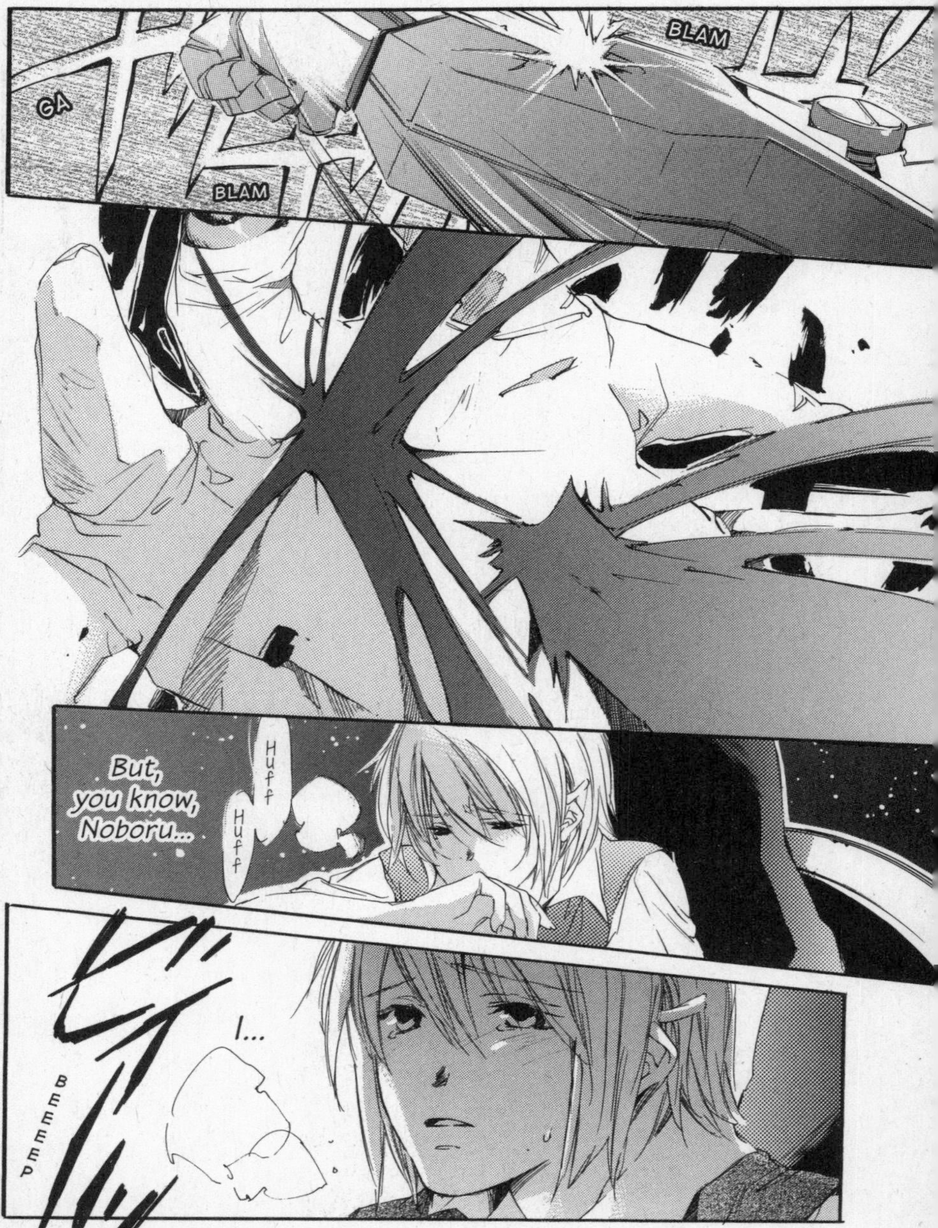
BLAM
GA
BLAM
Huff
Huff
But, you know, Noboru...
I...
BEEEEP

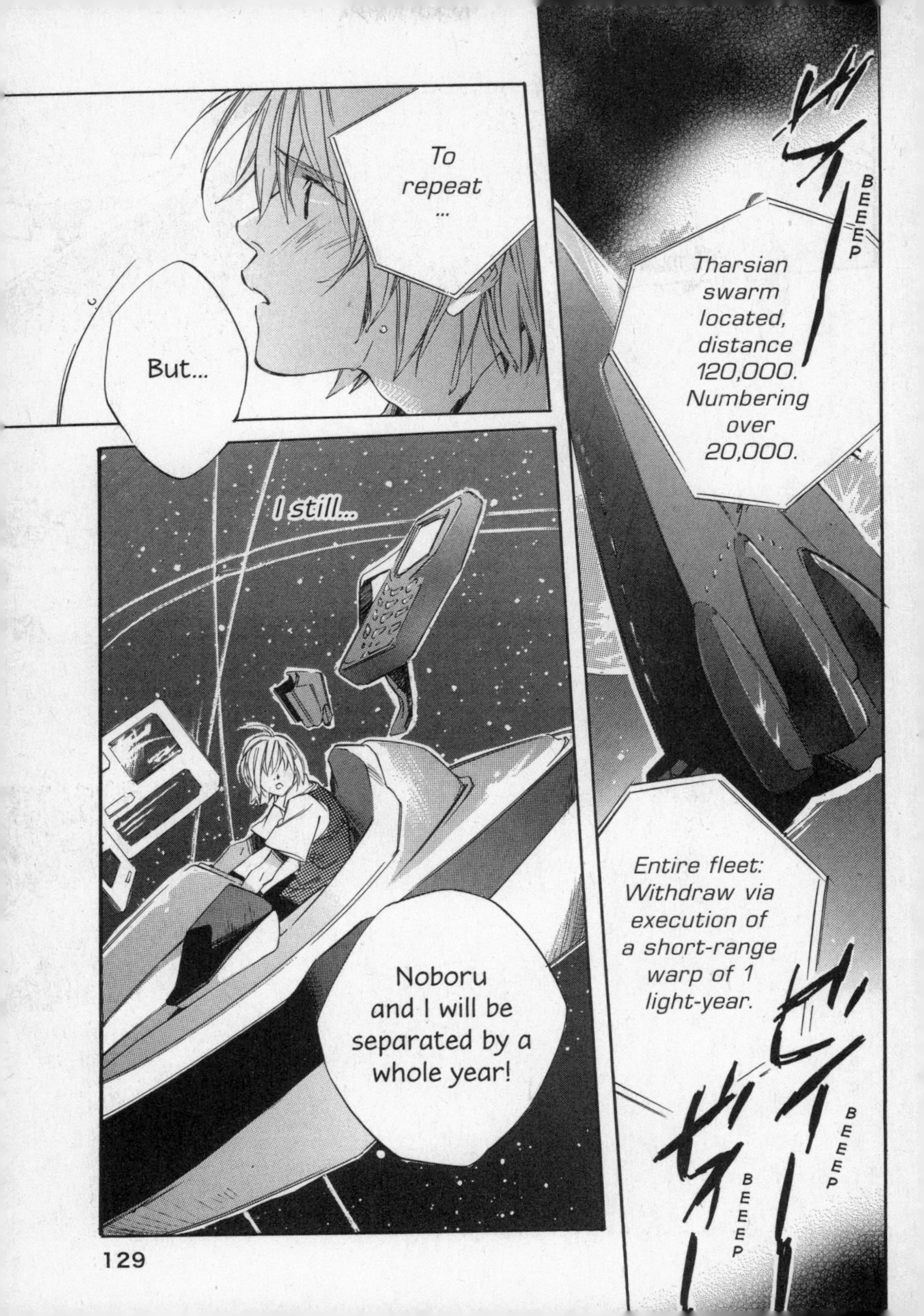
BEEEP
Tharsian swarm located, distance 120,000. Numbering over 20,000.
Entire fleet: Withdraw via execution of a short-range warp of 1 light-year.
BEEEP
BEEEP
To repeat ...
But...
I still...
Noboru and I will be separated by a whole year!

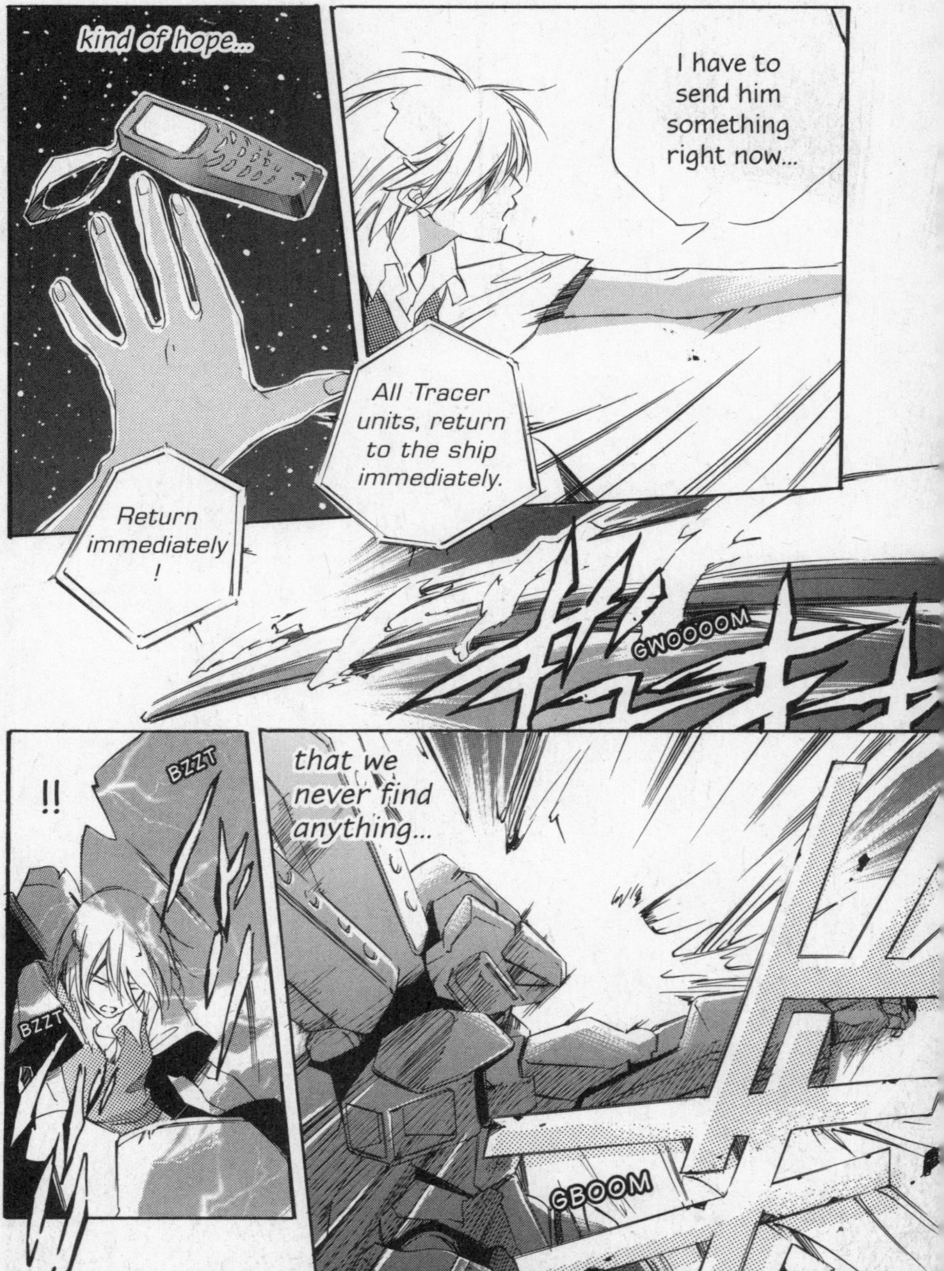
I have to send him something right now...
kind of hope...
All Tracer units, return to the ship immediately.
Return immediately !
GWOOOOM
that we never find anything...
GBOOM
BZZT
!!
BZZT

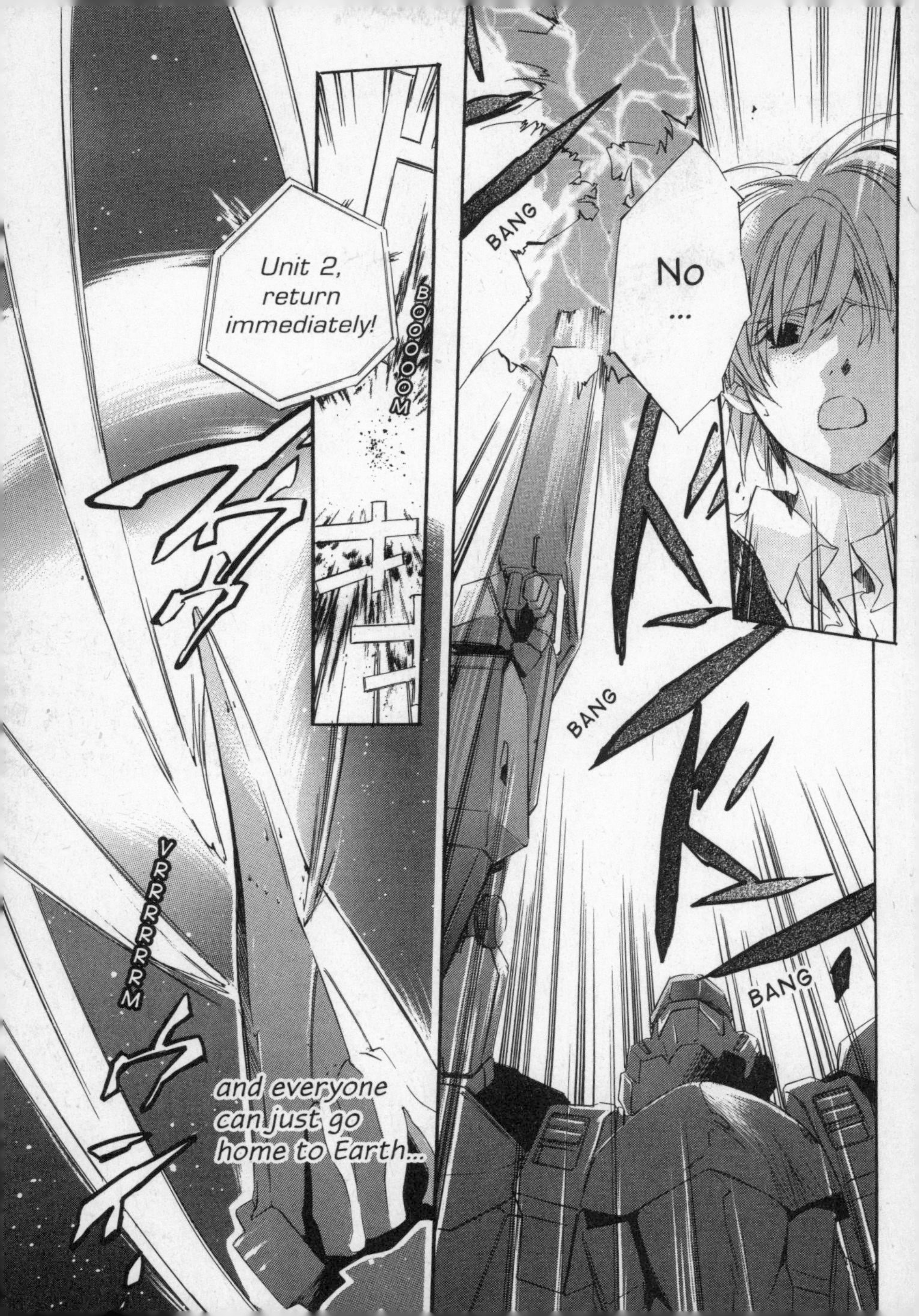
BANG
No ...
BANG
BANG
Unit 2, return immediately!
BOOOOOOM
VRRRRRRRM
and everyone can just go home to Earth...

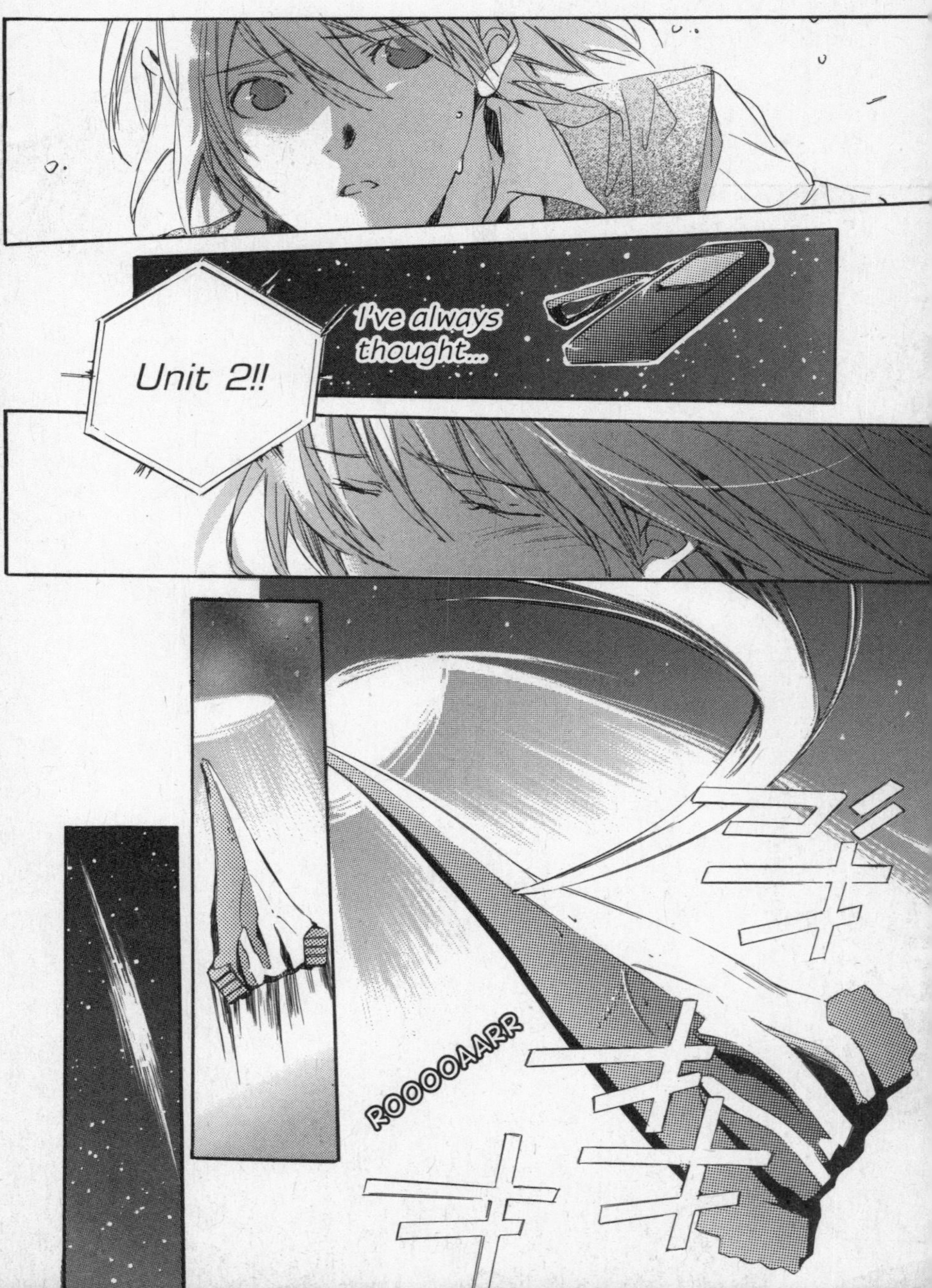
I've always thought...
Unit 2!!
ROOOOAARR

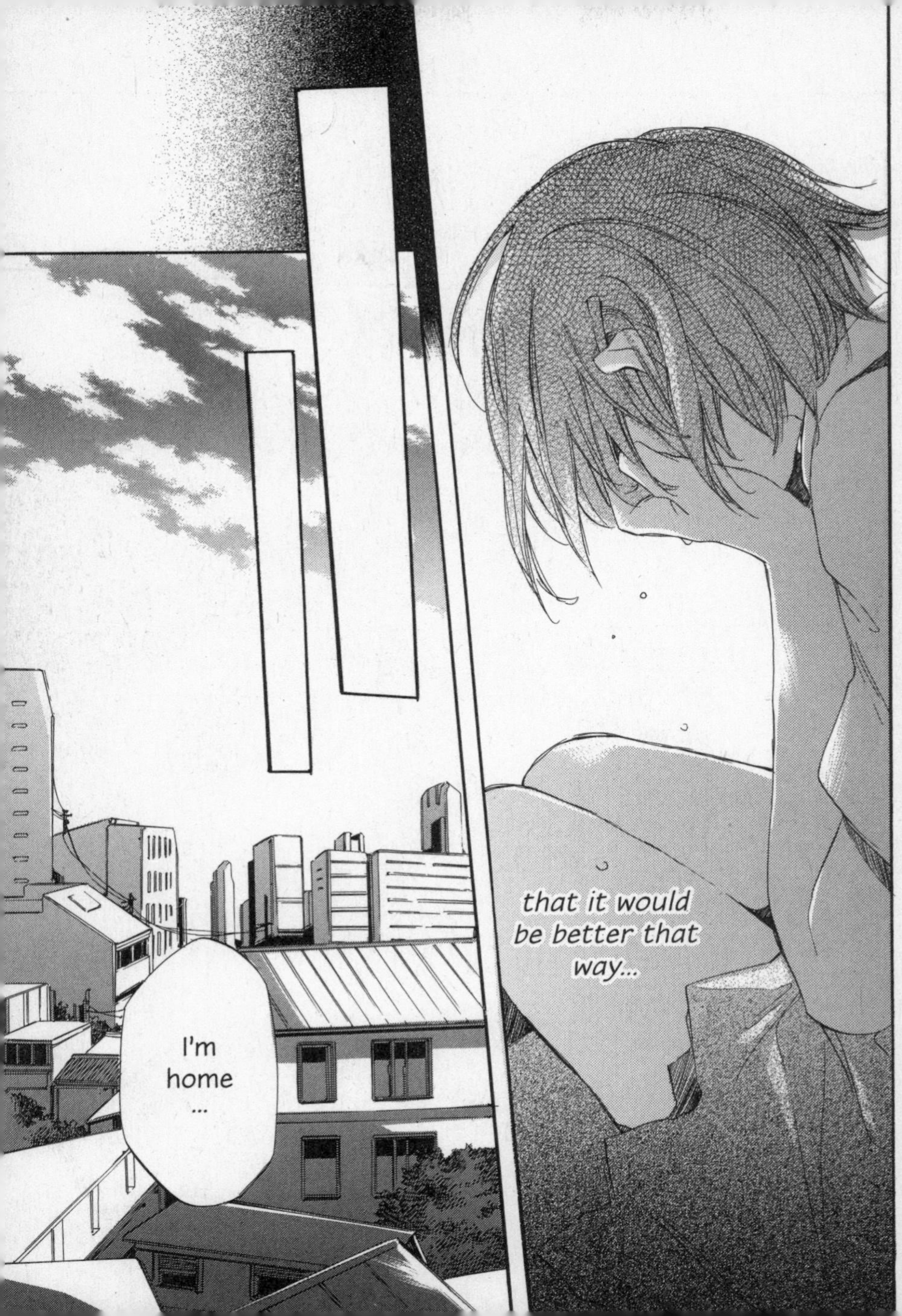
that it would be better that way...
I'm home ...

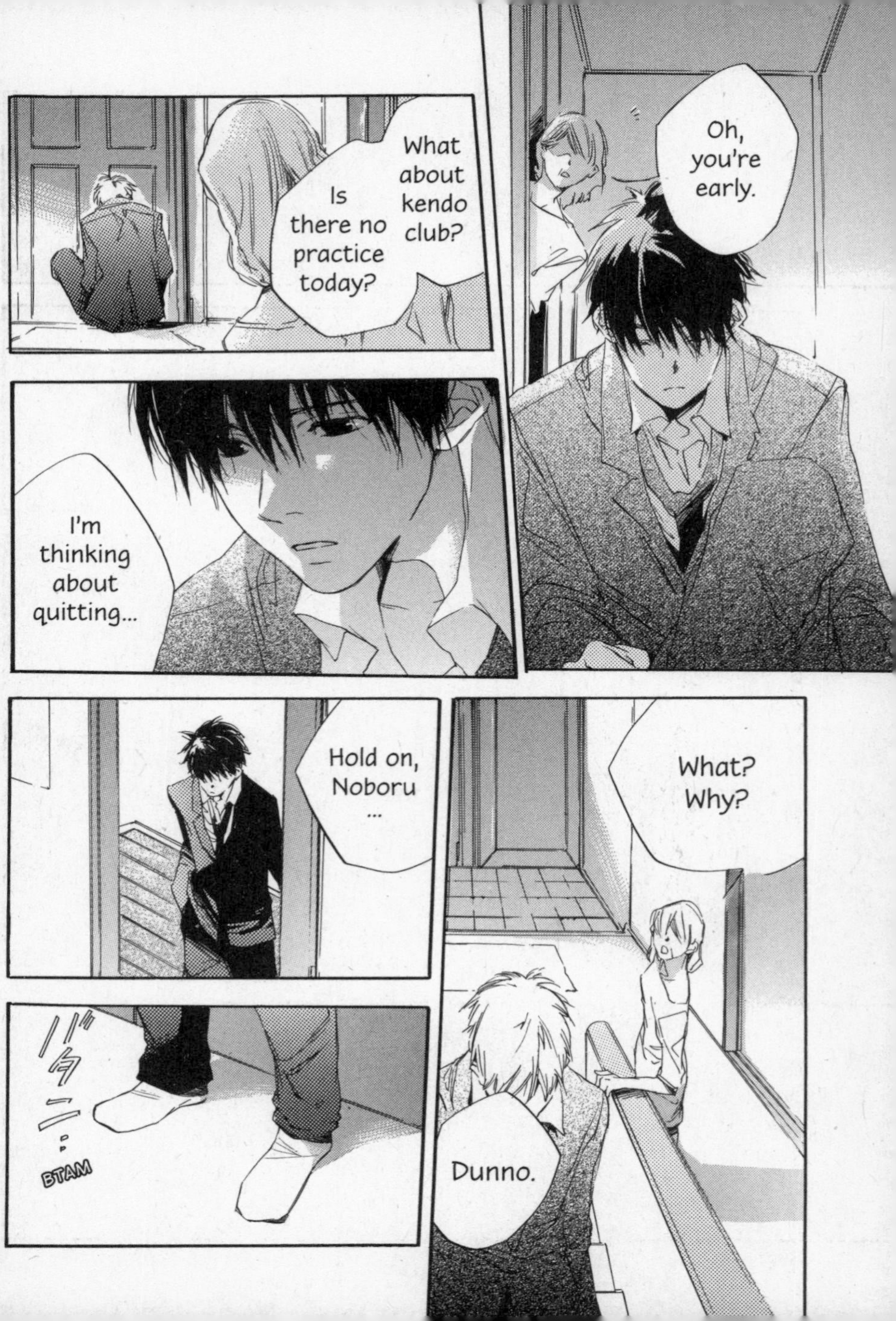
Oh, you're early.
What about kendo club?
Is there no practice today?
I'm thinking about quitting...
What? Why?
Dunno.
Hold on, Noboru ...
BTAM

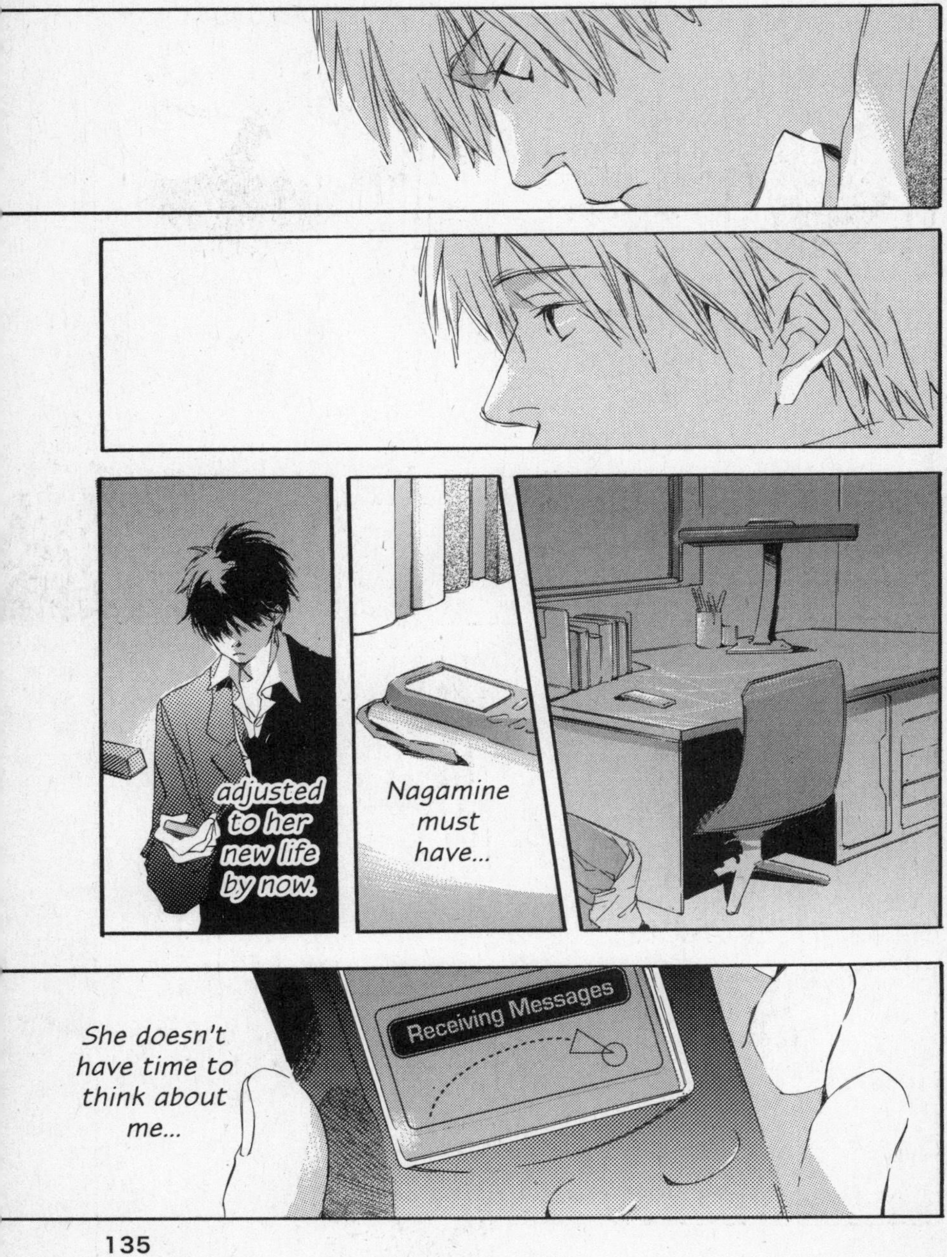
Nagamine must have...
adjusted to her new life by now.
Receiving Messages
She doesn't have time to think about me...

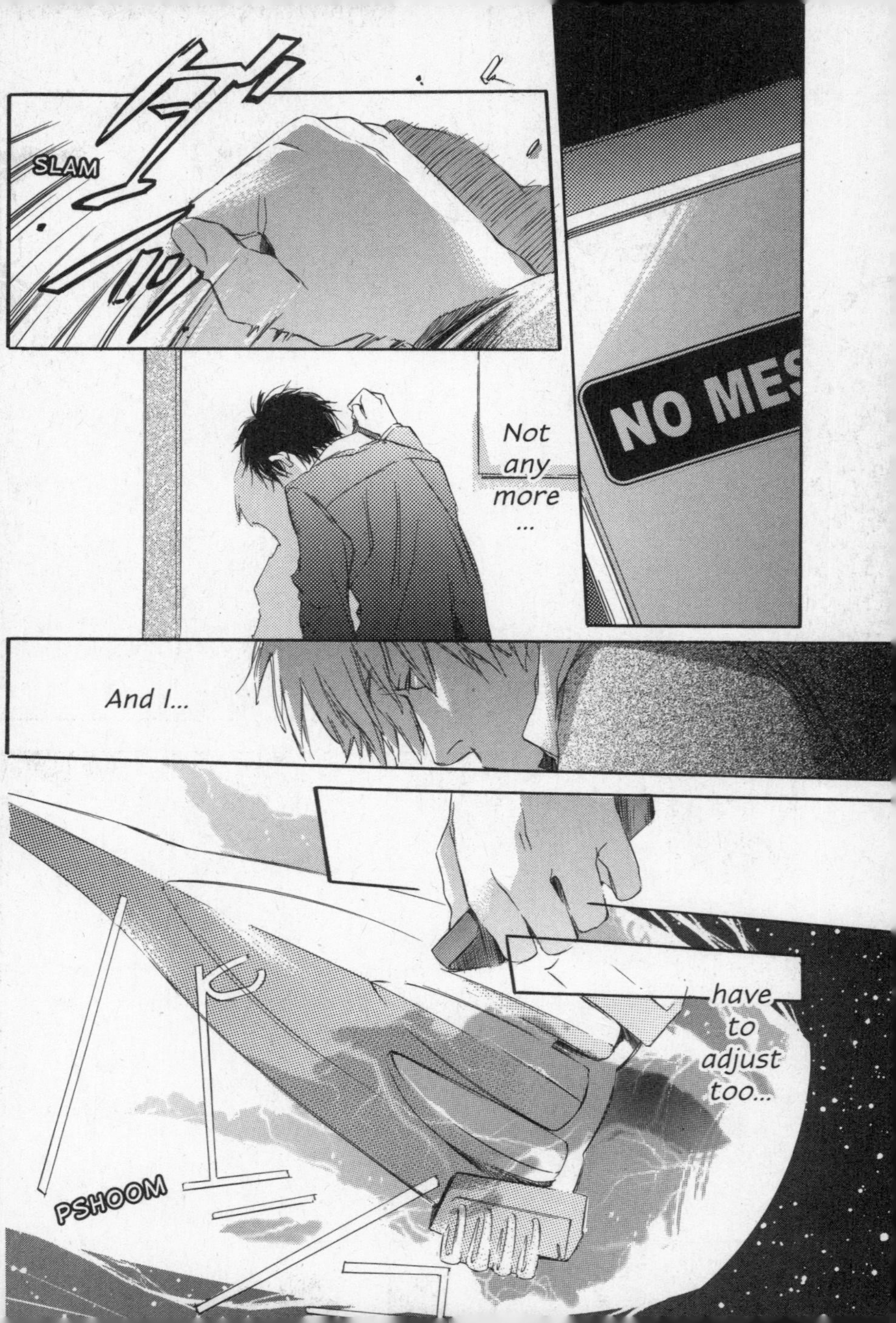
NO MES
SLAM
Not any more ...
And I...
have to adjust too...
PSHOOM

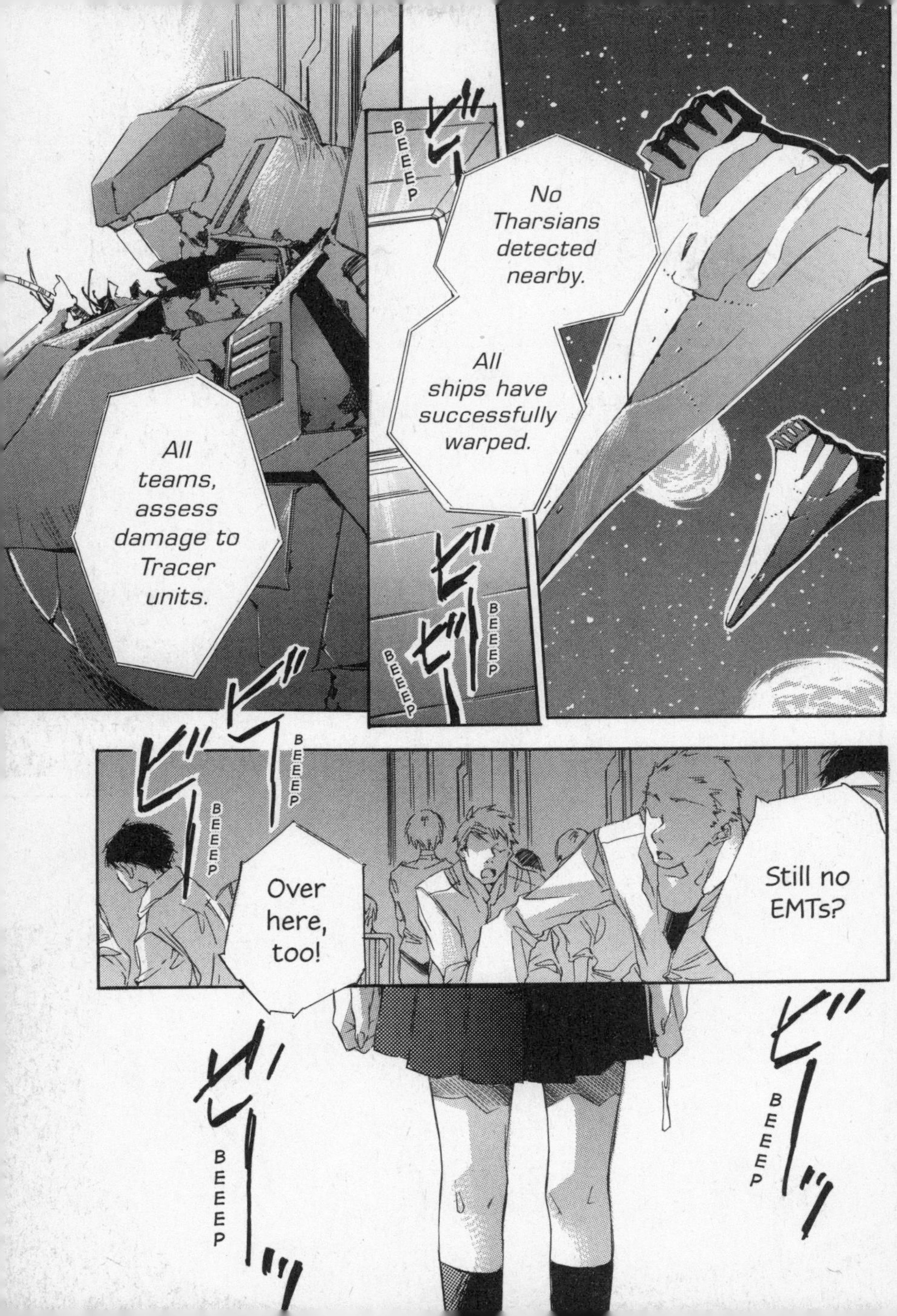
BEEEP
No Tharsians detected nearby.
All ships have successfully warped.
BEEEP
BEEEP
All teams, assess damage to Tracer units.
BEEEP
BEEEP
Still no EMTs?
Over here, too!
BEEEP
BEEEP

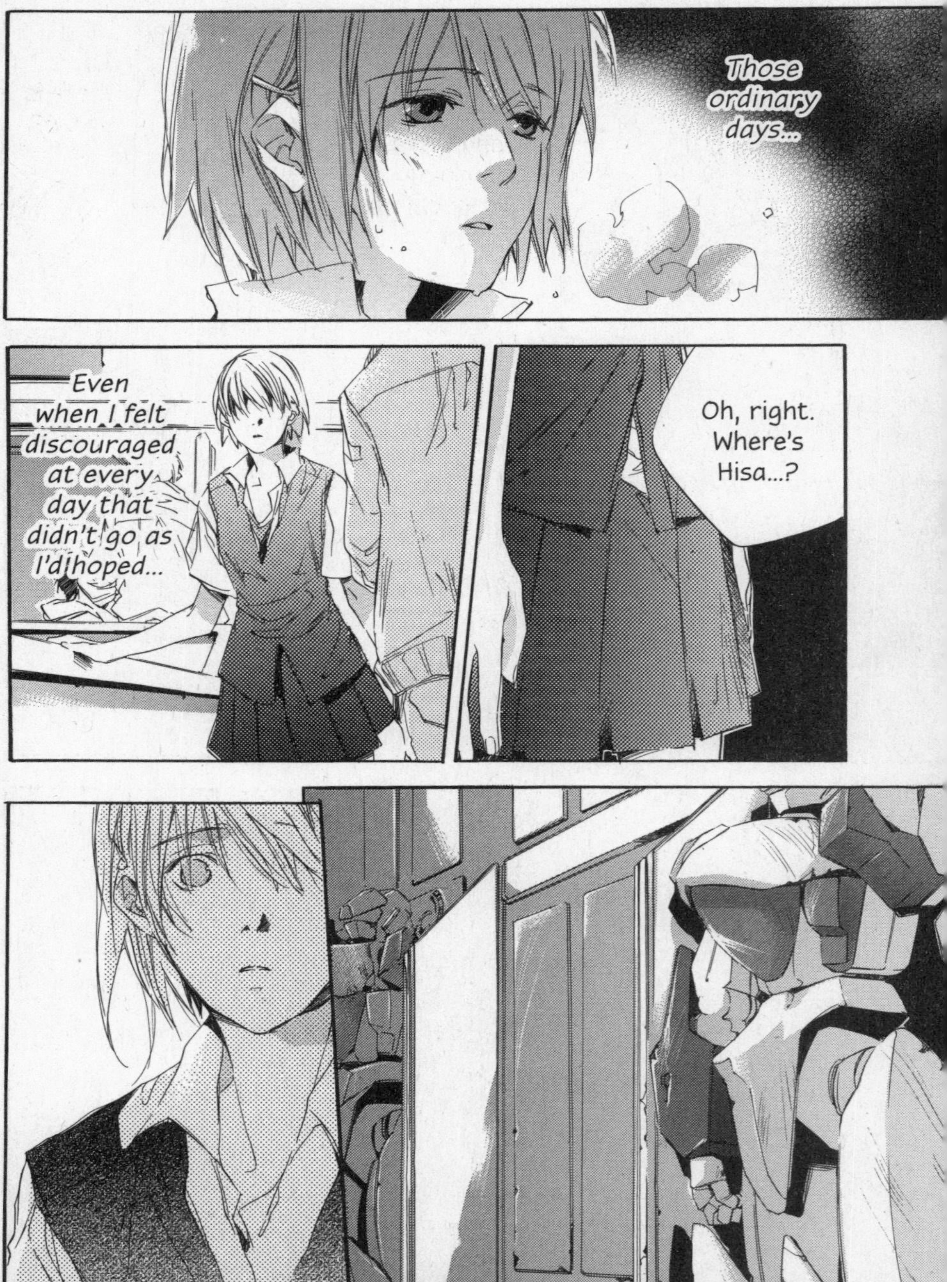
Those ordinary days...
Oh, right. Where's Hisa...?
Even when I felt discouraged at every day that didn't go as I'd hoped...

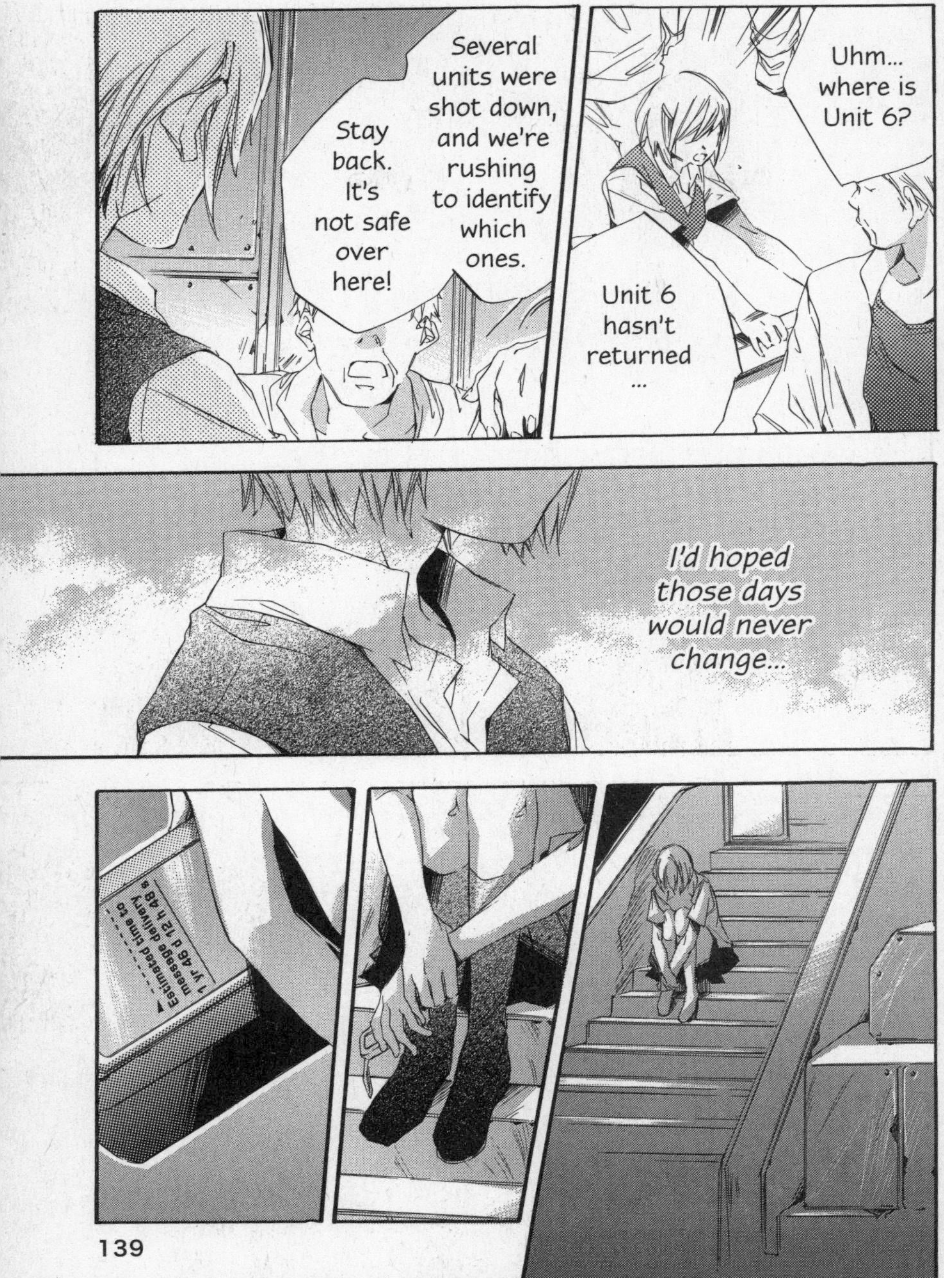
Uhm... where is Unit 6?
Unit 6 hasn't returned ...
Several units were shot down, and we're rushing to identify which ones.
Stay back. It's not safe over here!
I'd hoped those days would never change...
Estimated time to message delivery
1 yr 48 d 12 h 48 s

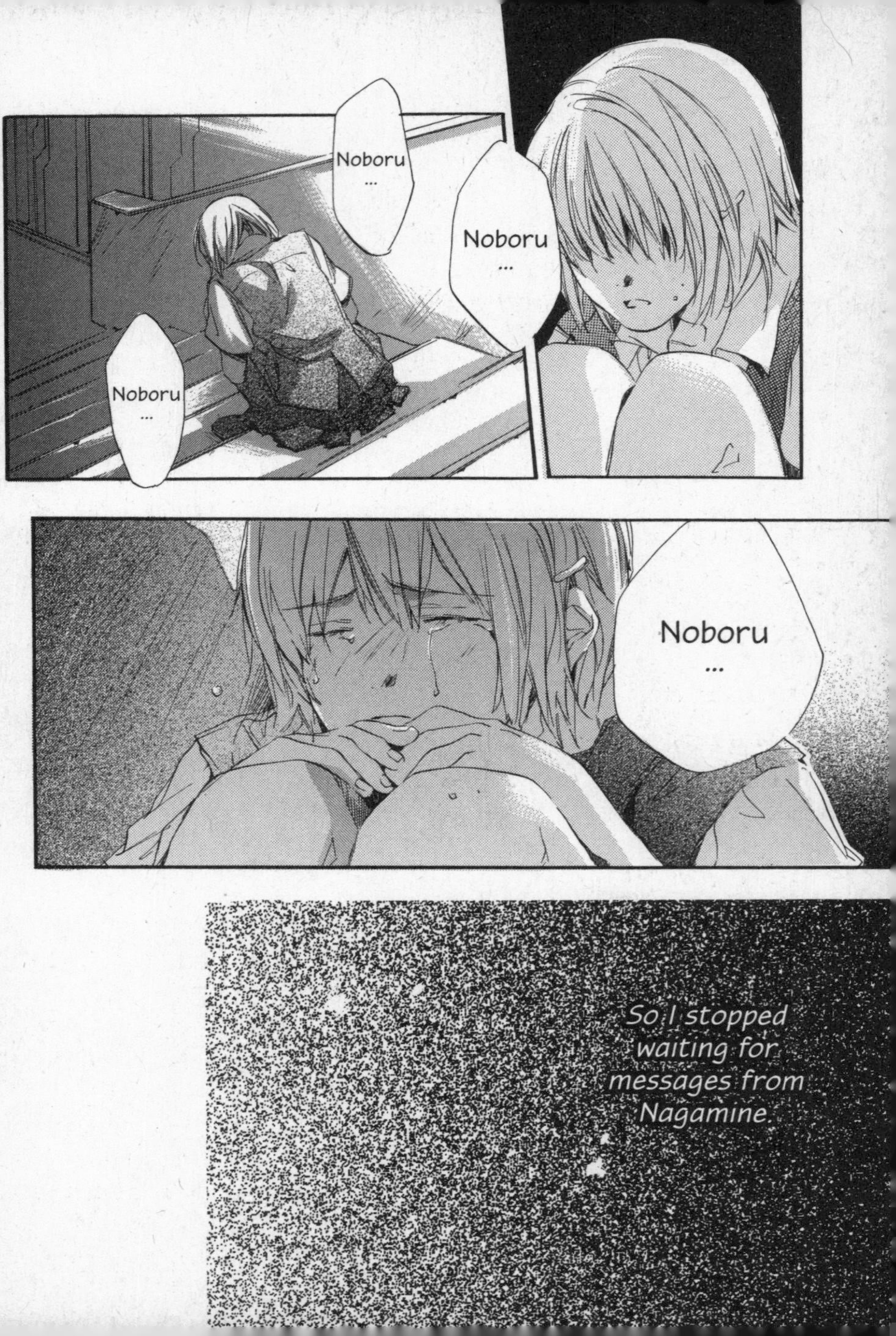
Noboru ...
Noboru ...
Noboru ...
Noboru ...
So I stopped waiting for messages from Nagamine.

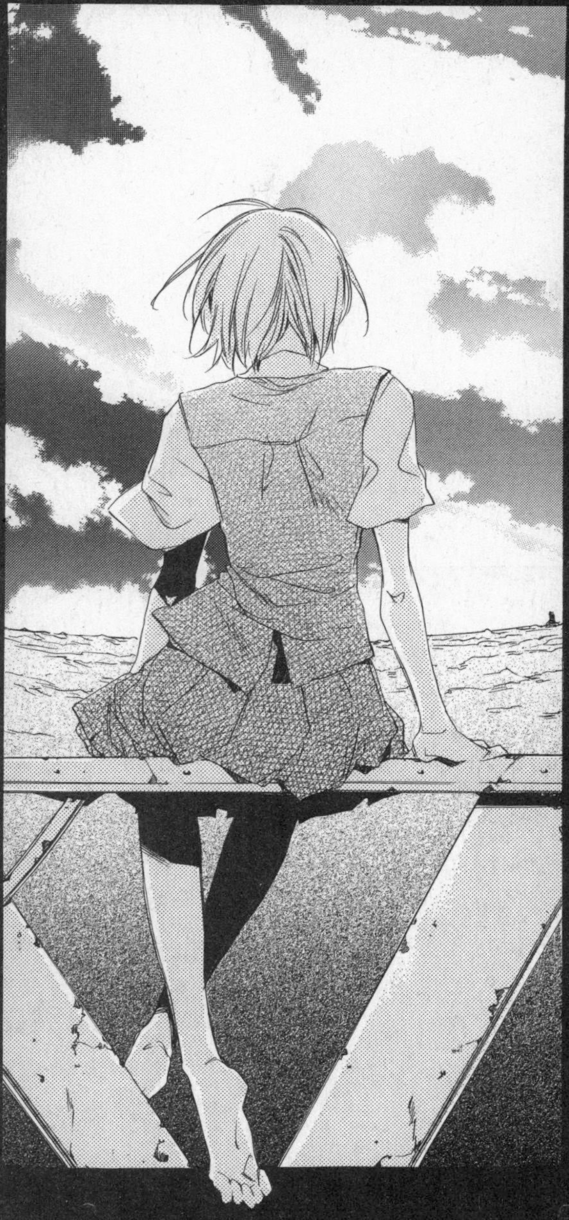

Voices of a Distant Star

Chapter 6

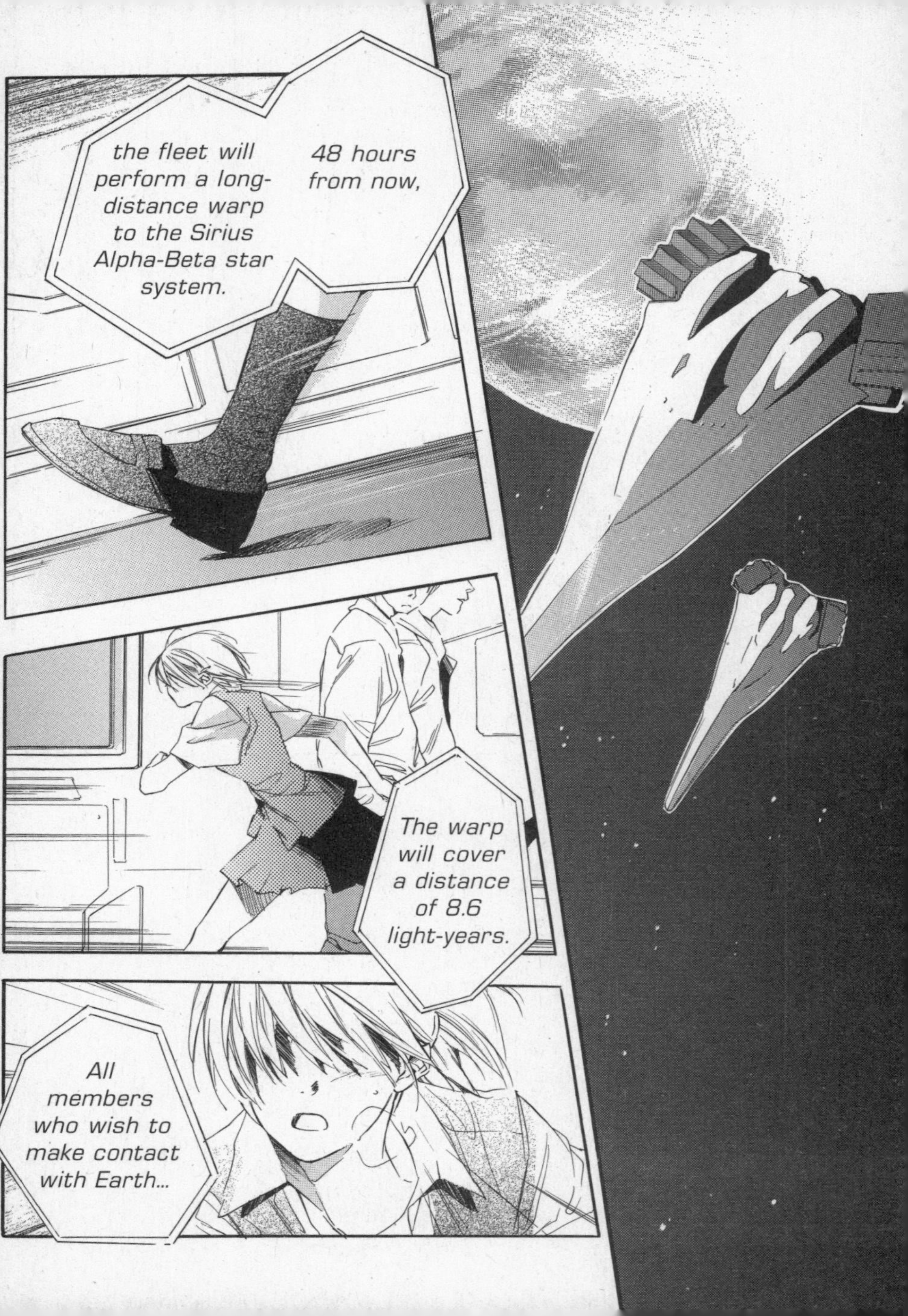
48 hours from now,
the fleet will perform a long-distance warp to the Sirius Alpha-Beta star system.
The warp will cover a distance of 8.6 light-years.
All members who wish to make contact with Earth...

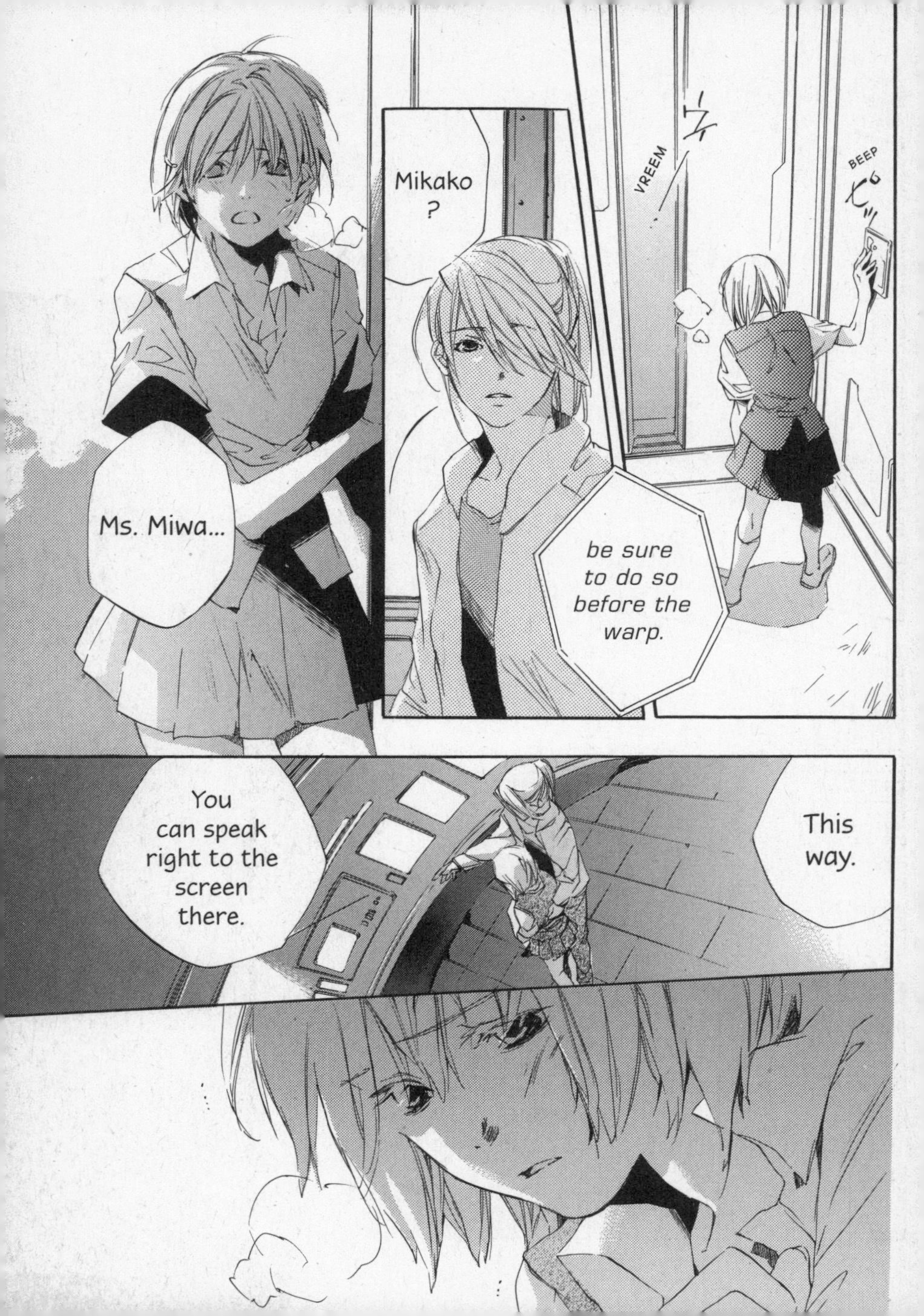

VREEM
BEEP
Mikako ?
be sure to do so before the warp.
Ms. Miwa...
This way.
You can speak right to the screen there.

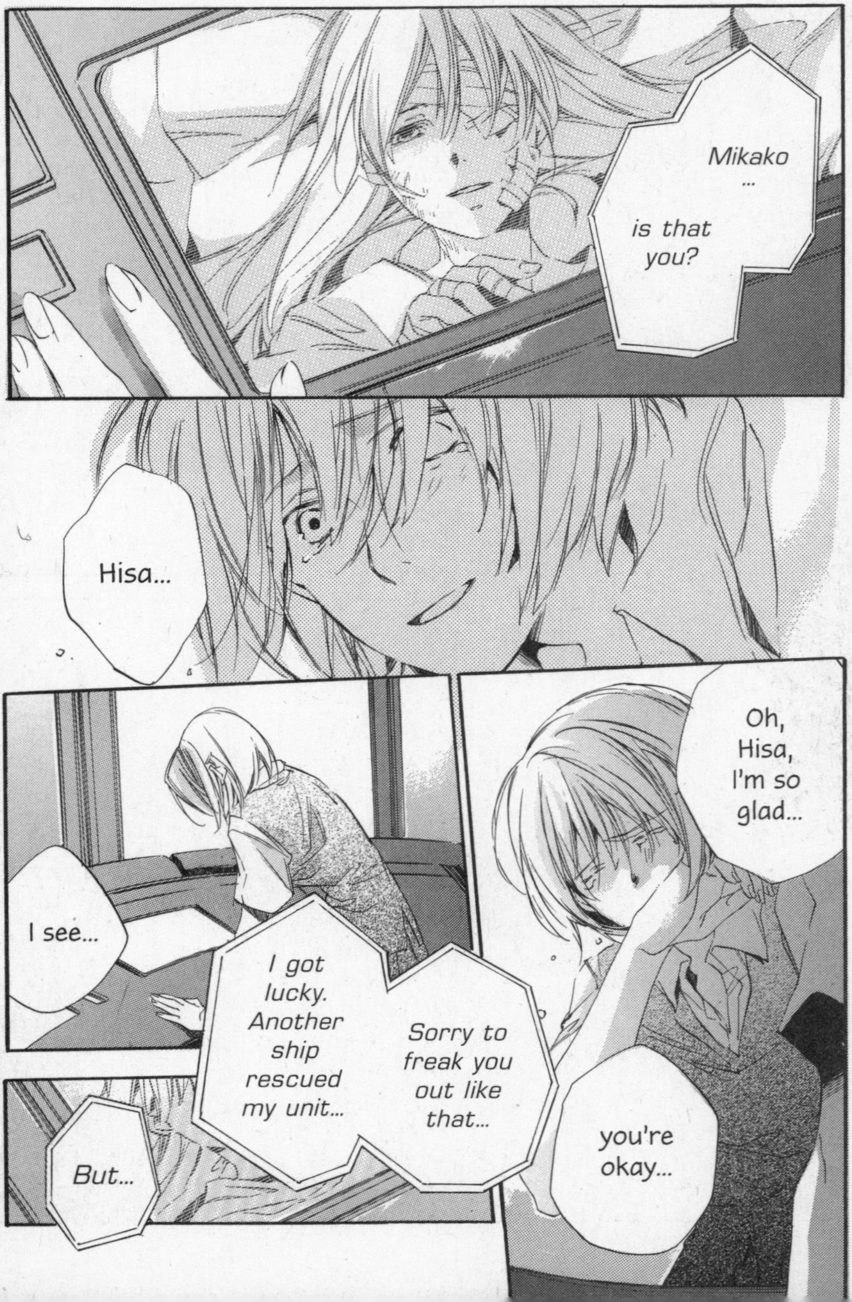
Mikako ... is that you?
Hisa...
Oh, Hisa, I'm so glad...
you're okay...
I see...
Sorry to freak you out like that...
I got lucky. Another ship rescued my unit...
But...

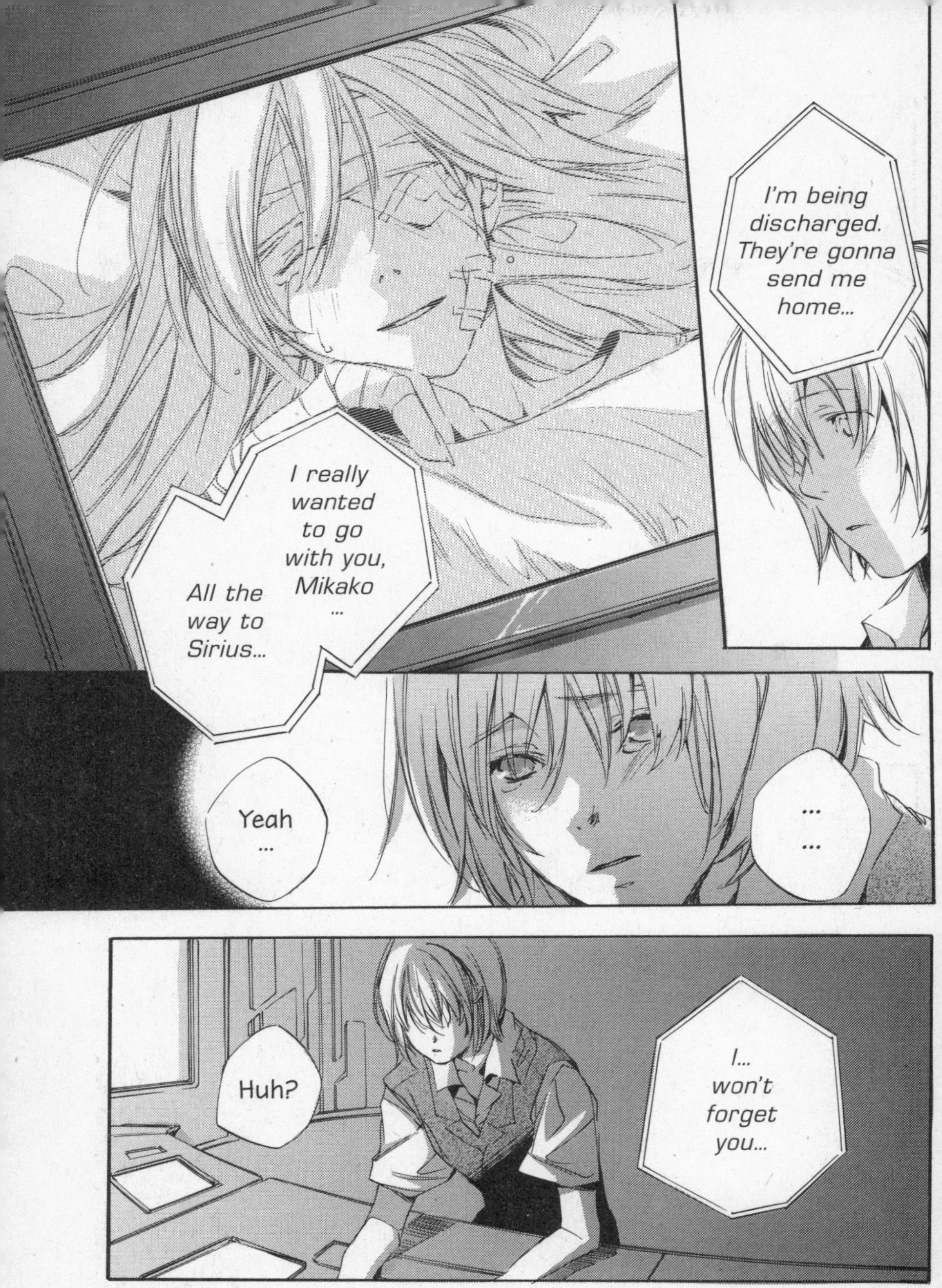
I'm being discharged. They're gonna send me home...
I really wanted to go with you, Mikako ...
All the way to Sirius...
… …
Yeah …
I… won't forget you…
Huh?

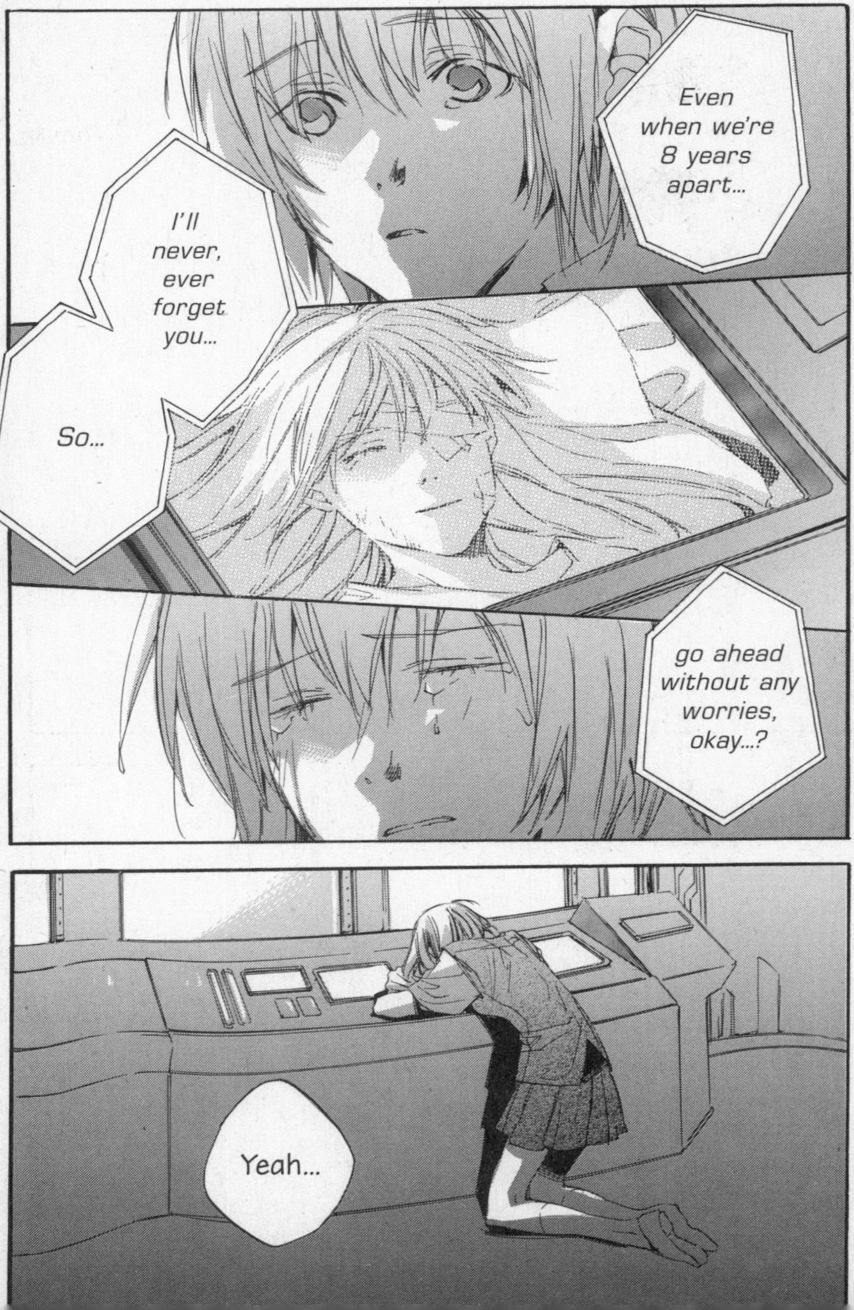
Even when we're 8 years apart...
I'll never, ever forget you...
So...
go ahead without any worries, okay...?
Yeah...

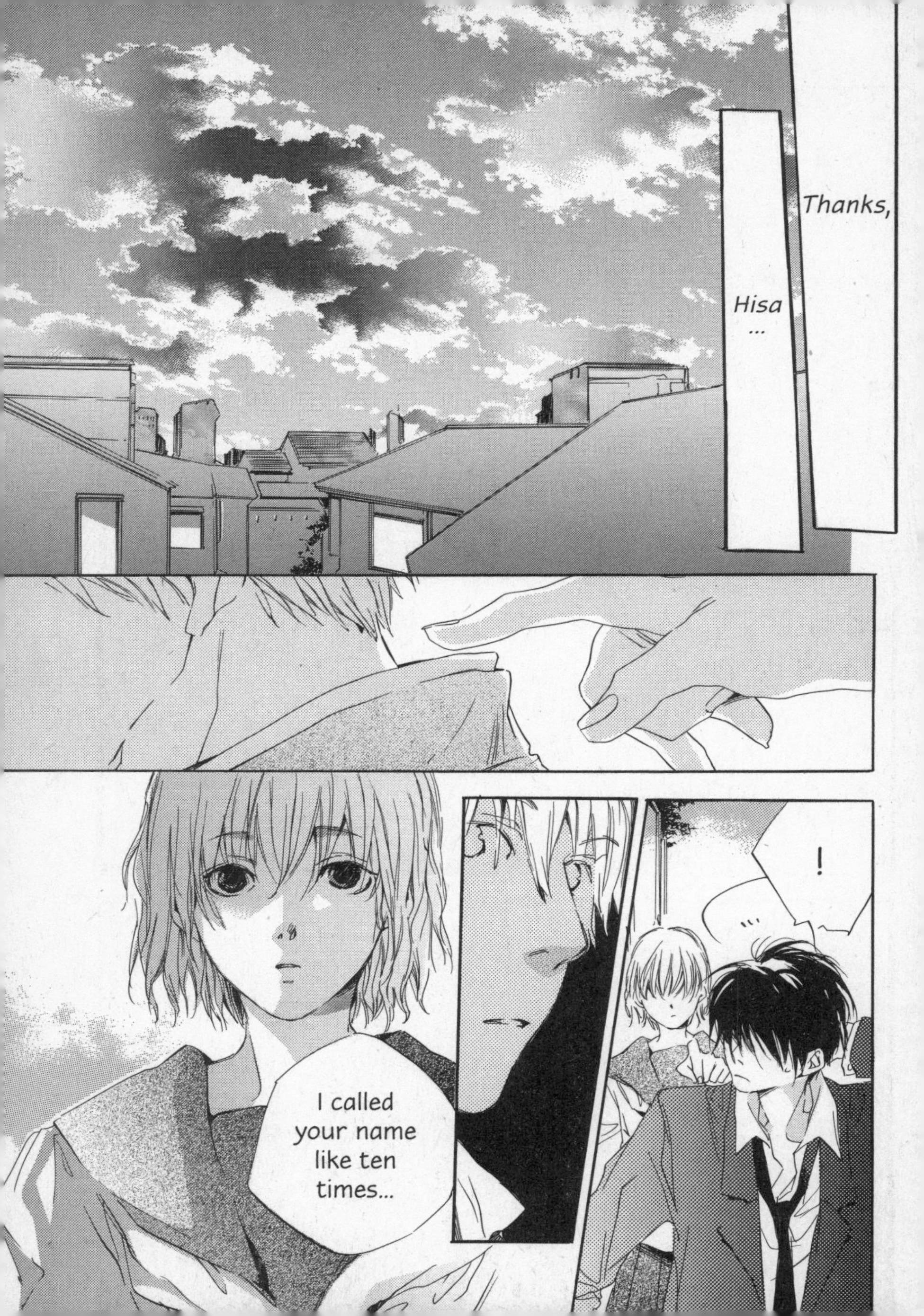
Thanks,
Hisa ...
!
...
I called your name like ten times...

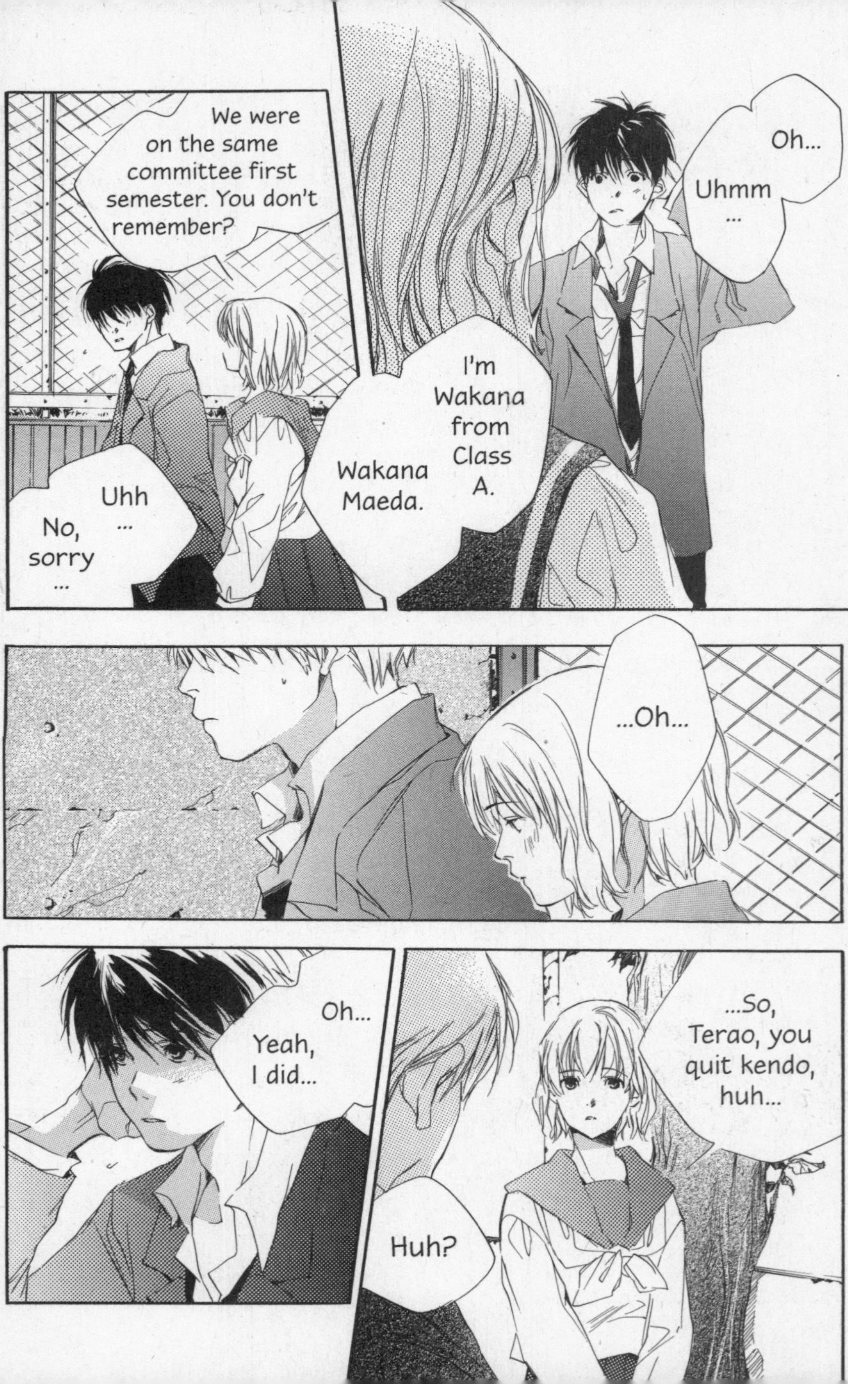
Oh... Uhmm ...
I'm Wakana from Class A.
Wakana Maeda.
We were on the same committee first semester. You don't remember?
Uhh ...
No, sorry ...
...Oh...
...So, Terao, you quit kendo, huh...
Huh?
Oh... Yeah, I did...

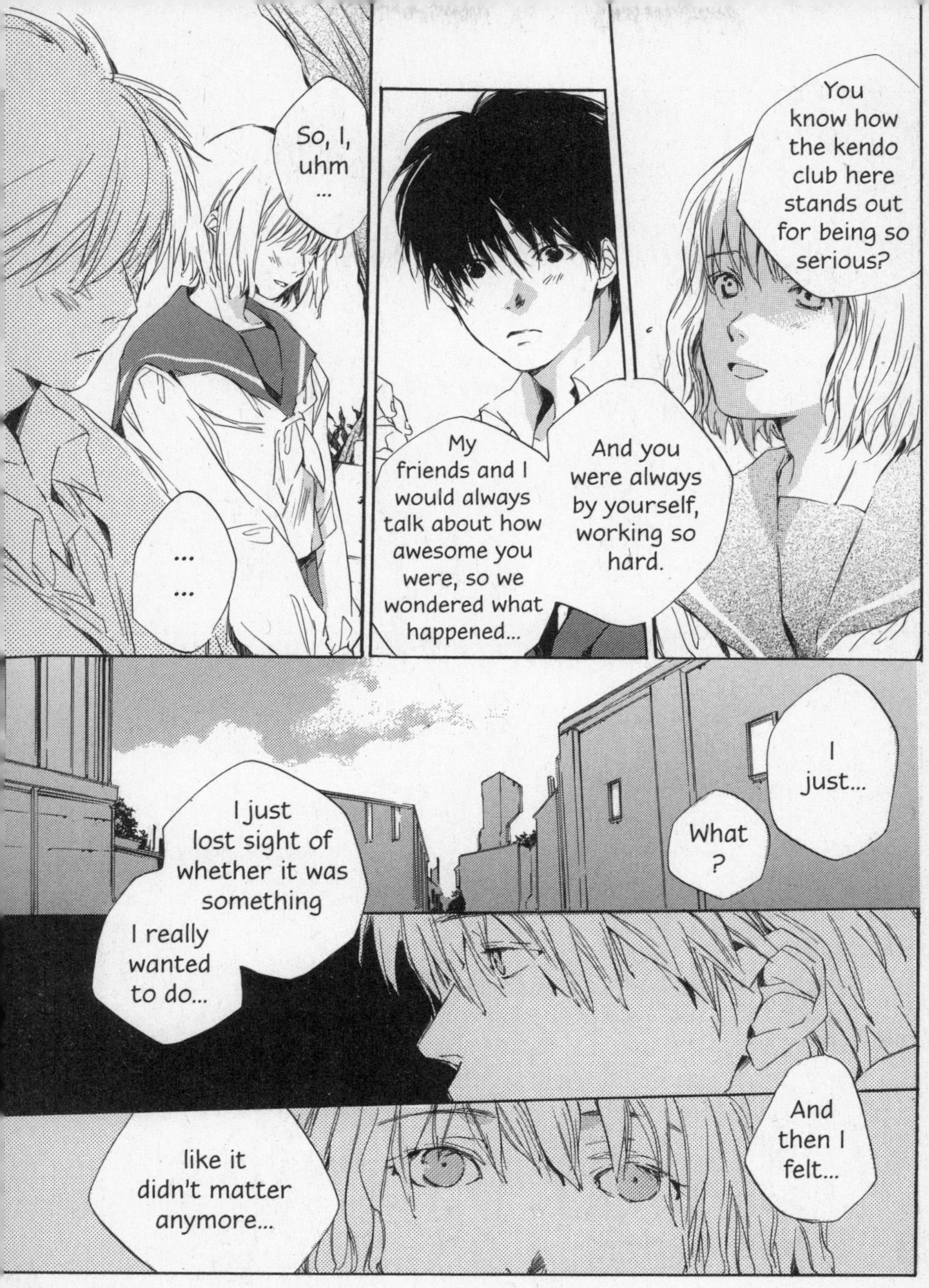

You know how the kendo club here stands out for being so serious?
And you were always by yourself, working so hard.
My friends and I would always talk about how awesome you were, so we wondered what happened...
So, I, uhm ...
... ...
I just...
What?
I just lost sight of whether it was something I really wanted to do...
And then I felt...
like it didn't matter anymore...

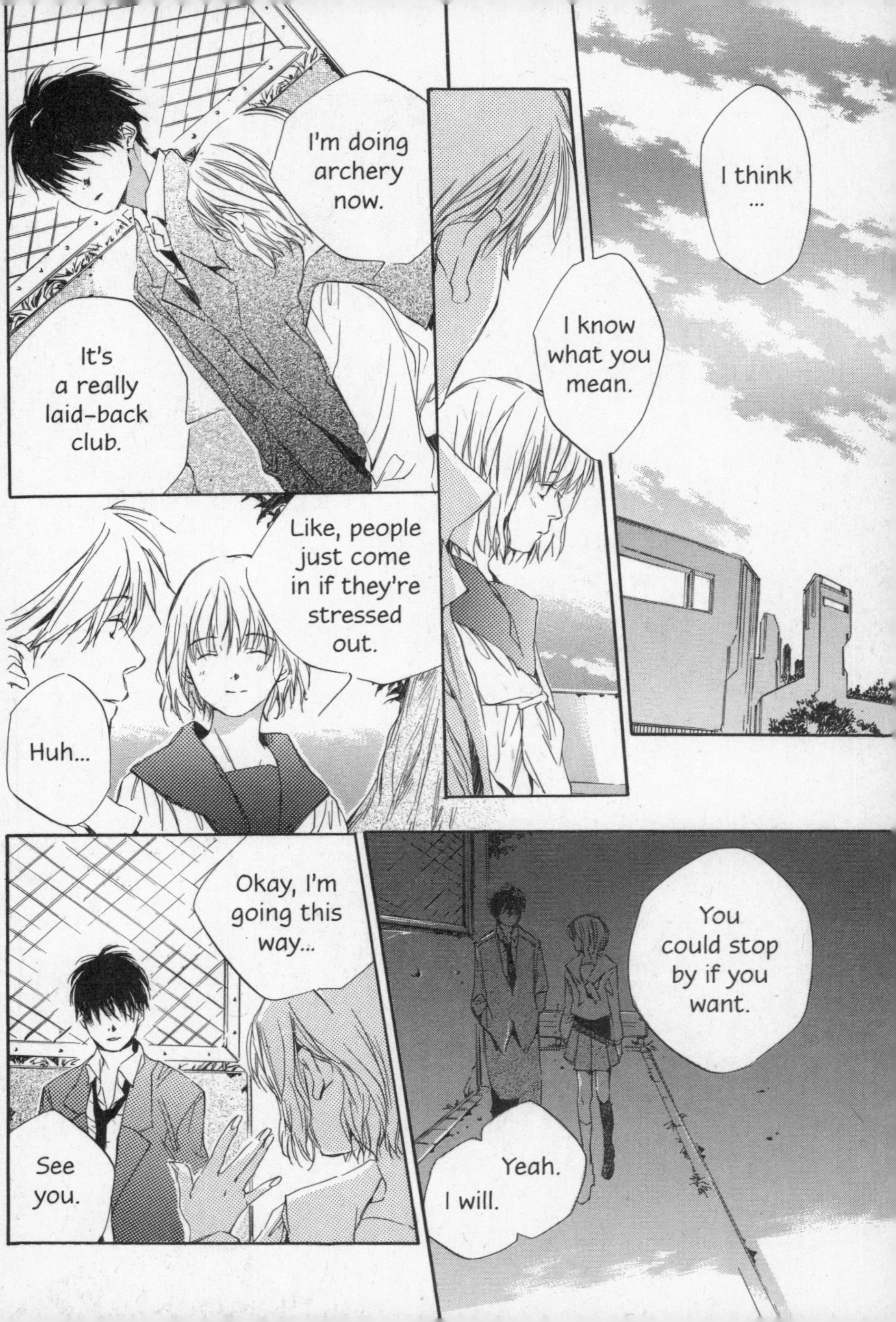
I think ...
I know what you mean.
I'm doing archery now.
It's a really laid-back club.
Like, people just come in if they're stressed out.
Huh...
You could stop by if you want.
Yeah.
I will.
Okay, I'm going this way...
See you.

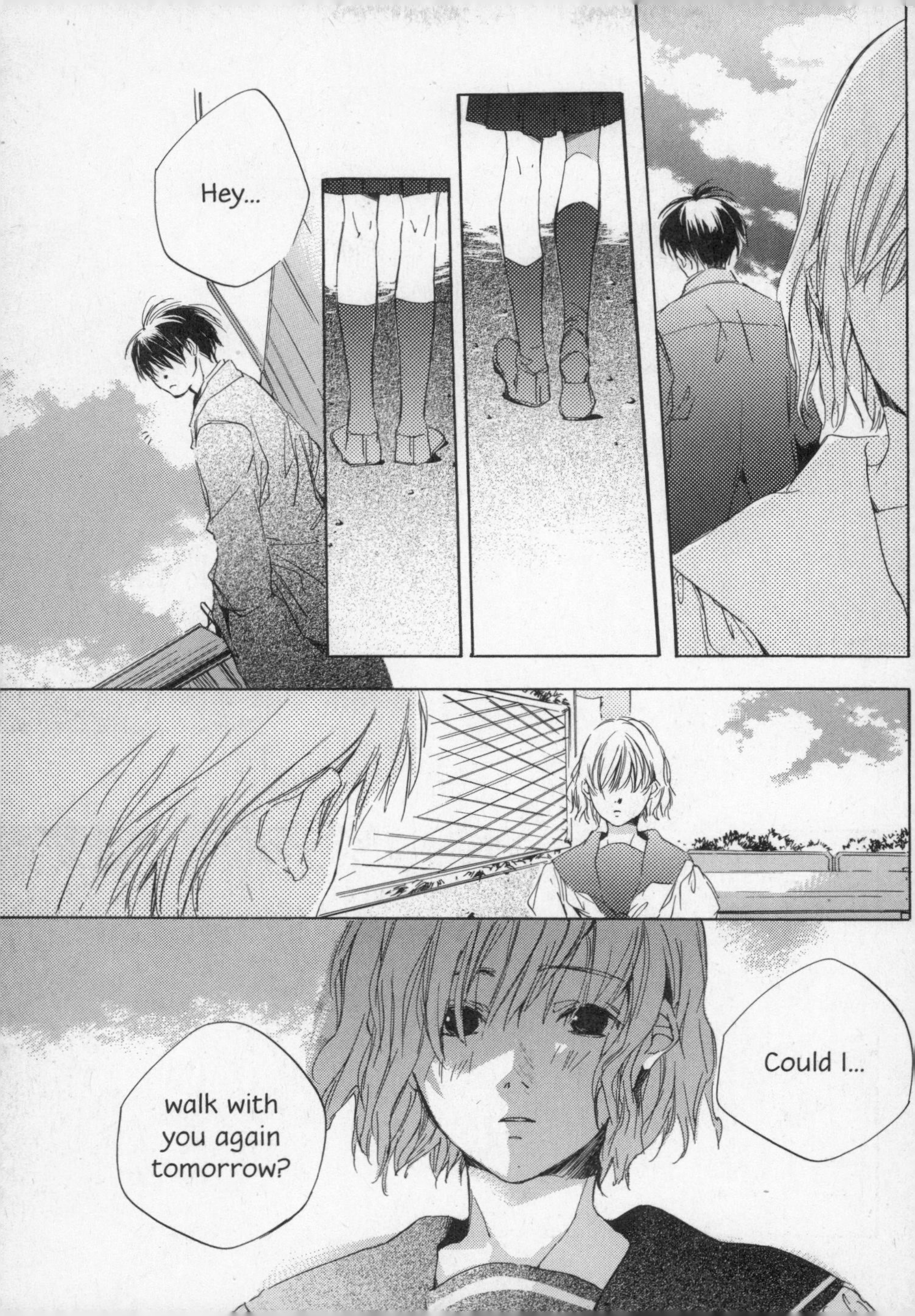
Hey...
Could I...
walk with you again tomorrow?

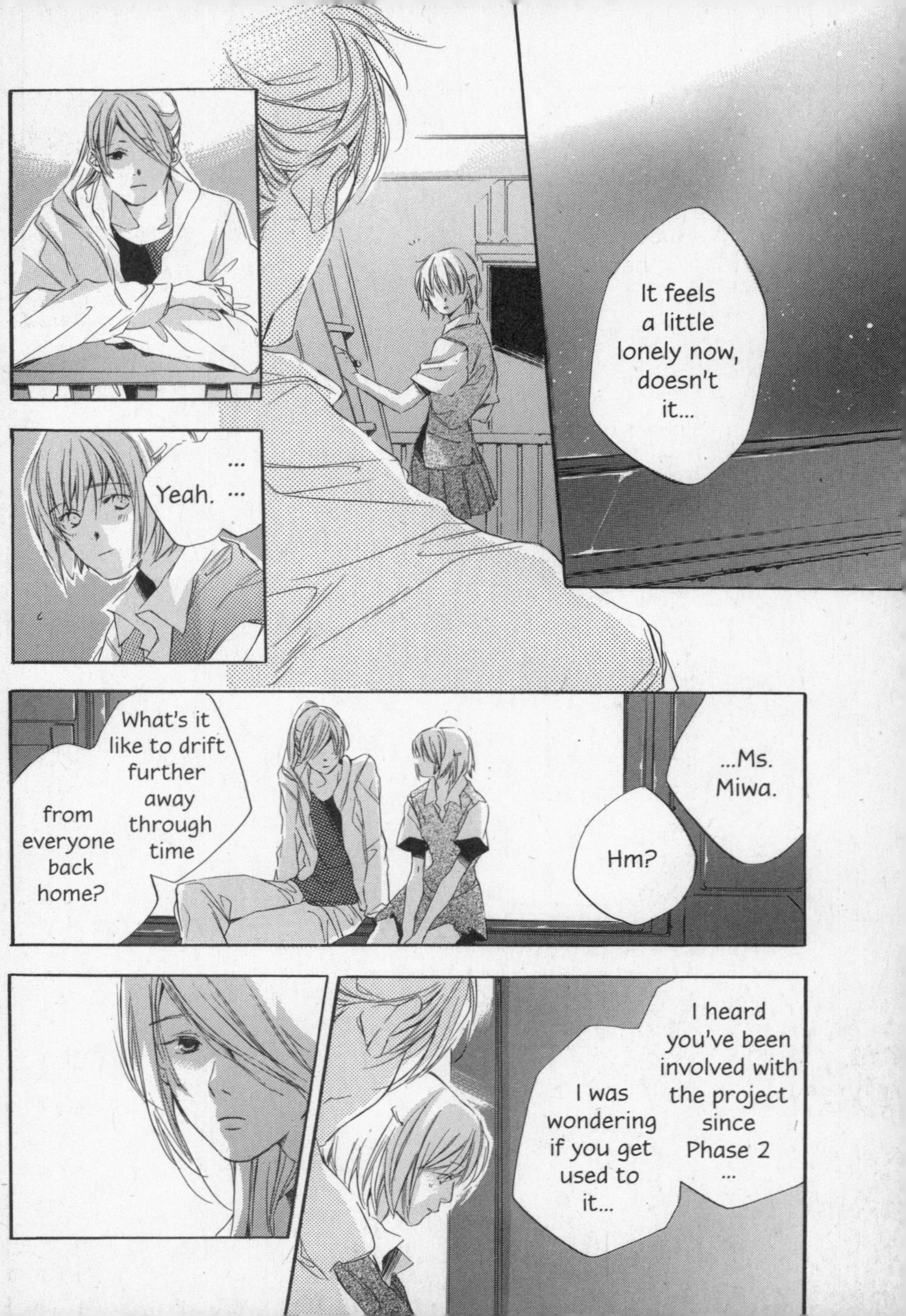
It feels a little lonely now, doesn't it...
... Yeah. ...
...Ms. Miwa.
Hm?
What's it like to drift further away through time from everyone back home?
I heard you've been involved with the project since Phase 2 ...
I was wondering if you get used to it...

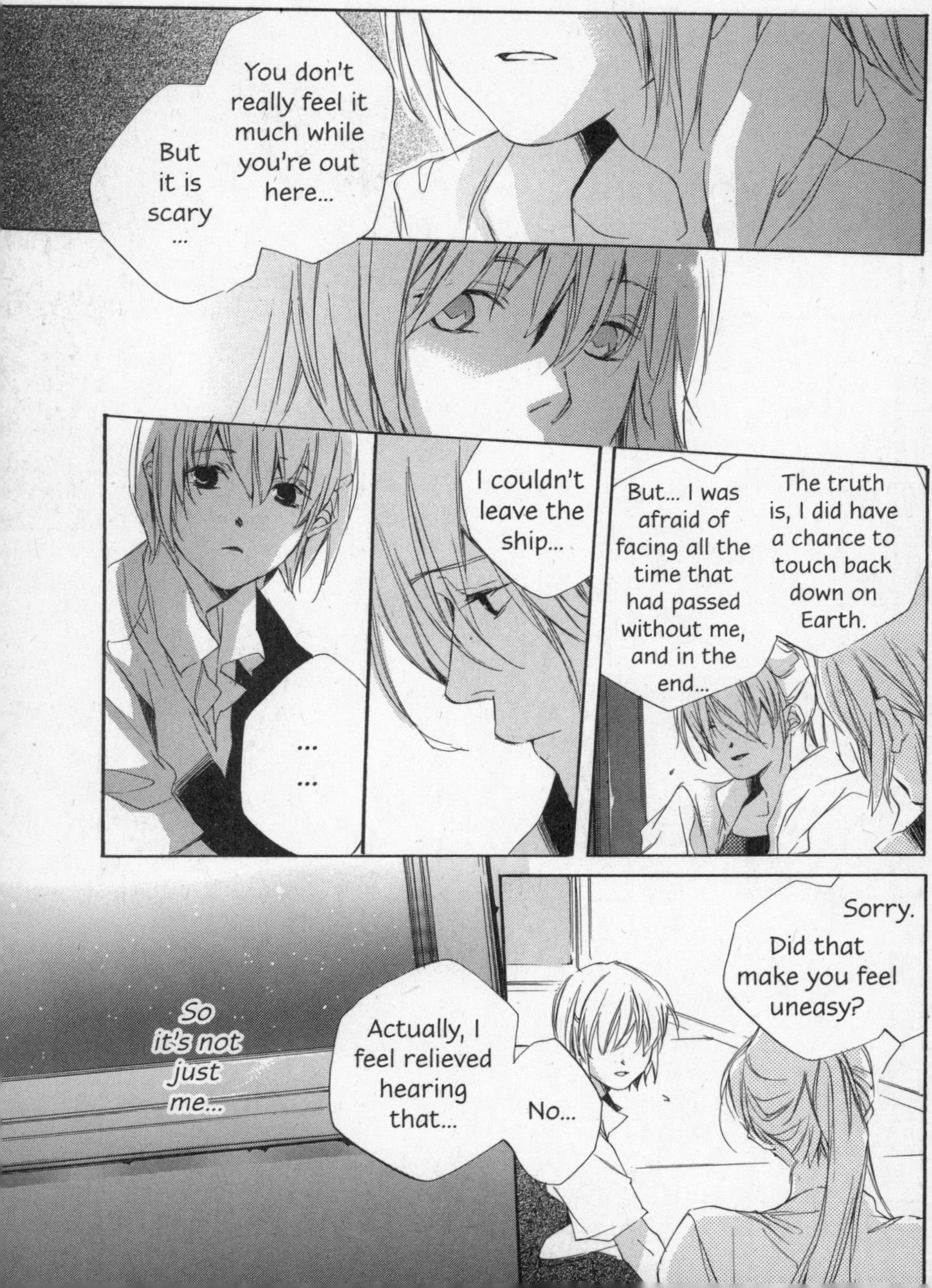
You don't really feel it much while you're out here...
But it is scary...
The truth is, I did have a chance to touch back down on Earth.
But... I was afraid of facing all the time that had passed without me, and in the end...
I couldn't leave the ship...
... ...
Sorry.
Did that make you feel uneasy?
No...
Actually, I feel relieved hearing that...
So it's not just me...

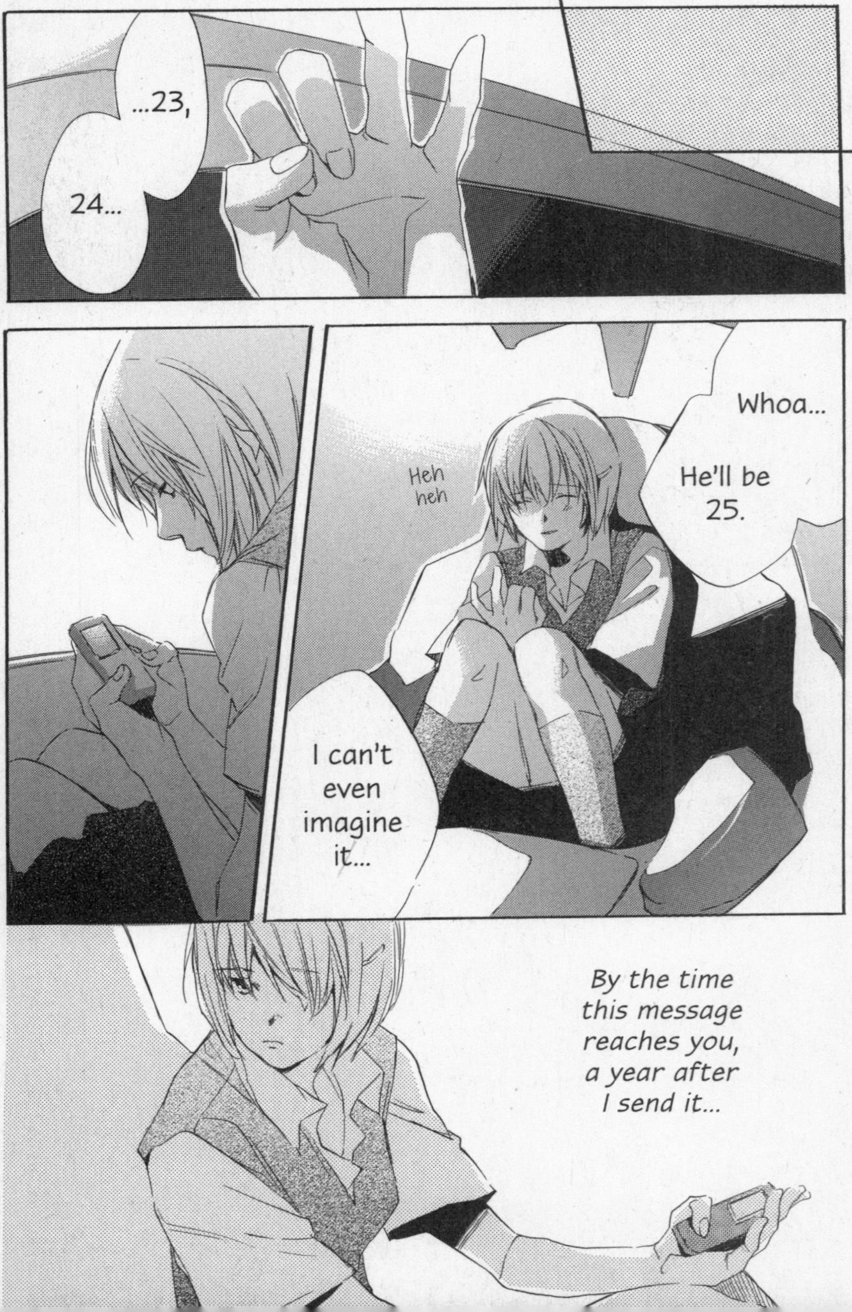
...23,
24...
Whoa...
He'll be 25.
Heh heh
I can't even imagine it...
By the time this message reaches you, a year after I send it...

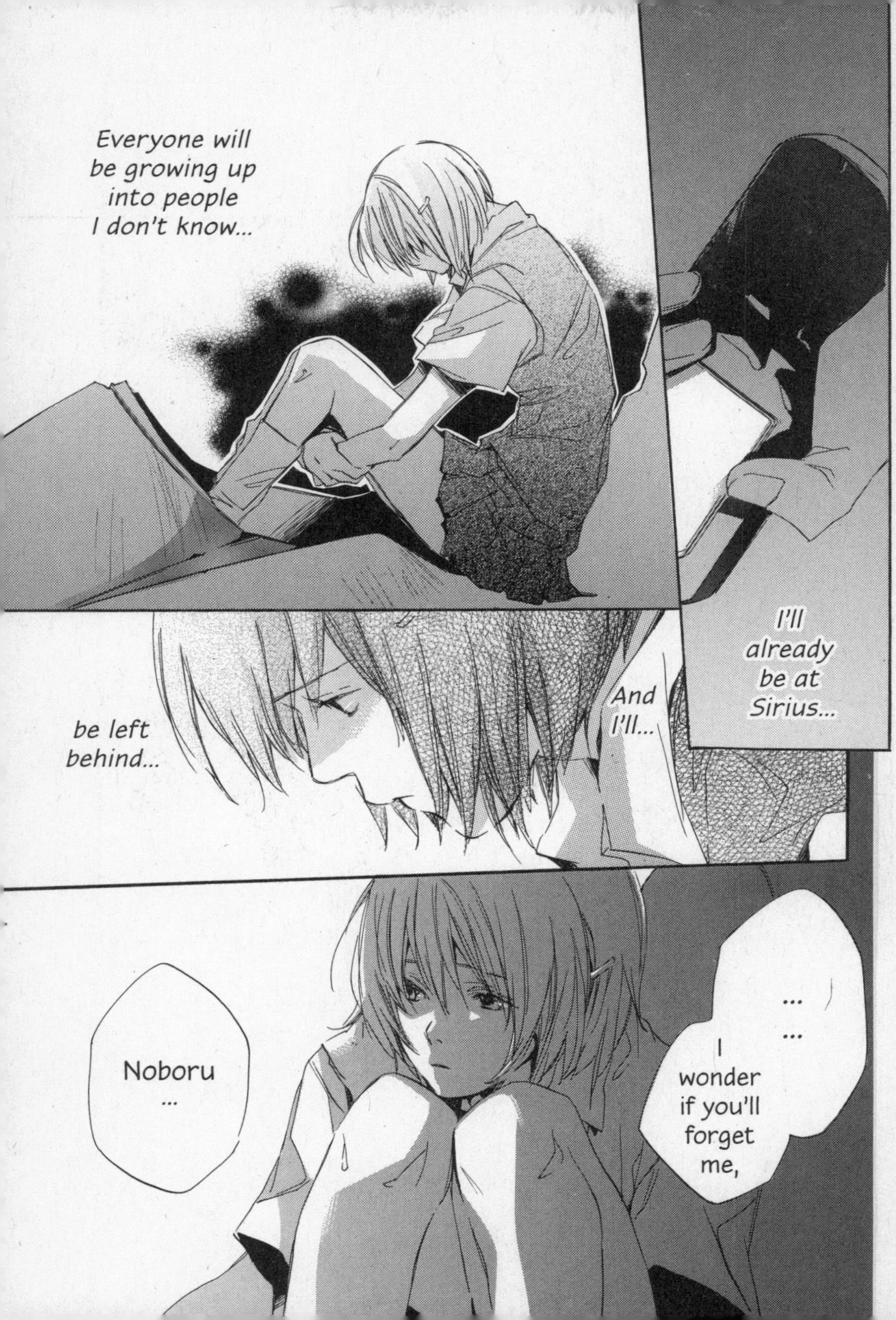
I'll already be at Sirius...
Everyone will be growing up into people I don't know...
And I'll...
be left behind...
... ... I wonder if you'll forget me,
Noboru ...

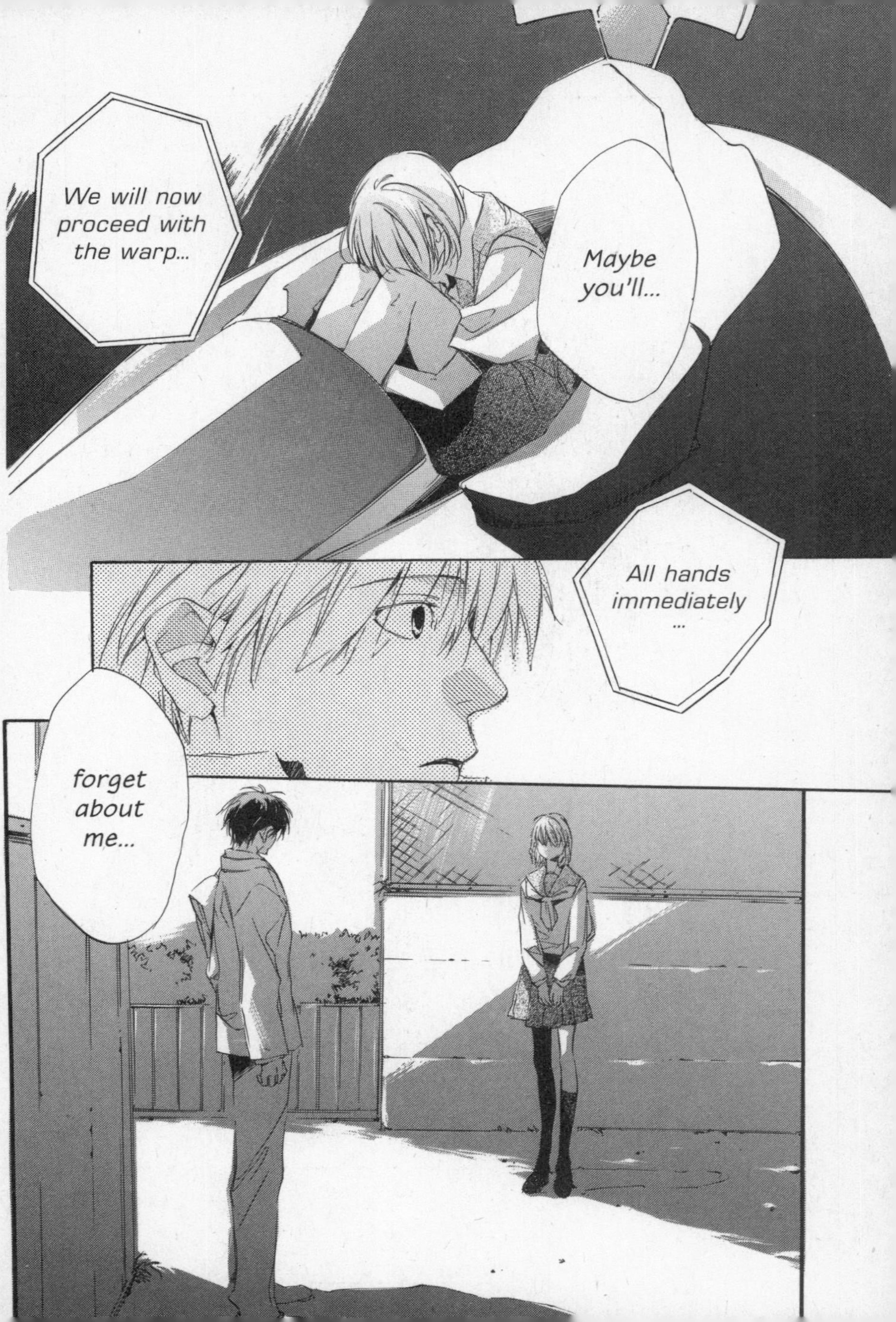

Maybe you'll...
We will now proceed with the warp...
All hands immediately ...
forget about me...

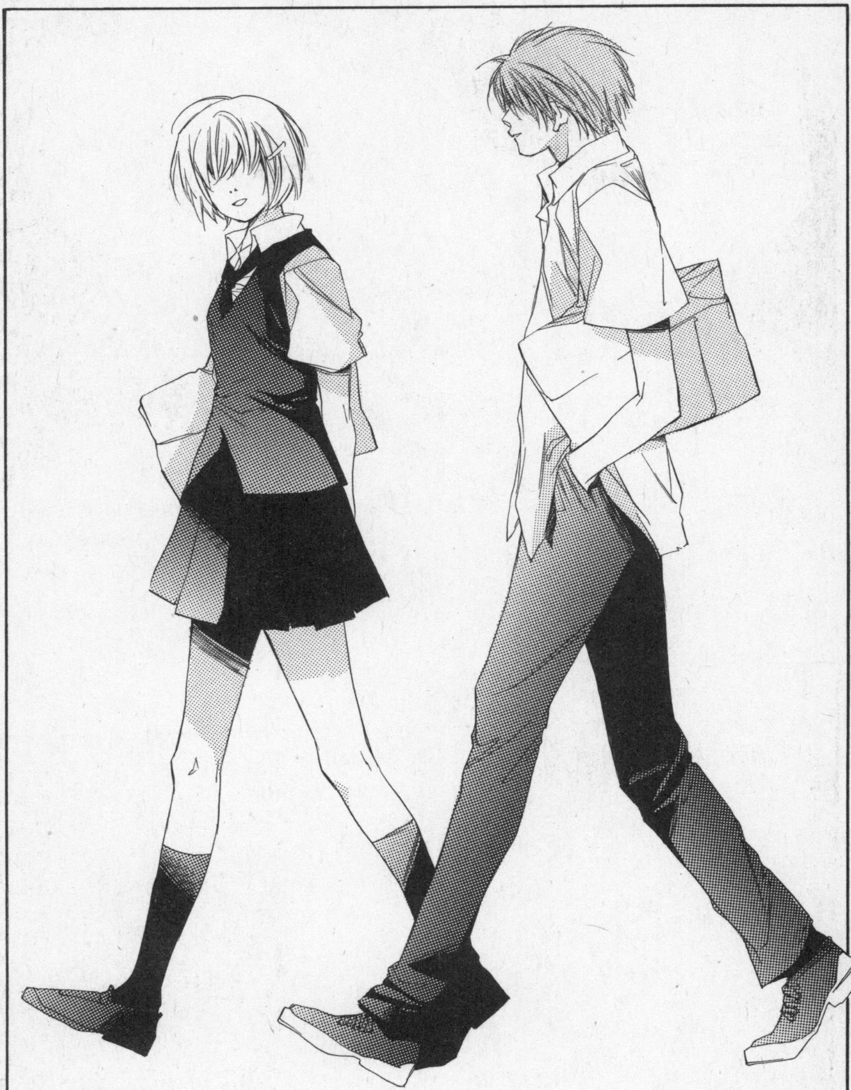

Voices of a Distant Star

Chapter 7

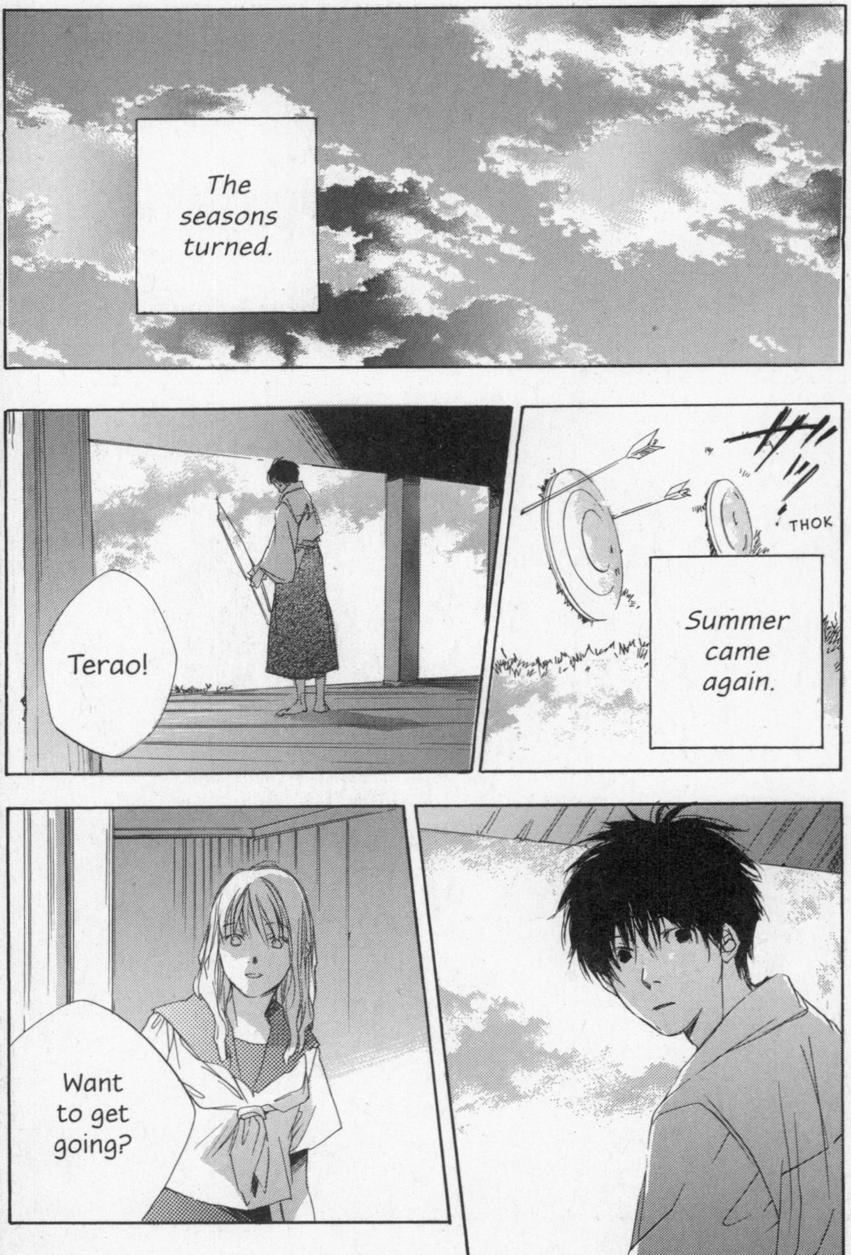
The seasons turned.
THOK
Summer came again.
Terao!
Want to get going?

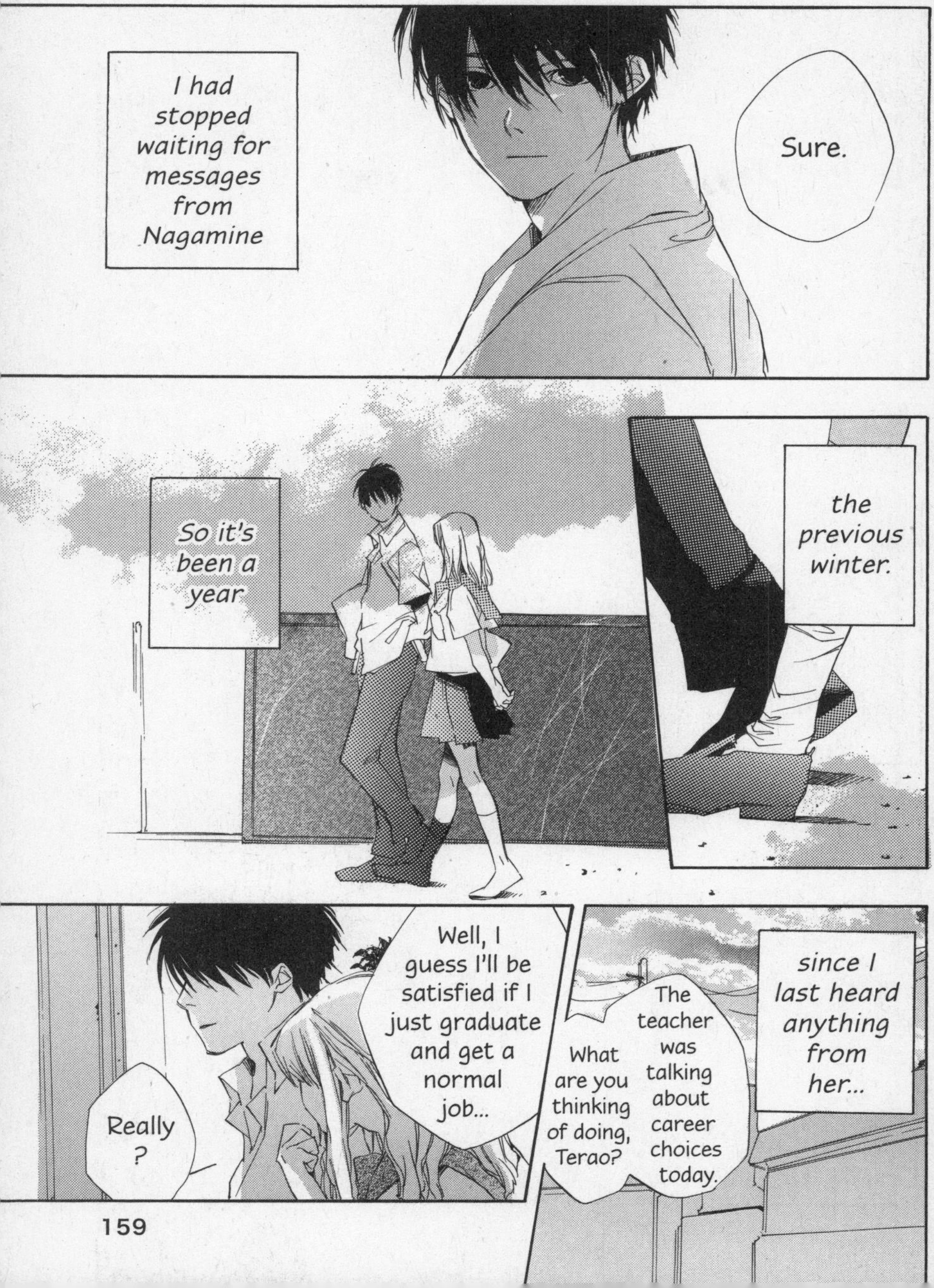
Sure.
I had stopped waiting for messages from Nagamine
the previous winter.
So it's been a year
since I last heard anything from her...
The teacher was talking about career choices today.
What are you thinking of doing, Terao?
Well, I guess I'll be satisfied if I just graduate and get a normal job...
Really ?

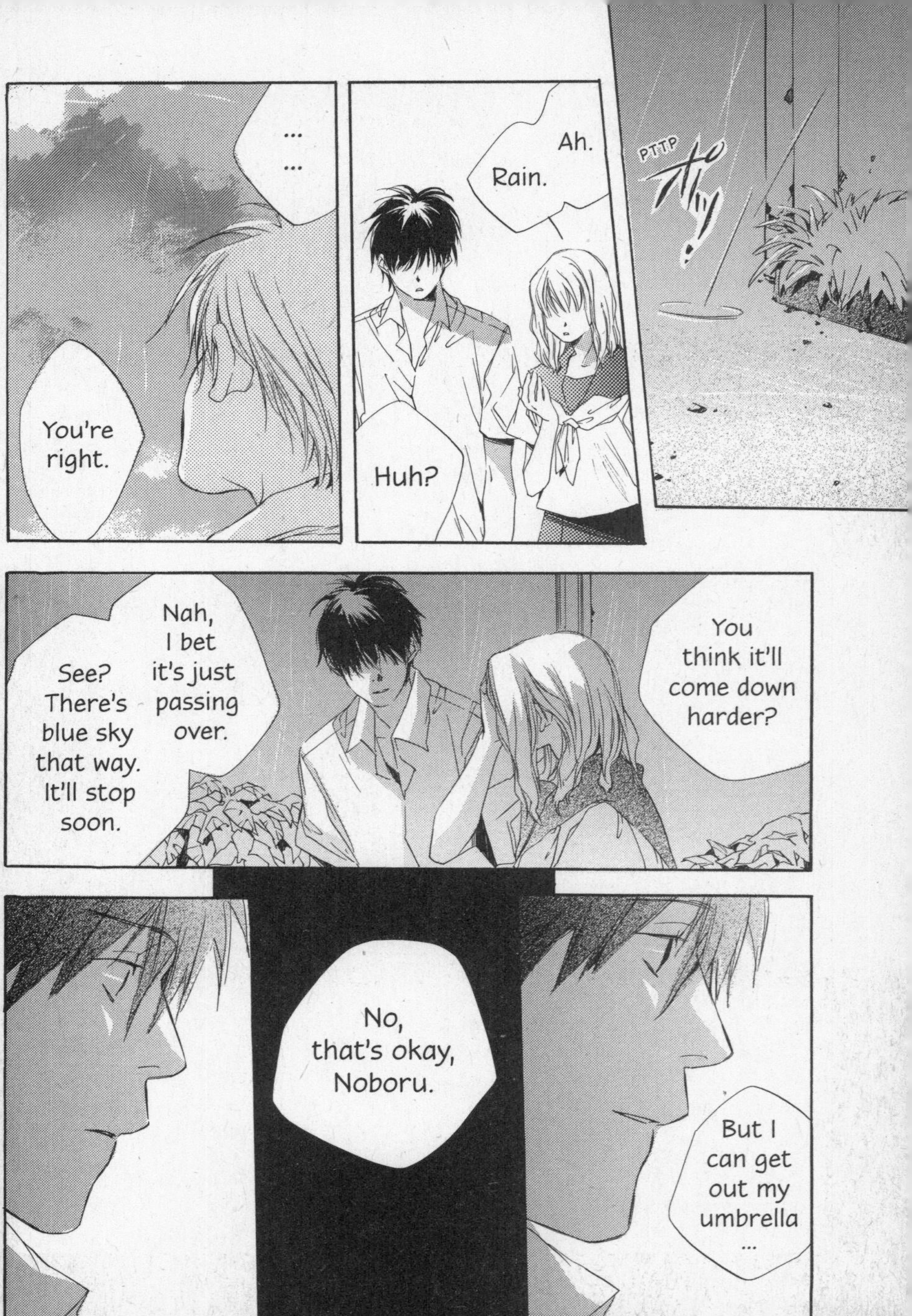
PTTP
Ah.
Rain.
Huh?
...
...
You're right.
You think it'll come down harder?
Nah, I bet it's just passing over.
See? There's blue sky that way. It'll stop soon.
But I can get out my umbrella ...
No, that's okay, Noboru.

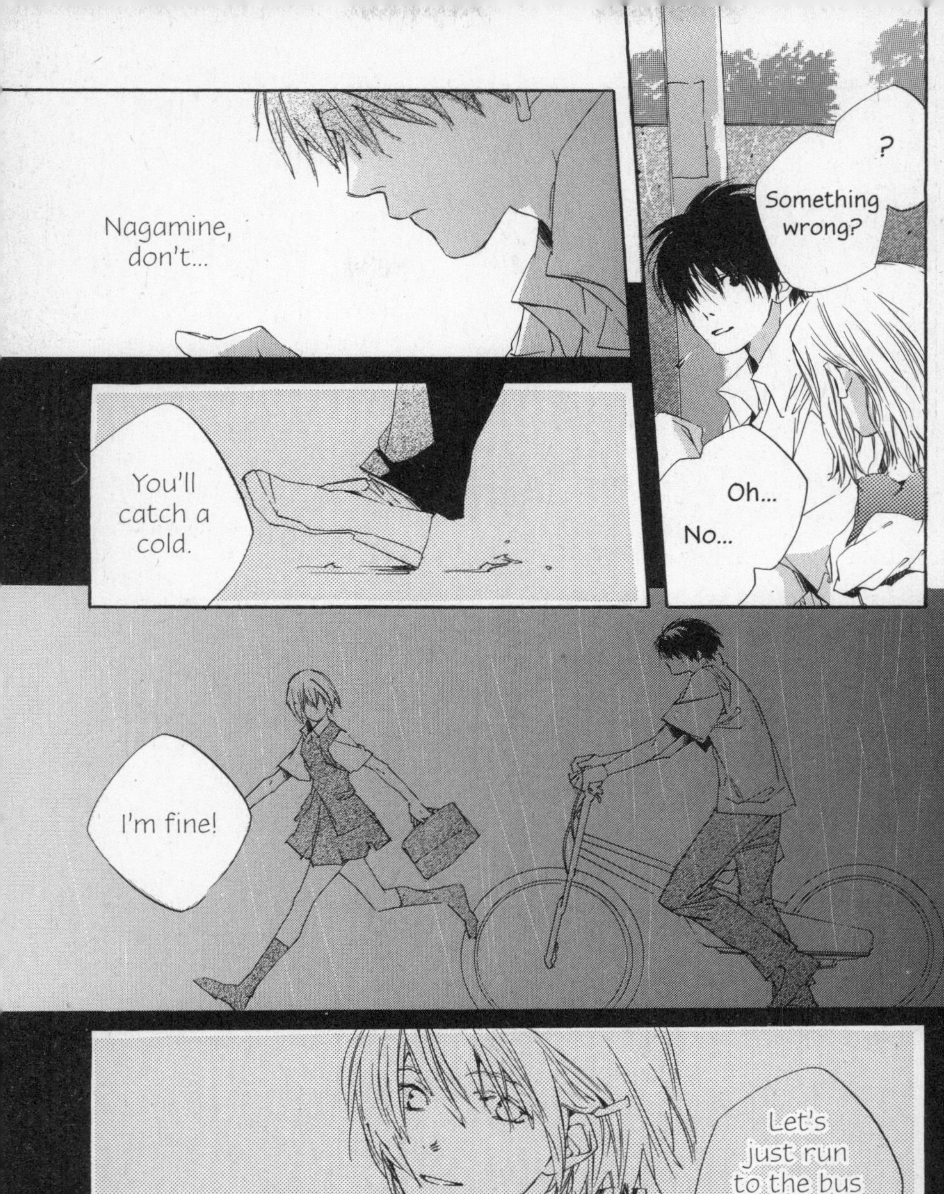
?
Something wrong?
Oh...
No...
Nagamine, don't...
You'll catch a cold.
I'm fine!
Let's just run to the bus stop.

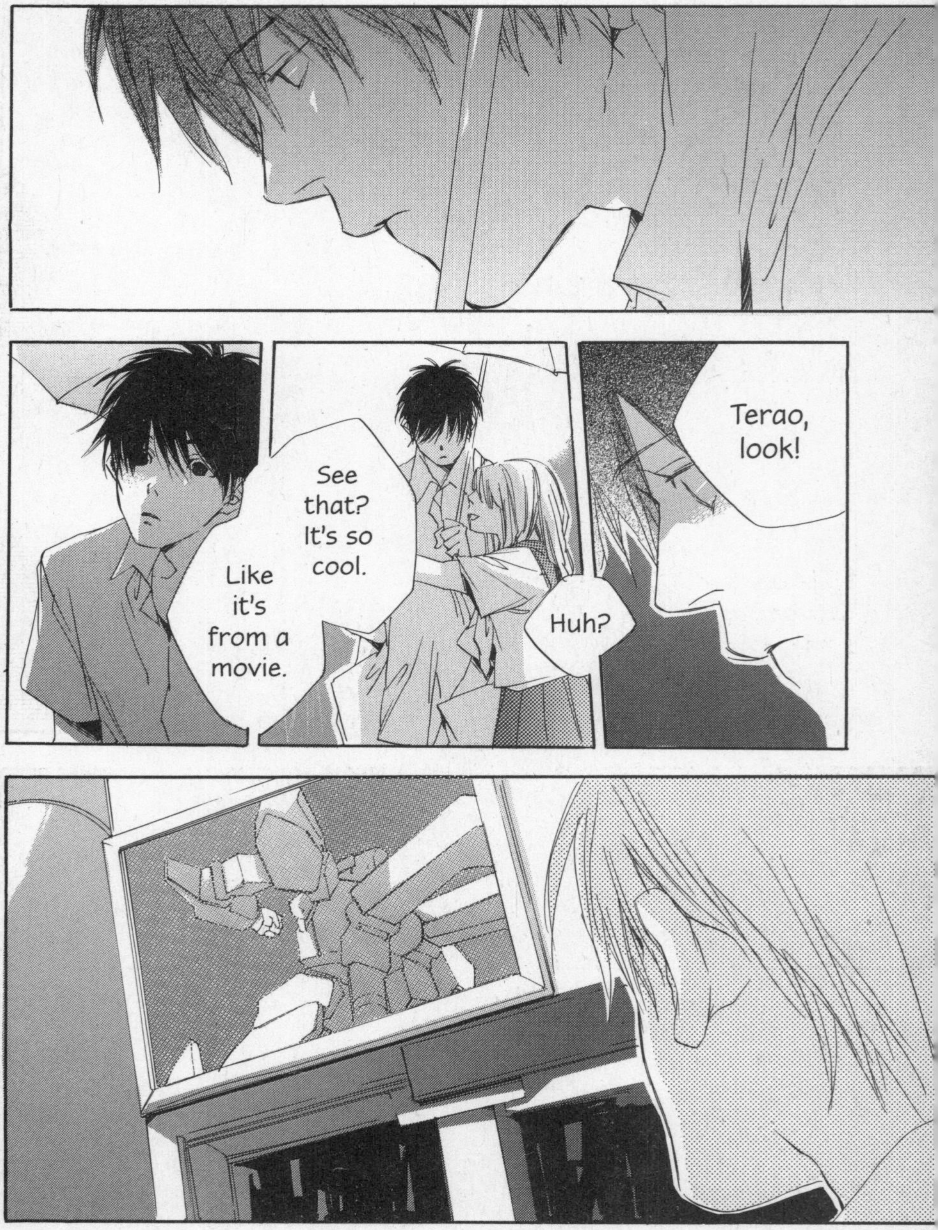
Terao, look!
Huh?
See that? It's so cool.
Like it's from a movie.

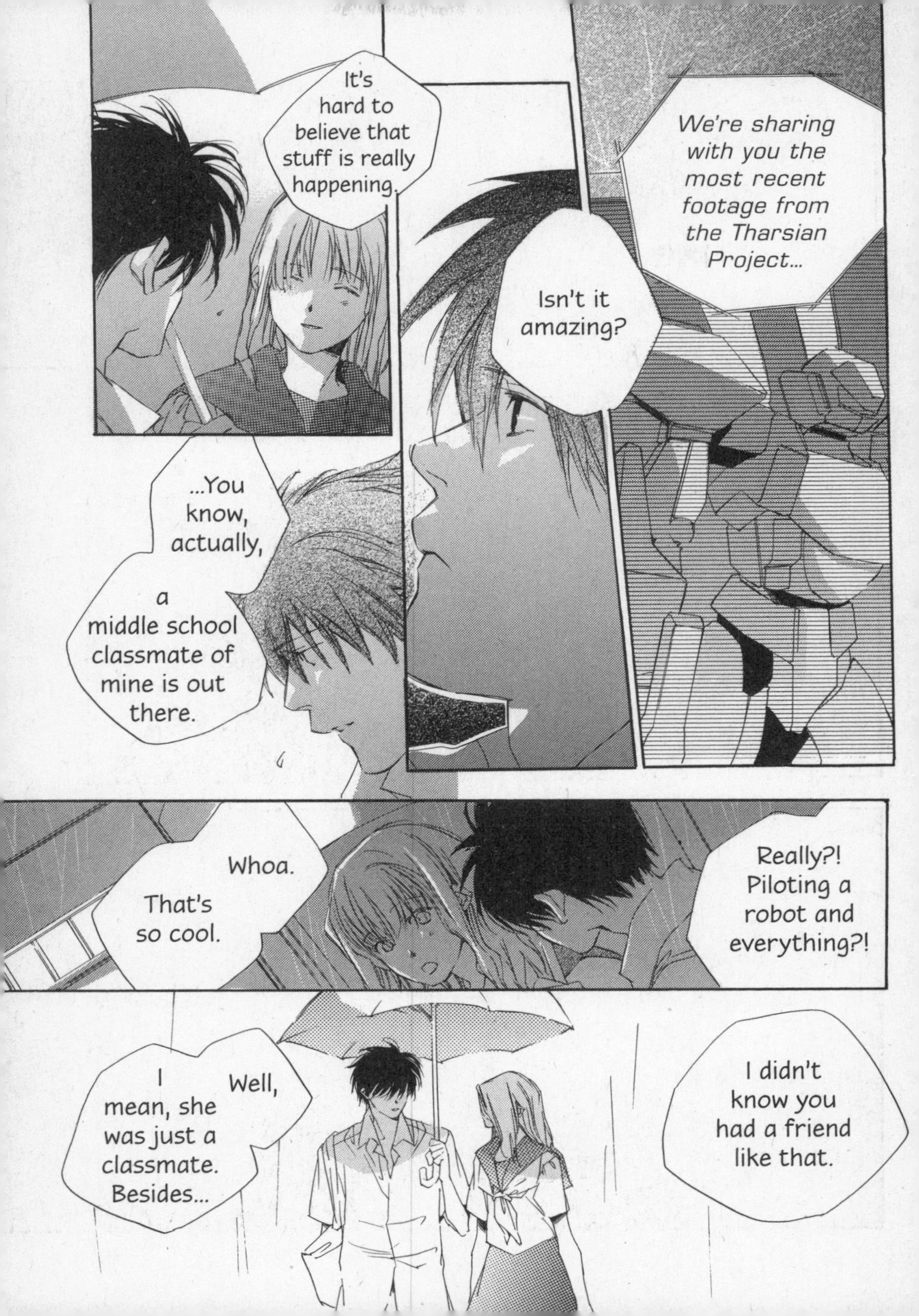
We're sharing with you the most recent footage from the Tharsian Project...
Isn't it amazing?
It's hard to believe that stuff is really happening.
...You know, actually,
a middle school classmate of mine is out there.
Really?! Piloting a robot and everything?!
Whoa.
That's so cool.
I didn't know you had a friend like that.
Well,
I mean, she was just a classmate. Besides...

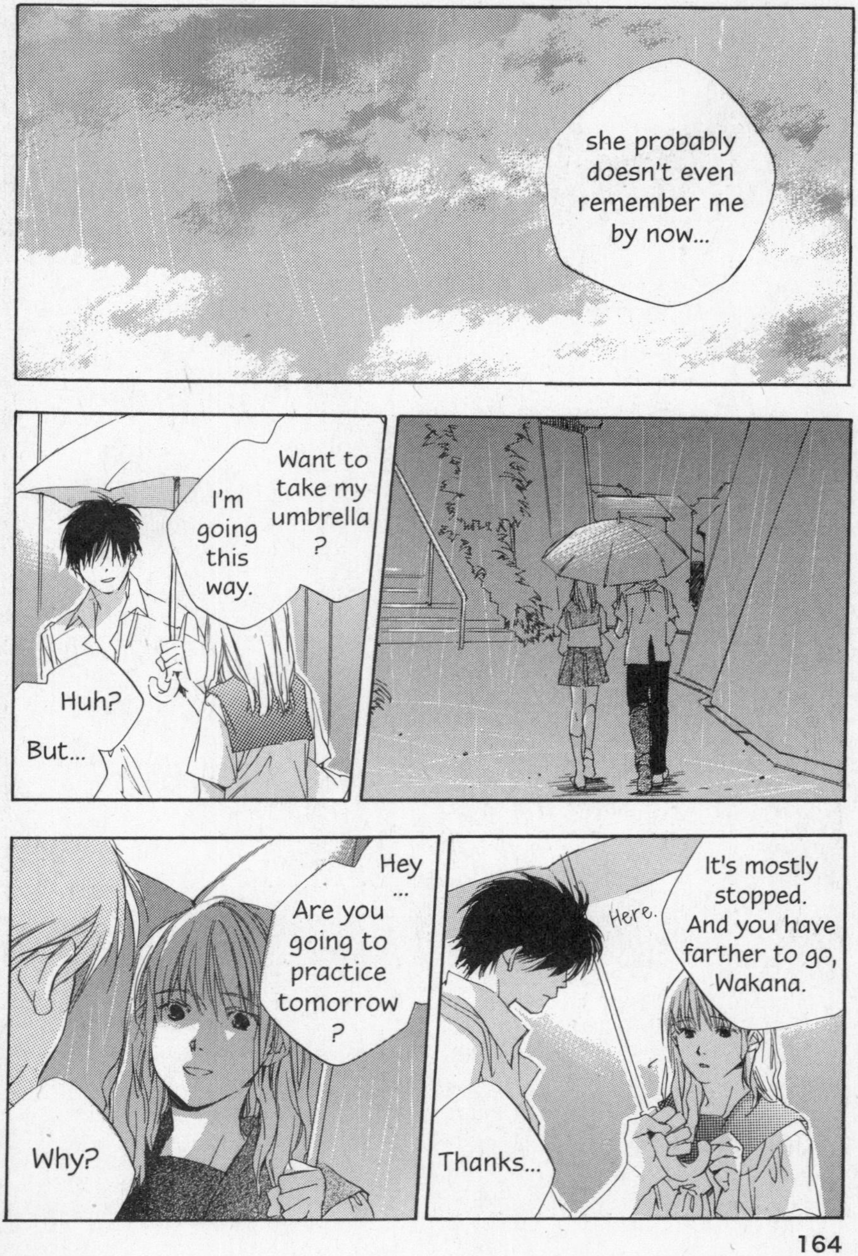
she probably doesn't even remember me by now...
Want to take my umbrella?
I'm going this way.
Huh?
But...
It's mostly stopped. And you have farther to go, Wakana.
Here.
Thanks...
Hey ...
Are you going to practice tomorrow?
Why?

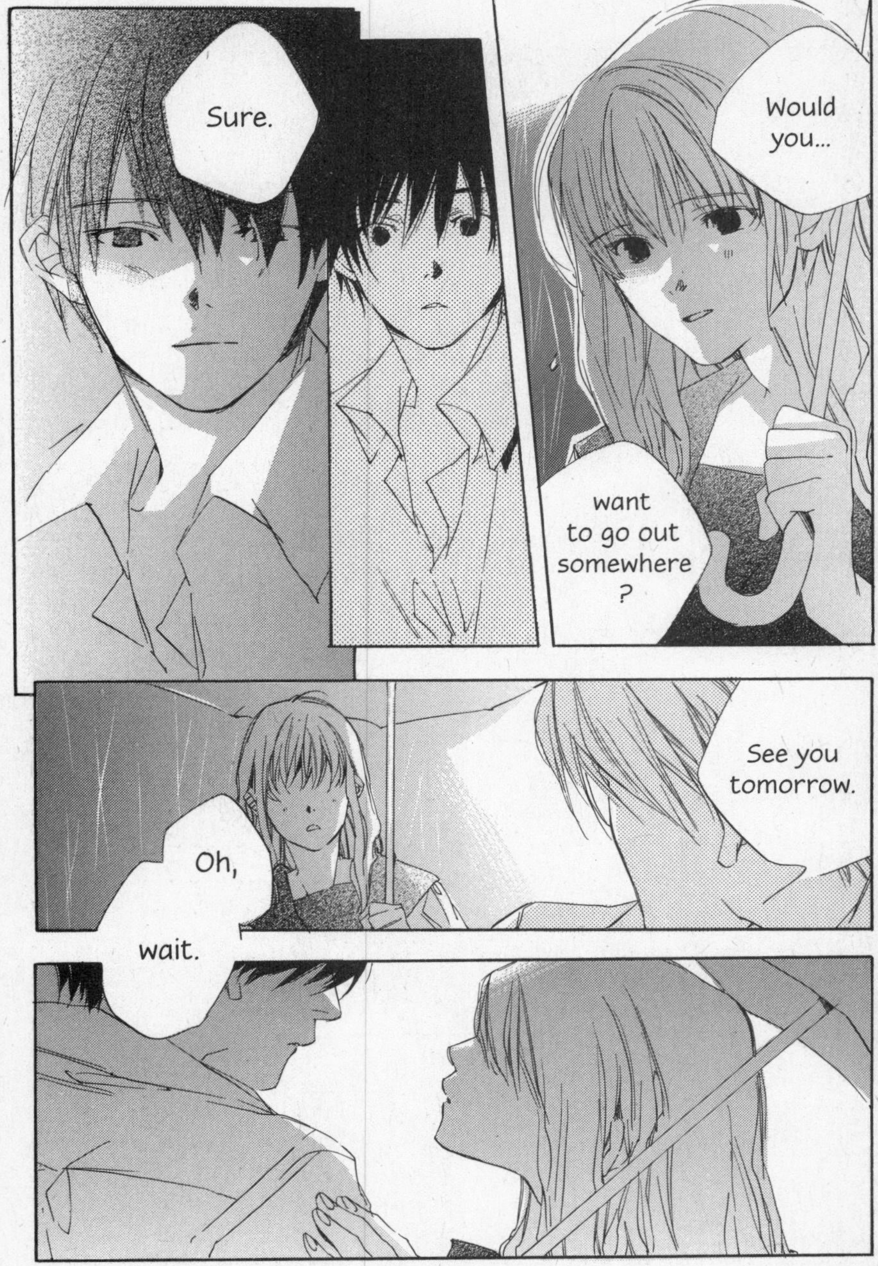
Would you...
want to go out somewhere?
Sure.
See you tomorrow.
Oh,
wait.

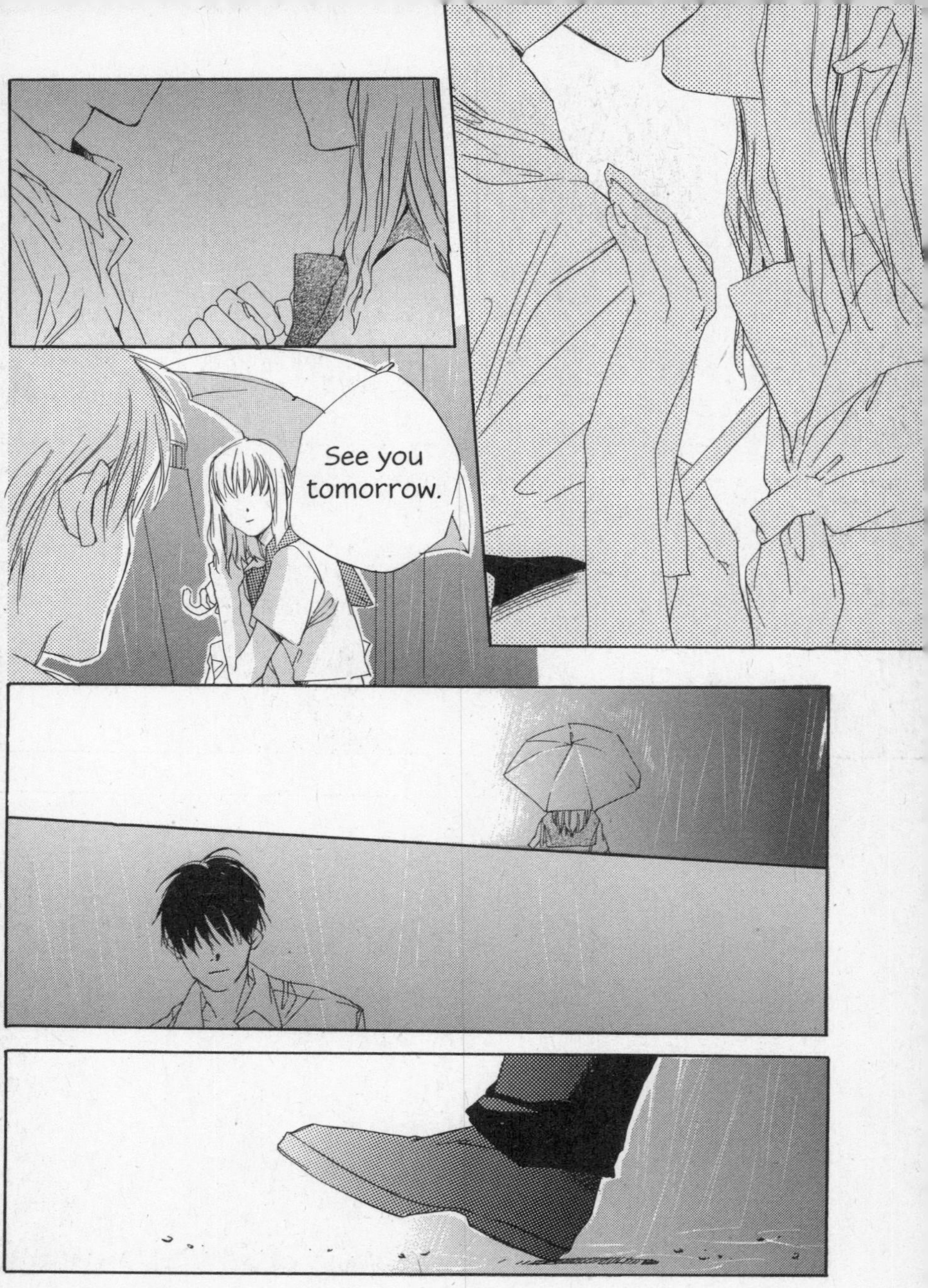
See you tomorrow.

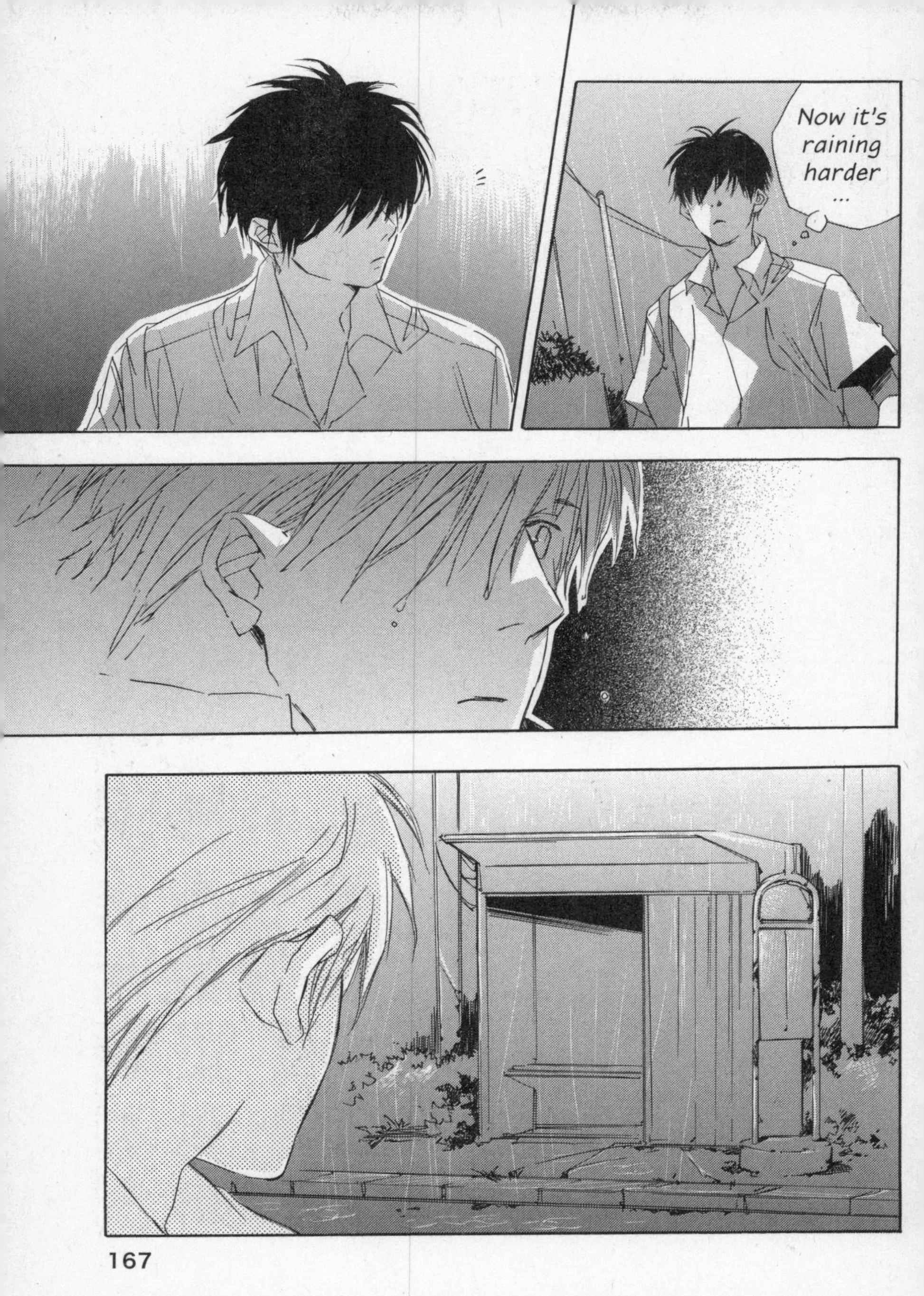
Now it's raining harder ...

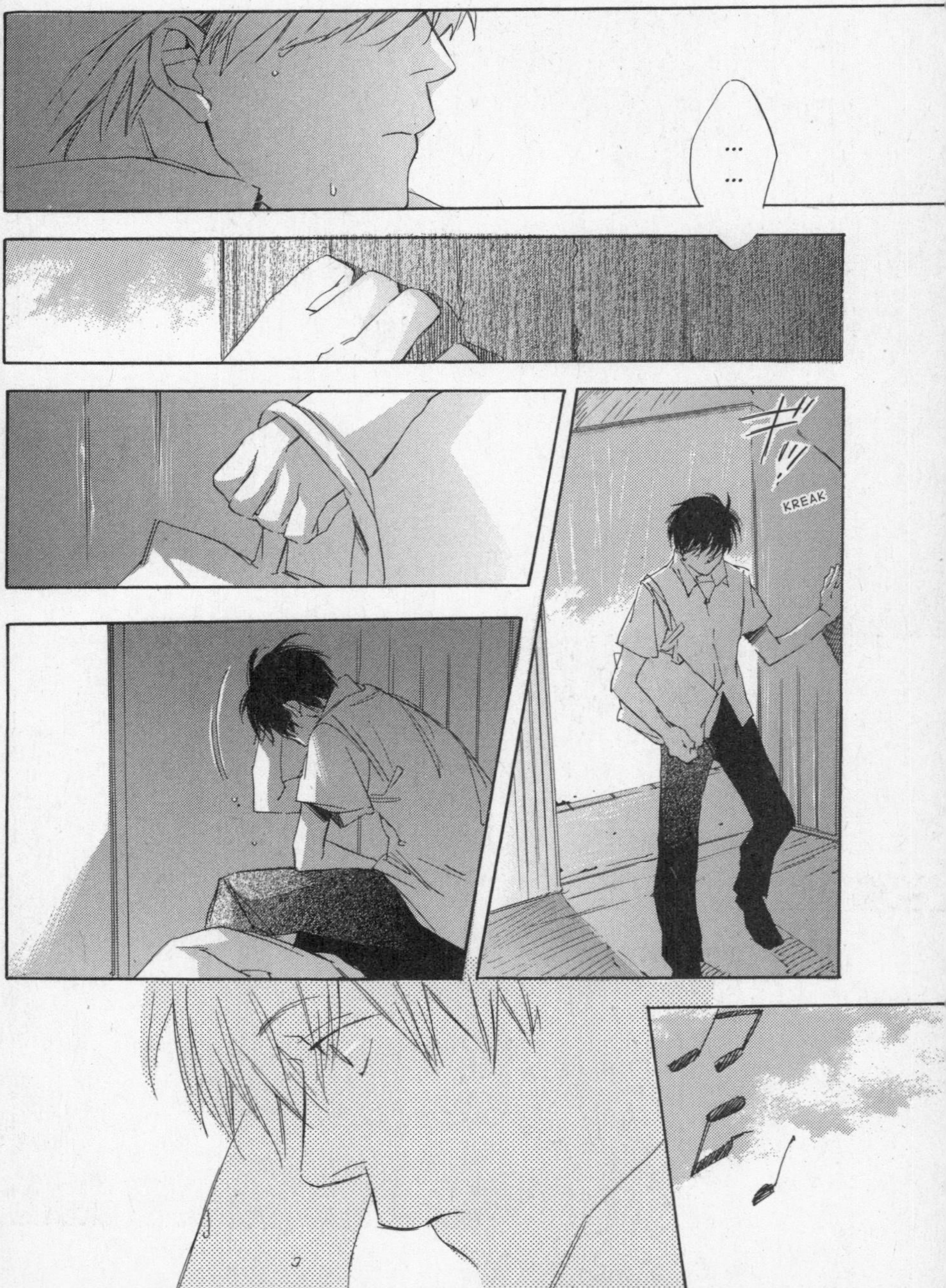
...
...
KREAK

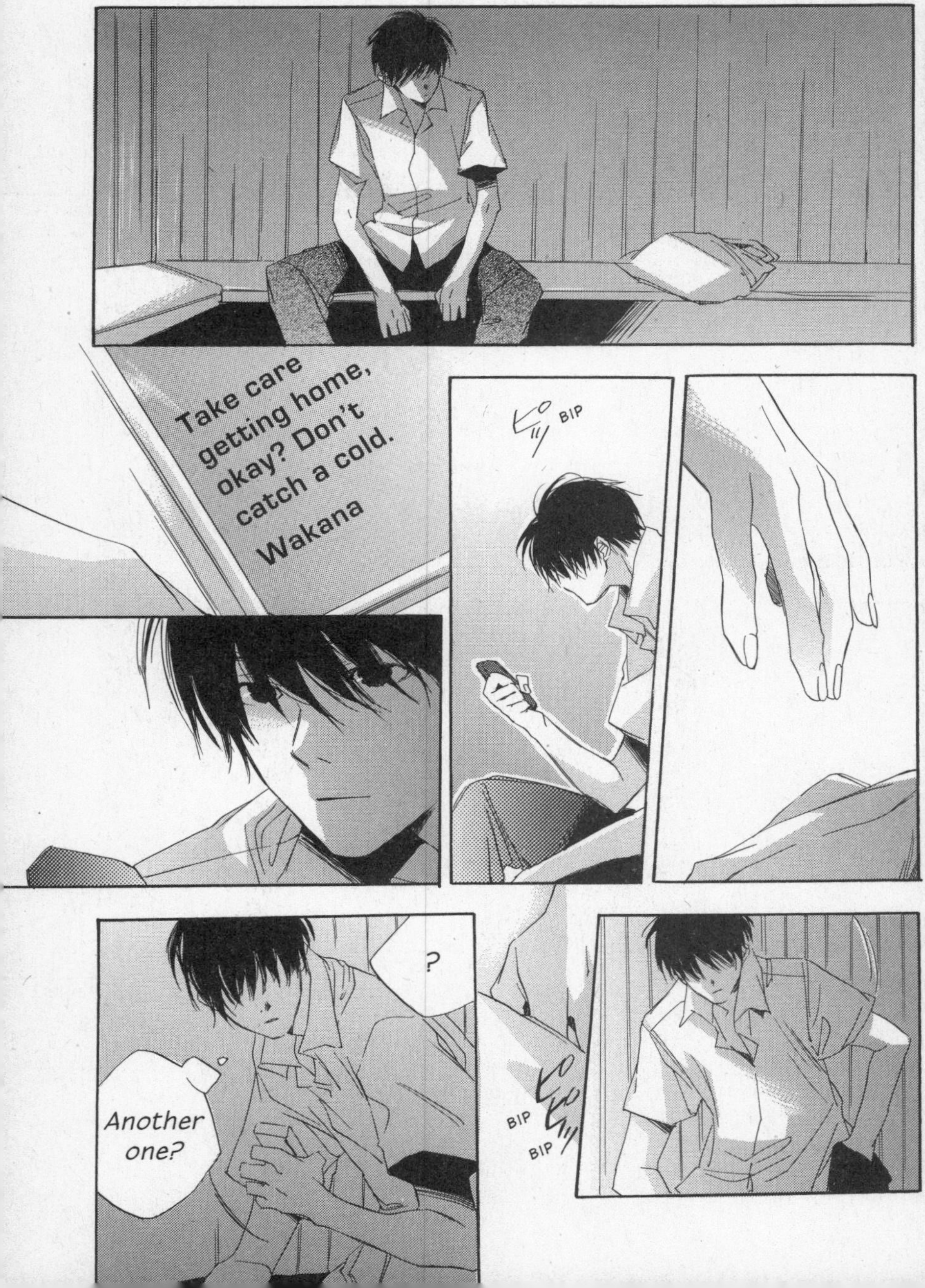
BIP
Take care getting home, okay? Don't catch a cold.
Wakana
BIP
BIP
?
Another one?

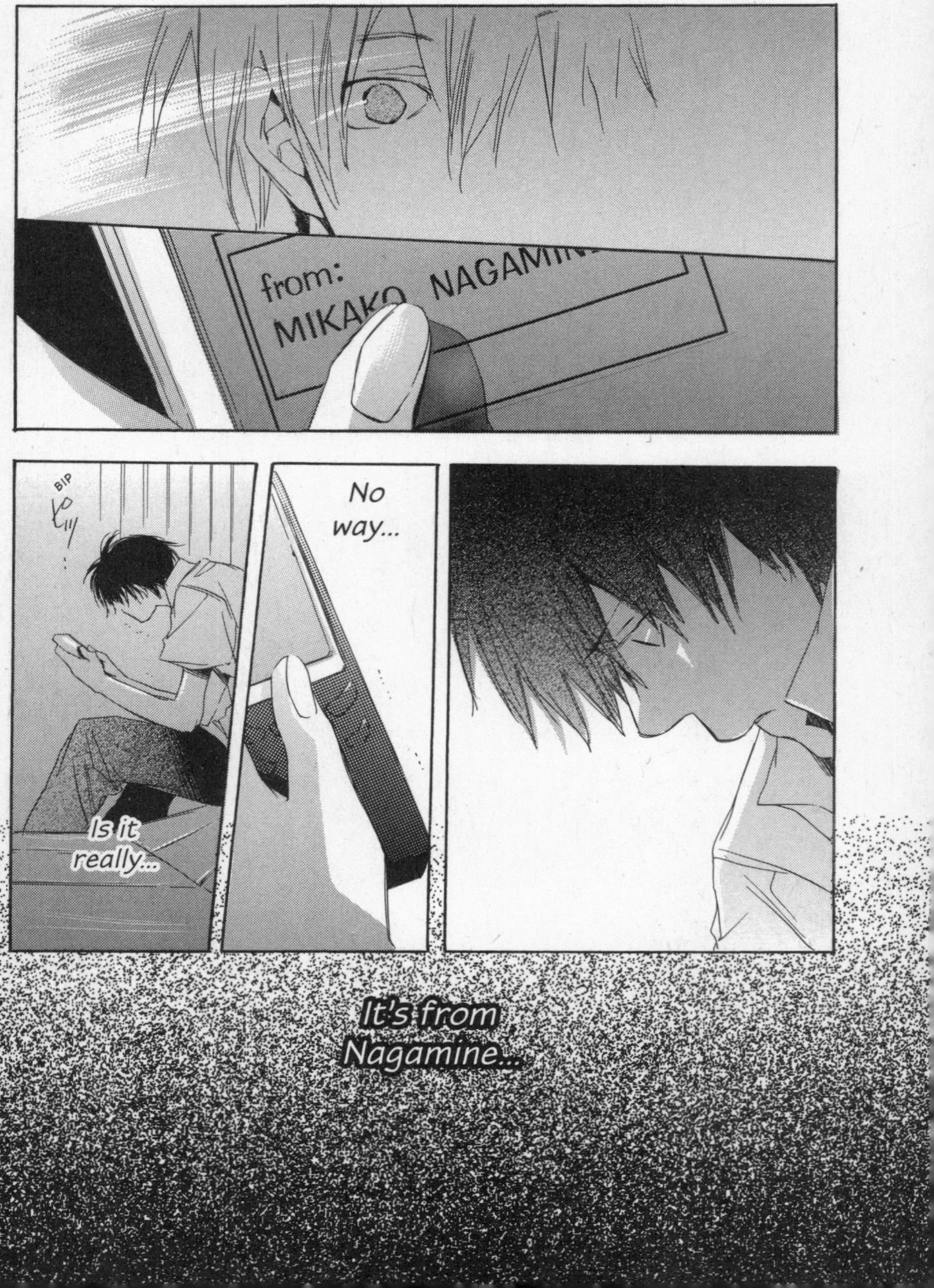
from:
MIKAKO NAGAMIN
No way...
BIP
Is it really...
It's from Nagamine...

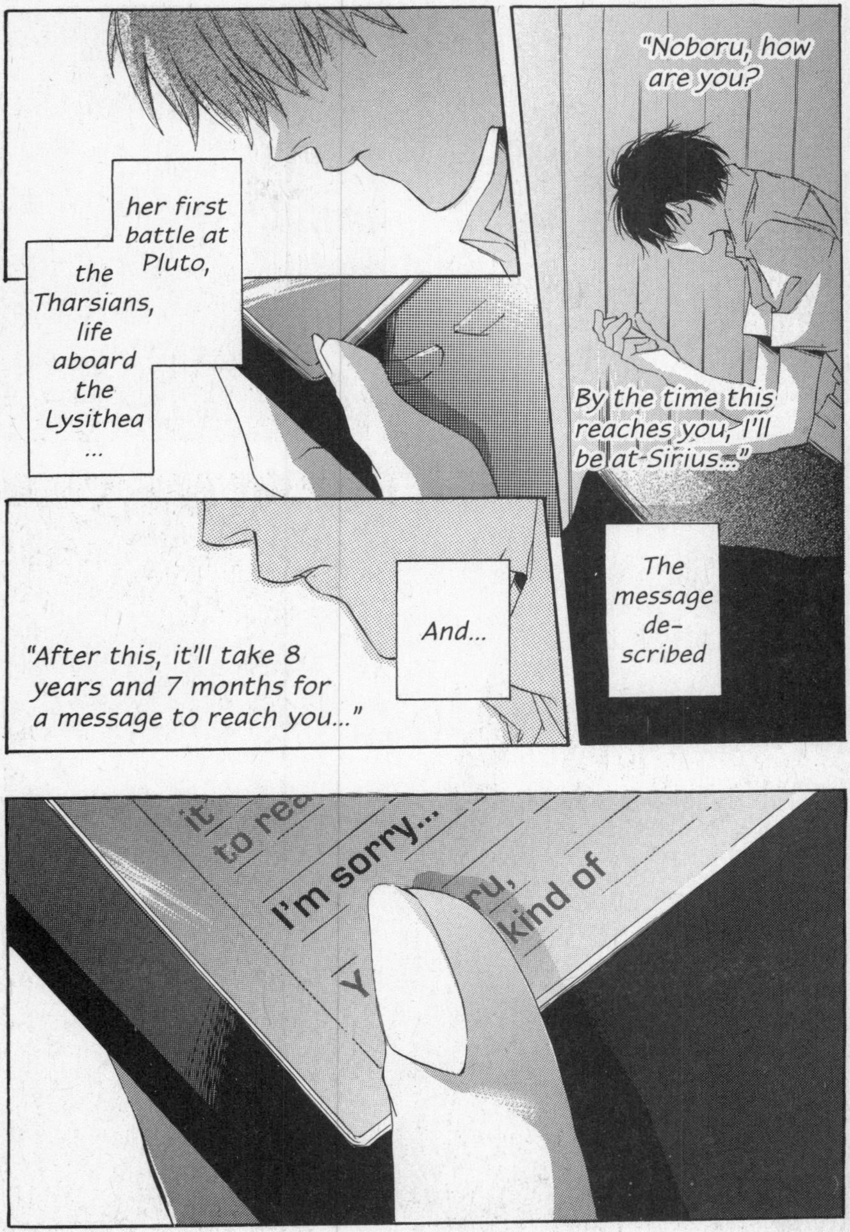
"Noboru, how are you?
By the time this reaches you, I'll be at Sirius..."
The message de-scribed
her first battle at Pluto,
the Tharsians, life aboard the Lysithea ...
And...
"After this, it'll take 8 years and 7 months for a message to reach you..."
I'm sorry...
kind of

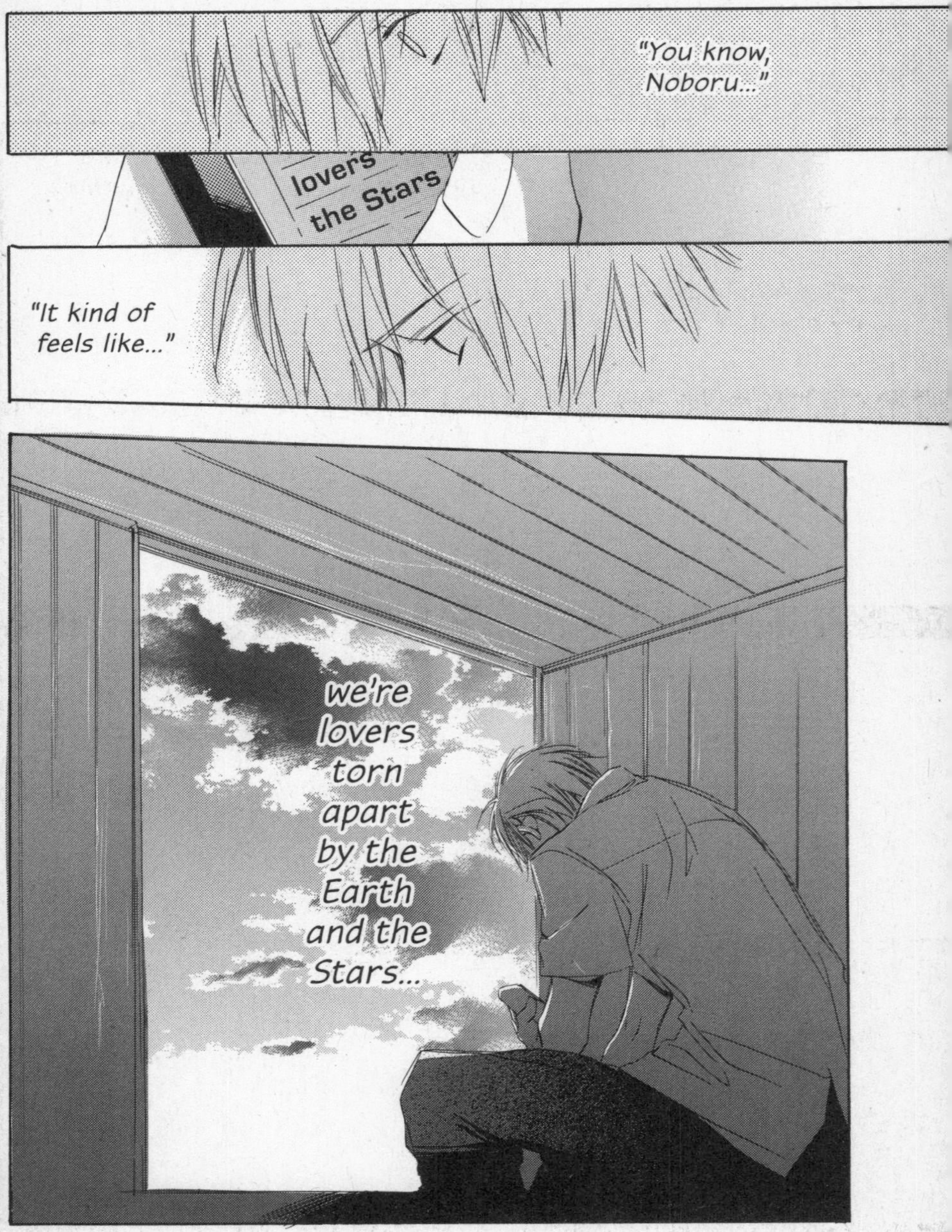
"You know, Noboru..."
lovers
the Stars
"It kind of feels like..."
we're lovers torn apart by the Earth and the Stars...

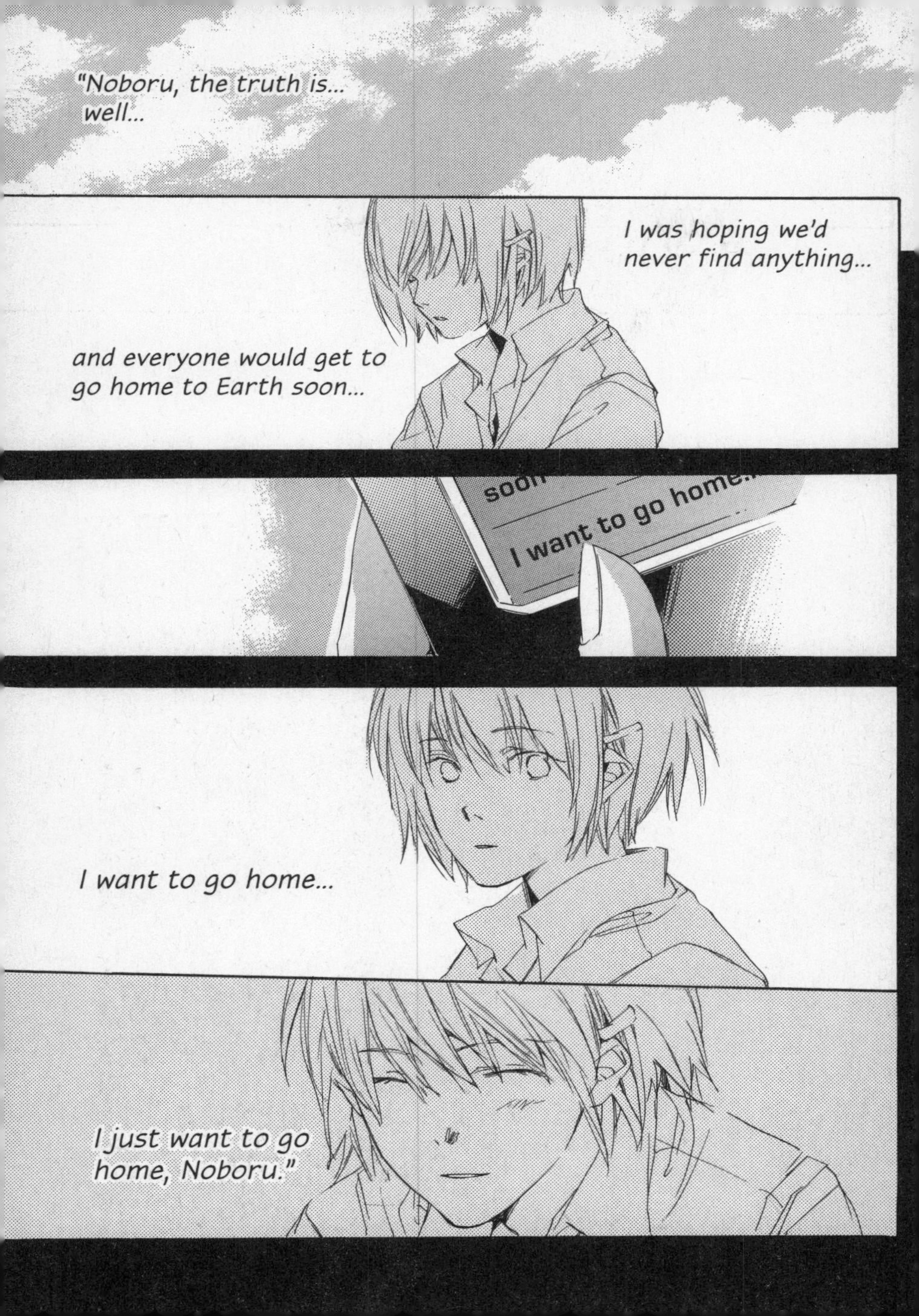
"Noboru, the truth is... well...
I was hoping we'd never find anything...
and everyone would get to go home to Earth soon...
soon
I want to go home...
I want to go home...
I just want to go home, Noboru."

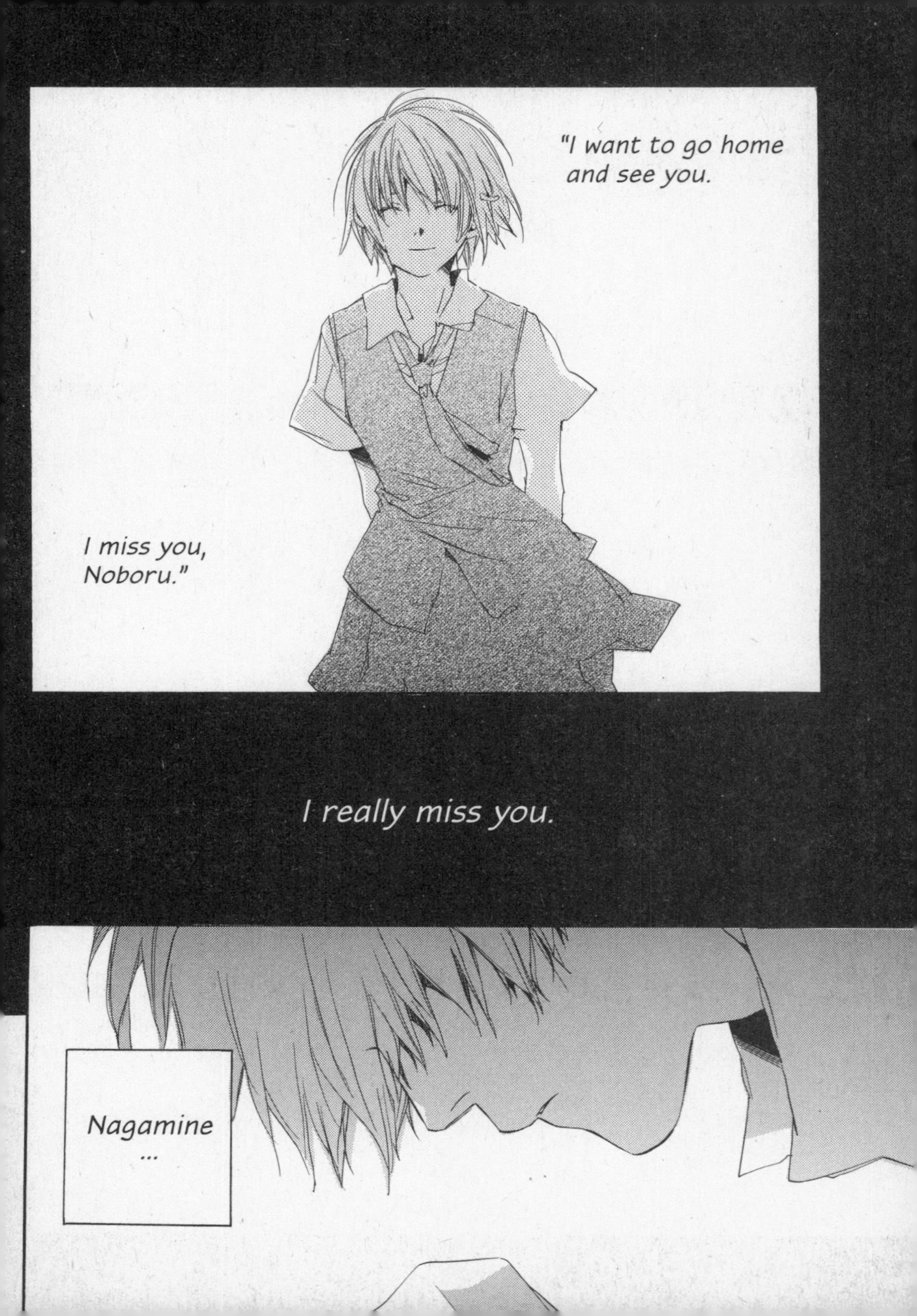
"I want to go home and see you.
I miss you, Noboru."
I really miss you.
Nagamine ...

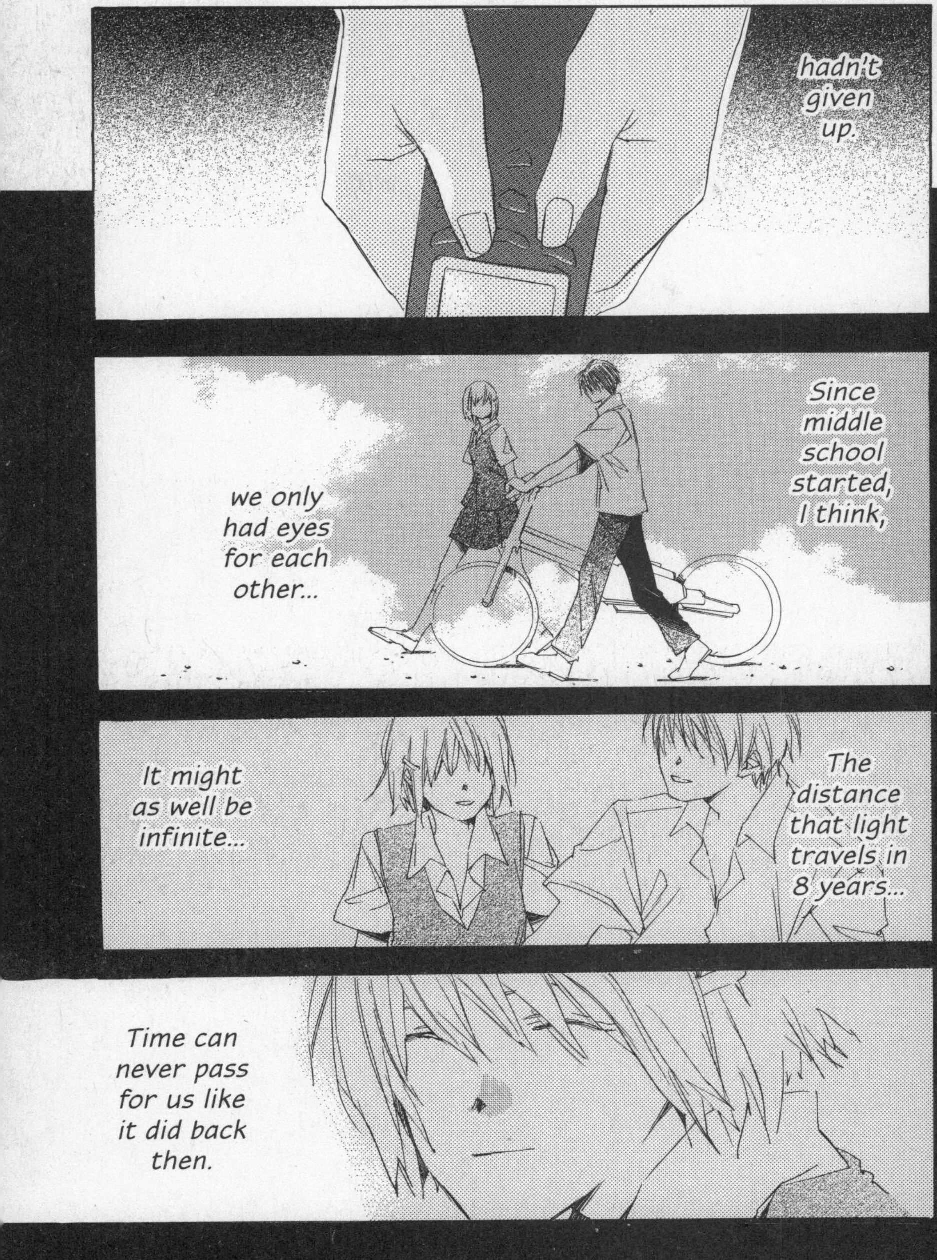
hadn't given up.
Since middle school started, I think,
we only had eyes for each other...
The distance that light travels in 8 years...
It might as well be infinite...
Time can never pass for us like it did back then.

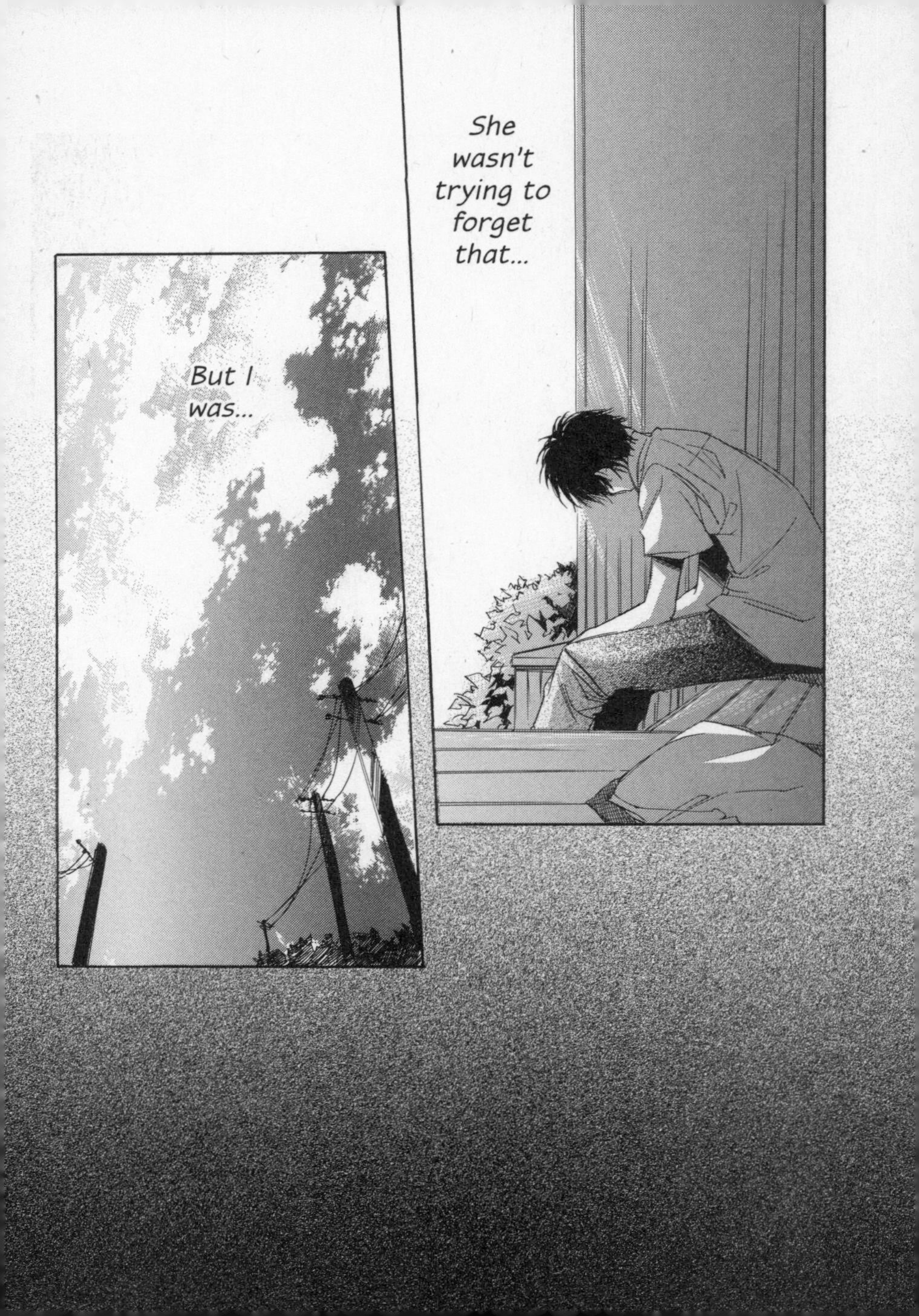
She wasn't trying to forget that...
But I was...

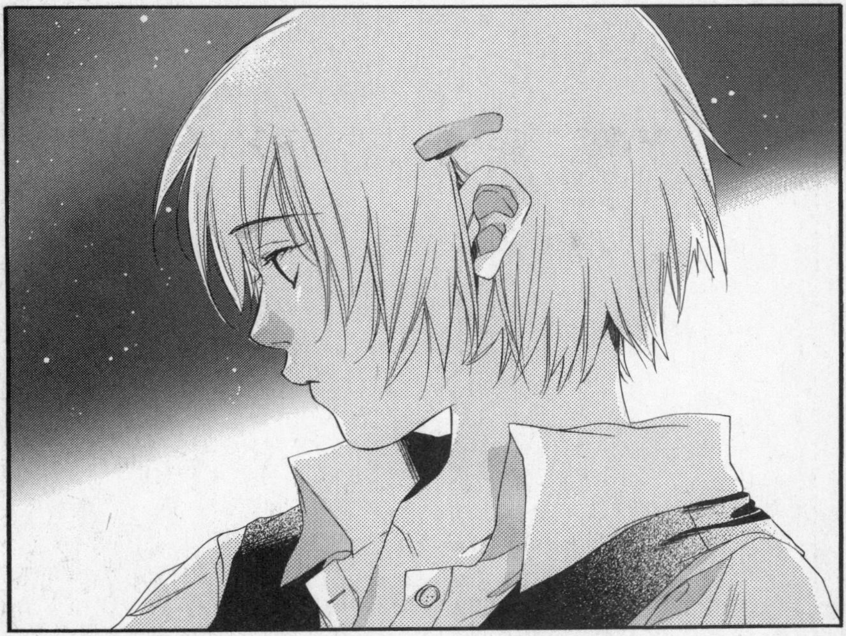

Voices of a Distant Star

Chapter 8

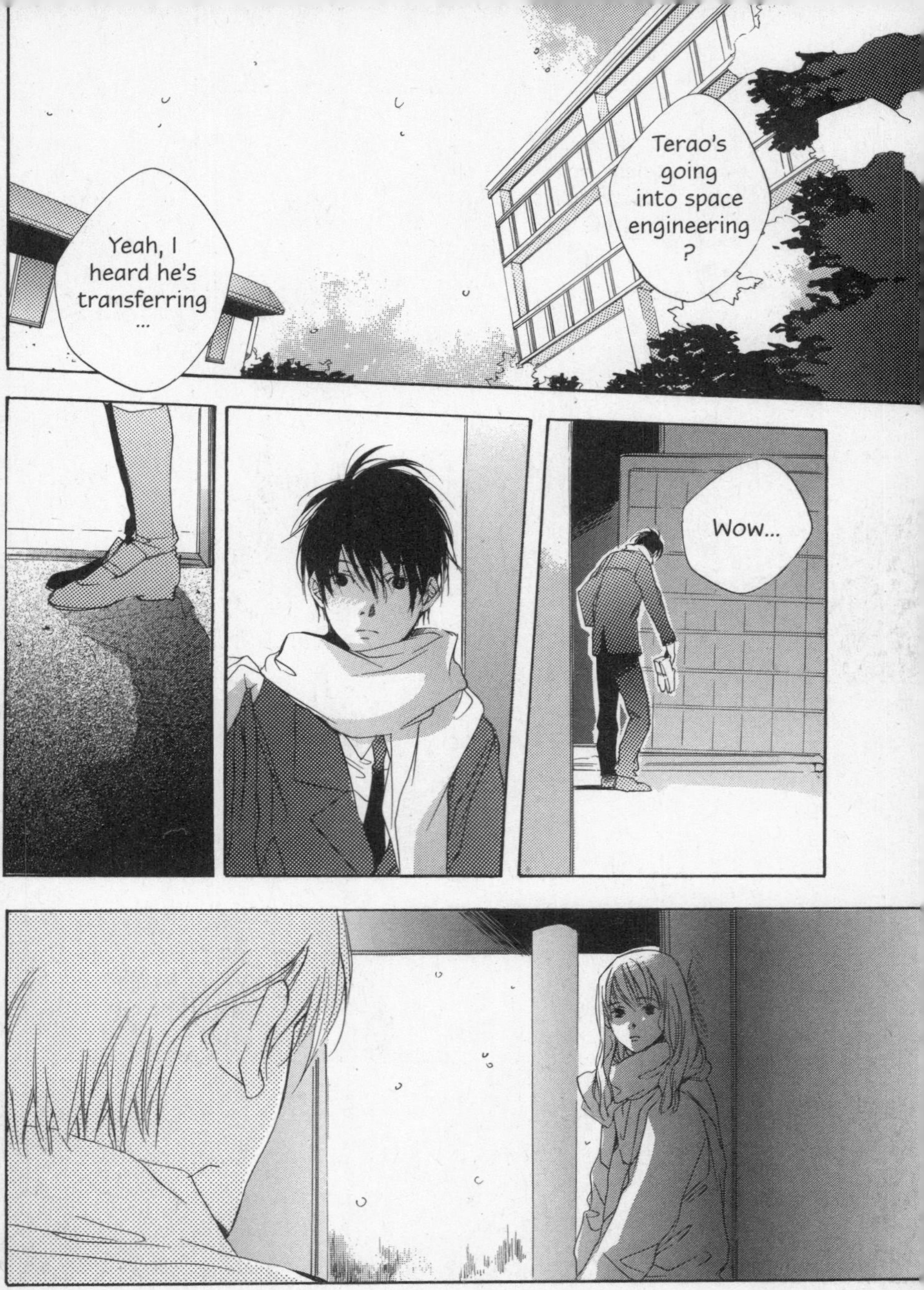
Terao's going into space engineering ?
Yeah, I heard he's transferring ...
Wow...

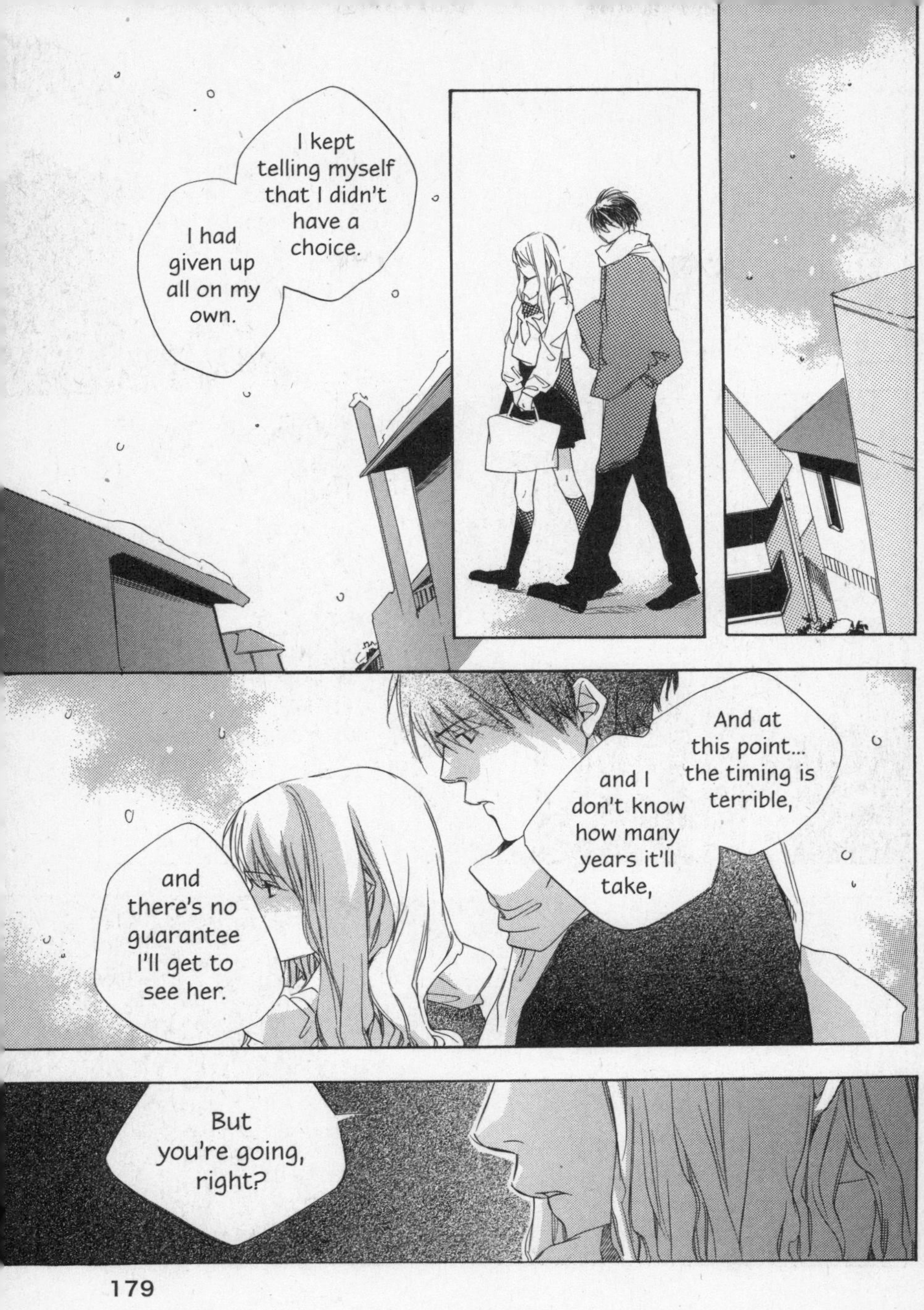
I kept telling myself that I didn't have a choice.
I had given up all on my own.
And at this point... the timing is terrible,
and I don't know how many years it'll take,
and there's no guarantee I'll get to see her.
But you're going, right?

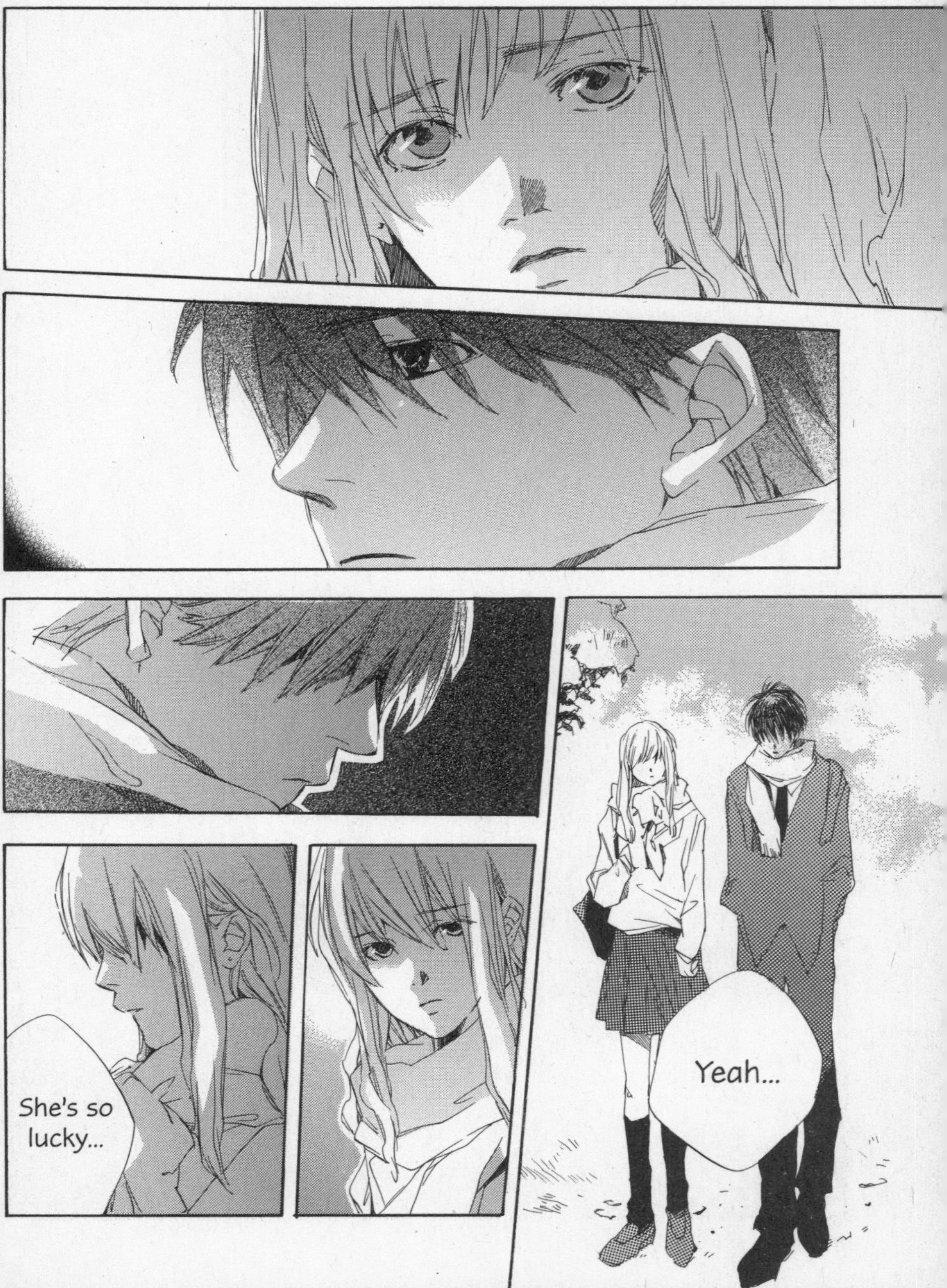
Yeah...
She's so lucky...

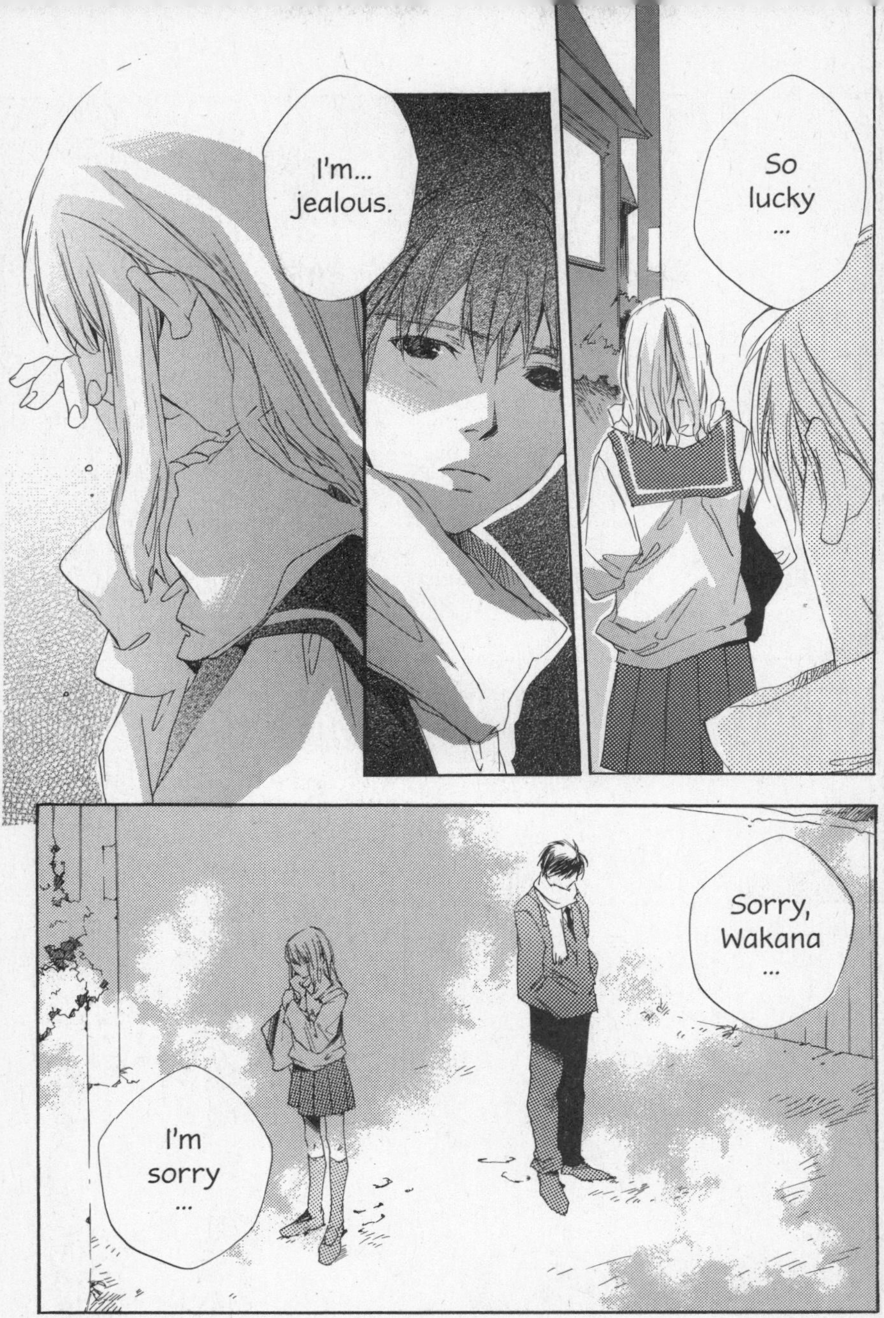
So lucky ...
I'm... jealous.
Sorry, Wakana ...
I'm sorry ...

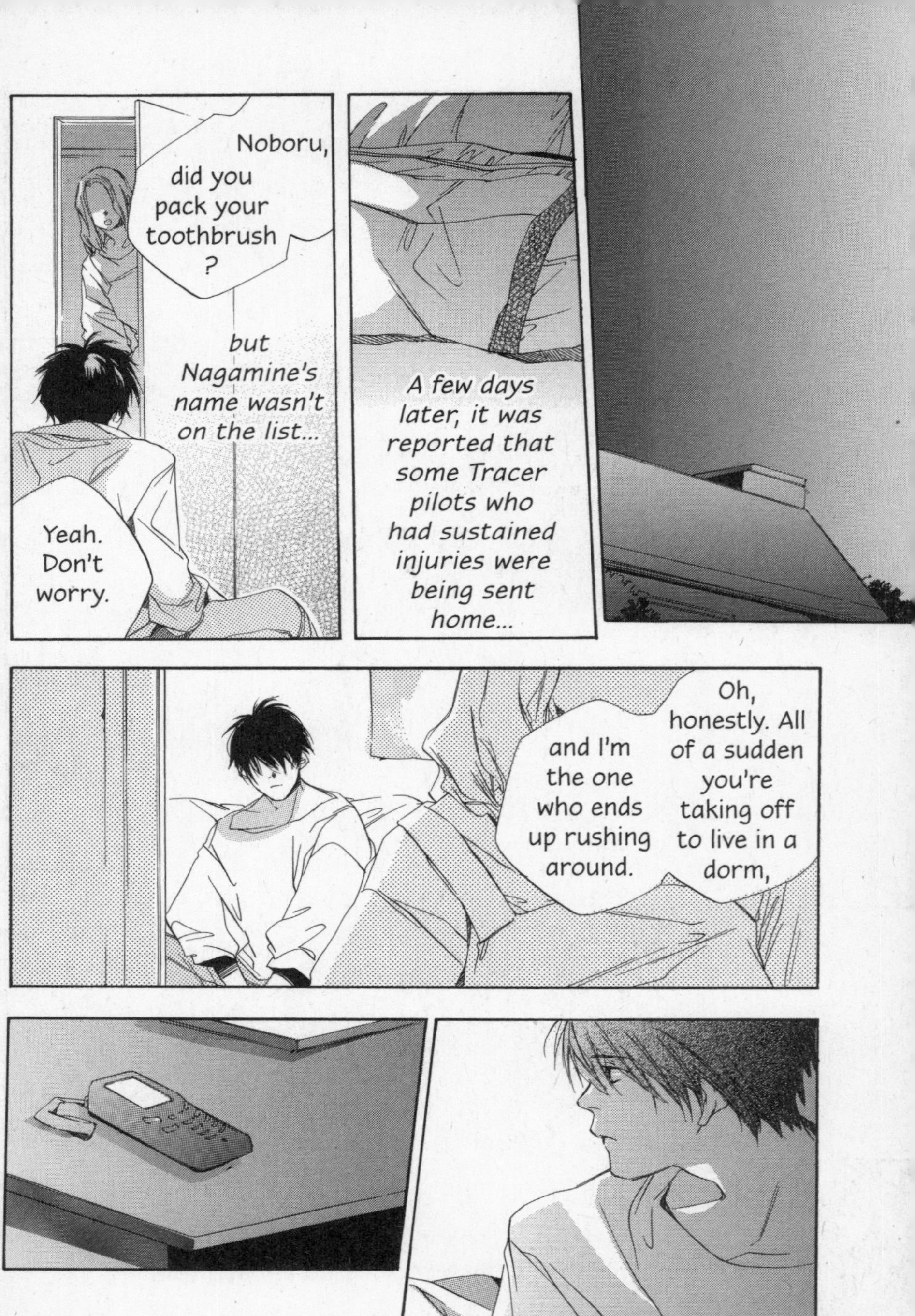
A few days later, it was reported that some Tracer pilots who had sustained injuries were being sent home...
Noboru, did you pack your toothbrush?
but Nagamine's name wasn't on the list...
Yeah. Don't worry.
Oh, honestly. All of a sudden you're taking off to live in a dorm,
and I'm the one who ends up rushing around.

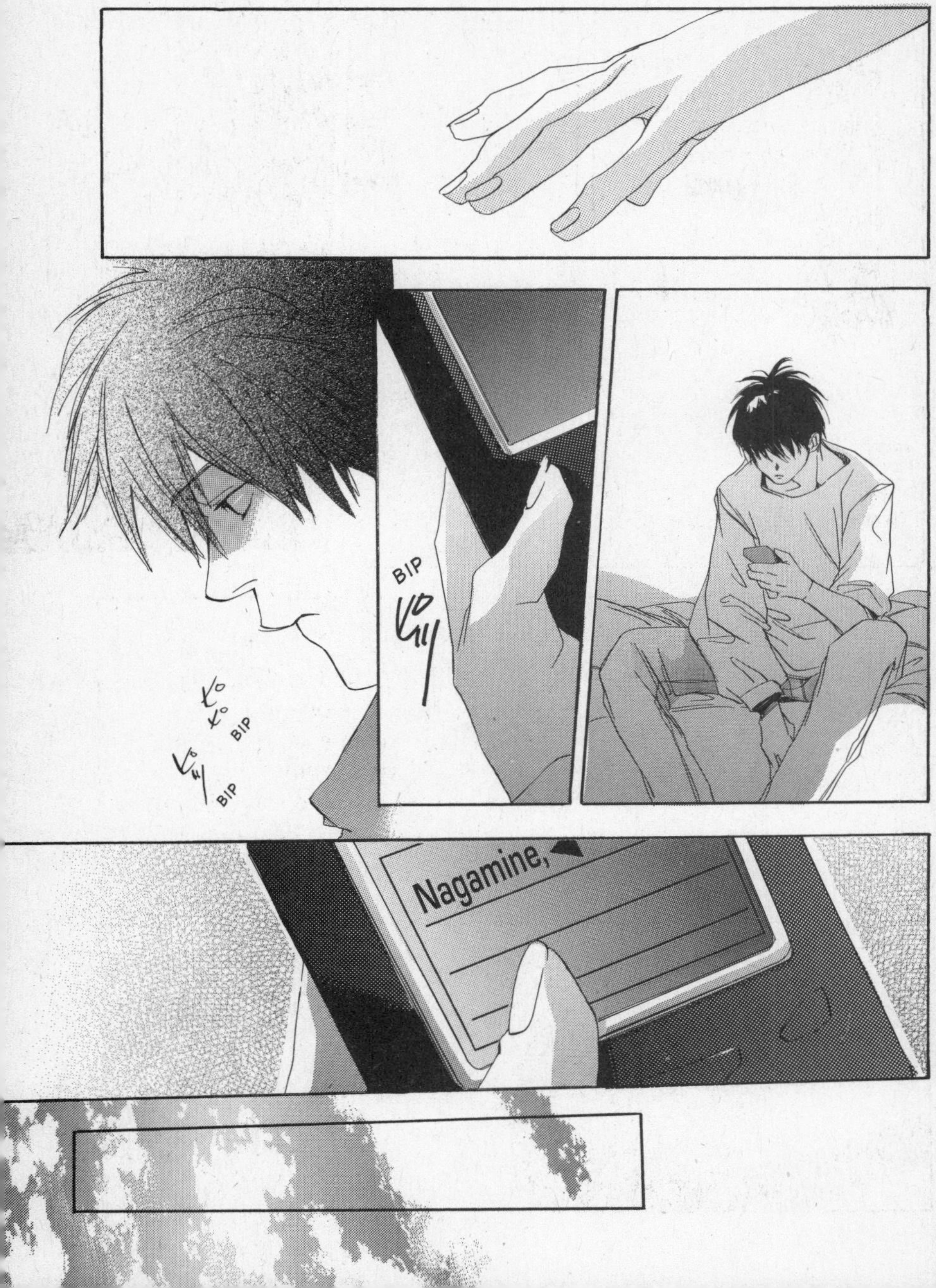
BIP
BIP
BIP
Nagamine,

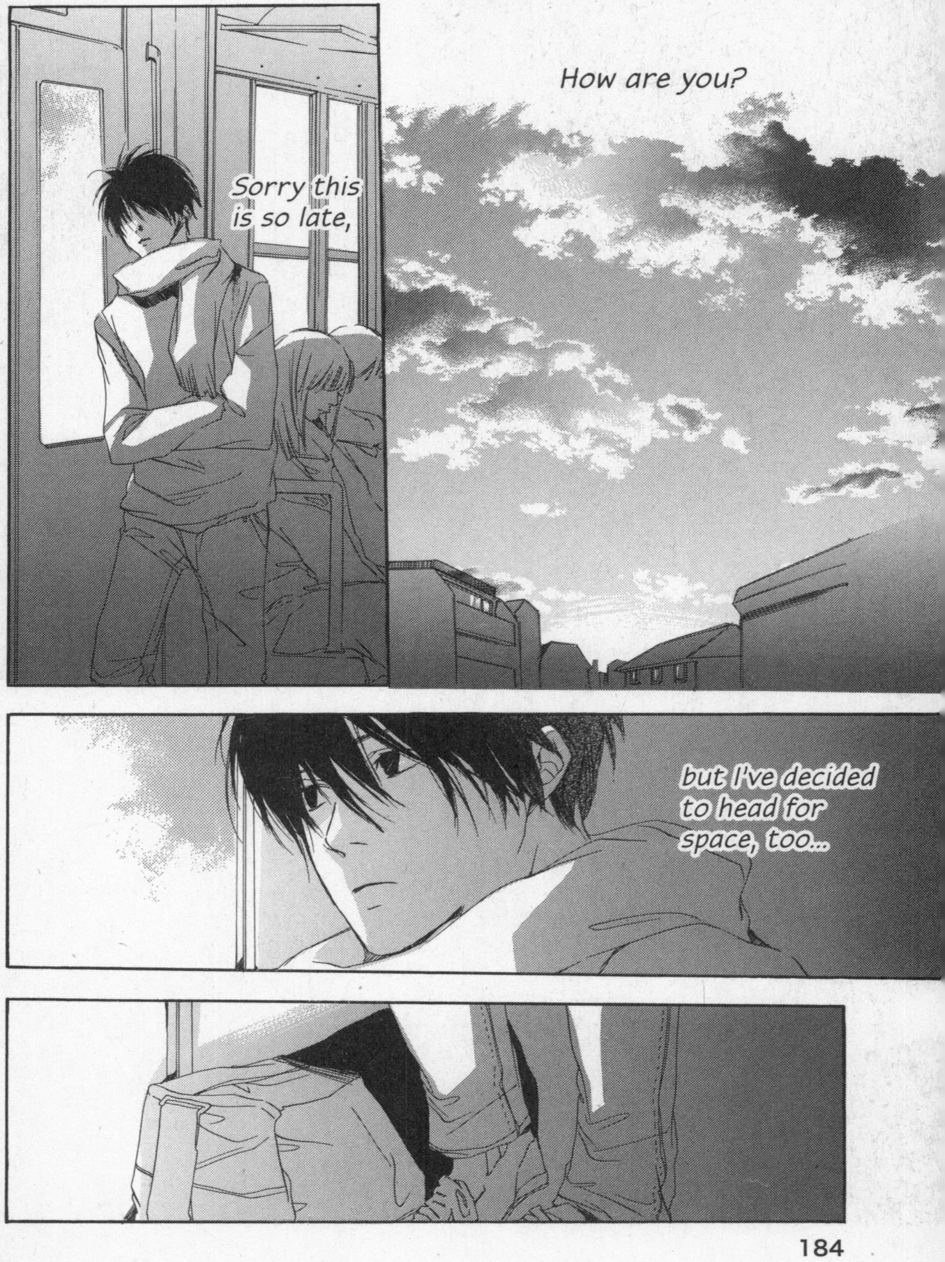
How are you?
Sorry this is so late,
but I've decided to head for space, too...

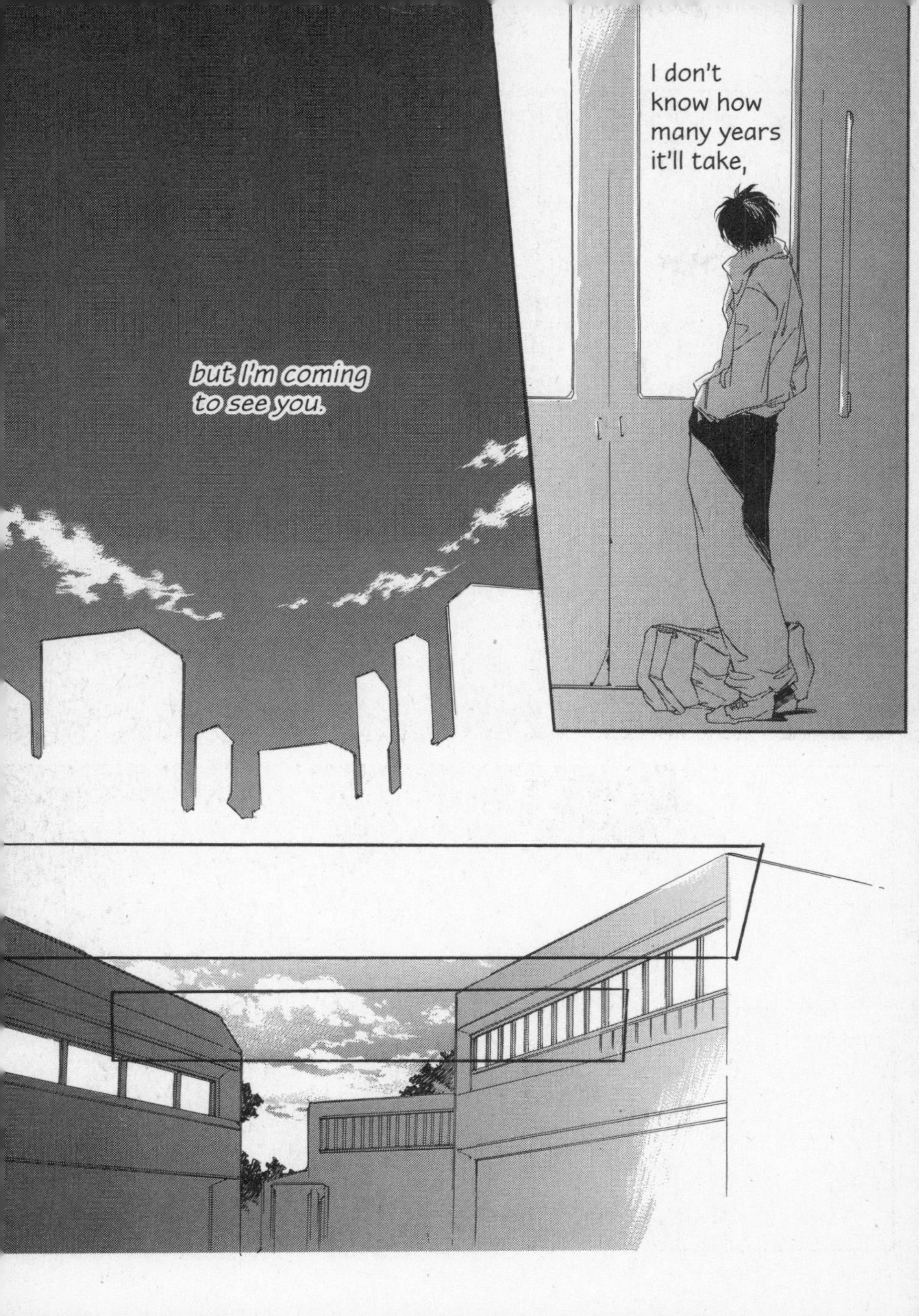
I don't know how many years it'll take,
but I'm coming to see you.

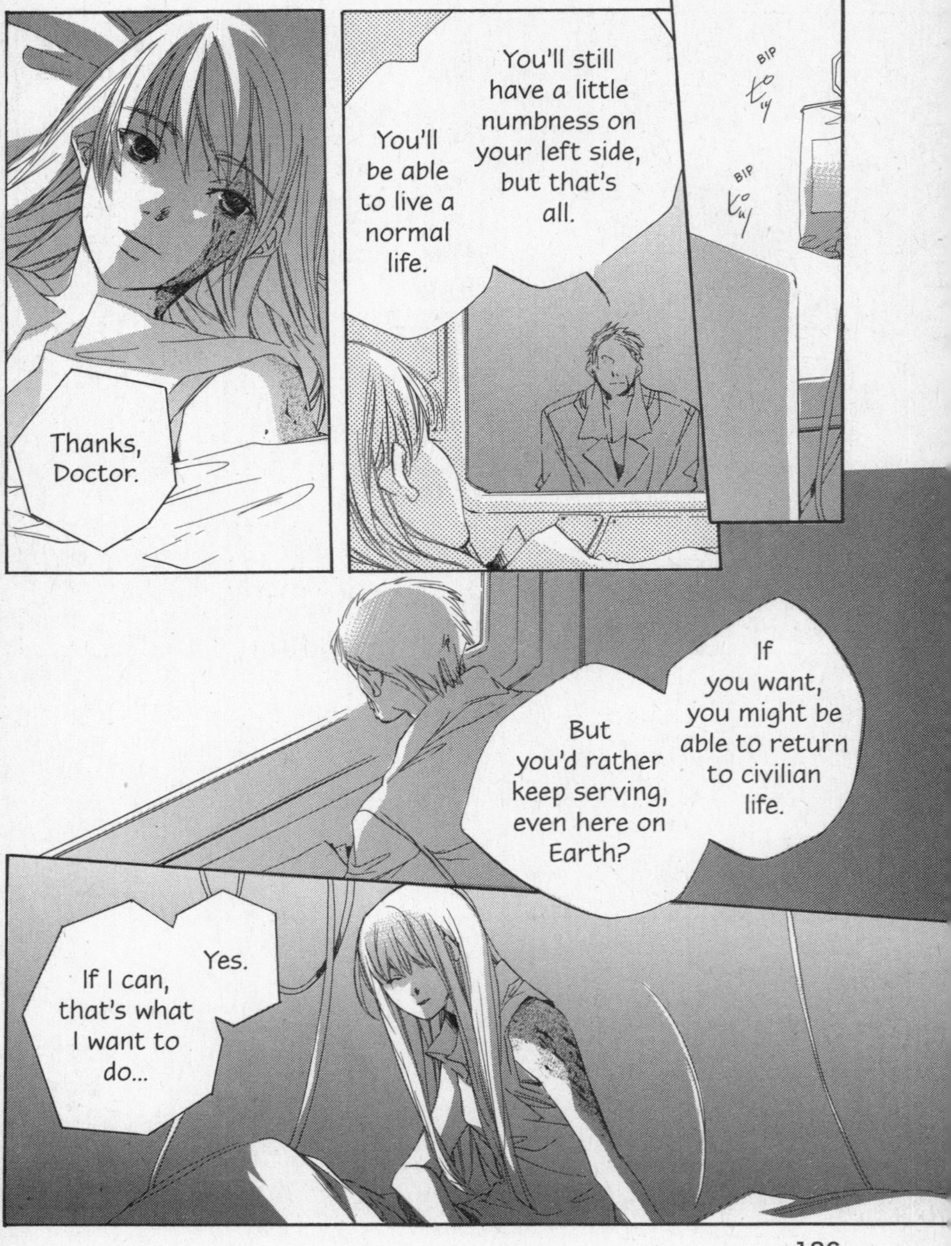
BIP
BIP
You'll still have a little numbness on your left side, but that's all.
You'll be able to live a normal life.
Thanks, Doctor.
If you want, you might be able to return to civilian life.
But you'd rather keep serving, even here on Earth?
Yes.
If I can, that's what I want to do...

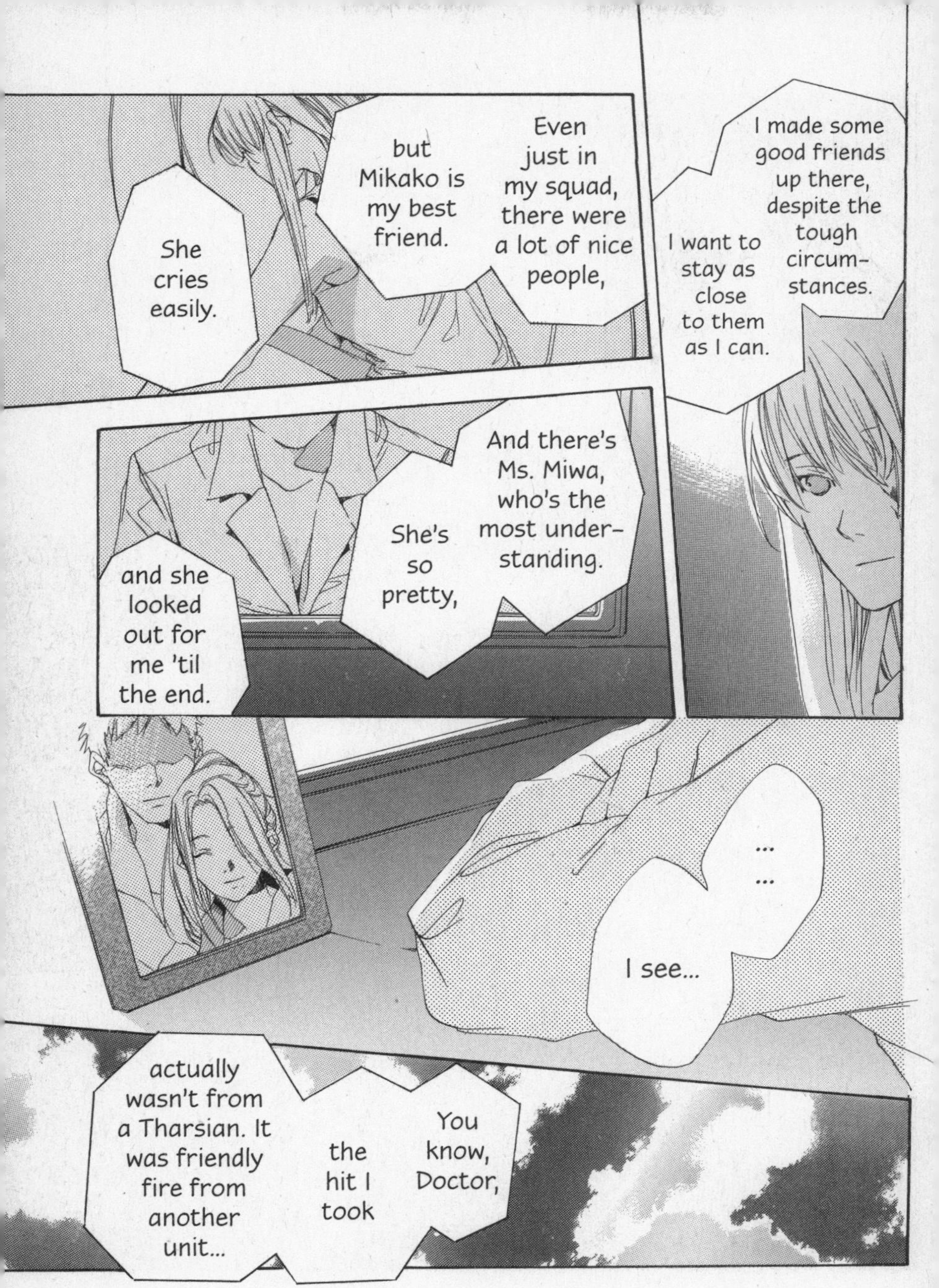
I made some good friends up there, despite the tough circumstances.
I want to stay as close to them as I can.
Even just in my squad, there were a lot of nice people,
but Mikako is my best friend.
She cries easily.
And there's Ms. Miwa, who's the most understanding.
She's so pretty,
and she looked out for me 'til the end.
...
...
I see...
You know, Doctor,
the hit I took
actually wasn't from a Tharsian. It was friendly fire from another unit...

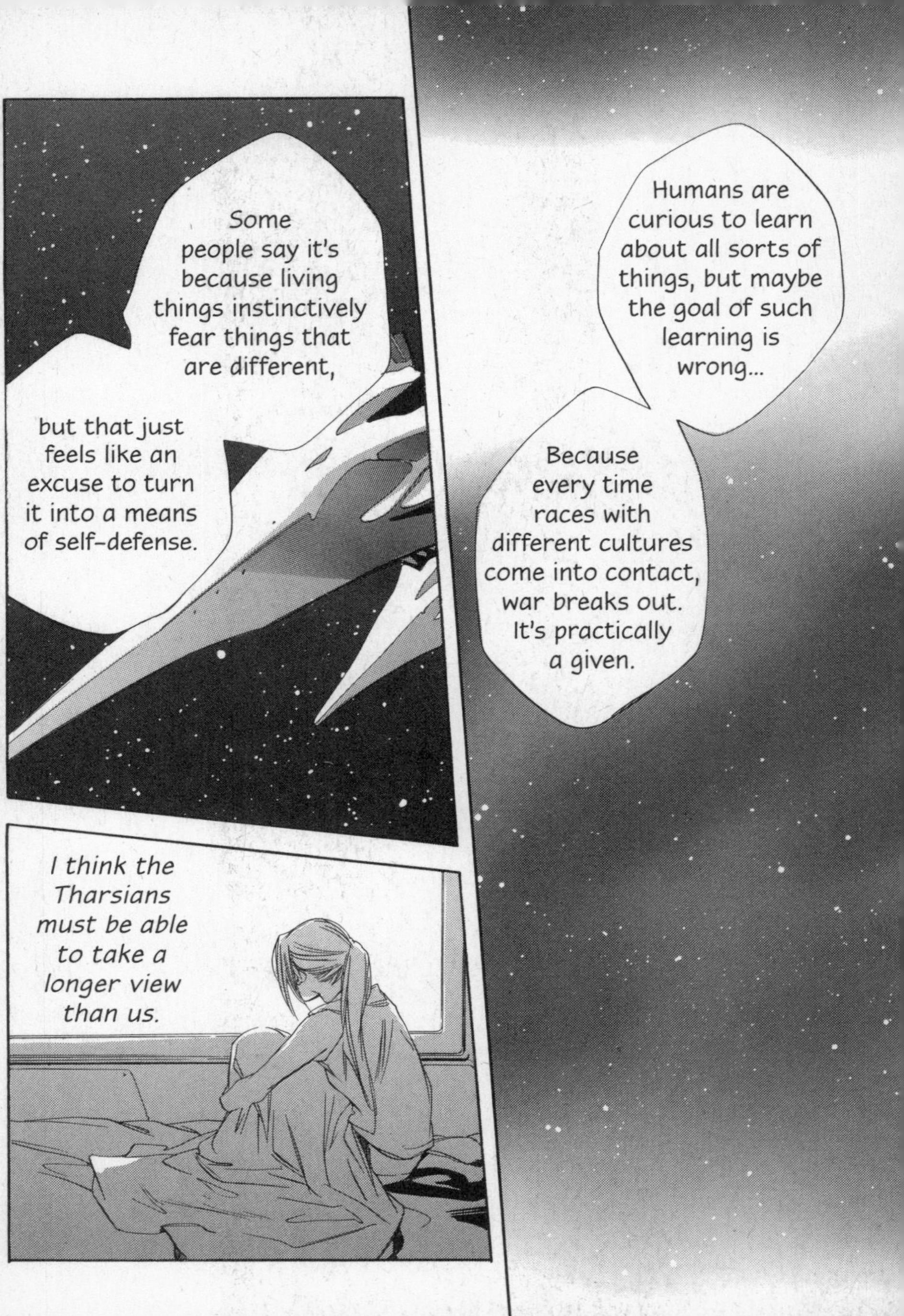
Humans are curious to learn about all sorts of things, but maybe the goal of such learning is wrong...
Because every time races with different cultures come into contact, war breaks out. It's practically a given.
Some people say it's because living things instinctively fear things that are different,
but that just feels like an excuse to turn it into a means of self-defense.
I think the Tharsians must be able to take a longer view than us.

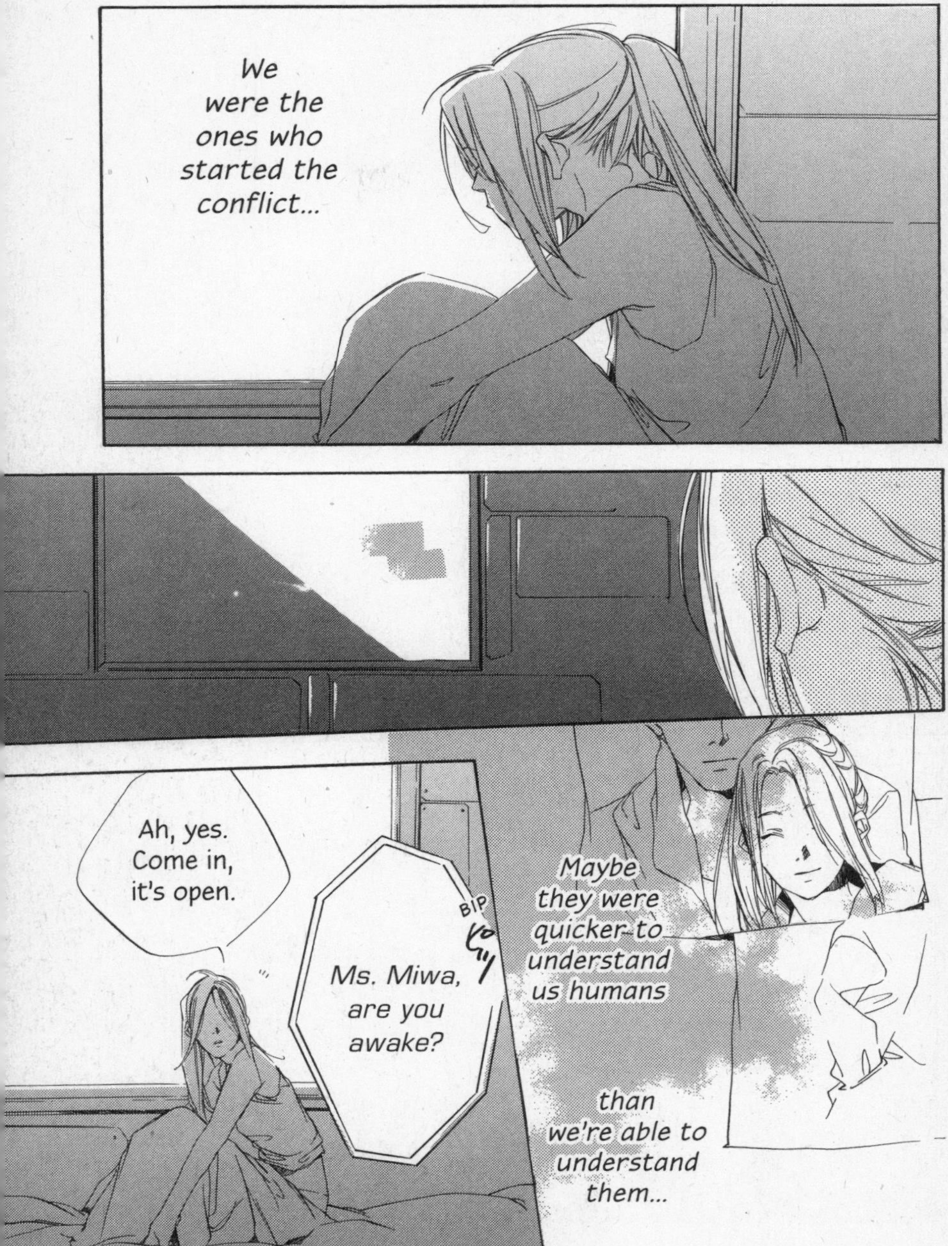
We were the ones who started the conflict...
Maybe they were quicker to understand us humans
than we're able to understand them...
BIP
Ms. Miwa, are you awake?
Ah, yes. Come in, it's open.

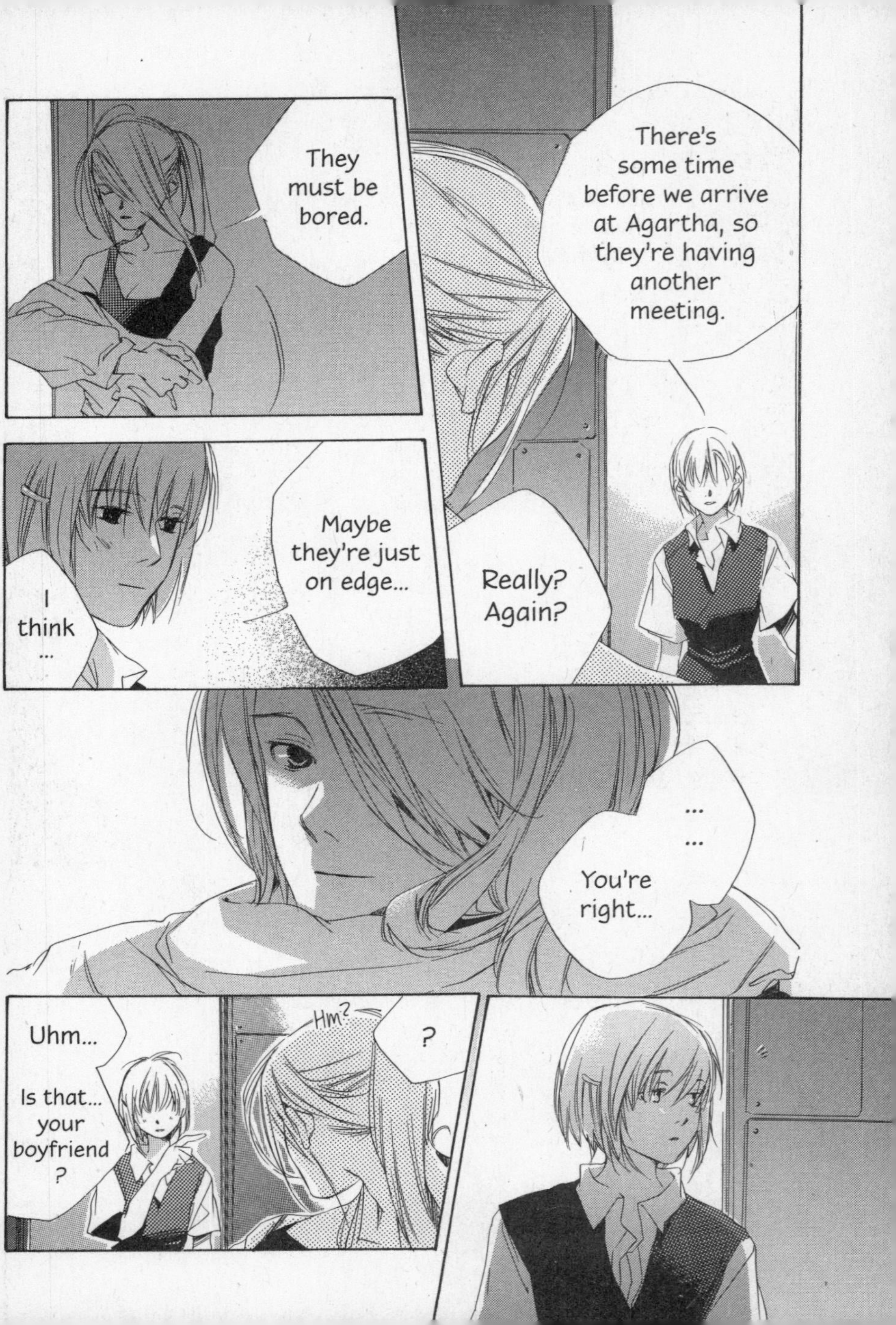
There's some time before we arrive at Agartha, so they're having another meeting.
Really? Again?
They must be bored.
Maybe they're just on edge...
I think ...
...
...
You're right...
?
Hm?
Uhm...
Is that... your boyfriend ?

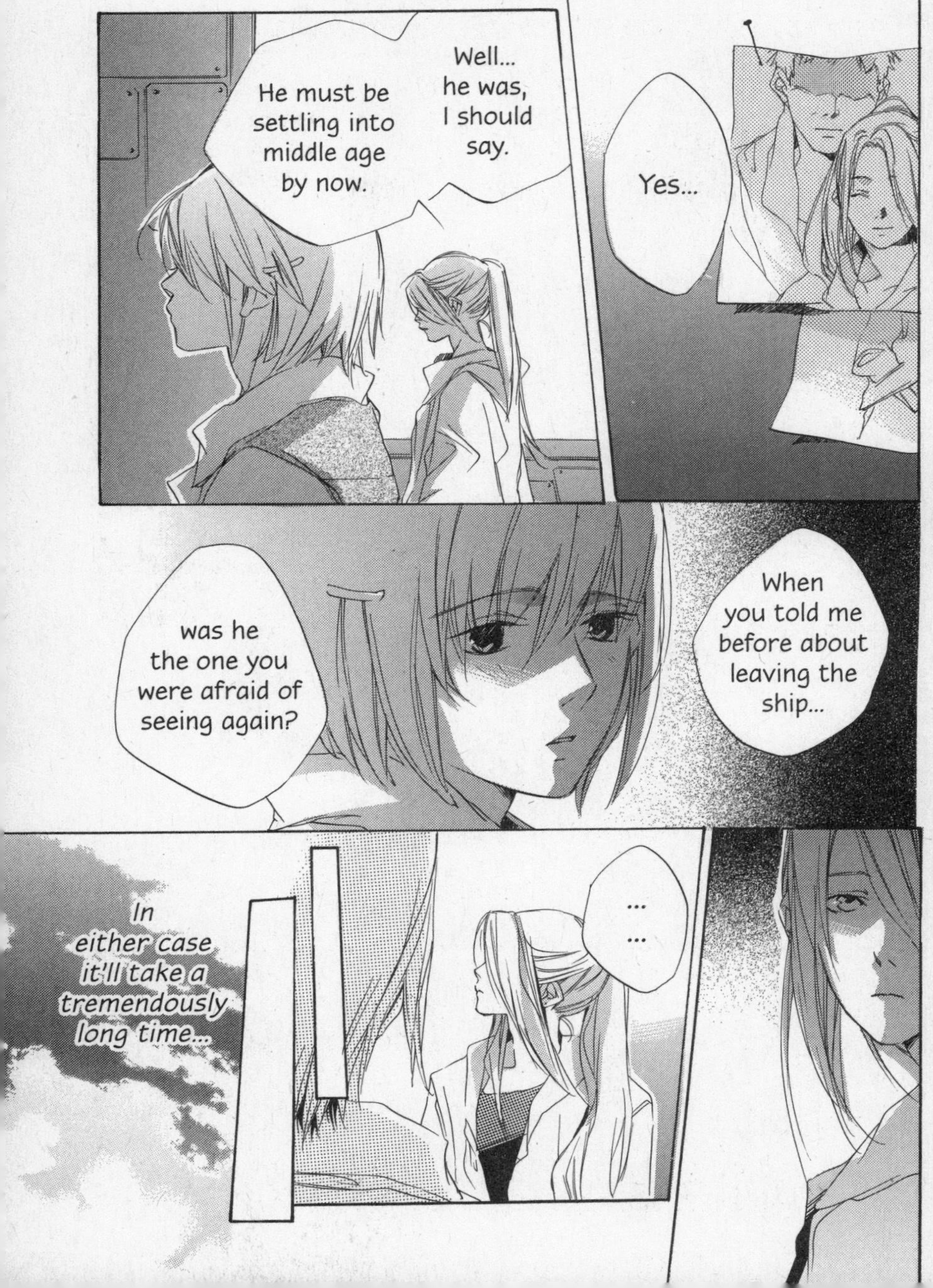
Yes...
He must be settling into middle age by now.
Well... he was, I should say.
When you told me before about leaving the ship...
was he the one you were afraid of seeing again?
... ...
In either case it'll take a tremendously long time...

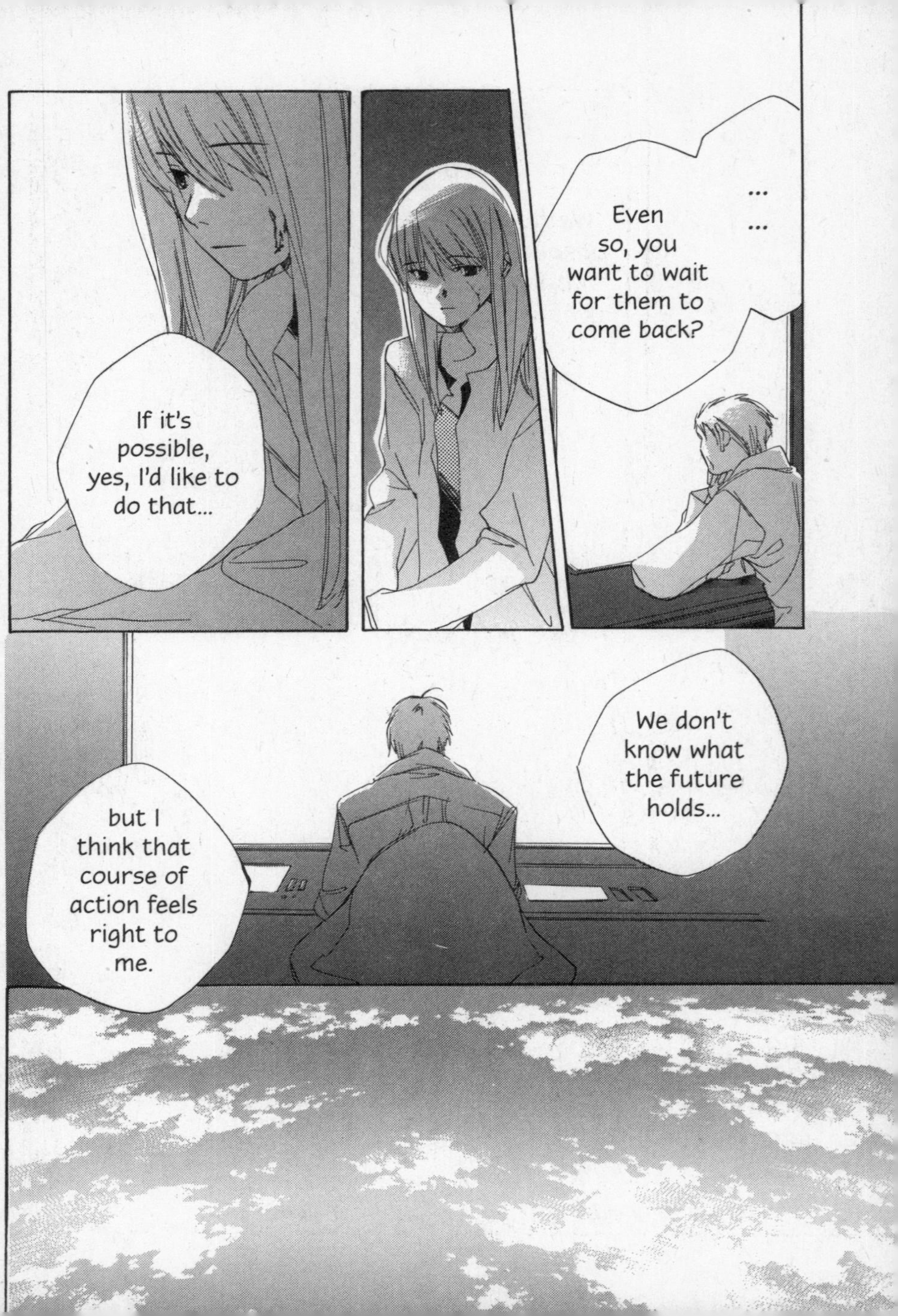
... ...
Even so, you want to wait for them to come back?
If it's possible, yes, I'd like to do that...
We don't know what the future holds...
but I think that course of action feels right to me.

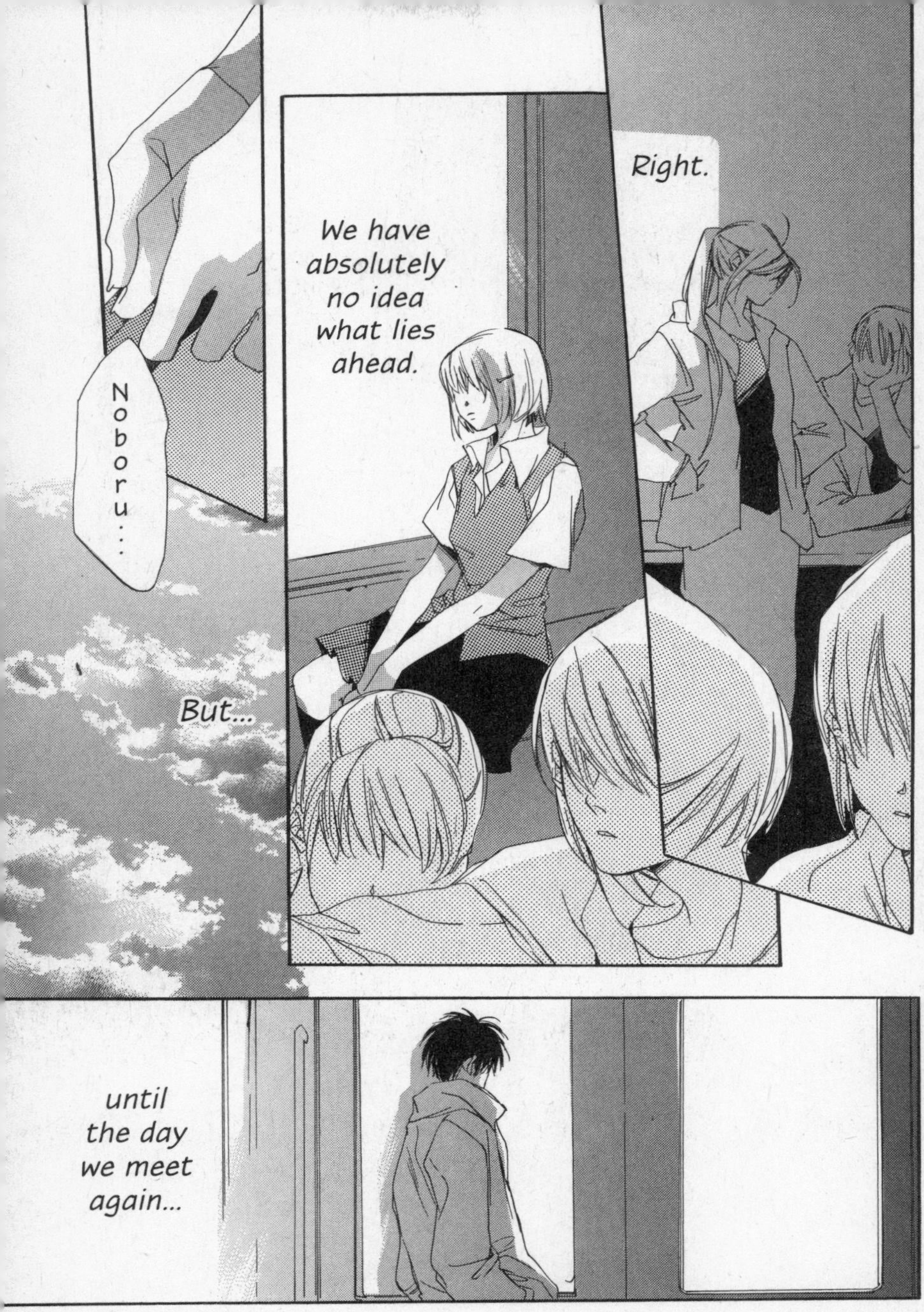
Right.
We have absolutely no idea what lies ahead.
Noboru...
But...
until the day we meet again...

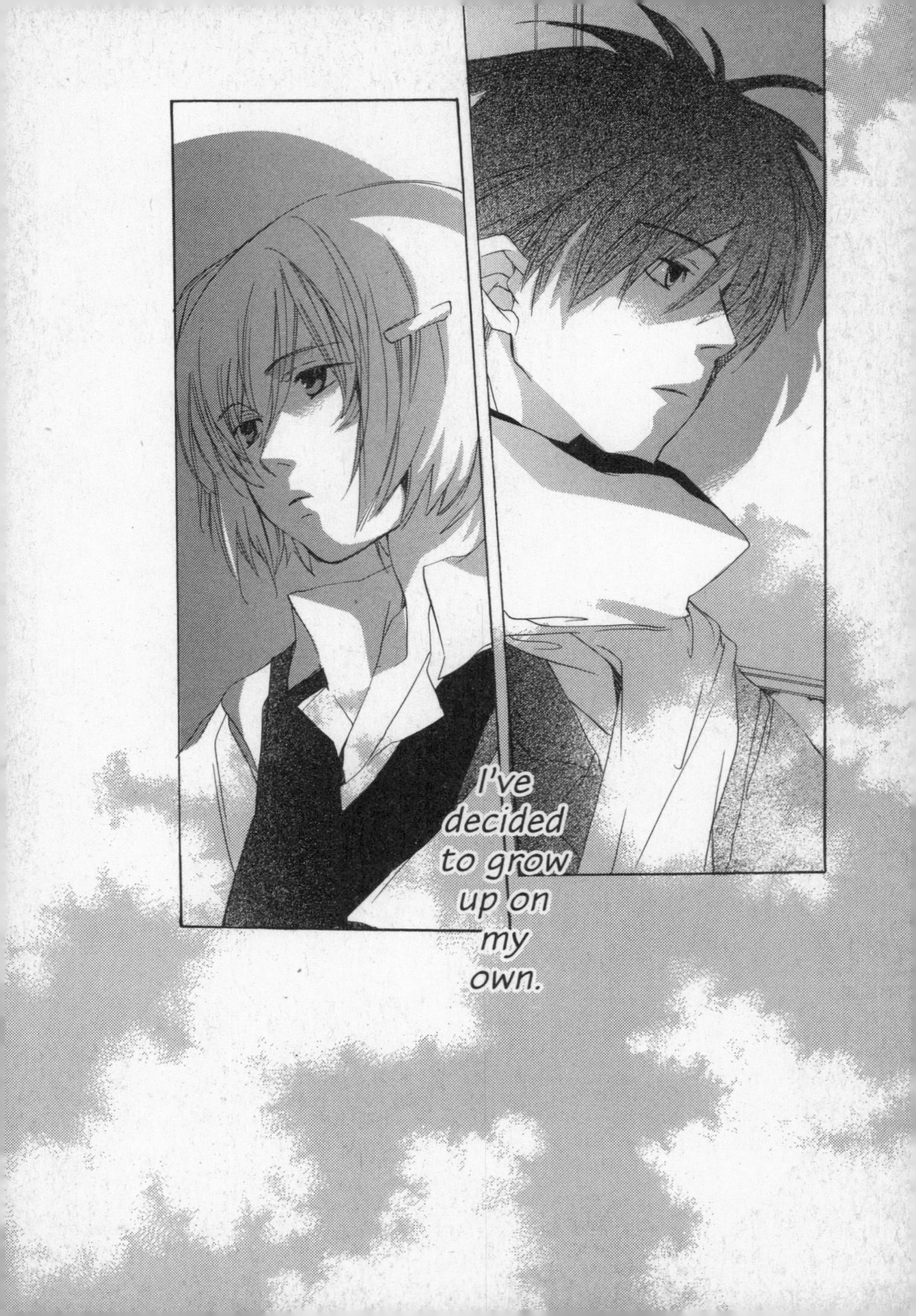
I've decided to grow up on my own.

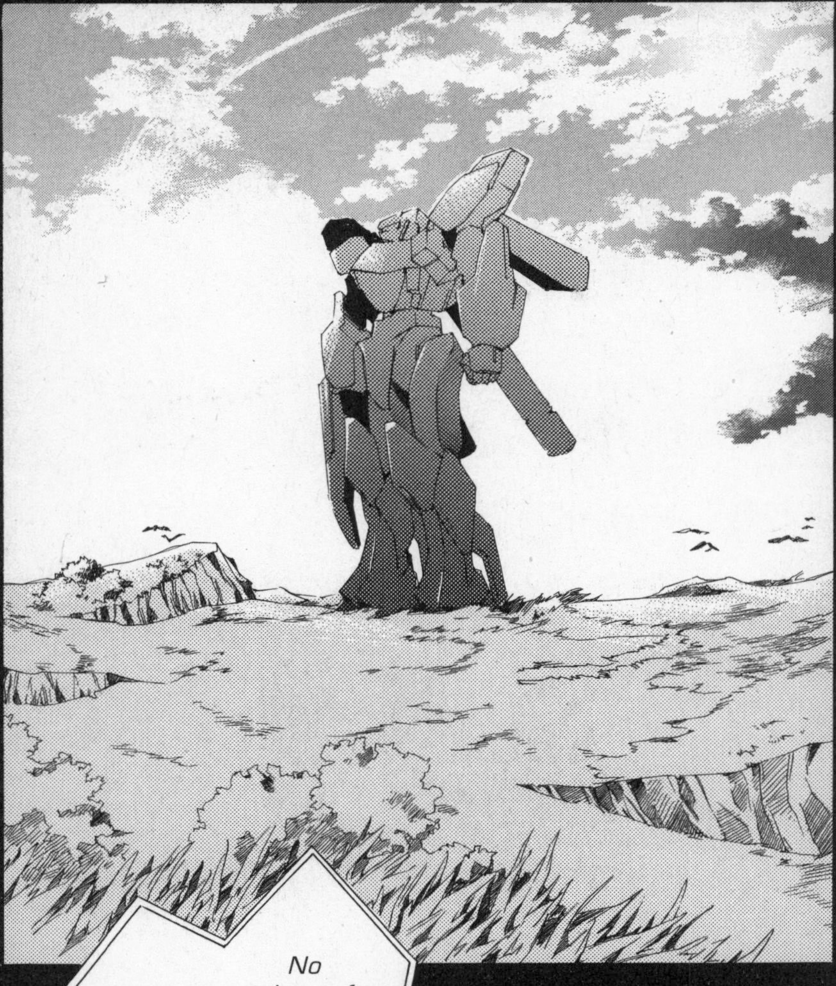
No signs of Tharsians detected yet.
All units, please continue with the investigation.

Voices of a Distant Star

Chapter 9

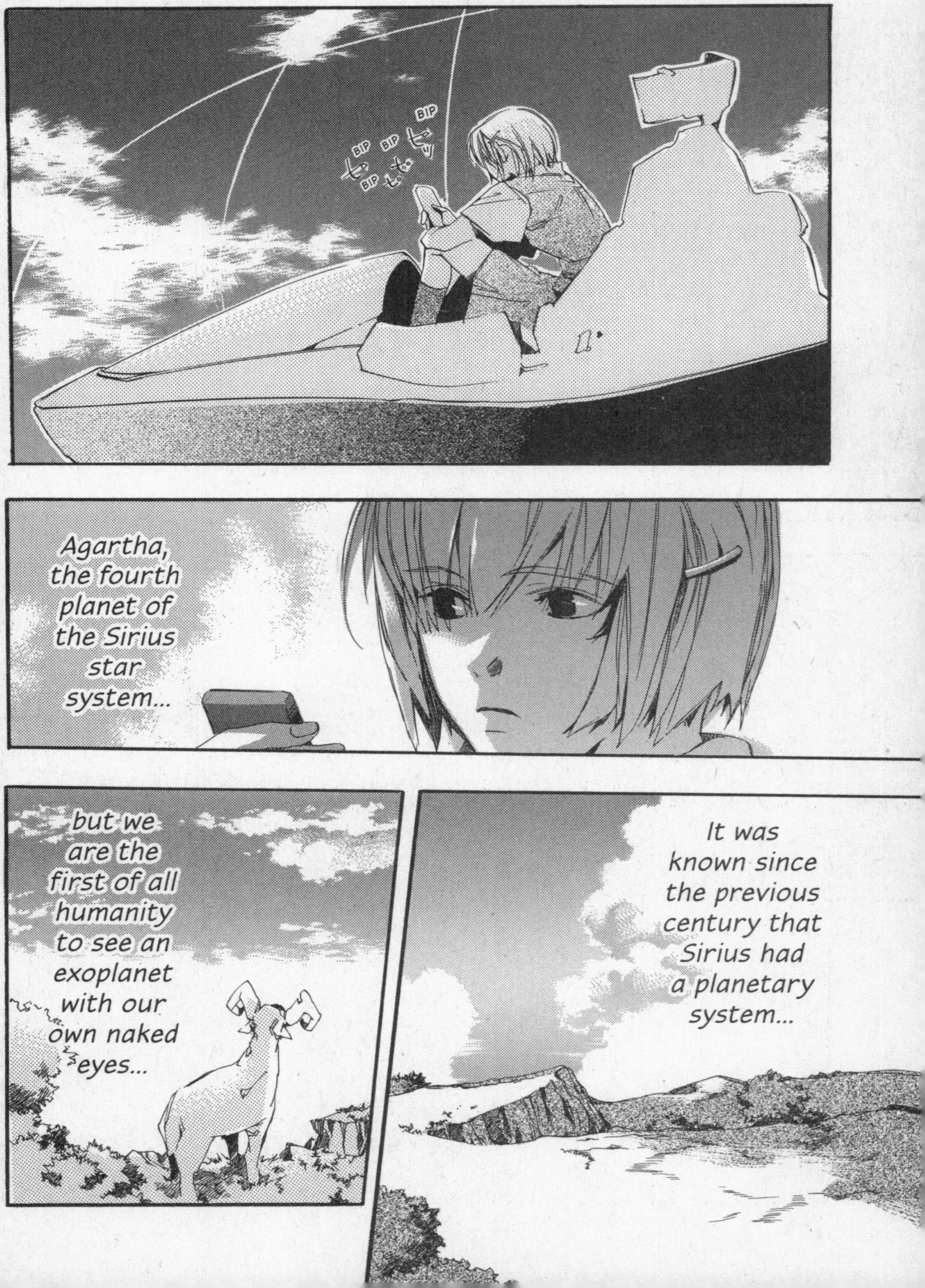
BIP
BIP
BIP
BIP
Agartha, the fourth planet of the Sirius star system...
It was known since the previous century that Sirius had a planetary system...
but we are the first of all humanity to see an exoplanet with our own naked eyes...

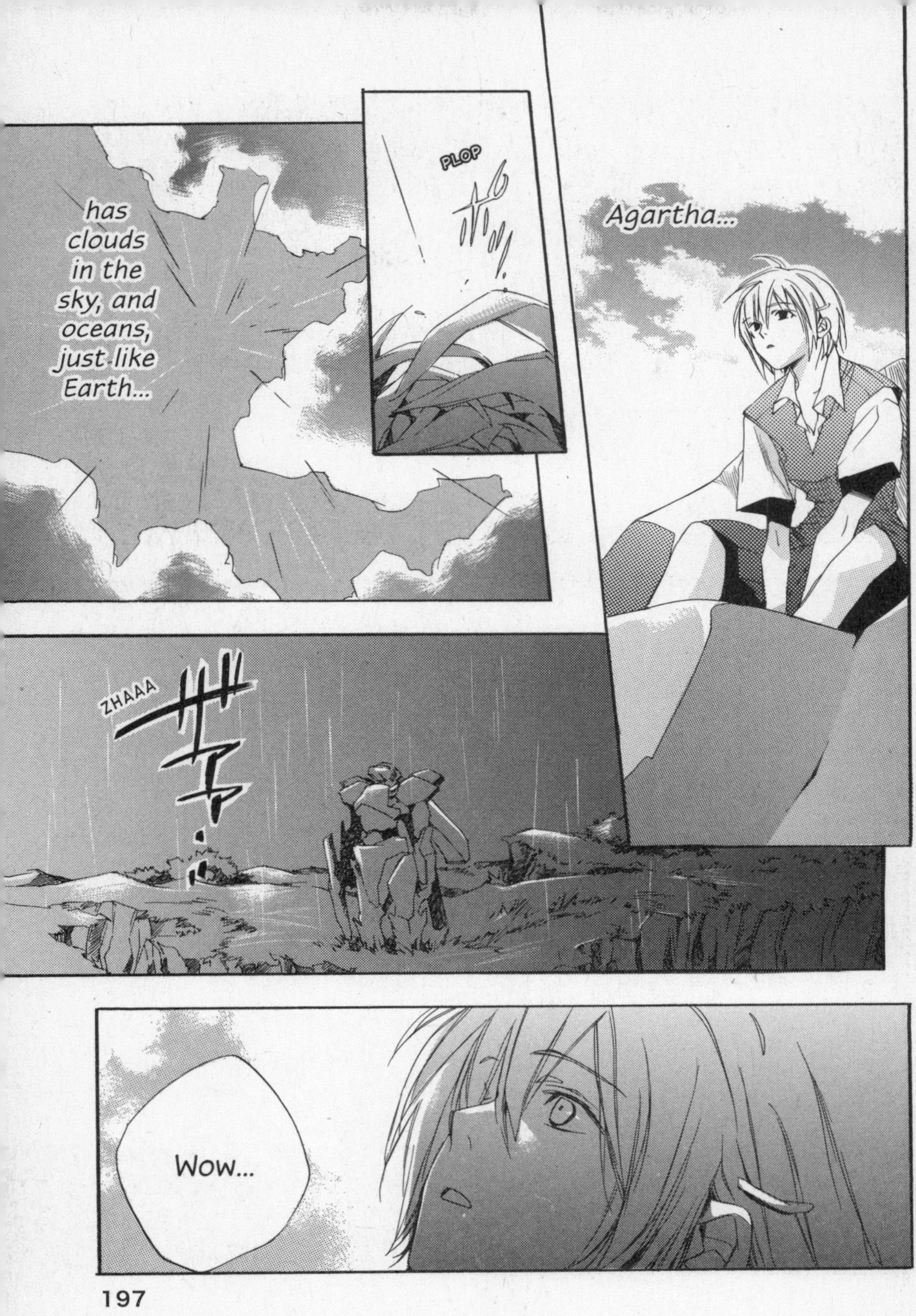
Agartha...
PLOP
has clouds in the sky, and oceans, just like Earth...
ZHAAA
Wow...

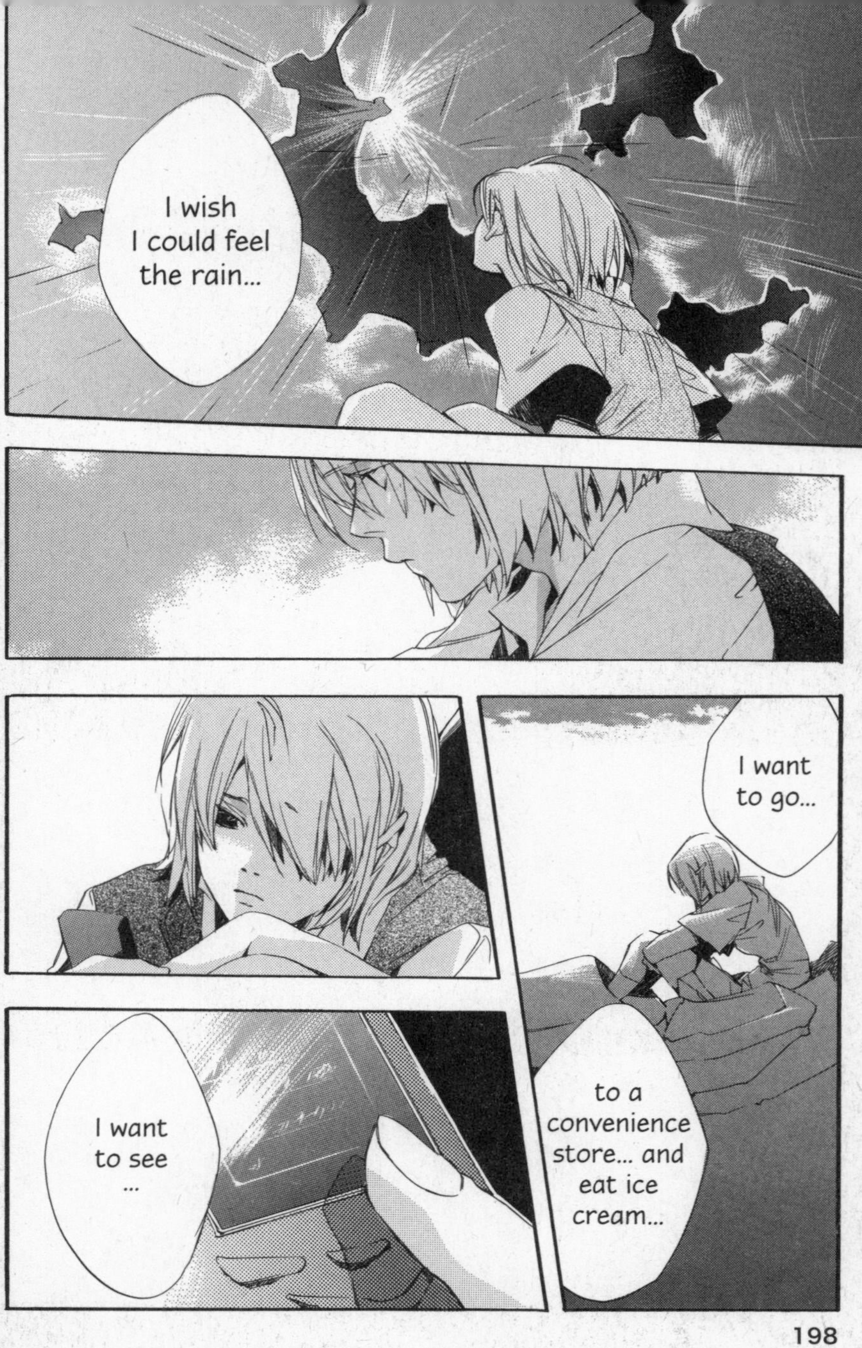
I wish I could feel the rain...
I want to go...
to a convenience store... and eat ice cream...
I want to see ...

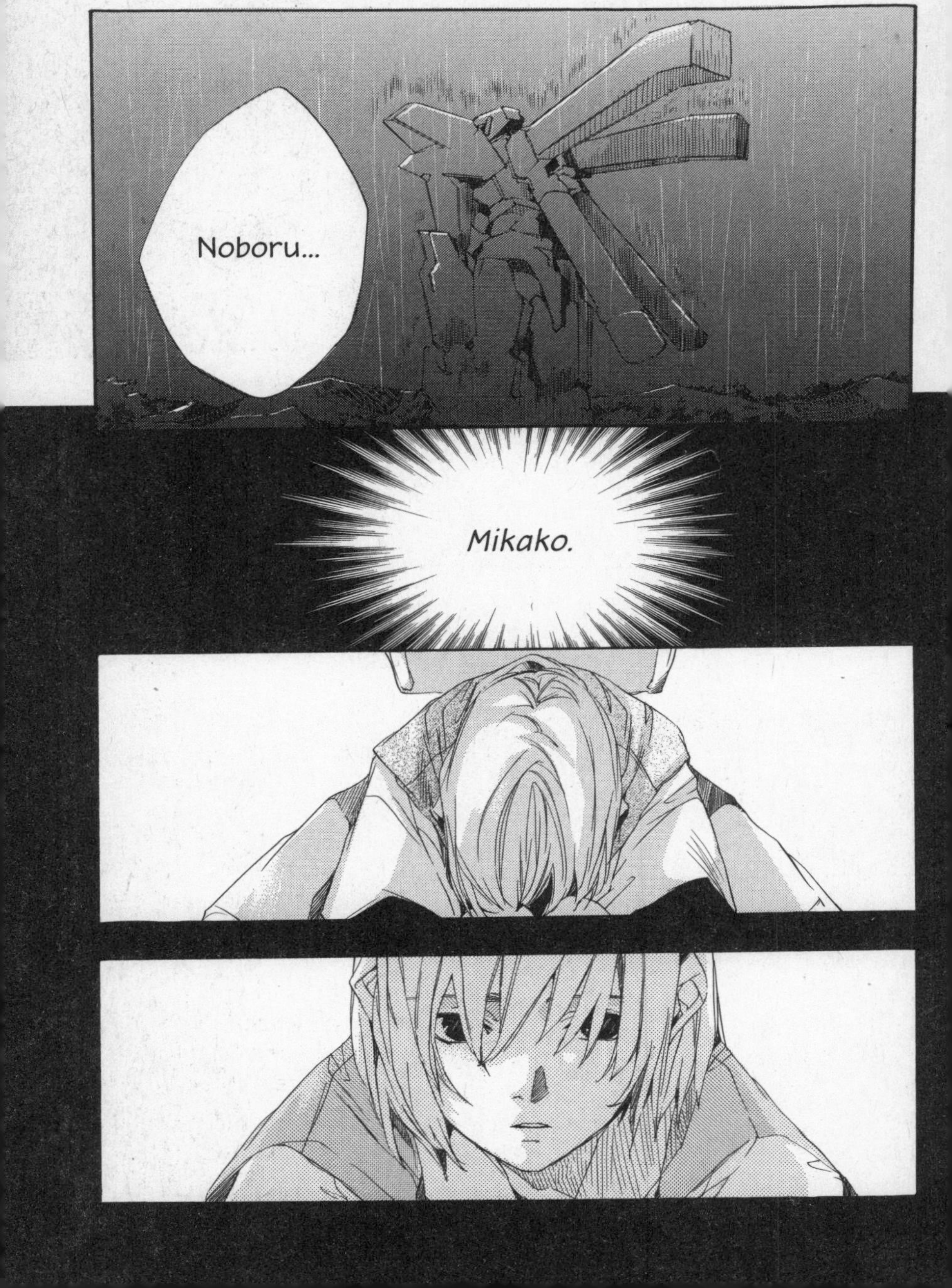
Noboru...
Mikako.

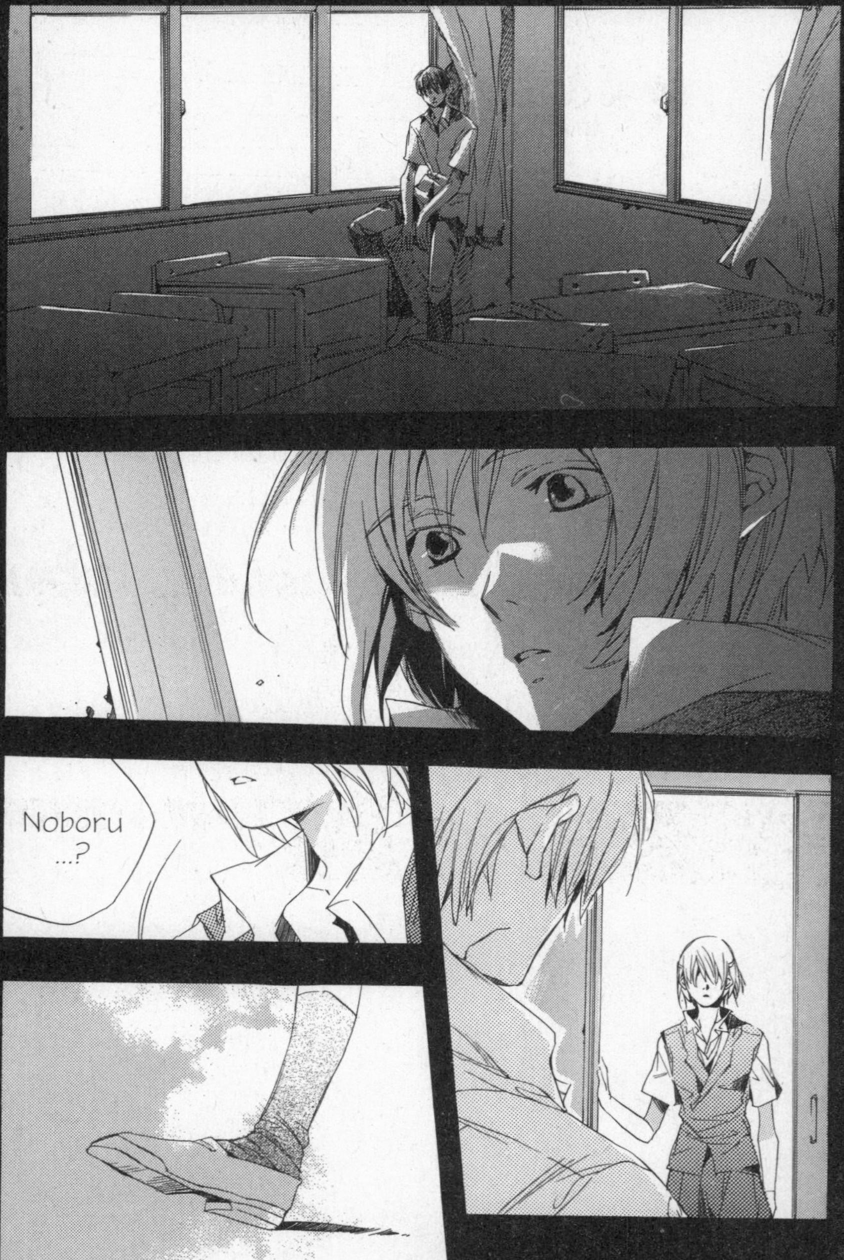
Noboru
...?

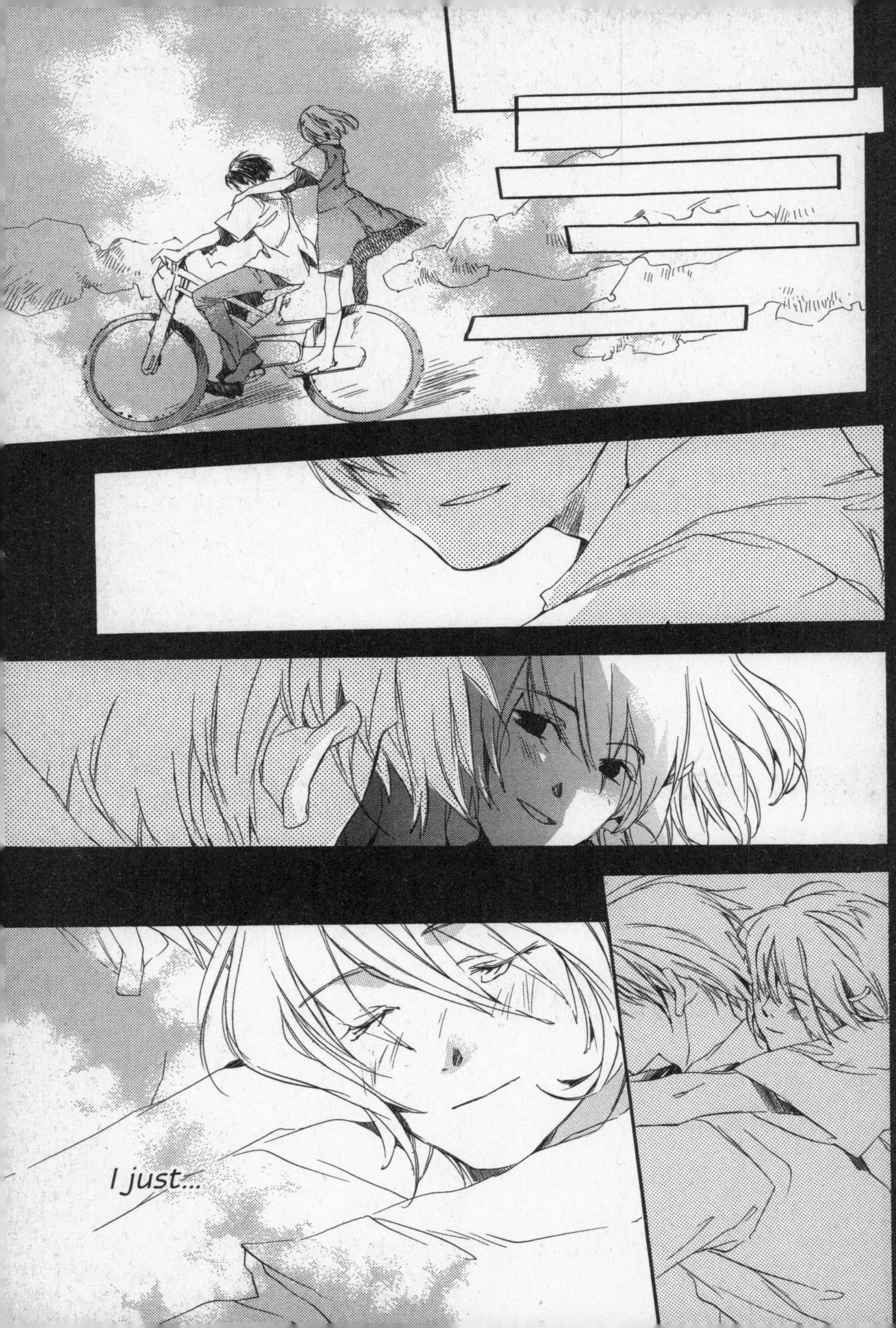
I just...

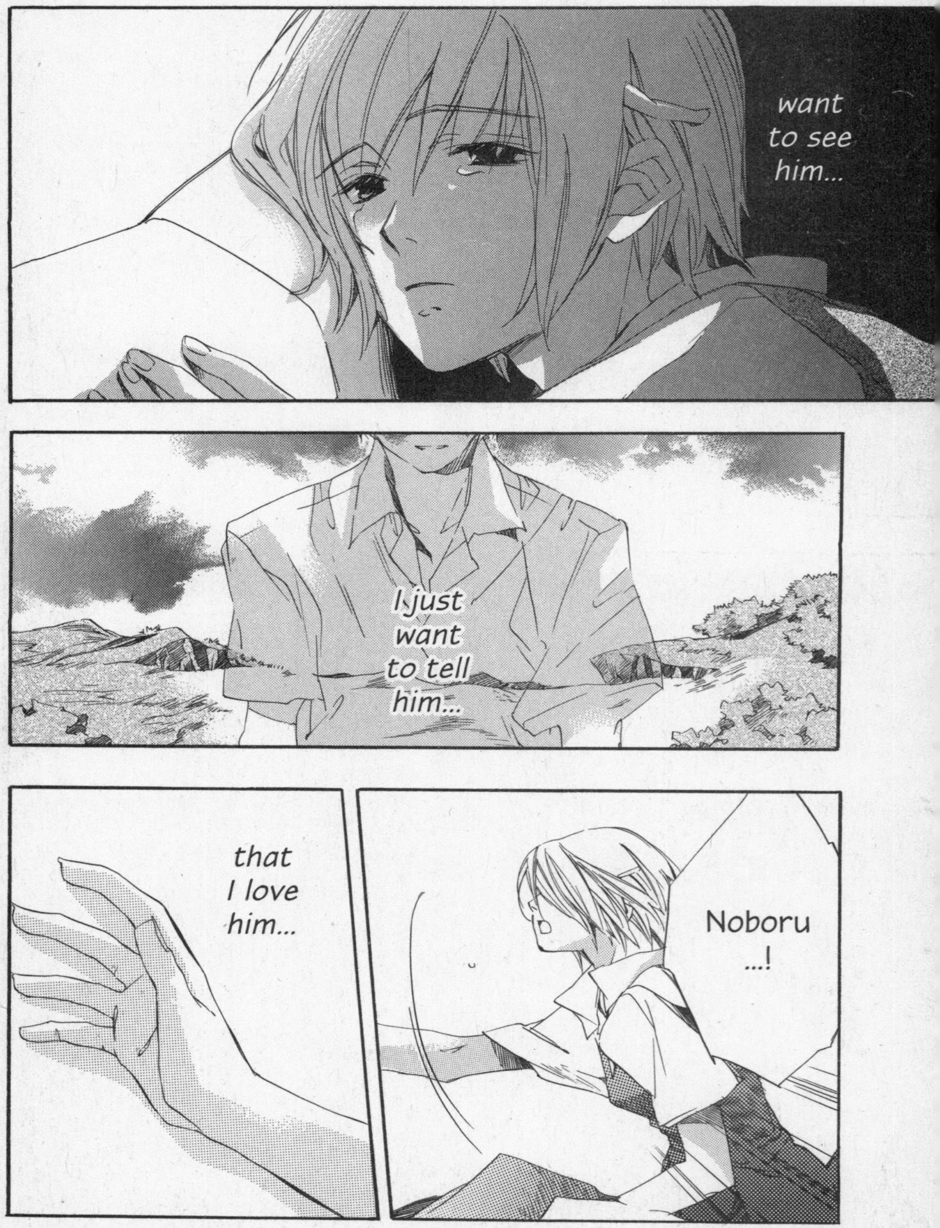
want to see him...
I just want to tell him...
Noboru ...!
that I love him...

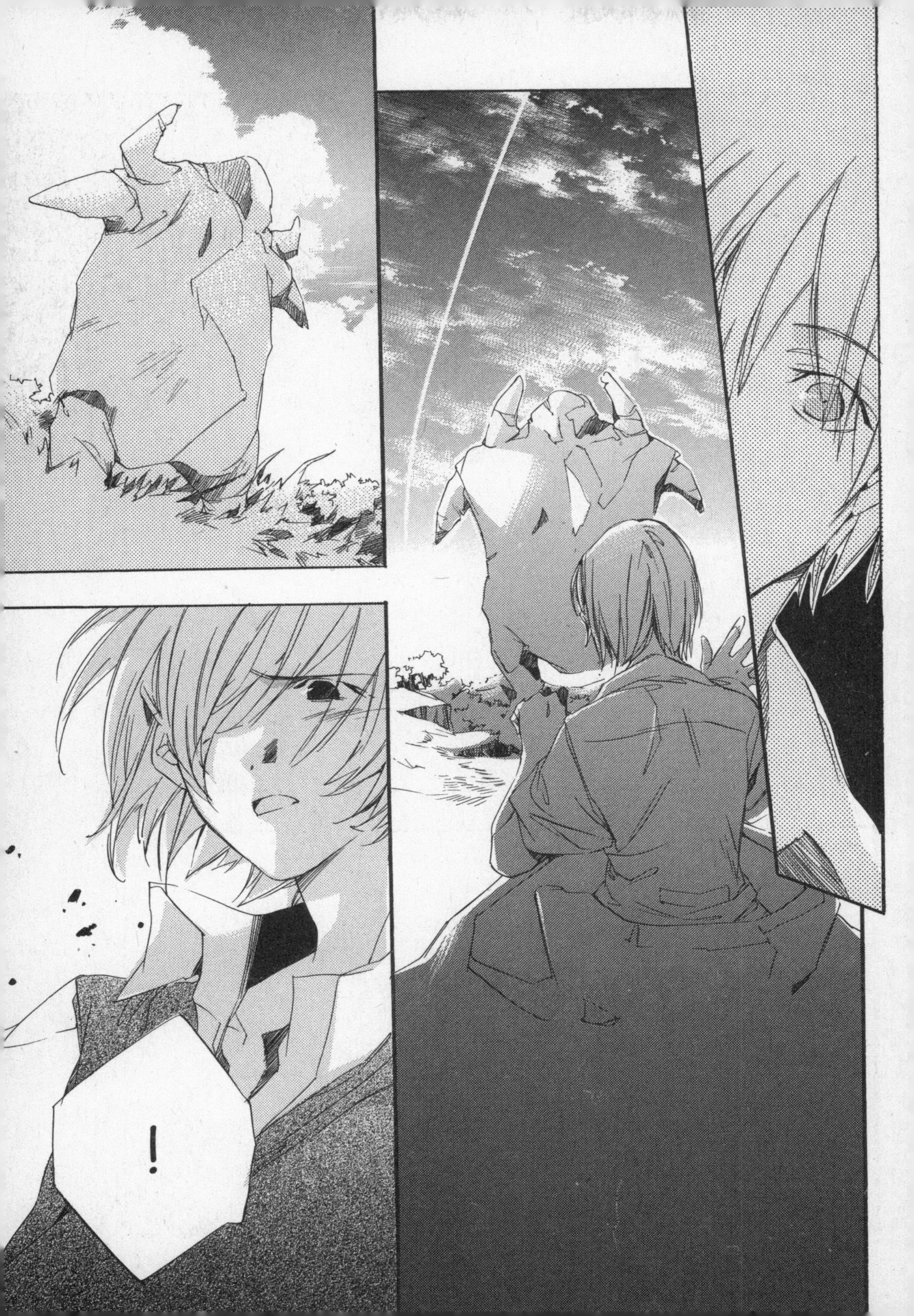
!

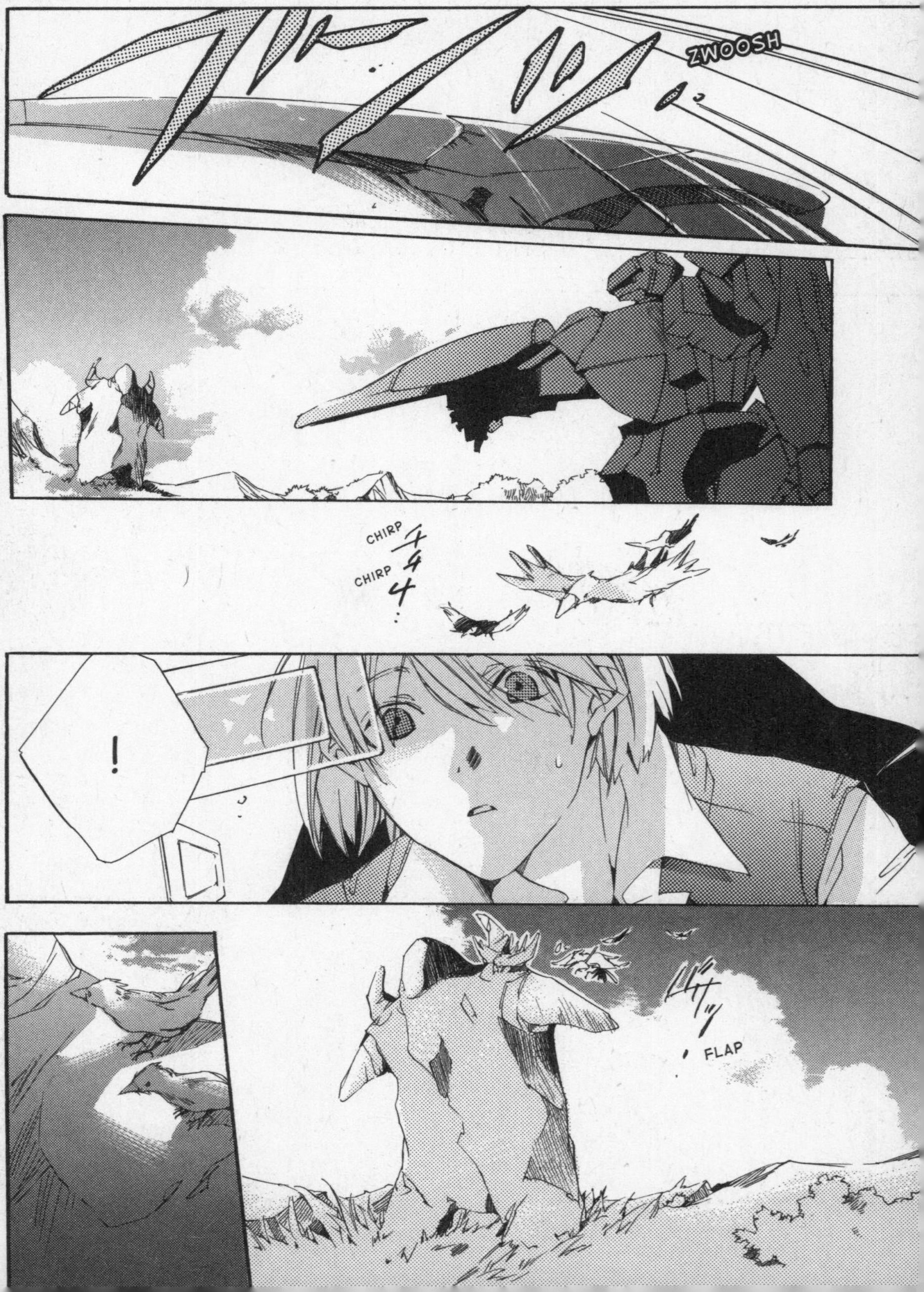
ZWOOSH
CHIRP
CHIRP
!
FLAP

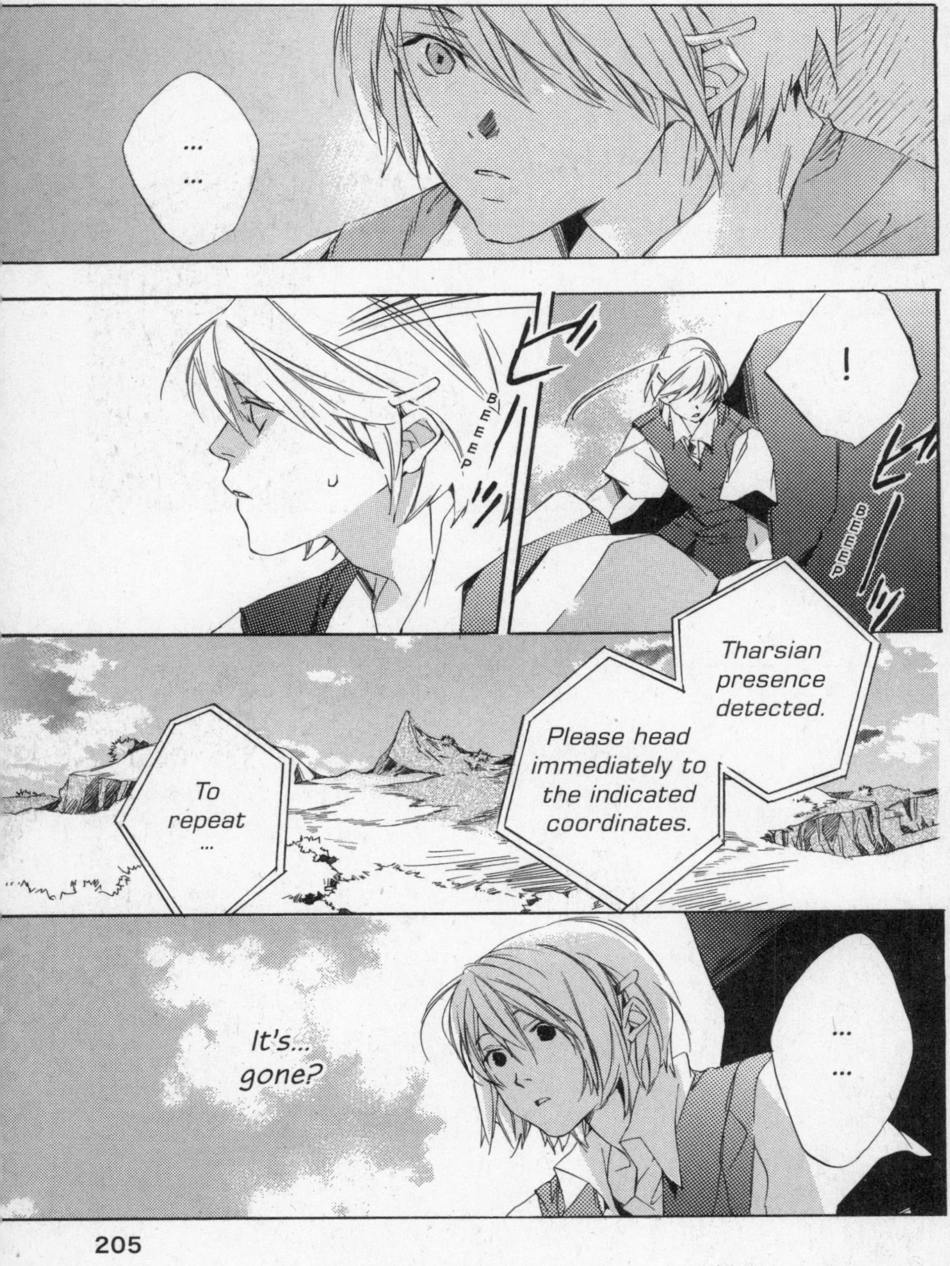
... ...
!
BEEEP
BEEEP
Tharsian presence detected.
Please head immediately to the indicated coordinates.
To repeat ...
... ...
It's... gone?

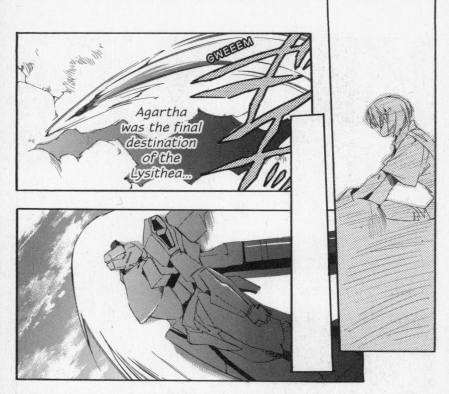

GWEEEM

Agartha was the final destination of the Lysithea...

to Earth ...

It's not like I want something to happen.

But... if we find something, maybe we'll get to go home...

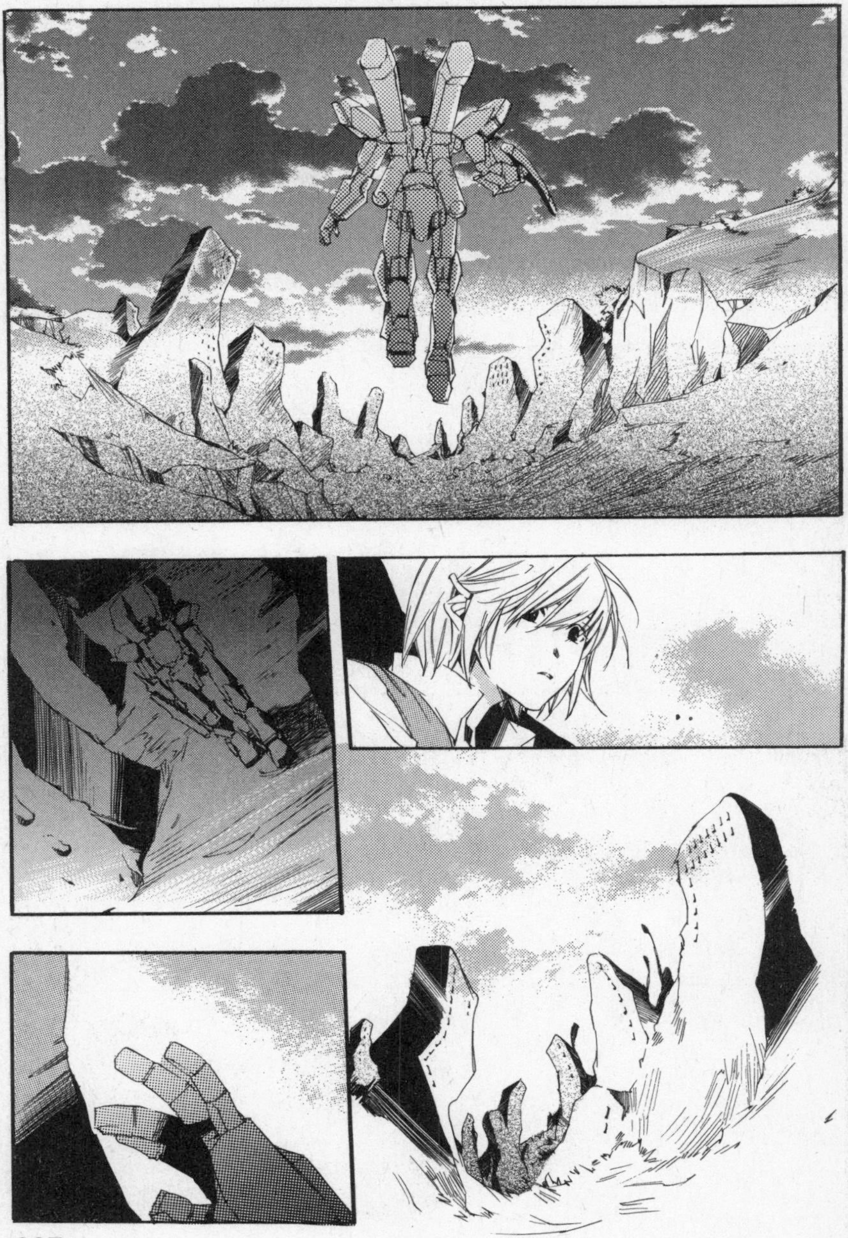

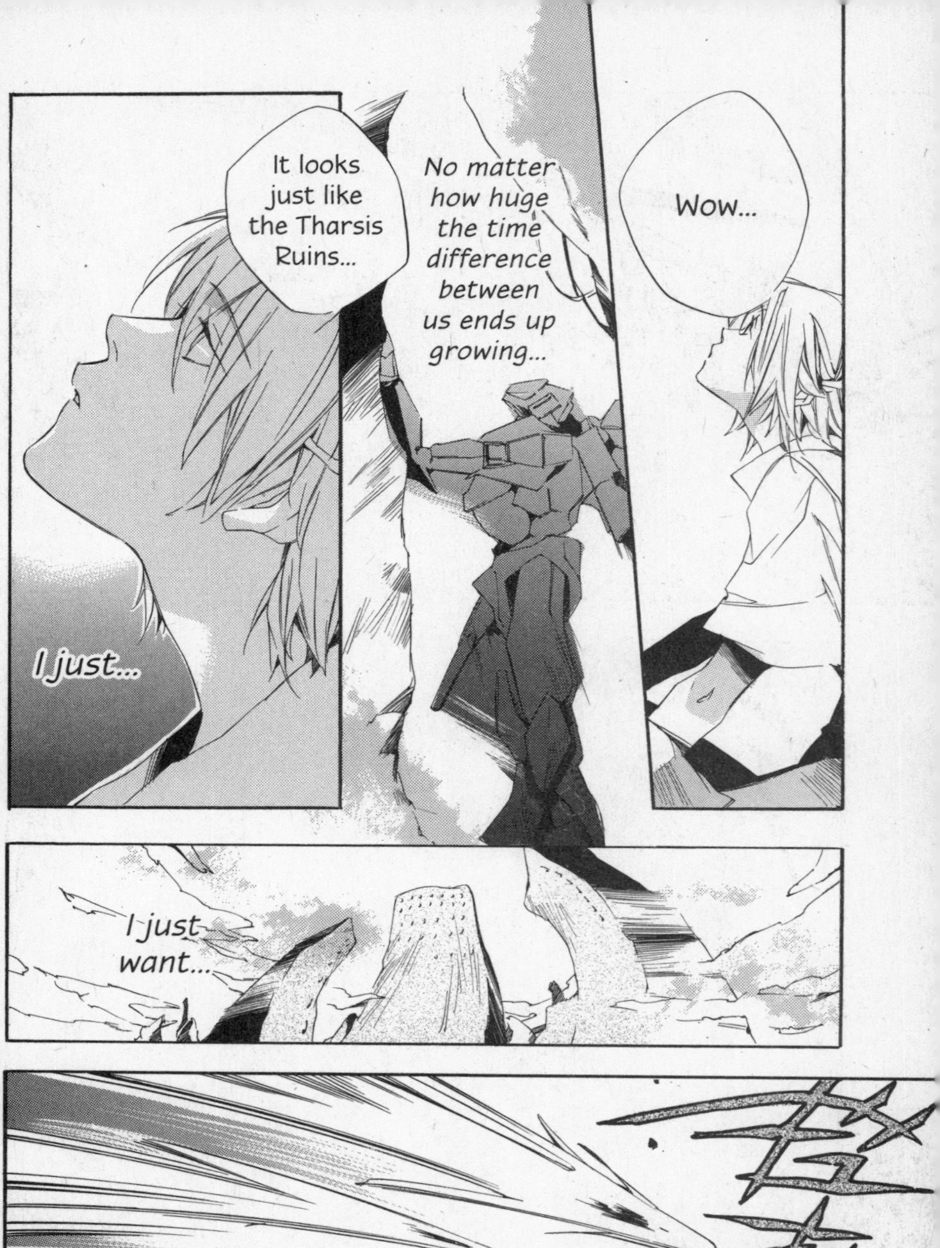
Wow...
No matter how huge the time difference between us ends up growing...
It looks just like the Tharsis Ruins...
I just...
I just want...
GWOOOSH

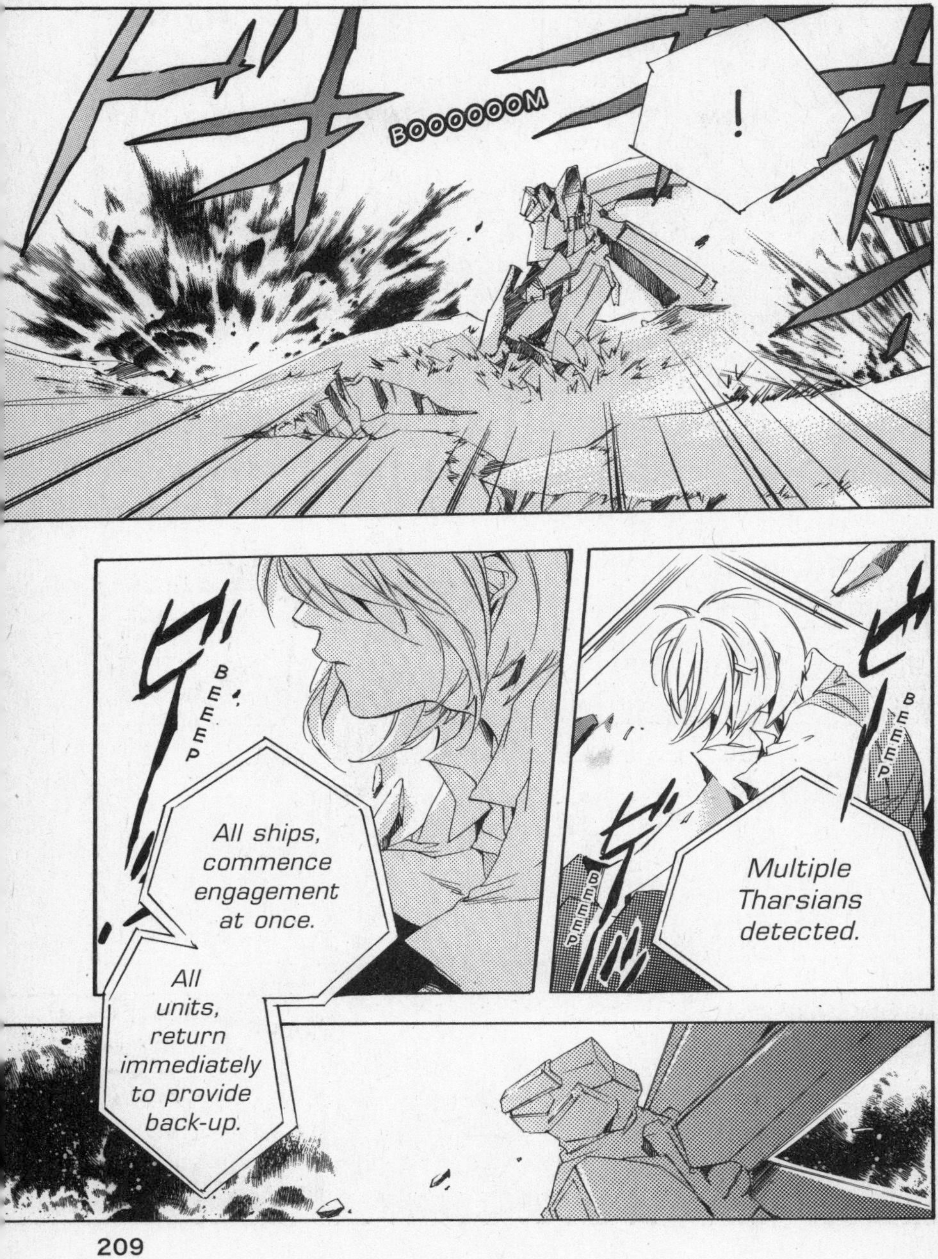

!
BOOOOOOM
BEEEP
BEEEP
Multiple Tharsians detected.
BEEEP
All ships, commence engagement at once.
All units, return immediately to provide back-up.

I just want...

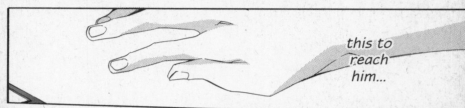

this to reach him...

Hello,
25-year-old
Noboru.

It's 16-year-old
Mikako.

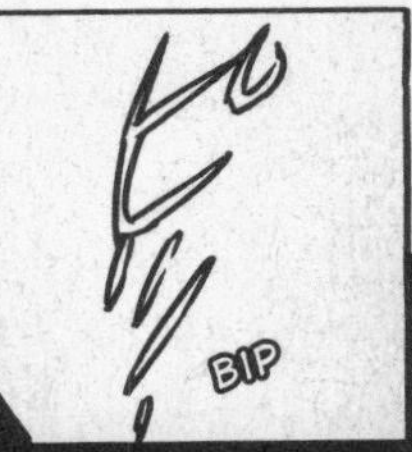
BIP

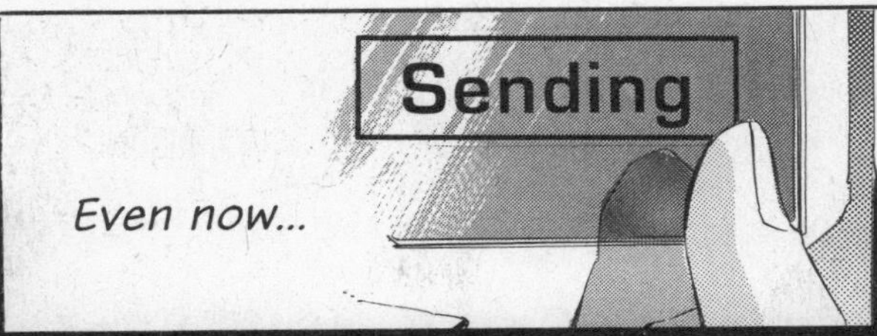
Sending
Even now...

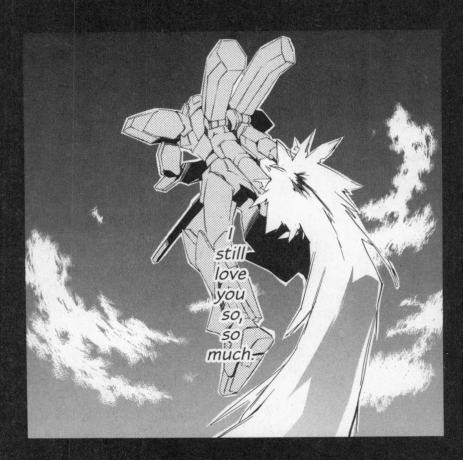

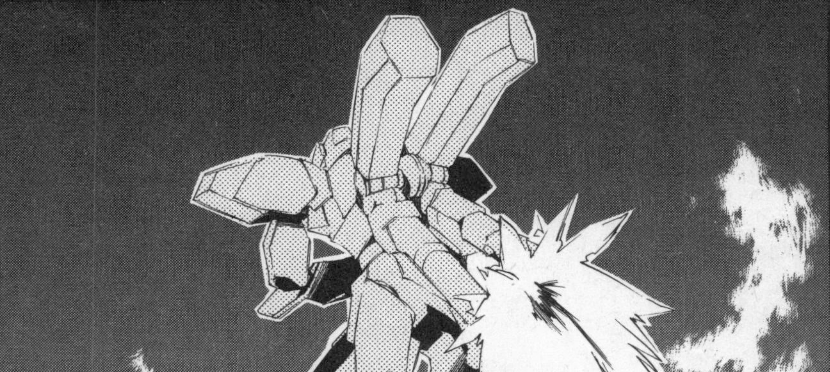
I still love you so, so much.

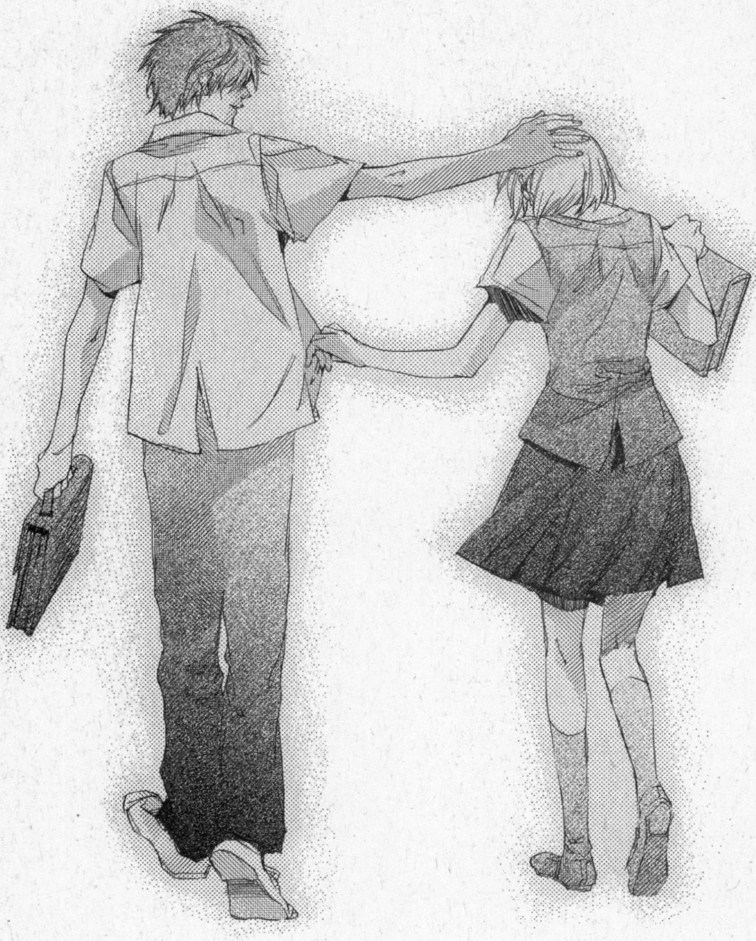

Voices of a Distant Star

Chapter 10

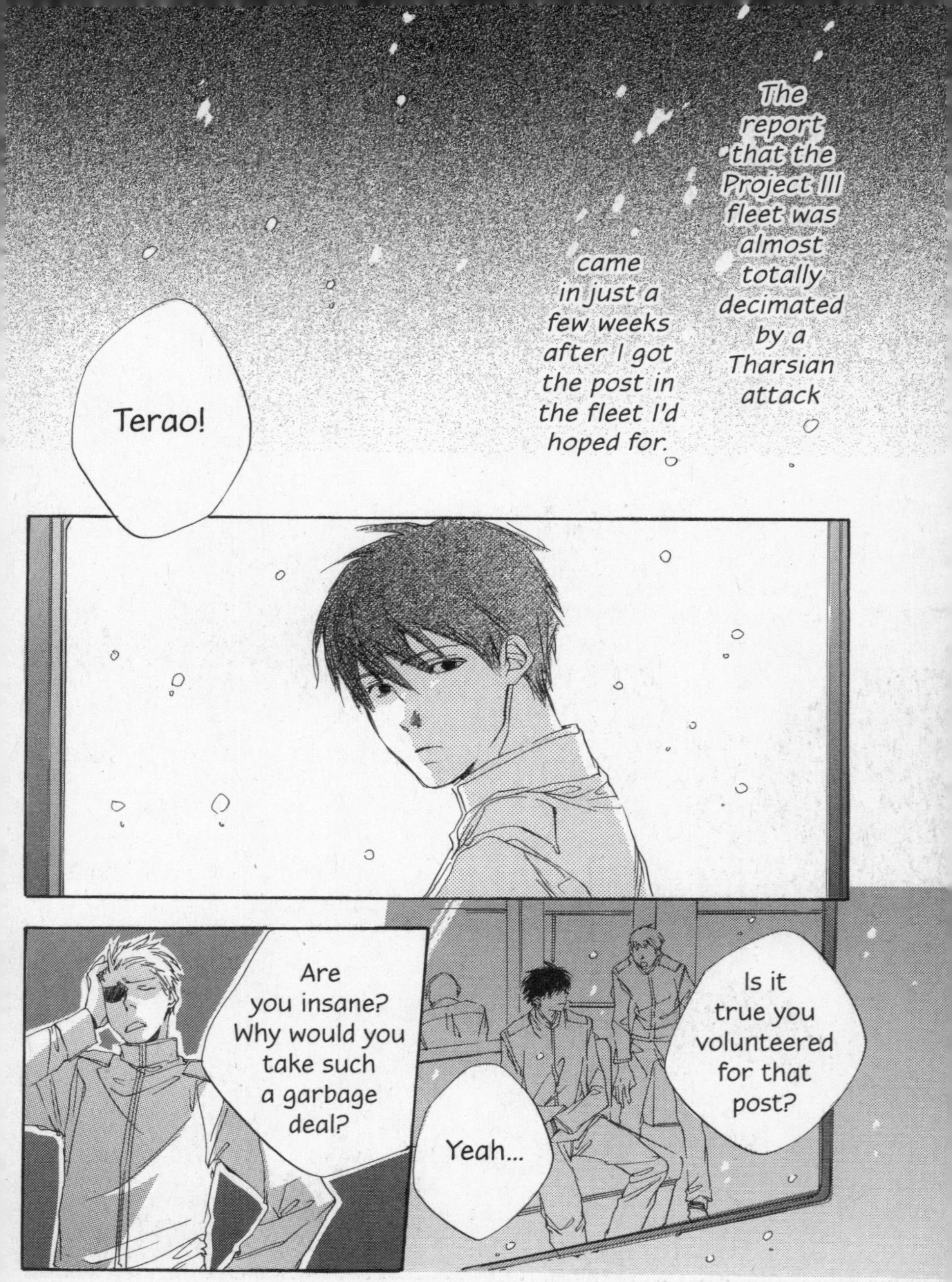
The report that the Project III fleet was almost totally decimated by a Tharsian attack
came in just a few weeks after I got the post in the fleet I'd hoped for.
Terao!
Is it true you volunteered for that post?
Yeah...
Are you insane? Why would you take such a garbage deal?

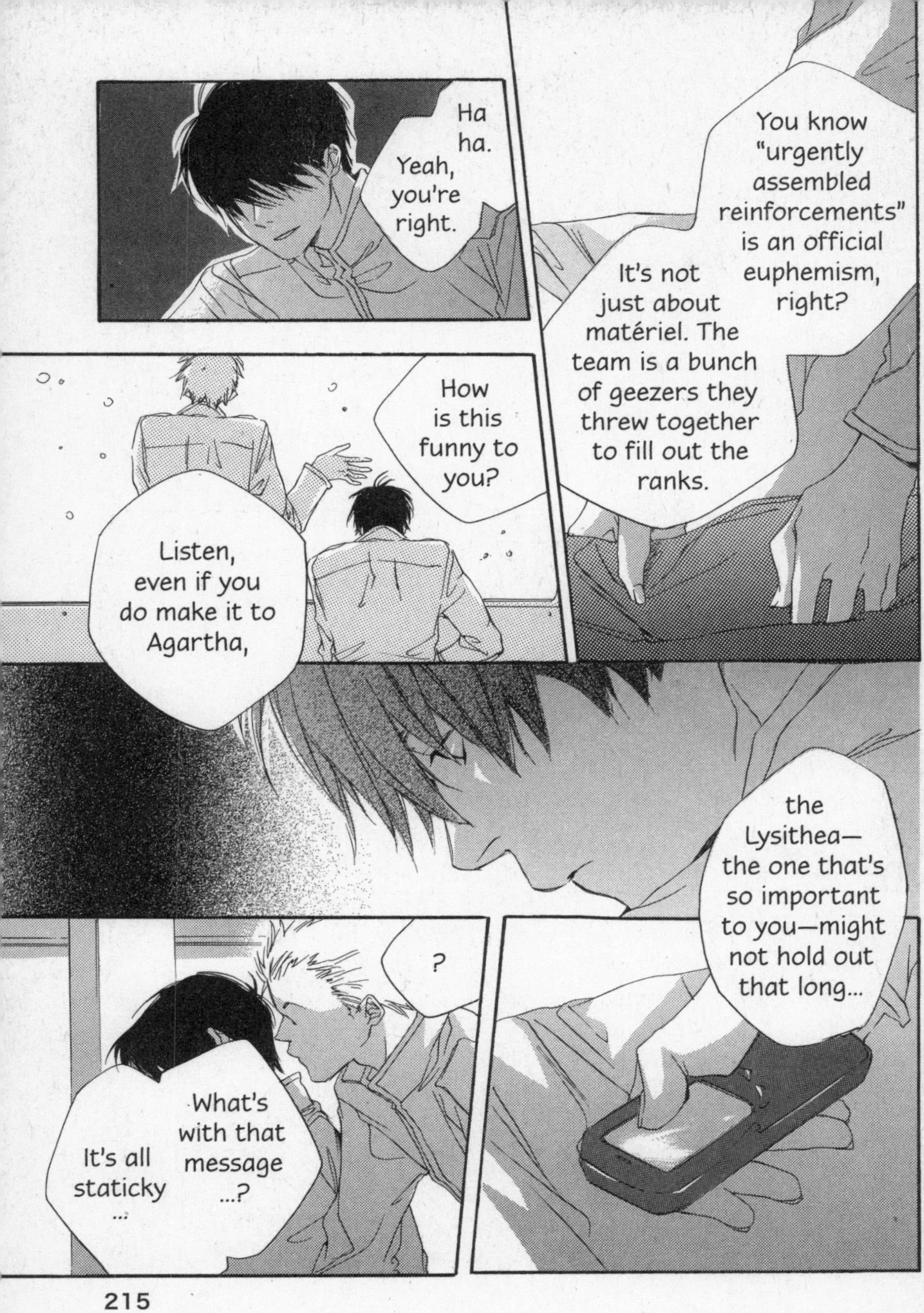

You know "urgently assembled reinforcements" is an official euphemism, right?
It's not just about matériel. The team is a bunch of geezers they threw together to fill out the ranks.
Ha ha. Yeah, you're right.
How is this funny to you?
Listen, even if you do make it to Agartha,
the Lysithea—the one that's so important to you—might not hold out that long...
?
What's with that message ...?
It's all staticky ...

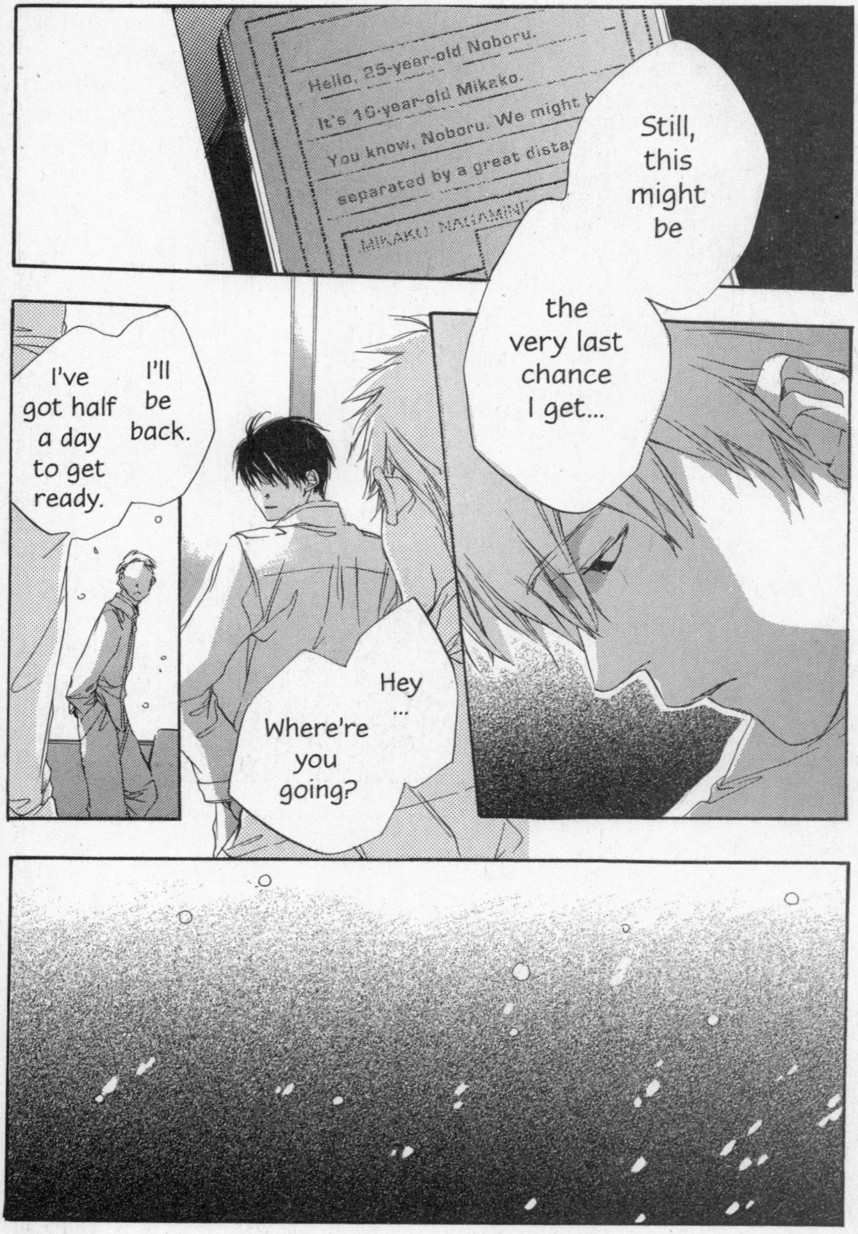
Hello, 25-year-old Noboru.
It's 16-year-old Mikako.
You know, Noboru. We might b
separated by a great dista
MIKAKO NAGAMINE
Still, this might be the very last chance I get...
Hey... Where're you going?
I'll be back.
I've got half a day to get ready.

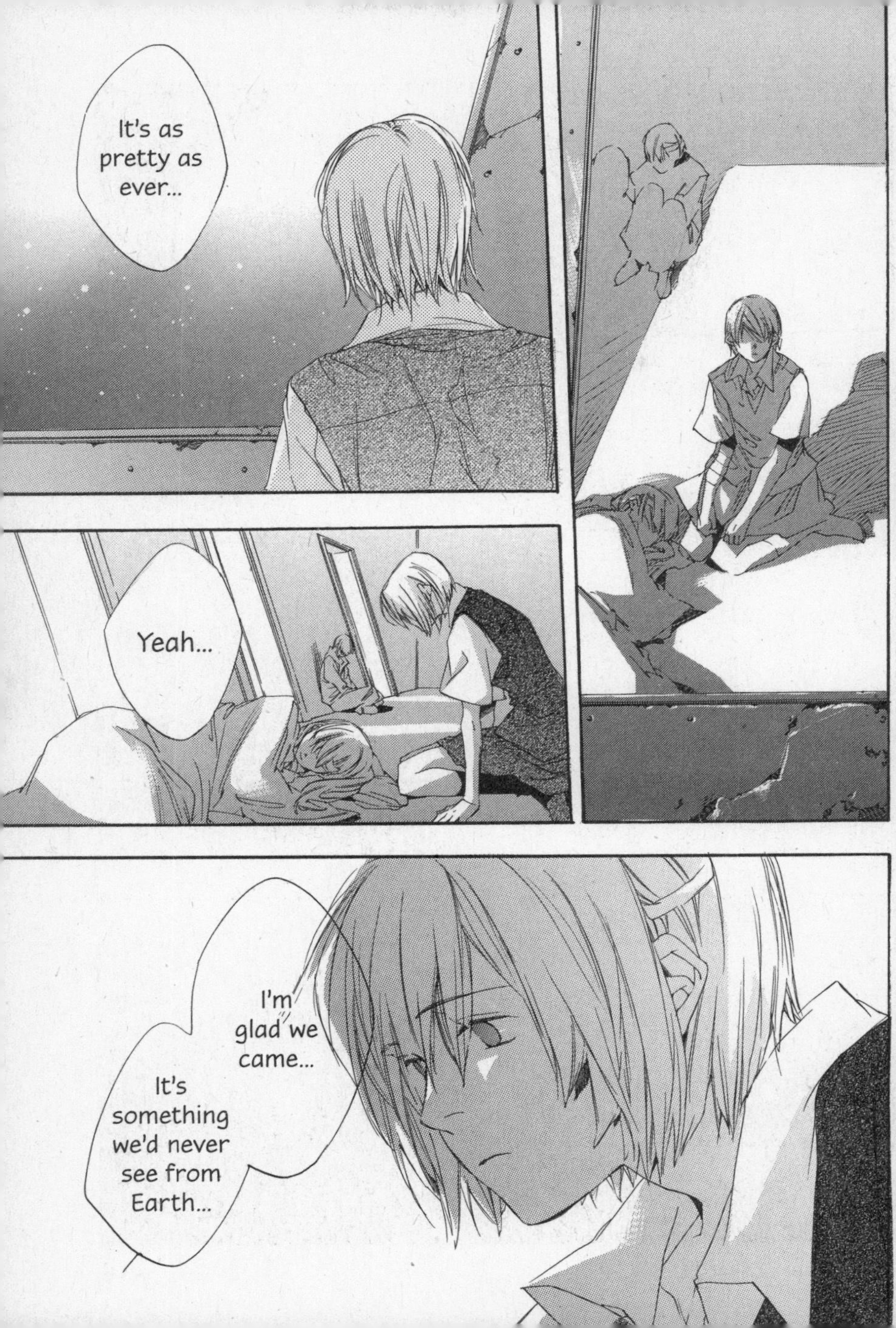
It's as pretty as ever...
Yeah...
I'm glad we came...
It's something we'd never see from Earth...

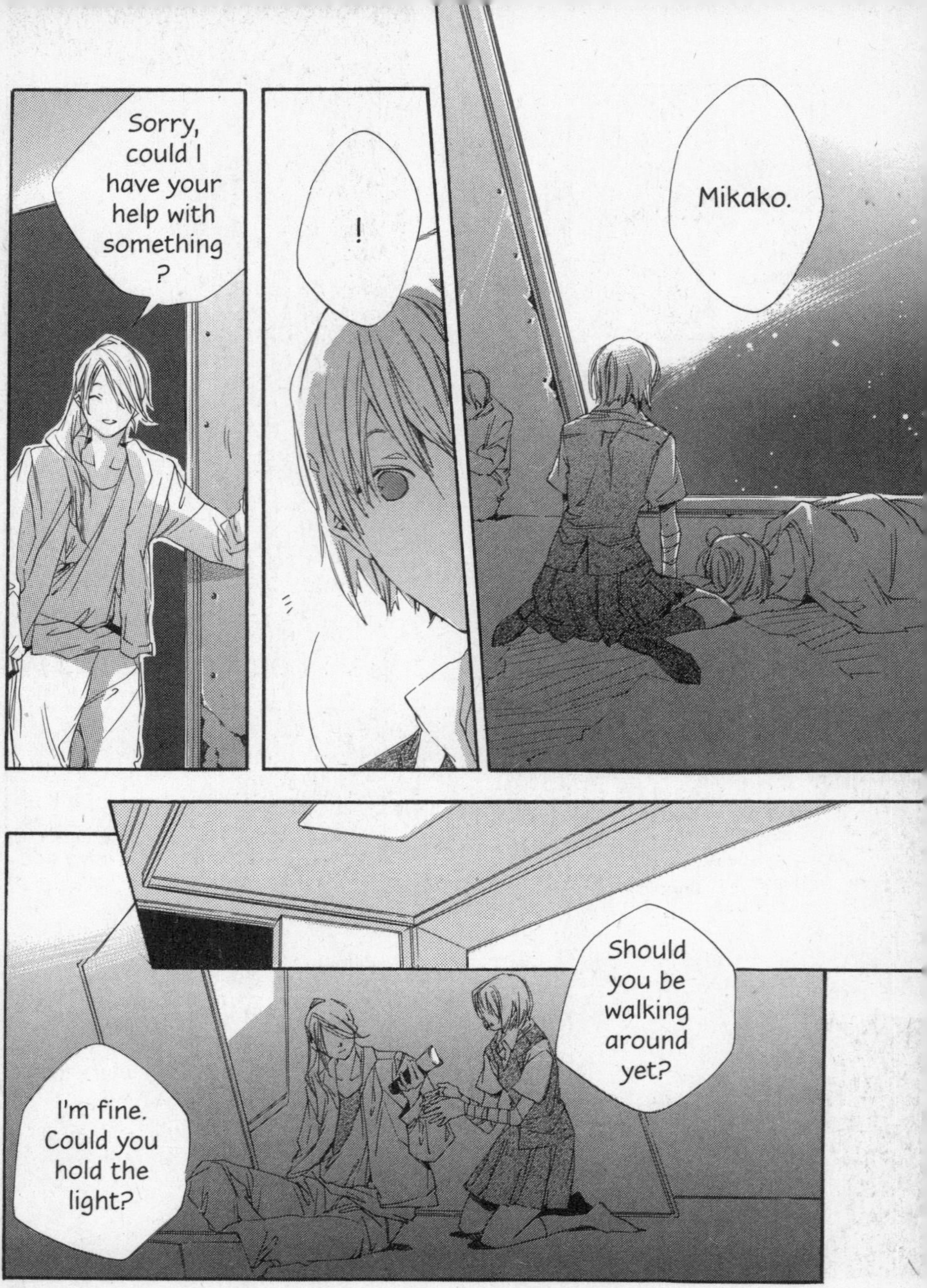
Mikako.
!
Sorry, could I have your help with something?
Should you be walking around yet?
I'm fine. Could you hold the light?

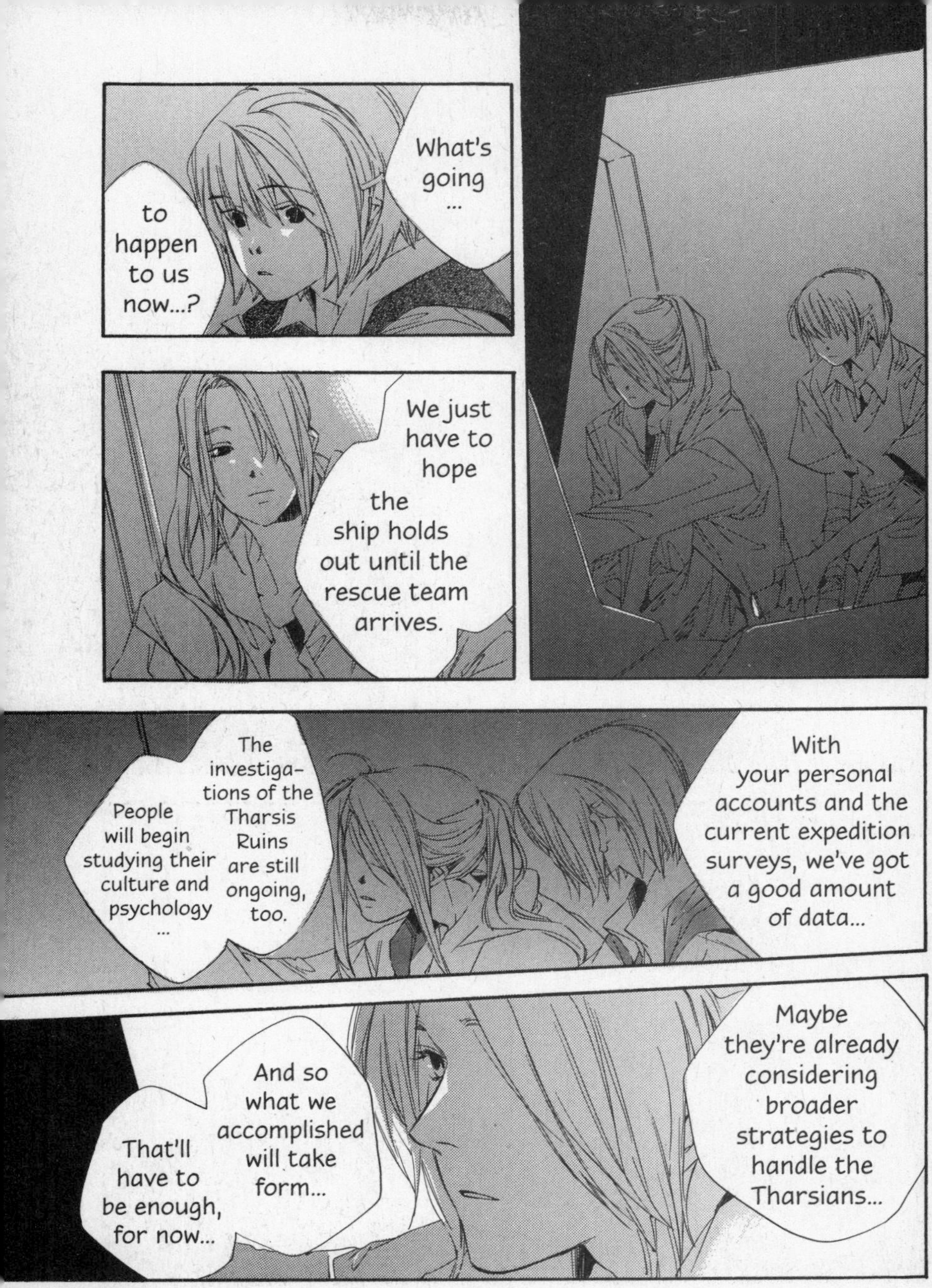
What's going ...
to happen to us now...?
We just have to hope
the ship holds out until the rescue team arrives.
With your personal accounts and the current expedition surveys, we've got a good amount of data...
The investigations of the Tharsis Ruins are still ongoing, too.
People will begin studying their culture and psychology ...
Maybe they're already considering broader strategies to handle the Tharsians...
And so what we accomplished will take form...
That'll have to be enough, for now...

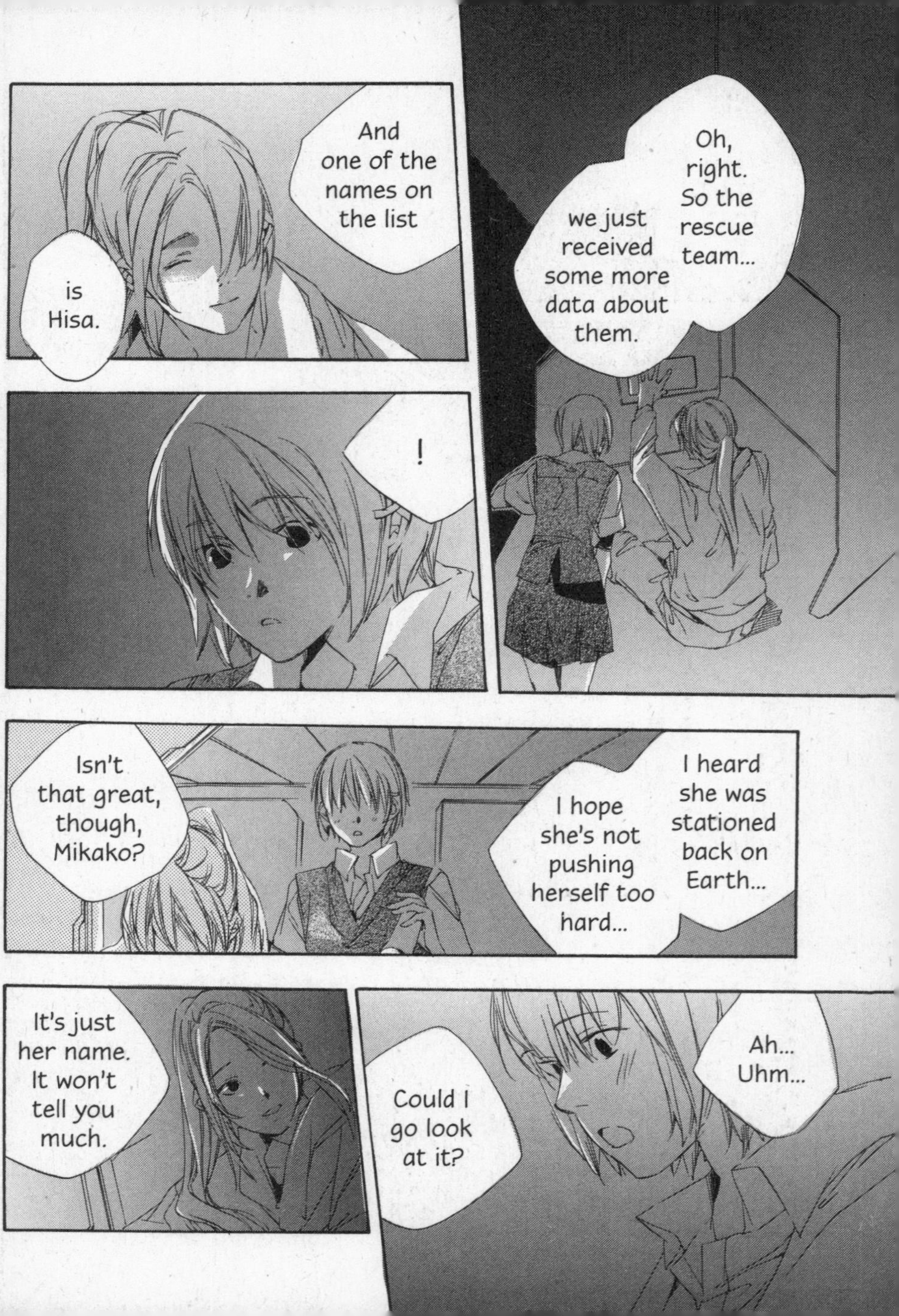
Oh, right. So the rescue team...
we just received some more data about them.
And one of the names on the list
is Hisa.
!
I heard she was stationed back on Earth...
I hope she's not pushing herself too hard...
Isn't that great, though, Mikako?
Ah... Uhm...
Could I go look at it?
It's just her name. It won't tell you much.

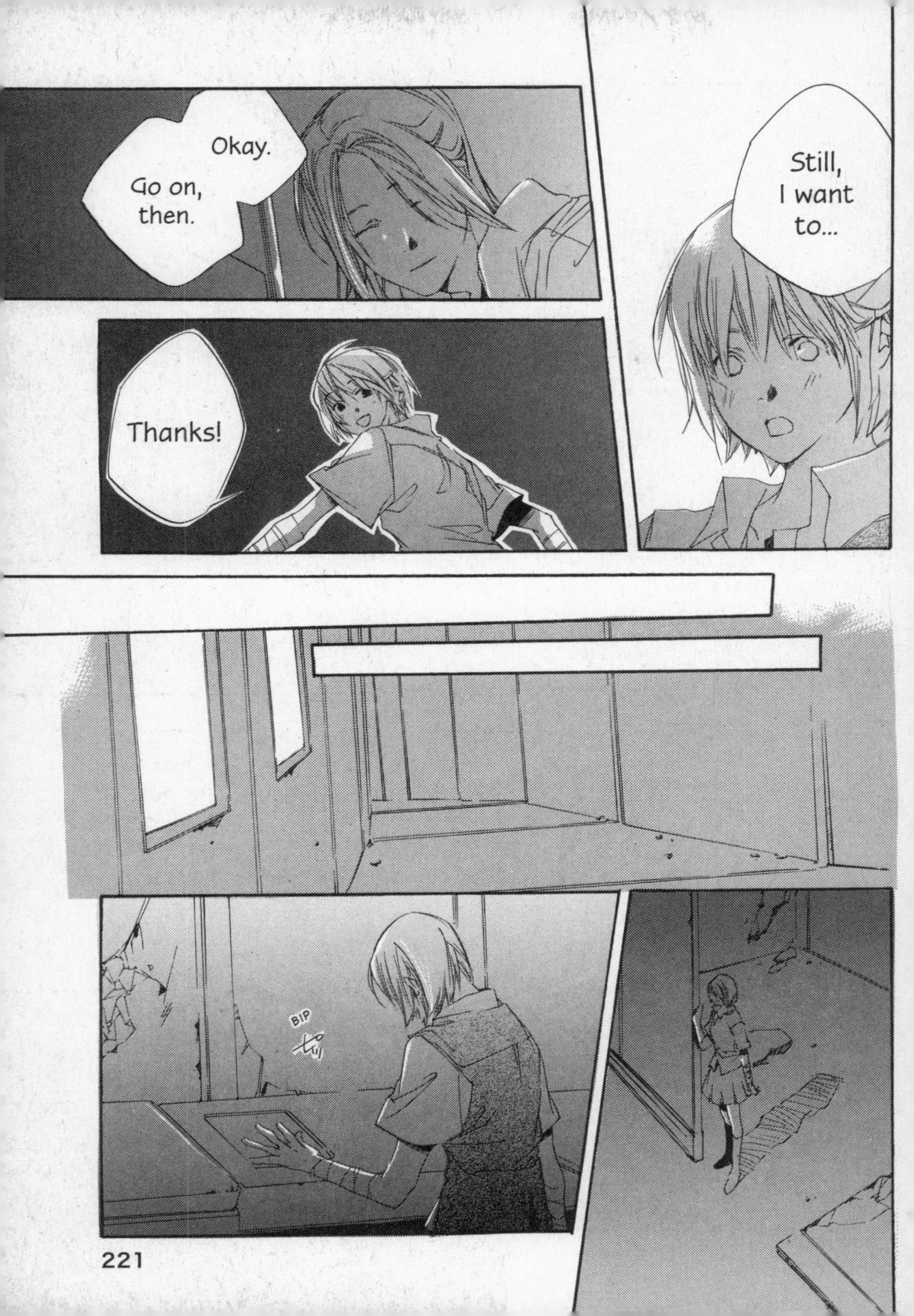
Still, I want to...
Okay.
Go on, then.
Thanks!
BIP

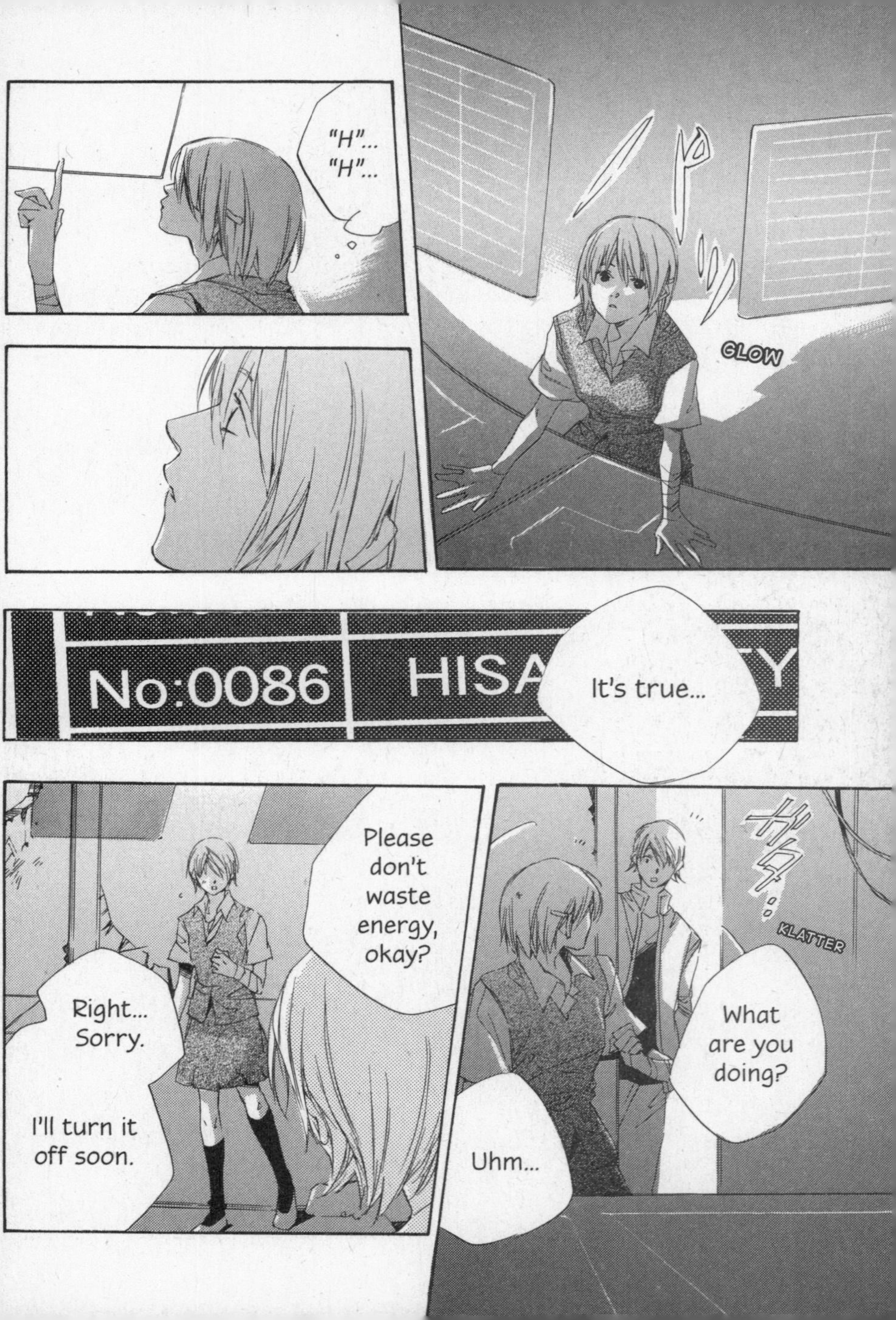
GLOW
"H"...
"H"...
No:0086
It's true...
KLATTER
What are you doing?
Uhm...
Please don't waste energy, okay?
Right... Sorry.
I'll turn it off soon.

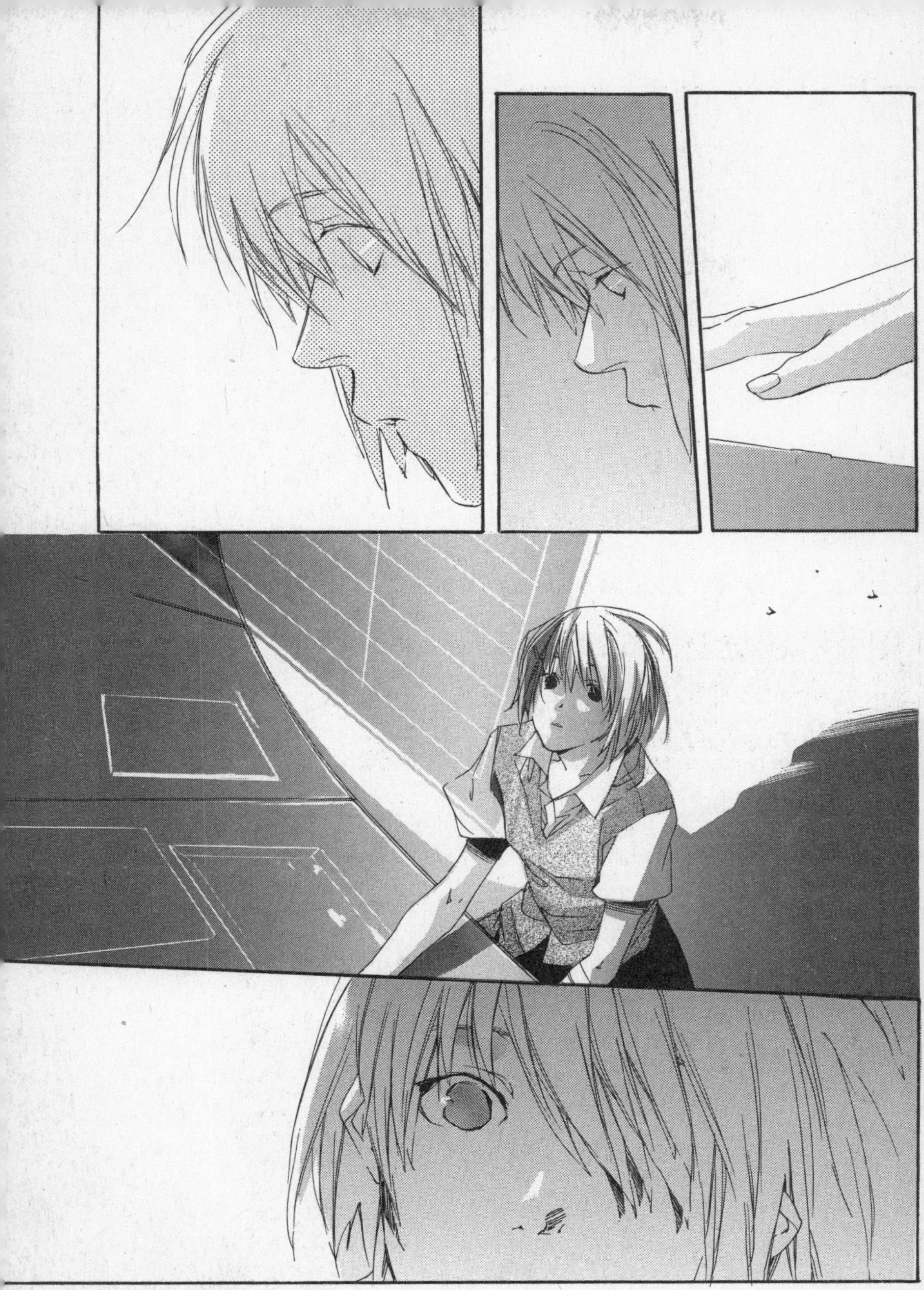

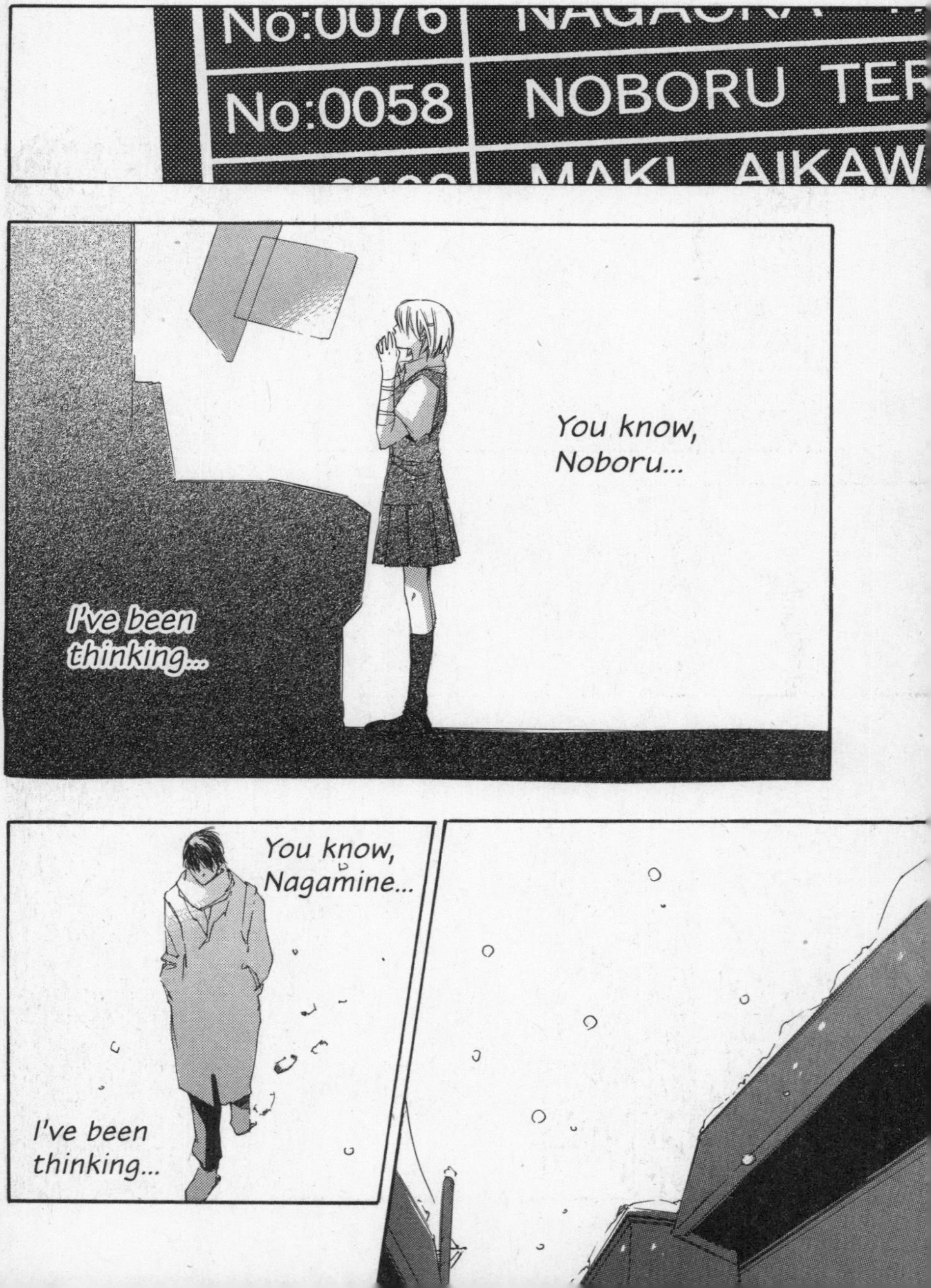
No:0076
No:0058
NOBORU TER
MAKI AIKAW
You know, Noboru...
I've been thinking...
You know, Nagamine...
I've been thinking...

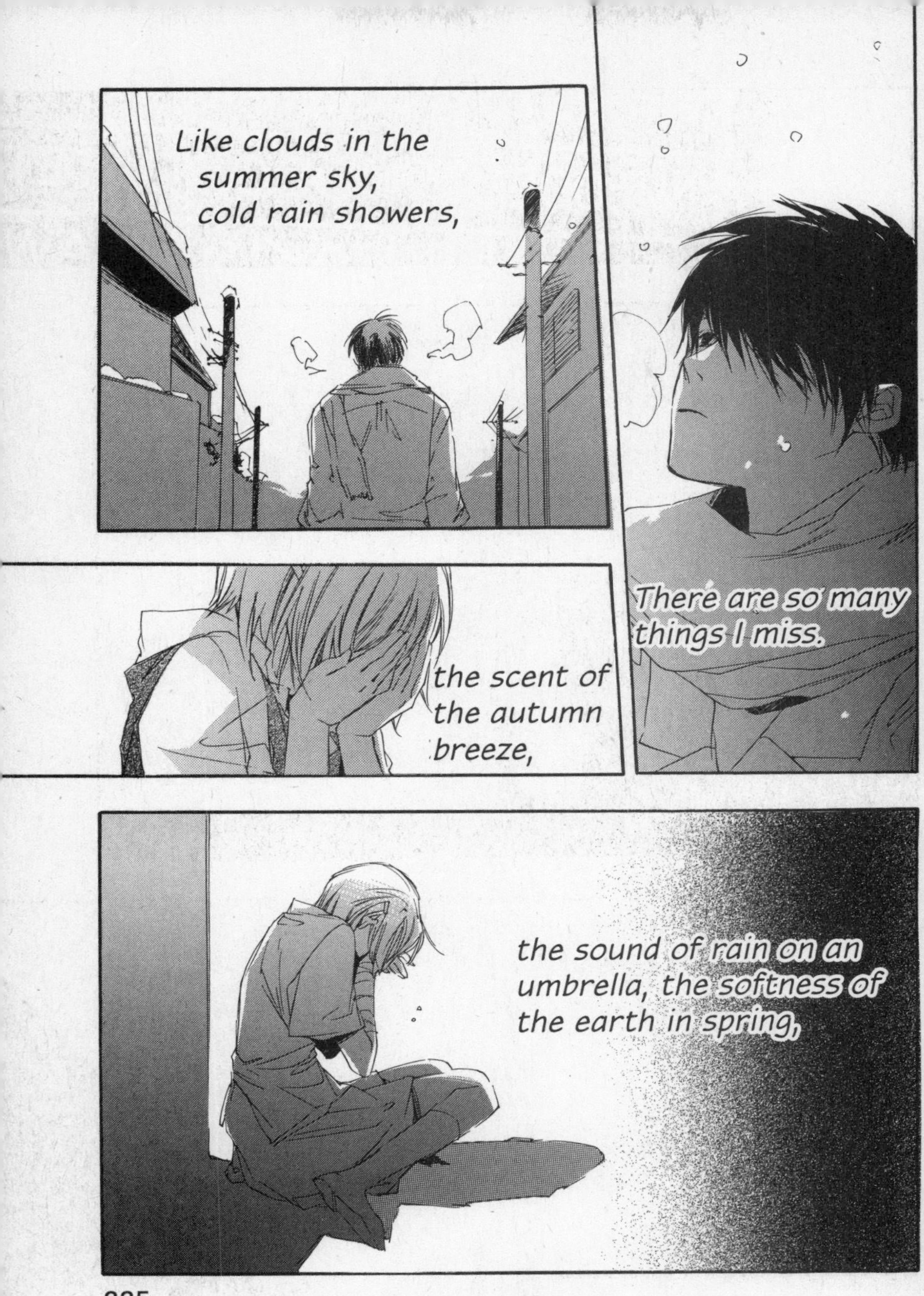
There are so many things I miss.
Like clouds in the summer sky, cold rain showers,
the scent of the autumn breeze,
the sound of rain on an umbrella, the softness of the earth in spring,

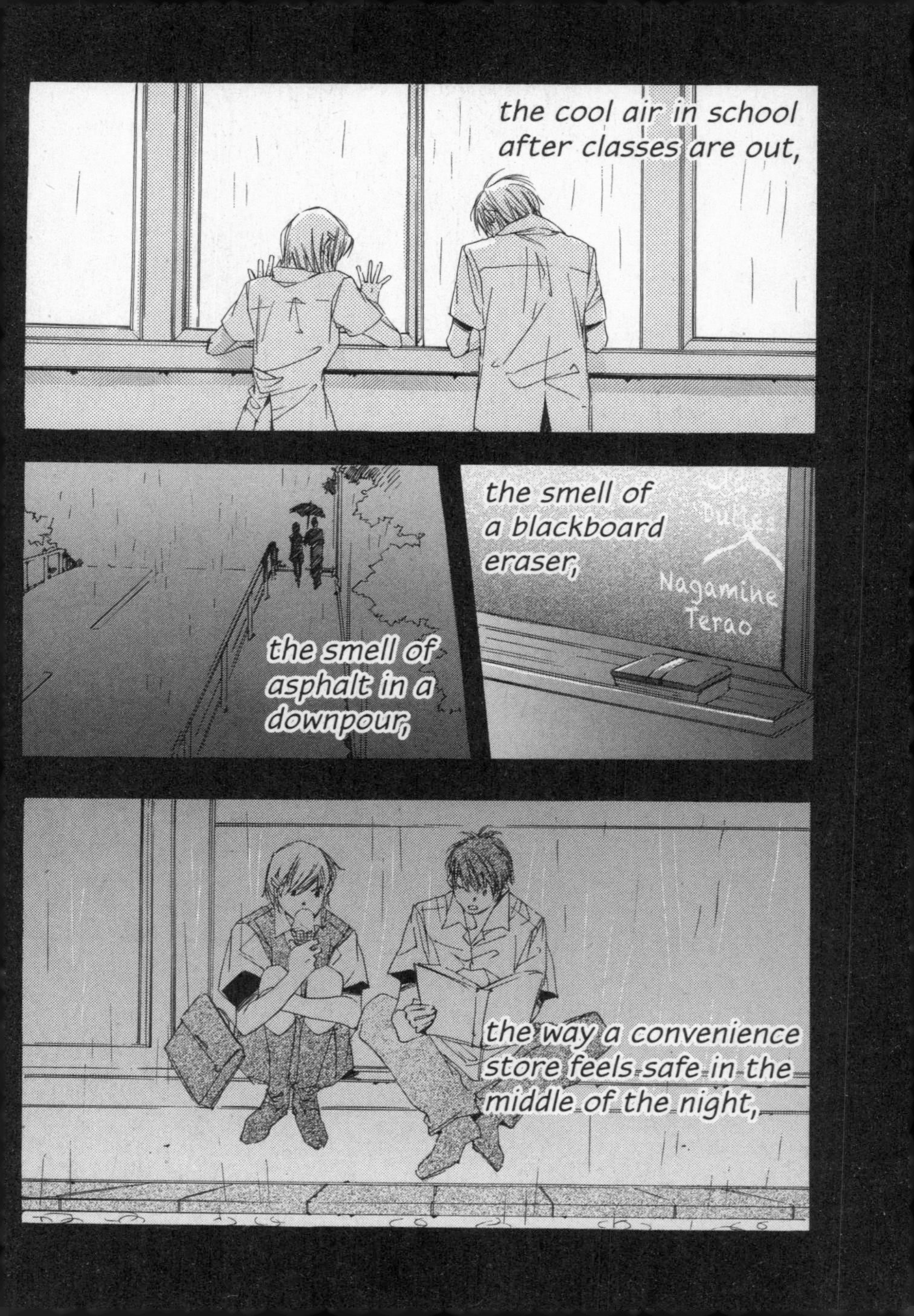
the cool air in school
after classes are out,
the smell of
a blackboard
eraser,
Nagamine
Terao
the smell of
asphalt in a
downpour,
the way a convenience
store feels safe in the
middle of the night,

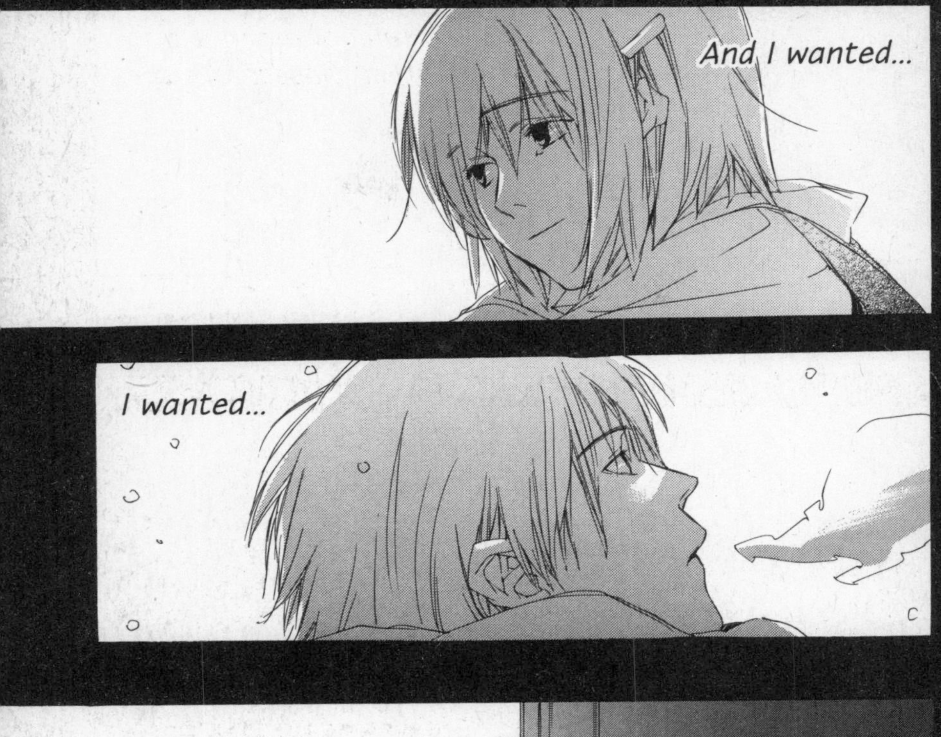
And I wanted...
I wanted...
to keep feeling those things with you, forever...

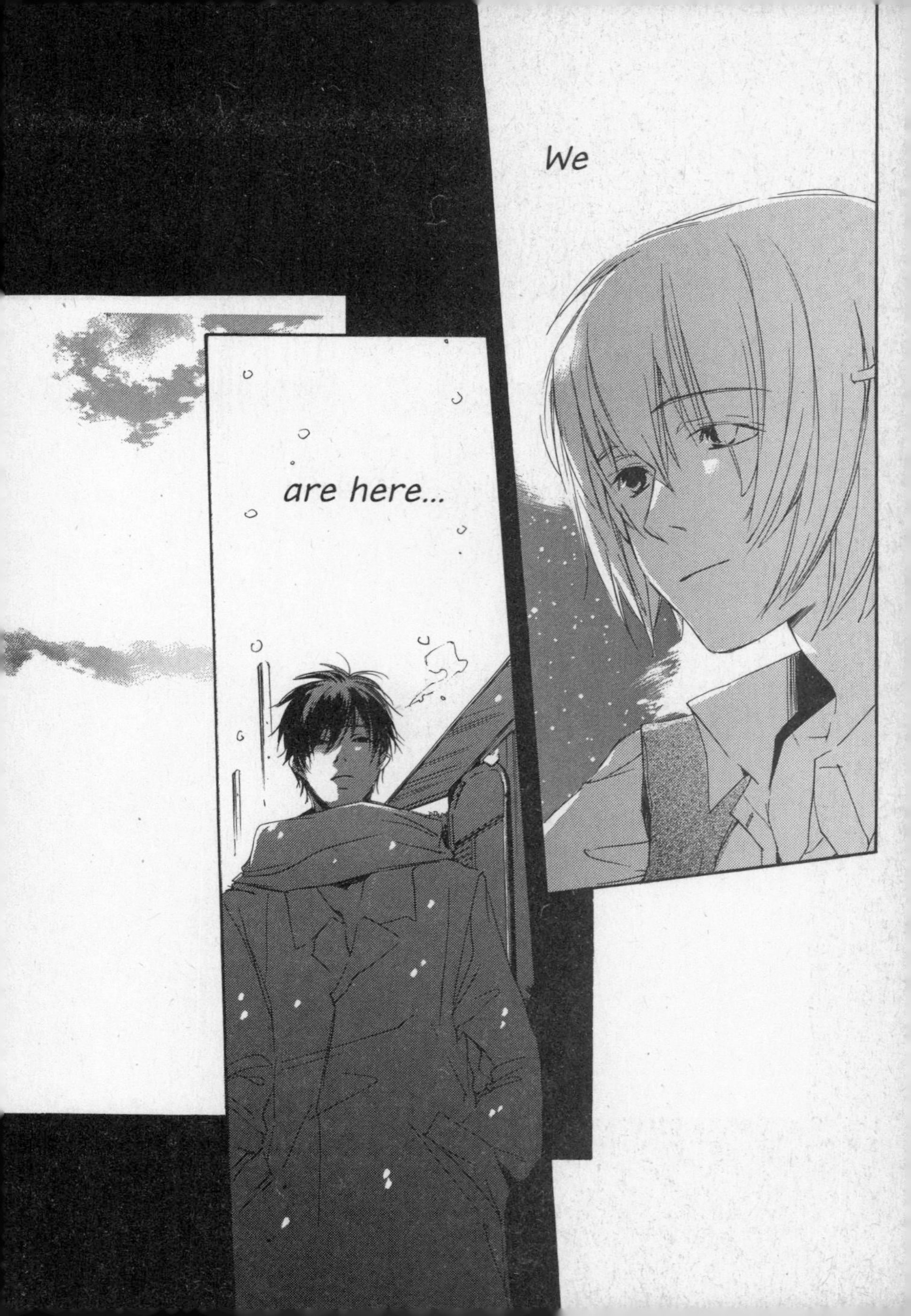
We
are here...

And someday,
I know we'll meet again...

Voices of a Distant Star

End

Sort of an Afterword:

First of all, I'm so grateful for the experience of adapting this story.

I'm still learning, so I have some misgivings about things I didn't get quite the way I wanted, but I did the best that I could, and for that I'm happy.

For fans of the *Voices of a Distant Star* film, I imagine there are some aspects that feel lacking or disappointing, but I hope you can look on it kindly.

Heartfelt thanks to Mr. Shinkai for all his support, to Nishimura and Kuchii of the Modeling Society at the University of Electro-Communications for their help with Tracer figurines; to my editor, my friends, and everyone.

Mizu Sahara

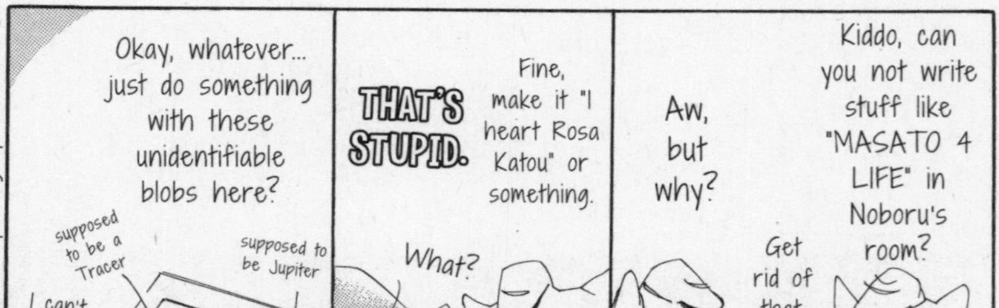
Kiddo, can you not write stuff like "MASATO 4 LIFE" in Noboru's room?
Aw, but why?
Get rid of that.
k-1 LOVE
Fine, make it "I heart Rosa Katou" or something.
THAT'S STUPID.
What?
loves the pretty ladies
Okay, whatever... just do something with these unidentifiable blobs here?
supposed to be Jupiter
supposed to be a Tracer
I can't tell what they are.

It was like this the whole time...
Thanks for putting up with me!

voices of a distant star

"It was the start of spring. It was raining. That was the day that she brought me home."

This is the story of Miyu, a woman who lives alone with her cat, Chobi. As Miyu navigates the world of adulthood, she discovers both the freedom and loneliness that come with living independently, and Chobi learns of the outside world through her actions. Time drifts slowly for Miyu and her cat, but the harsh realities of the world soon catch up...

"Shinkai has been hailed as the next Miyazaki, and his dreamy mindscapes often equal or surpass the anime maestro in breadth of detail and depth of emotion."   —*Variety*

Available Now!

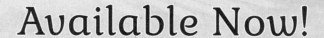

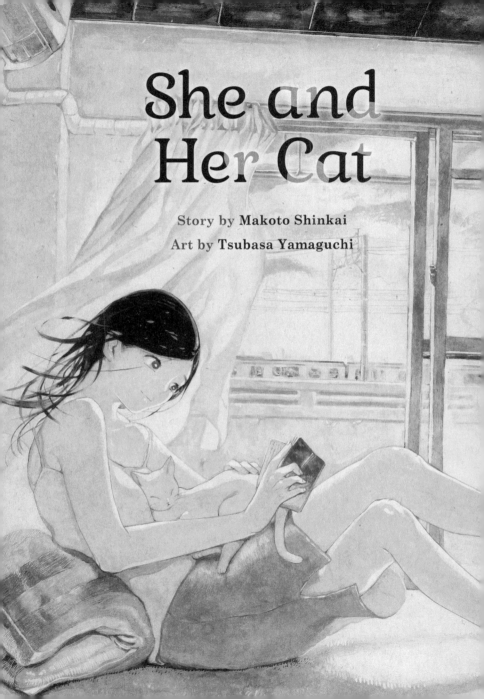

She and Her Cat

Story by Makoto Shinkai

Art by Tsubasa Yamaguchi

Makoto Shinkai

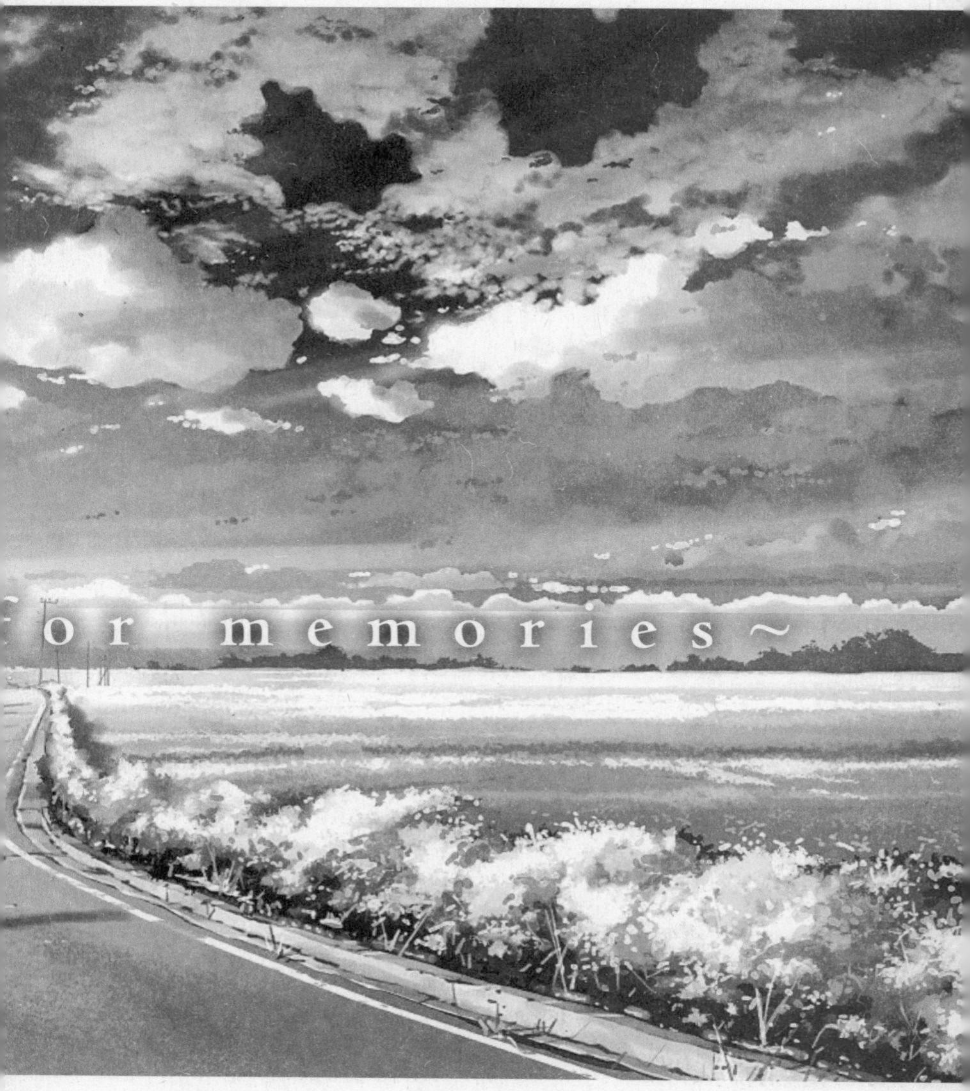
or memories~

A Sky Longing for Memories is a Makoto Shinkai fan's dream!

AVAILABLE NOW!

The Art o

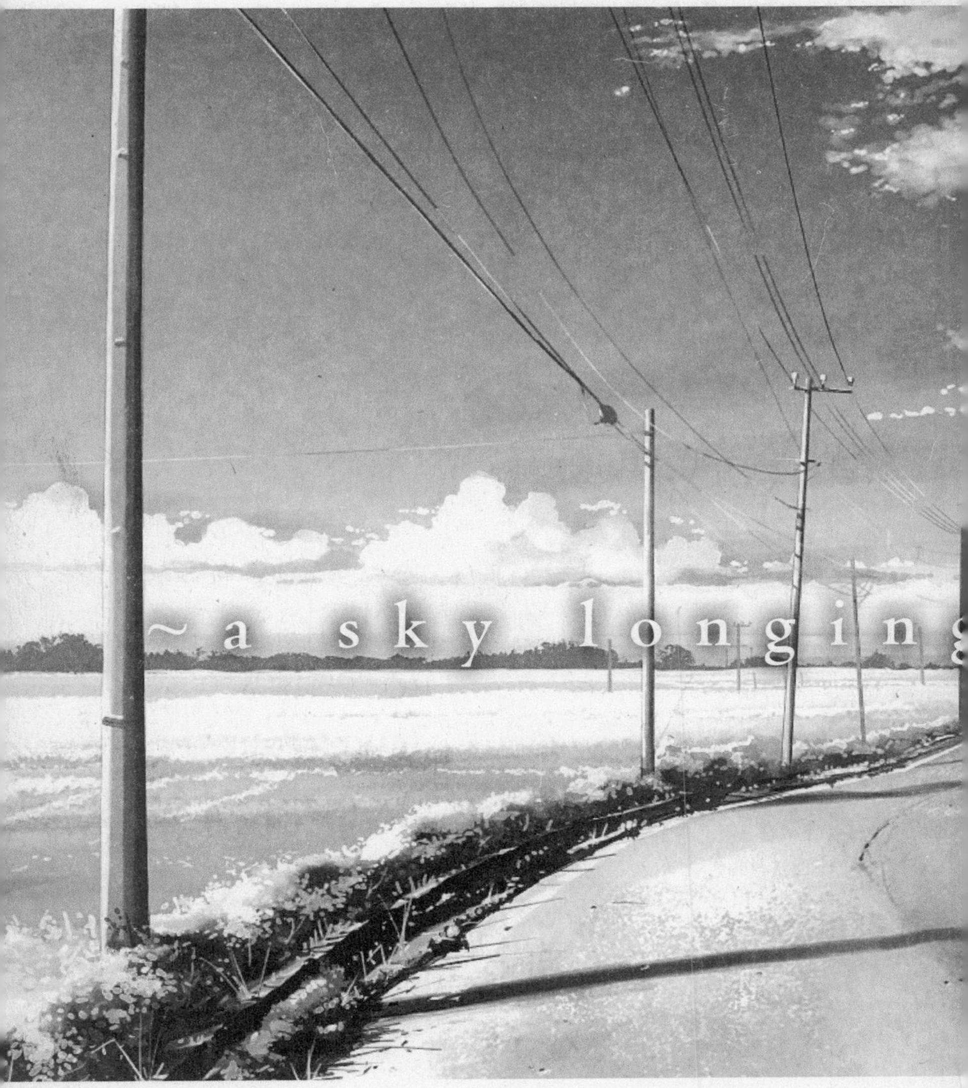
~a sky longing

Featuring works created by the beloved director, this full-color art book is packed with art from the many movies he directed, including *5 Centimeters per Second, The Place Promised in Our Early Days,* and *Voices of a Distant Star.*

V

A

Translation: Melissa Tanaka
Production: Grace Lu
         Anthony Quintessenza

First published in Japan in 2005 by Kodansha, Ltd., Tokyo
Publication for this English edition arranged through Kodansha, Ltd., Tokyo
English language version produced by Vertical, Inc.

Translation provided by Vertical Comics, 2018
Published by Vertical Comics, an imprint of Vertical, Inc., New York

Originally published in Japanese as *Hoshi no Koe* by Kodansha, Ltd., 2005
Hoshi no Koe first serialized in *Afternoon*, Kodansha, Ltd., 2004-2005

This is a work of fiction.

ISBN: 978-1-945054-66-2

Manufactured in Canada

First Edition

Vertical, Inc.
451 Park Avenue South
7th Floor
New York, NY 10016
www.vertical-inc.com

Vertical books are distributed through Penguin-Random House Publisher Services.